. Your HP LaserJet Handbook

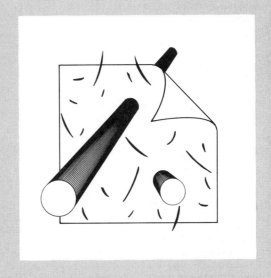

Your HP LaserJet Handbook

Alan R. Neibauer

San Francisco • Paris • Düsseldorf • London

Acquisitions Editor: Dianne King
Editor: Marilyn Smith
Technical Editor: Dan Tauber
Word Processors: Chris Mockel and Scott Campbell
Book Designer: Eleanor Ramos
Technical Art: Jeffrey James Giese
Screen Graphics: Jeffrey James Giese
Typesetter: Elizabeth Newman
Proofreaders: Patsy Owens and Chip Roberts
Indexer: Nancy Guenther
Cover Designer: Thomas Ingalls + Associates
Cover Photographer: David Bishop
Screen reproductions produced by XenoFont

To Barbara, for the last 26 years

ᐧ *Acknowledgments*

The in-depth coverage of hardware and software found in this book reflects the work of scores of professionals. No book is the work of one individual, no matter whose name appears on the cover. So while I get most of the credit, my thanks and appreciation go to the dedicated SYBEX team that made this book a reality.

These efforts were coordinated by Joanne Cuthbertson. Much of the organization and concise style can be attributed to editor Marilyn Smith. Perhaps only an author knows how it feels to read an edited draft of his writing, outwardly wondering why the editor made so many changes but inwardly recognizing that improvements were made.

The job of double-checking for technical accuracy belonged to Dan Tauber. His task was complicated by the range of printer models and software discussed here.

Transforming our manuscript into a finished book was accomplished through the efforts of Chris Mockel and Scott Campbell, word processors; Elizabeth Newman, typesetter; Jeffrey Giese, who produced some of the figures; Eleanor Ramos, book designer; and Patsy Owens and Chip Roberts, proofreaders.

A special thanks to the Boise (LaserJet) and Vancouver (DeskJet) Divisions of Hewlett-Packard for their invaluable information and support.

My appreciation to Aldus Corporation; Application Techniques; Ashton-Tate, Inc.; ASP Computer Products, Inc.; Martin C. Beattie; Bitstream, Inc.; Chinon America, Inc.; Digital Research, Inc.; Elfring Softfonts; Funk Software; FX Unlimited; Hybrid FAX, Inc.; Intellicom, Inc.; Keller Software; LaserGo, Inc.; LaserMaster, Corp.; Logitech, Inc.; Lotus Development Corp.; Darin May; Microsoft Corporation; Orbit Enterprises; Princeton Publishing Labs, Inc.; QMS, Inc.; Samna Corp.; Softcraft Inc.; Software Publishing Corp.; Software Publishing Corp.; Swfte International; Tall Tree Systems; Rip Toren; WordPerfect Corporation; XYWrite III Plus; and Z-Soft.

Special thanks to Jack Colton at Upstart Services in Cherry Hill, New Jersey, for his support and help.

Finally, but always first in my heart, thanks to Barbara Neibauer.

Contents at a Glance

Table of Contents

P·A·R·T   2

Using the LaserJet with Your Applications

• 6 *Printing with Microsoft Word* *144*

• 7 *Printing with Microsoft Windows* *174*

• 8 *Printing with WordStar* *194*

P·A·R·T   3

Enhancing Your System

P · A · R · T   4

**Programming Your
LaserJet**

• *Introduction*

• While the computer certainly brought about dramatic changes in our society, it was the advent of the laser printer that carried the technical revolution to a new plateau. Before the laser printer, computer users had to produce business documents in typewriter quality at best, and graphics using the coarse resolution of dot-matrix print heads.

But Hewlett-Packard began a new era in printers when it released the original LaserJet, ironically in 1984. While expensive—the original retail price was over $3,500—it was a token of things to come. Finally, there was a printer capable of high speed and quality printing of both text and graphics.

As new models were released and other manufacturers joined the market, prices fell and features increased from the ability to use softfonts starting with the LaserJet + to convenient duplex printing on the LaserJet IID (and affordable laser printing with the LaserJet IIP). Now, with affordable color laser printing just beyond the horizon, it is difficult to imagine how far this technology will bring us.

Still, there's been a price to pay, beyond dollars, for all this power. Using a laser printer to its fullest requires much more than connecting a cable and turning on the switch. Effective use of the printer is inexorably tied to either detailed knowledge of application software or a thorough understanding of the printer's internal programming language.

Although many software packages have the capability to use the Laser-Jet, they often require a special setup. And while all applications must ultimately communicate with the LaserJet in the same way—the PCL language—there are no standards in the way printer drivers are constructed, used, or modified.

It became obvious that what was needed was a comprehensive handbook that approached the subject of using LaserJet printers on several levels. These are the four levels represented by the parts in this book.

• *Book Structure*

This book is divided into four parts, followed by four appendices.

Part 1: The Basics

The four chapters in Part 1 present the basics of connecting and using LaserJet and compatible printers. Chapter 1 discusses the different Laser-Jet models, comparing their features and explaining fundamental concepts you'll need for mastering their use. Then in Chapter 2 you'll learn how to connect your LaserJet to your computer and how to use its control panel.

In Chapter 3, you'll learn how to use the LaserJet for common, everyday printing tasks such as printing screen dumps and envelopes. This chapter introduces a number of inexpensive software options, including those for printing two, four, or even eight pages of text on a single sheet of paper.

The final chapter in this section is a comprehensive guide to using fonts of all types. Chapter 4 discusses the use of internal fonts, cartridge fonts, and softfonts. Here you'll learn how to download and install fonts, create custom characters using editing programs, and even convert fonts between LaserJet and PostScript format. This is an important chapter if you plan on using softfonts.

Part 2: Applications

In Part 2, you'll learn how to use the LaserJet with application software. Many popular programs are discussed in detail, but even if you're using a package not discussed, the in-depth coverage of printer drivers can be applied to almost any program.

The chapters cover the following applications:

- Chapter 5: WordPerfect 5.0

- Chapter 6: Microsoft Word

- Chapter 7: Microsoft Windows

- Chapter 8: WordStar 5.5

- Chapter 9: MultiMate and XyWrite Plus

- Chapter 10: Xerox Ventura Publisher, Aldus Pagemaker, and PFS First Publisher

- Chapter 11: dBASE IV and earlier versions

- Chapter 12: Lotus 1-2-3 Release 3 and earlier versions

- Chapter 13: Harvard Graphics and Gem Presentation Team

Part 3: Power Uses

There's no need to be satisfied with just getting as much from your LaserJet as your applications allow. This part of the book covers the most up-to-date ways of enhancing your printing system for optimum efficiency and productivity.

Scanning, advanced graphics, and planning for color are discussed in Chapter 14. You'll learn about the types of scanners and how photographs and other gray-scale art can be processed for printing. This chapter also discusses the use of ready-made clip art and methods of converting graphics files from one format to another. You'll also find a section on hardware devices that modulate the laser's beam to produce publication-quality halftones.

Chapter 15 examines PostScript and adding PostScript capability to all LaserJet models. You'll discover how to add PostScript to your LaserJet using either hardware or software solutions. You'll also see how to get Post-Script and LaserJet capabilities on one printer, for no more (if not less) than the cost of a PostScript printer alone.

In Chapter 16, we'll focus on improving office productivity. You'll learn ways to share your LaserJet between more than one computer, increase printing speed, scan text, and print high-quality fax messages.

Part 4: PCL Programming

Using the LaserJet's PCL language is discussed in many of the earlier chapters. Part 4, however, is designed for programmers who want to access fonts and graphic capabilities in their own applications. Practical Basic programs are provided for most features.

An introduction to the PCL language and its structure is given in Chapter 17. It also includes a simple Basic program that you can use to create printer drivers for your own applications.

In Chapter 18, you'll learn how to control page size and cursor movement, as well as select and manipulate fonts. It includes programs for downloading fonts and using fonts to create special effects, such as three-dimensional printing.

The programming task of designing and downloading bit-map graphics is the subject of Chapter 19. Here you'll learn how to create custom logos and time-saving macros.

Chapter 20 presents a detailed inside look at softfonts. You'll learn the actual commands and codes that make up a softfont and how they communicate character design and shape to the printer. Read this chapter if you are considering designing your own special fonts and characters.

Additional Information

In Appendix A, you'll learn how to select paper and toner cartridges, as well as perform routine preventive maintenance. Appendix B shows the PC-8 and Roman-8 symbol sets, along with the corresponding decimal and hexadecimal codes.

A list of resources for hardware and software is presented in Appendix C. This includes names, addresses, and telephone numbers for manufacturers of the products discussed in the book, as well as many similar products.

Appendix D focuses on the DeskJet and DeskJet +, ink-jet printers that are similar to the LaserJet in many ways. If you have a DeskJet, also look for special margin notes explaining differences between the LaserJet material in the text and your own printer. This book serves as a DeskJet handbook as well.

Keep in mind that the DeskJet + was released just prior to publication of this book. So if you have a new version of an application, check its documentation or consult the software's manufacturer for up-to-the-minute information.

• *How to Use This Book*

It's unlikely that you'll have all the application programs discussed in this book. We suggest that you start by carefully reading Chapters 1 through 4, then go directly to the chapters that discuss the applications you are using. When you're ready to expand the capabilities of your printer, read Chapters 14 through 16. As you read, look for notes in the margins of the page. These present useful tips, special items of interest, or cautions.

If you are a programmer, start with Chapters 1 through 4, then skip to Part 4, Programming Your LaserJet. If you plan to write your own printer driver, study these chapters carefully, then read Chapters 5 through 13 to see how other manufacturers use printer drivers.

If you have a DeskJet printer, read Part 1, Appendix D, then the appropriate application chapters.

The LaserJet is really an exciting printer, with capabilities beyond many application programs. When you're finished reading this book, keep it near your printer as a handy guide. You can quickly refer to the appropriate application chapter for specific guidance.

DeskJet information appears in the margin next to related text.

Notes with additional information appear in the margin.

You will also see helpful tips in the margin.

Potentional problems are noted as warnings.

P · A · R · T   1

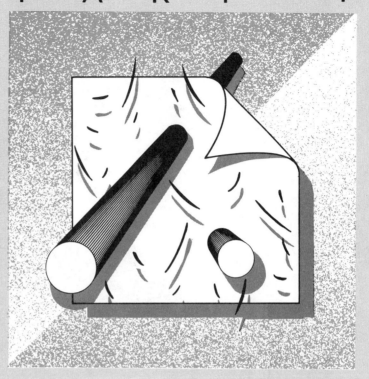

· An Introduction
to the LaserJet

The following four chapters cover fundamental concepts of laser printing and explain how to connect and use your LaserJet for basic printing tasks. These chapters lay the important groundwork for the more specific and advanced chapters in remaining parts. If you use cartridges or softfonts, read Chapter 4 carefully. It contains the information you'll need to get the most out of your printer and applications.

H·P L·A·S·E·R·J·E·T

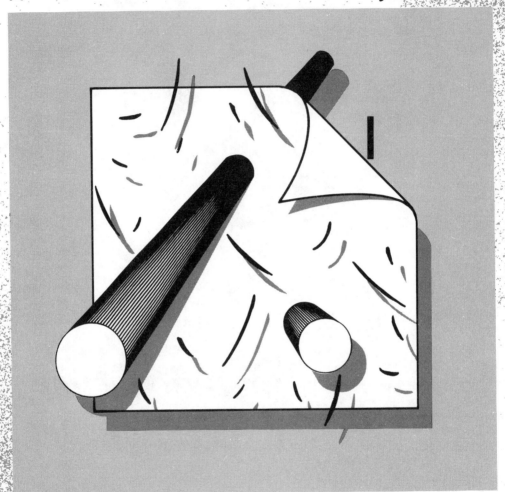

LaserJet Printer Basics

• Your LaserJet printer is a sophisticated piece of equipment. Before you begin working with it, you should understand the capabilities and limitations of your particular model, as well as some of the basic concepts and mechanics of laser printing. This chapter briefly describes the various LaserJet models and how they work. We'll cover general laser printing fundamentals, as well as the specific features of the different LaserJet models.

The Hewlett-Packard DeskJet + is an ink-jet printer that provides many of the same features as the LaserJet II. The similar features are noted throughout this book, and Appendix D discusses printing with the DeskJet + in more detail.

• *LaserJet Models*

Six models of the Hewlett-Packard (HP) LaserJet printer are in use today: the original LaserJet, LaserJet +, LaserJet 500 +, LaserJet II, LaserJet IID, and LaserJet 2000. A number of other printer manufacturers sell LaserJet-compatible printers that perform like one of the Hewlett-Packard models, although their actual degree of compatibility varies.

The original LaserJet offered high speed (for those days), outstanding quality text and graphics, and the ability to print in different typefaces, or fonts, using optional cartridges that plug into the printer. While expensive (almost $3,500) compared with other types of printers, it provided businesses with a perfect combination of quality and utility.

The LaserJet + and 500 + are great improvements over the original. Both models accept softfonts (or downloadable fonts), have more internal fonts and capabilities, and have serial as well as parallel interfaces. The LaserJet 500 + also has two paper trays.

In 1987, the LaserJet II was announced. It has two cartridge slots and more internal fonts and symbol sets. This printer is not only smaller and lighter than earlier models, but also costs about $1,000 less than the original LaserJet.

The LaserJet IID, the newest member of the family, is a duplex printer, which means that it can automatically print on both sides of the paper. It has two paper trays and can print all fonts in both landscape and portrait orientation.

Finally, the LaserJet 2000 is a high-speed (20 pages per minute) printer designed for high quantity work on a network or with a minicomputer system. With the D option installed, it even prints duplex. It's not a desktop model, but stands on the floor like a printing press—not the type of thing you would attach to your home computer in the recreation room.

Hewlett-Packard recently released a new model, the LaserJet IIP.

The DeskJet + accepts softfonts and has two font cartridge slots. However, DeskJet and LaserJet cartridges and softfonts are not interchangeable.

LaserJet models print
1/300-inch dots.

• *How Laser Printers Work*

Data is passed from your computer to your printer as electronic signals, called *bits*. A bit is either a one or a zero, and each character is represented by a series of 8 bits. The specific combination of ones and zeros is established by ASCII (American Standard Code for Information Interchange). For example, to print the capital letter A, the computer sends 01000001, which is the ASCII code for that character.

Laser printers use a photosensitive drum, electrostatic charges, and raster scanning (much like the way the image is put on your television screen) to convert the data to printed images. They reproduce images by transferring small dots of toner onto the paper. All graphics and text are converted into rows of dots, called *bit maps*. Figure 1.1 illustrates a bit-map pattern. Toner will be transferred to the paper for each one on the bit map shown in the figure, forming the image—the letter b—as a series of small dots.

By using bit maps, rather than remembering fully formed characters as typewriters or daisy-wheel printers do, laser printers can produce all

```
Row       Bit Map Pattern

01    11111100 00000000 00000000 00000000
02    11111100 00000000 00000000 00000000
03    00111100 00000000 00000000 00000000
04    00111100 00000000 00000000 00000000
05    00111100 00000000 00000000 00000000
06    00111100 00000000 00000000 00000000
07    00111100 00000000 00000000 00000000
08    00111100 00000000 00000000 00000000
09    00111100 00000000 00000000 00000000
10    00111100 00000000 00000000 00000000
11    00111100 00000000 00000000 00000000
12    00111100 00000000 00000000 00000000
13    00111100 00000000 00000000 00000000
14    00111100 00000000 00000000 00000000
15    00111100 00000111 11111110 00000000
16    00111100 00011111 11111111 00000000
17    00111100 00111111 11111111 11000000
18    00111111 11110000 00000000 11111100
19    00111111 11100000 00000000 00011110
20    00111100 00000000 00000000 00001111
21    00111100 00000000 00000000 00001111
22    00111100 00000000 00000000 00001111
23    00111100 00000000 00000000 00001111
24    00111100 00000000 00000000 00001111
25    00111100 00000000 00000000 00001111
26    00111100 00000000 00000000 00001111
27    00111111 11000000 00000000 00111110
28    00111111 11110000 00000000 01111100
29    00111100 01111000 00000001 11111000
30    00111100 00111111 11111111 10000000
31    11111100 00011111 11111111 00000000
32    11111100 00001111 11111110 00000000
```

• Figure 1.1: *Bit-map pattern for the letter b*

types of graphics. Any shape can be formed into a bit map and printed.

The performance of your particular printer depends on a variety of factors, including its memory, the available typefaces and fonts, and the software you're using.

• *Print Quality and Memory*

Using special hardware, the LaserJet can print at higher resolution.

The quality of the printed image is measured in *dpi* (dots per inch). The higher the *resolution*—the more dots printed per square inch—the better the image. All LaserJet printers can print in 75, 100, 150, and 300 dpi. The size of the image that can be printed at the highest resolution depends on your printer's memory.

Like your computer, the LaserJet has its own internal memory, or *RAM*. The memory holds any softfonts that are downloaded into the printer as well as the text of your page to be printed. If you're used to other types of printers, you probably think of memory strictly in terms of characters—a document with 2000 characters would only require 2000 bytes of memory. But this is not so with laser printers.

The DeskJet + can print in 300 dpi. It requires optional RAM cartridges for storing softfonts and can access up to 512K RAM using two 256K cartridges.

At 300 dpi, each square inch contains 90,000 dots, for a total of 7,560,000 dots on an 8- by 10½-inch page. Since each dot takes up 1 bit, you need 945,000 bytes of memory (7,560,000 divided by 8) to store the page in memory for it to be printed. Actually, a full page of graphics can take up more than 1.2 million bytes.

You can add more memory to your printer by purchasing expansion boards, as discussed in Chapter 16. The LaserJet models have the following standard and maximum memory:

LaserJet	128K, expandable to 2Mb
LaserJet + and 500 +	512K, expandable to 2Mb
LaserJet II	512K, expandable to 4Mb
LaserJet IID	640K, expandable to 4Mb
LaserJet 2000	1.5Mb, expandable to 5.5Mb

Note that not all this memory is available for your fonts and documents. The LaserJet uses some of it for its own purposes. Of the standard 512K or 640K available on most models, 395K is actually free for your use.

The LaserJet is a *page* printer, which means that the entire page (text and graphics) must be stored in the printer's memory before it is printed. Each dot of the printed page takes up memory, so a high-resolution document takes up more memory than one printed in a lower resolution.

With standard memory, only the LaserJet 2000 can print a full page of text in high resolution (300 dpi). The other models, with the exception of the original, can print just one half a page of text in high resolution. The original LaserJet prints a full page at 75 dpi, 1/2 page at 100 dpi, 1/4 page at 150 dpi, and 1/16 page at 300 dpi.

• *Text Appearance: Type Styles and Fonts*

Laser printers can reproduce a wide variety of type styles. The number of styles and sizes available to you depends on which LaserJet printer model you are using. We'll discuss type styles and how to use them in detail in Chapter 4. Here we'll review the terms used to describe type and explain the ways that fonts are made available to the LaserJet.

Type Terminology

Some users misinterpret advertisements regarding the number of fonts provided by a laser printer. They read "13 fonts," for example, and picture 13 different typefaces—Roman, Helvetica, Old English, etc. When they get their printer, they find that only two or three typefaces are actually supplied, but in several fonts each.

Typeface refers to the general shape or overall characteristics of printed characters. All characters in the same typeface share common design elements. Figure 1.2 illustrates three different typefaces. The Times typeface, shown at the top of the figure, has small serifs at the ends of lines, and each character has some thick lines and some thin ones. The Helvetica typeface, on the next line, doesn't have serifs (called *sans serif*), and all the strokes are the same thickness. The third typeface, Old English, has more elaborate characters.

The size of type is measured in *points*. There are approximately 72 points in an inch, so a 12-point typeface is about one-sixth of an inch.

A *font* is a collection of characters, numbers, and symbols in one size and style, such as Times 14-point bold. Fonts of the same basic style are collected into families. So all Times fonts are members of the Times family, even though each font is a different size or shape. Times 12-point and Times

---

TIMES
HELVETICA
𝔒𝔩𝔡 𝔈𝔫𝔤𝔩𝔦𝔰𝔥

• Figure 1.2: *Sample typefaces*

12-point italic, for example, are different fonts in the same family.

Sources of Fonts

The sources for DeskJet + fonts are the same. See Appendix D for details.

The LaserJet gets the bit maps of all fonts from three possible sources: internal fonts, plug-in cartridges, and softfonts on disk (except for the original LaserJet, which cannot use softfonts).

Internal Fonts

The LaserJet IID and 2000 can print all fonts in either orientation.

Internal fonts are bit maps that are permanently stored in the printer's ROM (read-only memory). They don't use up any RAM (random-access memory), and the default Courier font is immediately available when you turn on your printer.

You can select from the various internal fonts, but you can't change them. Some of these fonts may print in only one *orientation*, which refers to the direction of printing on the page, as illustrated in Figure 1.3. Portrait orientation, the default, prints across the page. Landscape prints down the side, lengthwise.

The internal fonts in the various LaserJet models are listed in Table 1.1. As you can see, except for the LaserJet 2000, the font selection is rather limited.

Cartridge Fonts

The S2 font cartridge is supplied with the LaserJet IID.

Cartridge fonts are plugged into the printer. Like internal fonts, they are available immediately when you turn on your printer. The original LaserJet, LaserJet +, and LaserJet 500+ have one cartridge slot; the LaserJet II and IID have two cartridge slots; and the LaserJet 2000 has three.

Softfonts

Softfonts (or *downloadable fonts*) are typefaces stored on a disk and transferred to your computer's memory when needed. They offer greater

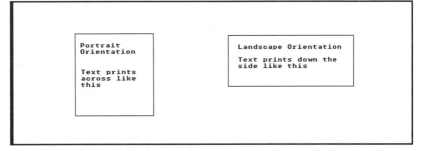

• Figure 1.3: *Printer orientation*

• Table 1.1: *LaserJet Internal Fonts*

PRINTER	INTERNAL FONTS
LaserJet	Courier, 10 pitch (12 point), portrait and landscape
LaserJet + and 500 +	Same as above, as well as Line Printer, 16.66 pitch (8.5 point) in portrait
LaserJet II	Same as above, as well as Courier Bold in portrait and landscape, and Line Printer in landscape
LaserJet IID	Courier Regular, Bold, and Italic, both 10 and 12 characters per inch (12 points) in portrait and landscape; and Line Printer in portrait and landscape
LaserJet 2000	34 internal fonts in portrait and landscape, including Courier in 10 and 12 pitch (10 and 12 points), Prestige Elite in 16.66 and 12 pitch (7 and 10 points), Line Draw in 16.66 and 10 pitch (8.5 and 12 points), Line Printer in 15 and 16.66 pitch (8.5 points), Times Roman proportionally spaced in 8 and 10 points, and Helvetica proportionally spaced in 14 points

variety but take time to load into your printer. Since they can consume a great deal of disk space, for all practical purposes, you should have a hard-disk drive to use softfonts. Chapter 4 describes how to install softfonts with softfont utilities, and other chapters cover how to use them with specific applications.

Maximum Fonts and Sizes

The number of fonts you can use at one time is determined by your printer. The maximum for each model is as follows:

LaserJet	8 fonts per page
LaserJet + and 500 +	16 per page, 16 in memory
LaserJet II	16 per page, 32 in memory

LaserJet IID	Limited only by memory
LaserJet 2000	Limited only by memory

The maximum point size you can print depends on your printer and the amount of memory it has installed. The LaserJet models can print the following type sizes:

LaserJet	18 points maximum
LaserJet + and 500 +	30 points maximum
LaserJet II	Fonts up to 14 inches
LaserJet IID	Limited only by memory
LaserJet 2000	Limited only by memory

Fonts and the Symbol Set

Each font can contain up to 255 different characters and other symbols. When your computer transmits a character to the printer, it sends the specific sequence of ones and zeros, the ASCII code for the particular character. The printer uses the font bit maps to find the character this sequence represents and prints it.

Since dealing with ones and zeros is often difficult for us humans, we also refer to each character by the decimal equivalent to the binary sequence. So the capital A, transmitted as 0100001, is also referred to as ASCII decimal number 65.

Most fonts assign the same binary sequence, and thus the same decimal number, to the letters, numbers, and other symbols you see on your keyboard. These are in the ASCII code range from 32 to 127. So it is more than likely, for example, that when the computer sends the ASCII code for 65, the bit map matching that in the printer will produce the letter A.

But the characters below 32 and above 127 may not be represented by the same codes in different fonts. In one font, the bit map for ASCII code 172 may produce Ç; in another font, the same code will print |. No matter what character you see on the screen, the LaserJet will print the character with the matching code number in the bit map.

The specific assignment of characters to ASCII codes in a font is called the *symbol set*. The two most common symbol sets are shown in Appendix B. By default, all LaserJet printers start with the Roman-8 set, which doesn't assign a character to every ASCII code. The PC symbol set contains all the characters that you can display on your computer screen, but this set is not built in to the earlier LaserJet models. If you want to use a symbol set that's not in the internal fonts, you'll have to use a font cartridge or softfont, as discussed in Chapters 3 and 4.

The LaserJet models have the following internal symbol sets:

LaserJet	Roman-8
LaserJet + and 500 +	Roman-8, ASCII, Roman Extended
LaserJet II	Roman-8, ASCII, IBM-US (PC), IBM-DN, ECMA-94, 17 ISO sets, and 2 HP sets
LaserJet IID	Same as above, as well as Legal and IBM-850
LaserJet 2000	Same as above, as well as Line Draw, OEM-1 (for DEC computers), Math-8, Technical-1 (for DEC computers), and PC8 Danish/Norwegian

• *Printer Mechanics: Speed, Output, and Nonprintable Areas*

Along with the quality of your printed pages and the type styles they contain, there are some basic printer mechanics that affect your work with the LaserJet. These include the speed of printing, the way paper is output, the way individual pages are output, and the areas of the page that cannot be printed on.

Printer Speed

While the speed of other printers is measured in characters per second (cps), laser printer speed is described in pages per minute. The LaserJet 2000 can print up to 20 pages a minute, the other models up to 8. The LaserJet IID can print up to 3.7 pages per minute in the duplex mode. These figures, and those quoted for other laser printers, are just general guidelines. The actual speed of printing—how long it takes for a page of data to be transferred from the computer and output on a sheet of paper—depends on the complexity and coverage of the page, the type of interface you're using, and if you have any optional accessories installed.

Paper Output

One major complaint people had about the original LaserJet and LaserJet + was that the printed sheets came out printed-side up. When you took the sheets from the output tray, the last page was on top, the first on the bottom. So, the job had to be recollated in the correct order.

This problem was addressed in later models. So, if you have a newer LaserJet 500 + , LaserJet II, or LaserJet IID, the paper will be output in the correct order. This is also true of the LaserJet 2000.

Page Output

The paper will also be ejected when certain other control codes are received, such as a change in orientation or paper sources or a command to reset the printer.

Printing is always page oriented, which means that the process doesn't start until the printer has all the information it needs for the complete page. After the page is printed, it is ejected from the printer so the next page can begin. What if you're printing less than a whole page? This is no problem if you're using a word processing package or other program that issues a form-feed command at the end of the page, letting the LaserJet know that's all for that sheet.

With other software, or when printing screen dumps or directory listings, you'll have to manually eject the page from the printer. You'll learn how to do this in Chapters 2 and 3.

Nonprintable Areas

Because of the way LaserJet printers are made, you can't print within 1/4 inch of the edges of the page, and the printer leaves default top and bottom margins of about 1/2 inch. So on 8 1/2-by-11-inch paper, you can print on only 8 by 10 1/2 inches. Table 1.2 shows the nonprintable areas (top, bottom, left, and right margins) for each model.

• Table 1.2: *Nonprintable Areas (in inches)*

MODEL	TOP	BOTTOM	LEFT	RIGHT
LaserJet	0.25	0.25	0.25	0.25
LaserJet +	0.25	0.25	0.16	0.32
LaserJet 500 +	0.25	0.25	0.16	0.32
LaserJet II	0.20	0.20	0.17	0.33

• Table 1.2: *Nonprintable Areas (in inches) (Continued)*

MODEL	TOP	BOTTOM	LEFT	RIGHT
LaserJet IID	0.17	0.17	0.17	0.17
LaserJet 2000	0.17	0.17	0.17	0.17

Most word processing programs that work with the LaserJet handle the situation without trouble. But this nonprintable area may present problems with some programs, especially those that attempt to print more than 60 lines on each page. Other programs may add their own top margin setting to the default ½ inch, or you may even lose some lines or get extra pages printed. In Chapter 3, you'll learn how to get around this limitation.

• *Printer Command Languages*

The original LaserJet cannot perform advanced PCL commands for downloading fonts and certain types of graphics.

The DeskJet + is also a PCL printer, and it recognizes most of the commands used with LaserJet models.

All LaserJet printers understand commands in the Printer Control Language (PCL). For instance, if your word processor wants to print in eight lines per inch instead of the default six, it has to send the appropriate PCL command to the printer. There are PCL commands for selecting fonts, setting page margins, drawing lines and graphics, selecting symbol sets, and controlling every aspect of the printer's operation.

If all your application programs are designed for using the LaserJet, you may never have to "speak" in PCL yourself. But to get the most from your printer with other applications, or if you want to access printer features from within your own computer programs, you'll have to learn PCL.

PCL commands are discussed in later chapters about applications that don't explicitly work with the LaserJet, and details for programming in PCL are presented in Part 4 of this book.

PostScript is another laser printer language introduced with the Apple LaserWriter printer. Its main advantage over PCL is that it can dynamically scale and manipulate fonts and graphics any way you want. You can print a font in any size and create special effects "on the fly." Chapter 15 discusses using PostScript (or emulating its advantages).

Now we'll move from discussion to action. In the next chapter, you'll learn how to connect your computer and printer, configure your printer, and use its controls.

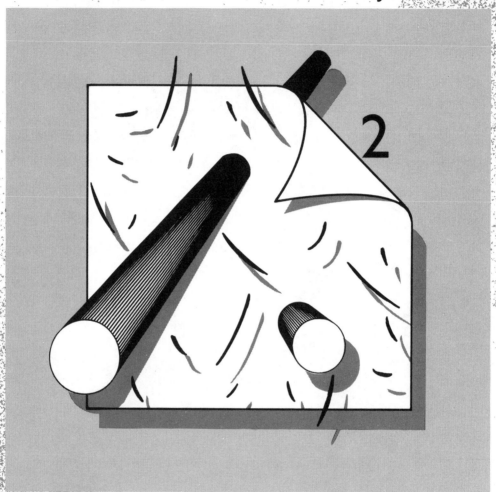

H·P L·A·S·E·R·J·E·T

2

Connecting and
Controlling Your Printer

• Getting ready to print with your LaserJet involves setting up your computer so that it can communicate with the printer, configuring the printer to accept the data your computer sends, and learning how to operate the printer's controls. This chapter explains how to set up and control each of the LaserJet models.

• *Connecting Your Computer and Printer*

The DeskJet+ has both parallel and serial connections, and it interfaces with your computer as discussed here.

How you set up your printer depends on whether you're using a serial or parallel interface and on the particular model you have. First we'll discuss the differences between the interfaces, and then you'll learn how to connect your model to the proper one.

Instructions for unpacking your printer are in the Hewlett-Packard printer manuals. Make sure you've read those sections thoroughly before you begin. If you have a printer advertised as LaserJet compatible, check the literature that came with it to see which Hewlett-Packard model it is compatible with and whether it has serial, parallel, or both connections. Then refer to your own manual to confirm the proper setup procedure as you read along here.

Your computer may have a serial or parallel connection, called a *port*, on its back, or it might have both. The serial port will be labeled serial, modem, or COM1. The parallel port will be labeled parallel, printer, or LPT1. The terms *serial* and *parallel* refer to the way data (your characters and graphics) is passed from your computer to your printer.

Technically, the baud rate is a measure of the signal rate change, the speed at which electronic signals can go from one to zero. While it is not necessarily the same as bits per second (bps), most people use the terms interchangeably.

In a serial transmission, your computer sends the bits one at a time over one wire, as illustrated in Figure 2.1. The speed at which the bits travel is the *baud rate*. Your computer and printer must be set at the same baud rate so the printer accepts bits at the same speed the computer is sending them.

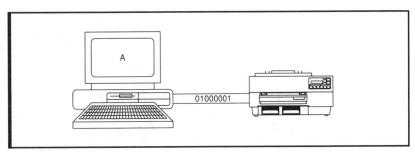

• Figure 2.1: *Serial transmission*

In a parallel transmission, the 8 bits that make up each character are sent out simultaneously over eight separate wires, as illustrated in Figure 2.2. Because 8 bits leave the computer at one time, parallel transmission is much faster than serial—an average of two to three times the fastest serial baud rate.

With the exception of the original LaserJet, which has only a serial interface, LaserJet printers can be set up for either serial or parallel transmission. The LaserJet II and IID also have an I/O port for connecting optional interfaces, as we'll discuss in Chapter 16. The LaserJet 2000 can use a Dataproducts interface, but it must be purchased separately.

Choosing a Port

If your computer has both a serial and parallel port, and you're not using the original LaserJet, you can use either one. However, since parallel transmission is so much more efficient and serial connections present some complications, you should use the parallel port unless your printer is more than 15 feet away from your computer.

Chapter 16 discusses connecting your printer to more than one computer for maximum productivity.

Because they are susceptible to noise and signal degradation, normal parallel connections are not as effective over a distance of more than 15 feet or so. If your computer and printer are further apart than this, you're better off using a serial connection unless you want to purchase additional hardware. (In Chapter 16, I'll describe hardware solutions to using parallel connections over greater distances.) But even serial cable has its limitations. Most sources recommend a maximum distance from 50 to 80 feet, but the actual maximum depends on the speed of the transmission. If you must go further than 80 feet, select a slow transmission (baud) rate when configuring your system. The slower the baud rate, the greater the distance a signal can travel without being affected.

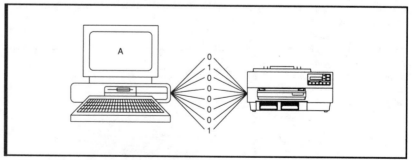

• Figure 2.2: *Parallel transmission*

Using a Single Serial Port for Multiple Devices

Most computers today come with one serial and one parallel port. While the parallel port is typically used only for printing, the serial port can accept a variety of other devices. Modems, mice, digitizer tablets, and plotters, for example, can also be connected to your computer's serial port.

If you are going to connect your LaserJet to your computer's only serial port, you may want to be able to use that port for other devices as well.

You could add another serial (or parallel) port, but that requires purchasing a circuit card that is installed inside your computer, taking up an available slot. You would then have to configure your software to send its data to the appropriate port, for example, the port for accepting mouse coordinates or the one for sending printer data.

One alternative is to purchase some type of switching mechanism that allows you to use more than one device in a single port. An A-B switch, for example, can connect two printers to one computer or two computers to a printer. Figure 2.3 illustrates the setup for attaching two printers to the same port. When you want to use one printer, you turn the switch to the A setting. To use the other, flip the switch to B.

But if you are using a mechanical switch, don't just flip it at any time. These types of switches have metal contacts that slide from one position to the other. Turning the switch may generate voltage spikes that can damage the printer (or other interface equipment). If you have this type of switch, *only turn it when your printers are off.*

Electronic switches don't generate the same type of voltage spikes and are generally safe to use. Some have small touch pads rather than a knob to turn or can be controlled from your computer.

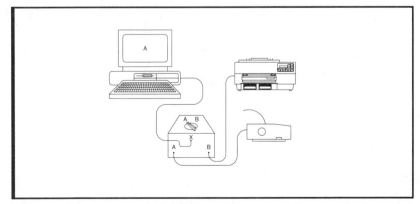

• Figure 2.3: *Using an A-B switch to connect two printers to the same port*

The other option is to unplug one device and plug in the other every time you want to change. Just make sure your printer is turned off when you're plugging in cables because this can generate the same dangerous voltage spikes that you get with mechanical switches.

Unfortunately, using a single port for several serial devices is not as easy as just turning a switch or plugging in a new cable. As you'll learn shortly, if you are using a serial port for your printer, you must set the baud rate and direct the printer output to this port each time you start your computer. You can have this done automatically through a batch file, but these settings may not work with other serial devices, such as a modem, mouse, or a different printer. For example, if one printer is set for 9600 baud and the other for 2400, each time you turn the switch (or change that cable), you'll also have to change your computer's baud rate and perhaps some other settings.

Connecting Your LaserJet to the Serial Port

If you want to set up your printer for serial operation (or have no other option), you'll be using the connector on the printer shown in Figure 2.4. This is a female-gender serial connector that accepts a 25-pin cable. The serial connector on your computer might be a 25-pin or 9-pin male connector, as shown in Figure 2.5.

Gender refers to whether the connector has pins (male) or receptacles (female). The connector and the end of the cable that attaches to it must complement each other.

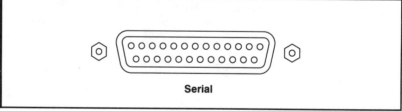

Serial

• Figure 2.4: *Printer's serial connector (25-pin female)*

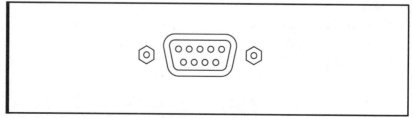

• Figure 2.5: *Computer's serial connector (9-pin male)*

Use these instructions even if your serial interface is an RS-422. You'll learn how to configure the printer for that interface later in this chapter.

The first thing you'll need is the proper cable to connect the two. The ends of the cable must be the correct gender, size, and type for the computer and printer.

If you have a 9-pin connector or a female serial port, you'll also need a special attachment for most serial cables. Your computer store can sell you an adapter to connect a 25-pin cable to a 9-pin serial port. It's a short cable with 9 pins on one end, 25 pins on the other. You might also need a gender changer, which is a device that allows a female cable to connect to a female serial port.

With some computers, you can use a standard cable to connect your LaserJet. These include the DEC Rainbow, Apple IIe, and Apple III. But don't try to use a serial cable that comes with a modem, even if it looks like it would work.

When you get a cable, be sure to tell the salesperson the name and model number of your computer. If possible, take the model number of the cable from the Hewlett-Packard manual. At a minimum, write down the gender and number of pins of the computer port and be sure the gender on the cable is opposite the one on the computer (male to female). If you have more than one serial port, note whether your printer is attached to the first (COM1) or second (COM2) one.

After you have connected the proper cable to the computer and printer, you must set up your operating system for serial printing.

Setting Up the AUTOEXEC File

Because IBM-compatible computers are set for parallel printing, you have to tell your computer how you want to communicate with your serial printer each time you start up. This is done through a program called AUTOEXEC.BAT, a small batch command file used by the operating system when your computer is turned on or rebooted. To use the LaserJet as a serial printer, with the default serial transmission settings, the file AUTOEXEC.BAT must have these two lines:

```
mode    com1:9600,n,8,1,p
mode    lpt1: = com1:
```

Here's how these lines work:

mode   Both lines begin with the DOS Mode command.

com1:   The name of the serial port attached to the printer. If your printer is attached to a second serial port, use com2: in the command line.

9600	Data will be transmitted at 9600 baud.
n	There is no parity. Parity is a communications system for checking the accuracy of transmitted data. Other possible settings are e (even) and o (odd).
8	Each transmitted character will contain 8 bits.
1	Each character will have 1 extra bit to signify when it ends, called the stop bit.
p	The serial port is being used for serial printing, not data communications.
lpt1: = com1:	All characters going to the lpt1: port (the default parallel port) should be redirected to the serial port. (Again, use com2: if it's going to the second serial port.)

This file must be on the root directory of your hard disk, or on the floppy disk that you use to start your computer.

Before creating this AUTOEXEC.BAT file, check to see if one already exists on your disk. You might already have one that sets up the serial port for use with the mouse, controls the directory path, or requests the date and time. In most cases, you can add the two lines to the existing AUTOEXEC.BAT file rather than replacing it.

Follow these steps to create or modify the AUTOEXEC.BAT file:

1. Start your computer as normal. If you have a floppy-disk system, use the same floppy disk that you'll be using whenever you start your system.

2. Type

   dir autoexec.bat

3. If the file is listed on the screen, add the two commands to it. Type

   copy autoexec.bat + con: autoexec.bat

   and press ⏎. You'll see

   autoexec.bat
   con

4. If you saw the "file not found" message, the file doesn't exist on your disk. Type

   copy con: autoexec.bat

   and press ◄─┘. (The cursor will go to the next line but nothing else will happen; don't worry—that's normal.)

5. Now type

   mode com1:9600,n,8,1,p

   mode lpt1: = com1:

   Next, press Ctrl-Z (hold down the Ctrl key, and then press Z). The characters ^Z will appear on the screen, signifying the end of your input. Finally, press ◄─┘.

6. The AUTOEXEC.BAT file now contains those two lines. To make sure, type **TYPE AUTOEXEC.BAT** to confirm the file is on your disk and that the two Mode commands have been added.

Now whenever you start your computer, you'll see a message similar to

   redirecting lpt1: to com1:

If you want to use your printer right now, you have to reboot to activate those commands. Press Ctrl-Alt-Del.

The exact wording depends on the version of your operating system.

These serial transmission settings agree with the default setup of your LaserJet. Most users will be able to start printing without making any changes to the printer itself. However, if you want to change the baud rate—perhaps because your printer is further than 80 feet from the computer—you have to enter the new baud rate in the AUTOEXEC.BAT file and reconfigure the LaserJet itself, as explained later in the chapter.

Connecting Your LaserJet to the Parallel Port

If you want to connect your printer to a second parallel port, the command mode lpt1: = lpt2: must be in your AUTOEXEC.BAT file. Refer to the previous section about setting up the AUTOEXEC file.

The parallel port on your printer is shown in Figure 2.6. Instead of pins like the serial port, it has a slot with metallic contacts. The parallel port on the computer, however, looks just like its serial port, except it's usually female gender. Cables for parallel printers are relatively standard. They have a pin-type connector at the end that attaches to the computer, and a

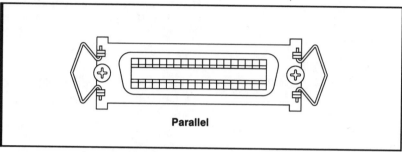

Parallel

• Figure 2.6: *Printer's parallel port*

parallel-type that inserts into the printer, so you can't plug it in the wrong way. Just confirm the type and gender before purchasing your cable.

Since the LaserJet is set up as a serial printer, you will have to tell it you're using parallel transmission. Depending on the model of your printer, this is done by changing switches inside the machine (LaserJet + and 500 +) or through the control panel, as explained in the following sections.

• *Changing the LaserJet, LaserJet +, and LaserJet 500 + Printer Interface*

See Appendix D for details on configuring DeskJet + printers.

To modify the interface configuration in the earlier models, you have to remove the printer's back panel and change the position of dip (dual-inline package) switches. You'll need a small Phillips screwdriver and about ten minutes. It's not a difficult task, but you must be careful to set the switches correctly. Remember, you only have to modify the configuration if you plan to use the LaserJet + or 500 + as a parallel printer (the original LaserJet only has a serial interface) or you want to change the default serial interface.

Accessing the Dip Switches

Follow these steps to access the printer's dip switches:

1. Unplug the printer. Don't take any chances by just turning it off.

2. Remove the four small screws that attach the back panel.

3. Remove the screw holding the metal vertical support bracket in the center of the printer.

You'll see a small bank of eight little switches. Figure 2.7 shows these switches in the default position set by the factory for a LaserJet + . (The switches may be different for the original LaserJet.) The positions of the switches determine the interface you're using and the type of serial communications.

A switch is on when it is in the up position, off when it is in the down position. The switches are numbered from left to right, with switch 1 at the far left and switch 8 on the right.

To move the switches, use a thin, rigid object like the end of a paper clip. Don't try it with a pencil because the point could break and fall into the printer.

Using the Parallel Interface

To set up the LaserJet + or 500 + for parallel printing, flip dip switch 1 on by putting it in the up position. Don't touch the other switches; just leave them in the default position. Replace the vertical support bracket and the back cover, and you're ready to print.

Changing the Serial Configuration

To change the default baud rate for serial communications on an original LaserJet, LaserJet + , or LaserJet 500 + , first make sure that dip switch 1 is in the off position, pointing down. The baud rate is determined by the position of switches 2, 3, and 4, as listed in Table 2.1. Set the switches to the same baud rate you entered in the DOS Mode command in the AUTOEXEC.BAT file. For example, to use a baud rate of 2400, switch 2 should be off (down), and 3 and 4 on (up).

Although a baud rate of 19,200 is listed in the table, you should only use this speed if you have a short cable connecting the printer and computer.

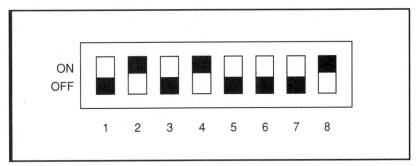

• Figure 2.7: *LaserJet + dip switches (in default position)*

• Table 2.1: *Dip Switch Settings for Serial Communications Baud Rates*

BAUD RATE	SWITCH 2	SWITCH 3	SWITCH 4
300	off	off	off
600	off	off	on
1200	off	on	off
2400	off	on	on
4800	on	off	off
9600	on	off	on
19200	on	on	off

If you have any trouble printing at this setting, change the Mode command and dip switch settings to 9600.

Generally, the baud rate is the only adjustment you will have to make. But if you've connected your printer directly to a modem or your system has special requirements, you might need to change other switch settings.

The other switches serve the following purposes:

Switch 7 is not used on the LaserJet + and 500 + , and switches 1, 5, 6, and 7 serve no purpose on the original LaserJet.

• Switch 5 controls the auto-continue function. In the default off position, the printer will stop on certain error conditions and flash a message until you press Continue. When this switch is in the on position, the printer will automatically continue after the message flashes ten times.

• Switch 6 is called the Robust Xon switch. When the printer is free to accept characters, it sends the computer a signal called Xon (Xoff means it's not ready to print). When this switch is off, only one Xon signal is transmitted. When it's on, the factory setting, the Xon signal is repeated every second while the printer is waiting for data. If your printer continues to eject blank pages, set this switch to the off position.

• Switch 8 controls the data terminal ready (DTR) signal sent from the printer to the computer. Before any information can be transmitted by the computer, the printer must send a DTR signal on pin 20 of the serial connector. By default, the LaserJet places a "high" state on the pin to signify that it is turned on and ready. If your system's serial interface requires a "low" state on the DTR pin, set this switch to the off position.

Changing to an RS-422 Interface

Another configuration adjustment you can make with the original LaserJet, LaserJet +, and LaserJet 500 + is to change the serial interface from an RS-232, the most common, to an RS-422, another type of serial interface that can transmit over longer distances. To the left of the printer's dip switch bank are four sets of pins, as illustrated in Figure 2.8. The sets are numbered 1 to 4, starting at the left. By default, two small jumpers connect the pins of sets 1 and 3, signifying an RS-232 interface.

To configure your printer as a RS-422 device, pull the jumpers off of sets 1 and 3, then place them on sets 2 and 4. You might have to use a needle-nose pliers to grasp and remove the jumpers.

When all your configuration changes are complete, replace the vertical support bracket and the rear panel.

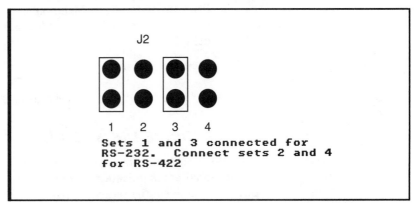

• Figure 2.8: *LaserJet, LaserJet +, and LaserJet 500 + pins for serial interface type*

• *Changing the LaserJet II and LaserJet IID Printer Interface*

Configuration changes to the LaserJet II and IID are made directly from the control panel. The following sections describe how to set up the printer for parallel communications and change the serial configuration. We'll describe the other controls later in the chapter.

Using the Parallel Interface

If you want to use your computer's parallel port, you have to change the LaserJet's factory settings. Follow these steps:

1. Turn the printer on.

2. Press the On Line button on the control panel until the light above the button goes off.

3. With the LaserJet II: Press and hold down the Menu button (about five seconds) until you see the message SYMBOL SET = ROMAN-8* on the display panel. Press the Menu button twice. The message I/O = SERIAL* appears in the display.

   With the LaserJet IID: Press and hold down the Menu button (about five seconds) until you see the message AUTO CONT = OFF*, and then press the Menu button again to see the message I/O = SERIAL*.

4. Press the + button to display the message I/O = PARALLEL.

5. Press the Enter/Reset Menu button. An asterisk appears next to the word Parallel on the display, indicating that this is the new default setting.

6. Press the On Line button.

Your printer is now ready for parallel transmissions.

Changing the Serial Configuration

If you set your computer to a baud rate other than 9600 or have some unique serial communications requirements, you'll have to change the printer's default configuration settings. Here's the procedure.

1. Turn the printer on.

2. Press the On Line button on the control panel until the light above the button goes off.

3. With the LaserJet II: Press and hold down the Menu button (about five seconds) until you see the message SYMBOL SET = ROMAN-8* on the display panel. Press the Menu button twice. The message I/O = SERIAL* appears in the display, confirming that you're using the serial interface. If I/O = PARALLEL* appears, press the + or − button to select a serial interface, and then press the Enter/Reset Menu button.

The printer must be "off line" when you use any of the control panel functions.

Changing to a RS-422 interface on a LaserJet II requires flipping a switch in the back of the computer, as explained shortly.

With the LaserJet IID: Press and hold down the Menu button (about five seconds) until you see the message AUTO CONT = OFF*. Press the Menu button to see the message I/O = SERIAL*. If I/O = PARALLEL* appears, press the + or − button to select a serial interface, and then press the Enter/Reset Menu button. Press the Menu button to see the message SERIAL = RS-232*. If you want to use an RS-422 interface, press the + or − button to display SERIAL = RS-422, and then press Enter.

4. Press the Menu button to display the message BAUD RATE = 9600*.

5. Press the + or − button until the baud rate you want to use appears in the display.

6. Press the Enter/Reset Menu button to place an asterisk next to the baud rate, indicating it is now the default setting.

The next two settings are for handshaking signals that your printer uses to indicate it is turned on and ready to accept characters. The first is Robust Xon. When this is set on, the printer transmits a signal to the computer every second that it can accept characters and none are being sent. (When the printer's buffer becomes full, it sends an XOFF telling the computer to stop sending data.)

Some not-so-compatible computers, or a modem connected directly to the printer, may have trouble interpreting this continual stream of XON signals and force blank pages to be ejected. If this happens, follow step 7 below.

The DTR (data terminal ready) signal is another handshaking signal telling the computer that your printer is turned on and ready. By default, the LaserJet sends a "high" signal out on pin 20 (the DTR pin), the most common setting used by computers. However, it's possible that a not-so-compatible computer may expect a "low" signal on pin 20 when the printer is ready. So using the factory setting, the printer appears perpetually turned off. If you can't get anything to print, follow step 8 below.

7. Press the Menu button to display the message ROBUST XON = ON*. Press the + or − button to display ROBUST XON = OFF, and then press the Enter/Reset Menu button to make the setting the new default.

8. Press the Menu button to display DTR POLARITY = HI*. Press the + or − button to display DTR POLARITY = LO, and then press the Enter/Reset Menu button.

9. Press the On Line button when you are finished making changes.

Using the RS-422 Interface on the LaserJet II

To use your LaserJet II with an RS-422 interface, you must make some changes to small switches in the back of the printer. You'll need a small Phillips screwdriver to access the switches and a rigid, pointed device, such as the end of a paper clip, to change their positions. Don't use a pencil because the point could break and fall into the printer.

Make sure that you've selected serial for the I/O option (follow steps 1 through 3 above), then turn off your computer and follow these steps:

1. On the back of the printer, near the bottom, is a small plate marked OPTIONAL I/O. Remove the two screws holding the plate in place.

2. On the right side of the opening, you'll see a switch labeled SW 1 with two tabs toward the bottom. Move these tabs to the up position.

3. Replace the OPTIONAL I/O plate.

• Controlling Your Printer

Most of the LaserJet controls are on its control panel. The control functions and their operations on the various printer models are detailed in the following sections.

Operating the LaserJet, LaserJet +, and LaserJet 500 +

The LaserJet 500 + has the same control panel as the LaserJet +, but the Manual Feed button is renamed Paper Select, and to the far right of the panel are four indicators: Auto, U Cassette, L Cassette, and Manual.

Figure 2.9 shows the control panel on the original LaserJet, and Figure 2.10 shows the one on the LaserJet +. Both control panels contain five buttons, a number of indicator lights, and a small display area. The buttons allow you to control the printer, and the display area and indicator lights indicate the printer's status or condition.

The Display Area

The display at the left of the control panel indicates certain status and error conditions. Most of the time, the display shows 00, meaning that the printer is on and ready. All the possible displays are shown in Tables 2.2, 2.3, and 2.4.

Table 2.2 shows status messages, which tell you about the condition of the printer. These are not error messages but reports about the current

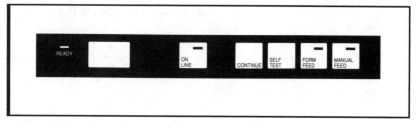

• Figure 2.9: *LaserJet control panel*

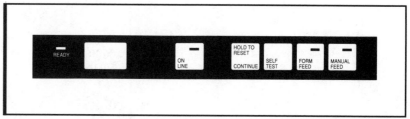

• Figure 2.10: *LaserJet + control panel*

• Table 2.2: *Control Panel Status Messages*

LASERJET, LASERJET +, AND LASERJET 500 + DISPLAY	LASERJET II AND LASERJET IID DISPLAY	MEANING
00	00 READY	The printer is ready to accept characters.
02	02 WARMING UP	Wait.
04	04 SELF TEST	The printer is continuously printing test sheets. Press On Line. When the last sheet is printed, the LaserJet will go back on line.

• Table 2.2: *Control Panel Status Messages (Continued)*

LASERJET, LASERJET +, AND LASERJET 500 + DISPLAY	LASERJET II AND LASERJET IID DISPLAY	MEANING
05	05 SELF TEST	The printer is going through a nonprinting self test.
06	06 PRINTING TEST	The printer is making a printed test of its internal characters.
06	06 FONT PRINTOUT	The printer is printing samples of its fonts.
07	07 RESET	You have reset the printer to its user-selected default settings and cleared the buffer.
	08 COLD RESET	The printer is returning to the factory-set defaults (2000).
	09 MENU RESET	All Printing menu settings are returned to their factory values.
15	15 ENGINE TEST	The printer is making a pattern test print.

state of the printer. Table 2.3 shows attendance messages, which require some action on your part. Table 2.4 lists error conditions that require special action or repair. Call for repair (or consider purchasing extra memory for condition 20) if any of these conditions occur repeatedly.

• Table 2.3: *Control Panel Attendance Messages*

LASERJET, LASERJET +, AND LASERJET 500 + DISPLAY	LASERJET II AND LASERJET IID DISPLAY	MEANING
	10 RESET TO SAVE	Indicates that you've made Printing menu changes while printing data (IID). Press Reset to activate your menu selections, or Continue to complete printing with the original settings.
11*	11 PAPER OUT*	The paper tray is empty.
LC 11*	LC EMPTY*	Lower paper cassette (500 + and IID) is empty.
UC 11*	UC EMPTY*	Upper paper cassette (500 + and IID) is empty.
12*	12 PRINTER OPEN*	The upper body of the printer is open. Close the printer and wait until the ready message is displayed.
13*	13 PAPER JAM*	Paper is jammed and must be cleared.
14*	14 NO EP CART*	No toner cartridge is installed.

• Table 2.3: *Control Panel Attendance Messages (Continued)*

LASERJET, LASERJET +, AND LASERJET 500+ DISPLAY	LASERJET II AND LASERJET IID DISPLAY	MEANING
	16 TONER LOW*	The cartridge is almost out of toner—you've got enough for about 30 to 100 more pages.
PC*	PC LOAD*	A different size paper cassette has been requested by the software.
PF*	PF FEED*	Manual feed has been requested—insert paper in the manual feed tray.
PE*	PE FEED*	Envelope feed has been requested; the size of the envelope will appear.
	EC LOAD*	Load and insert the envelope feeder (II).
	UE LOAD*	Load and insert the envelope feeder into the upper tray.
	LE LOAD*	Load and insert the envelope feeder into the lower tray.
	UE TRAY*	
	LE TRAY*	
	EE TRAY*	Confirm that the envelopes in the tray match the size requested in the display.

• Table 2.3: *Control Panel Attendance Messages (Continued)*

LASERJET, LASERJET +, AND LASERJET 500+ DISPLAY	LASERJET II AND LASERJET IID DISPLAY	MEANING
FC*	FC LEFT, RIGHT or BOTH*	Check that the font cartridge is inserted properly.
FE	FE CARTRIDGE	The font cartridge has been removed during operation. Make sure the printer is off line when you insert or remove font cartridges.
	UC LOAD*	Insert the proper paper in the upper tray.
	LC LOAD*	Insert the proper paper in the lower tray.
FF		Your printer cannot handle the amount of data sent to it. Turn the printer off, then on and try again.

• Table 2.4: *Control Panel Error Messages*

LASERJET, LASERJET +, AND LASERJET 500+ DISPLAY	LASERJET II AND LASERJET IID DISPLAY	MEANING
20*	20 ERROR*	The full page being printed requires more memory than

• Table 2.4: *Control Panel Error Messages (Continued)*

LASERJET, LASERJET +, AND LASERJET 500 + DISPLAY	LASERJET II AND LASERJET IID DISPLAY	MEANING
		available. Press continue to print the partial page. If this occurs, try reducing the resolution, the number of fonts, or the size of graphics that you're trying to print.
21*	21 ERROR*	Printer overrun—the page-formatting process is too slow; some data will not be printed. Press Continue.
22*	22 ERROR*	The printer's overflow buffer has overflowed—probably a handshaking or communications problem and data will be lost. Press Continue.
40*	40 ERROR*	A communications or configuration problem message indicating a data error has occurred. Press Continue.
41*	41 ERROR*	A temporary error has occurred on the page just printed. Press Continue.

• Table 2.4: *Control Panel Error Messages (Continued)*

LASERJET, LASERJET +, AND LASERJET 500 + DISPLAY	LASERJET II AND LASERJET IID DISPLAY	MEANING
	42 ERROR	
	43 ERROR*	A problem has occurred in an optional interface card. Press Continue, then check the installed card.
50	50 SERVICE	A malfunction in the fusing assembly. Turn the printer off for ten minutes then try again.
51*	51 ERROR*	A beam detect malfunction. Press Continue.
52*	52 ERROR*	A scanner malfunction. Press Continue.
53		A malfunction in the temperature-control circuits. Turn the printer off for ten minutes.
	53 ERROR	An error in an optional memory card. Turn the printer off and check the card.
54*		A main motor malfunction or the input cassette is overfilled. Press Continue.

• Table 2.4: *Control Panel Error Messages (Continued)*

LASERJET, LASERJET +, AND LASERJET 500 + DISPLAY	LASERJET II AND LASERJET IID DISPLAY	MEANING
	54 SERVICE	An error during duplexing; confirm that the correct size paper is loaded, then turn the printer off and on.
55*	55 ERROR*	A printer command error. Press Continue.
	56 SERVICE	An output selector error. Turn the printer off then on.
60		An internal bus error or an improperly seated cartridge. Try turning the printer off and reseating the cartridge.
61	61 SERVICE	A program ROM error. Turn the printer off then on.
62	62 SERVICE	A font ROM error.
63	63 SERVICE	A dynamic RAM error. Turn the printer off, then check any optional memory boards. Turn the printer back on and try again.
64	64 SERVICE	A scan buffer error. Turn the printer off then on.

• Table 2.4: *Control Panel Error Messages (Continued)*

LASERJET, LASERJET +, AND LASERJET 500 + DISPLAY	LASERJET II AND LASERJET IID DISPLAY	MEANING
65	65 SERVICE	A D-RAM controller error. Turn the printer off then on.
67	67 SERVICE	A miscellaneous interface error. Turn the printer off then on.
	68 SERVICE	An internal error. Turn the printer off then on.
	69 SERVICE	An error on the board installed in the I/O slot. Turn the printer off then on.
	70 ERROR	You are using a font cartridge not designed for the LaserJet. Turn the printer off then on.
	71 ERROR	A miscellaneous font cartridge error. Turn the printer off then on.
	72 SERVICE	A font cartridge error. Turn the printer off then on.
	79 SERVICE	A firmware error. Turn the printer off then on.

In Tables 2.3 and 2.4, the conditions marked with an asterisk can be cleared with the Continue button, as explained shortly.

The On Line Button and Indicator

When the printer is on line, the indicator light on the On Line button is lit and the printer is ready to accept characters from the computer. When the On Line indicator is off, the printer is called off line, and the computer will not transmit any characters. To switch between on and off line, press and release the On Line button.

To use any of the other controls on the panel, the printer must first be off line. The On Line indicator flashes when data is being accepted by the printer.

The Continue Button

You can continue printing after you remedy any of the conditions marked with an asterisk in Tables 2.3 and 2.4. Press and release the Continue button (marked Hold to Reset/Continue on the LaserJet+ and 500+) to clear the error and continue printing. For example, if your paper jams, clear the jammed paper, and then press Continue to print the page.

The Hold to Reset Button

With the LaserJet+ and 500+, hold down the Hold to Reset/Continue button to reset the printer, returning it to its original default settings. Any formatting or orientation settings and any temporary softfonts sent previously will be erased. After about 3 seconds, the display will show 07, and then the printer will return to the ready state. Softfonts loaded as permanent will remain in the printer's memory.

The Self Test Button

Press the Self Test button to have the printer perform a two-part test. During the first phase, 05 appears in the display as the printer tests its internal circuitry. Then 06 will appear while a full-page test pattern is printed. The complete test takes only a few seconds. When it's completed, the display shows 00 again, indicating the printer is in ready condition.

If any other messages appear during the test, refer to Tables 2.2, 2.3, or 2.4 to see what's wrong and how it can be corrected.

The Form Feed Button and Indicator

The indicator on the Form Feed button lights when data is being received from the computer. When the page becomes full or a form-feed

Most of the functions of the control panel can be performed directly from your keyboard using special utility software described in Chapter 3.

If you hold down the Self Test button too long, 06 will appear and the printer will continue making test prints until you press Self Test again or press On Line.

command is received from your software, the page is ejected and the Form Feed indicator light goes off.

If you've printed less than a full page and no form feed command is sent by your software, you have to eject the page yourself after it is printed. Press the On Line button to place the printer off line, press the Form Feed button to eject the paper, and then press the On Line button again to return the printer to the ready condition.

Pressing the Form Feed button also clears the LaserJet's internal buffer, which is the memory area where your document is stored after being received from the computer. So don't press the Form Feed button unless you're sure all the data has been transmitted and the page won't eject by itself. If you press the Form Feed button in the middle of a printing function, some of your text may be lost.

Never turn off your printer when the Form Feed indicator light is on because this means that there is data in the printer. Press the On Line button to place the printer off line; then press the Form Feed button to print whatever is there. You can then turn off the printer without losing any data.

The Manual Feed Button and Indicator

The LaserJet will automatically use the paper that's in the cassette tray. To feed paper or envelopes yourself, you must place the printer in the manual feed mode. Press the On Line button to put the printer off line, and then press the Manual Feed button. The indicator light on the button will go on.

In this mode, the message PF will flash on the display when you have to insert paper. The message alternates with a code indicating the type of paper expected: L for letter, LL for legal, A4 for A4, or B5 for B5. It is your responsibility to insert the correct paper. For example, if your document is formatted to print on legal-sized paper, the LL message will alternate with PF. If you insert letter-size paper, some of your document will not print.

When you see these codes flashing, it means that your text has been transmitted and is ready to print. Do not turn off or reset the computer until you load paper and print the page. Otherwise, your data will be lost.

The Paper Select Button and Indicators

The LaserJet 500+ has a Paper Select button in place of Manual Feed and four paper source indicators on the right of the control panel:

Auto   As long as both cassettes are the same size, the printer will switch to the second tray when the first runs out of paper.

U CASSETTE	Paper will be taken from the upper cassette. When the tray becomes empty, the printer will not switch to the next but alternately flash 11 and UC on the display.
L CASSETTE	Paper will be taken from the lower cassette. LC and 11 will flash when the tray becomes empty.
MANUAL	Set for manual feed, as explained in the previous section.

Other Controls and the Toner Indicator

There are two other operator controls on the printer: the density dial and the Test Print button. Both are located on the printer's left side. If you press the Test Print button, the printer will print a full page of vertical lines. The lines should be uniform throughout the page, with the same density at every spot and no irregularities.

The density dial controls the darkness of the printed image, and it has settings from 1 to 9. Turn it clockwise (to a higher number) for a lighter image, counter-clockwise (to a lower number) for darker. You won't actually see much difference between the two end positions, but the printer will use less toner at the lighter side.

Start with the dial at the center position, then lower it for a few test sheets. To extend toner cartridge life, keep the dial as low as possible. As your toner starts to run out, you'll have to turn the dial up to maintain printing quality.

Finally, when a toner cartridge is installed, you'll see a toner indicator on the right side of the printer. The indicator shows the number of times the drum has rotated, not the actual level of toner. However, it does provide a general guideline, going from green, to yellow, to red as you use the cartridge.

Operating the LaserJet II and IID

Figure 2.11 shows the control panel on the LaserJet II, and Figure 2.12 shows the one on the LaserJet IID. Notice that several buttons have labels on the top and bottom. To perform the function printed on top, press and release the button. Holding the button down for several seconds activates the function printed below.

The control panel also has a display area and indicator lights.

The Display Area

The display on the left side of the panel indicates certain status and error conditions. Most of the time, the display shows 00 READY, meaning

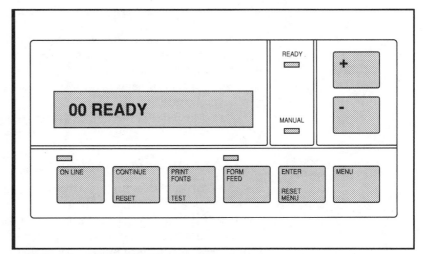

• Figure 2.11: *LaserJet II control panel*

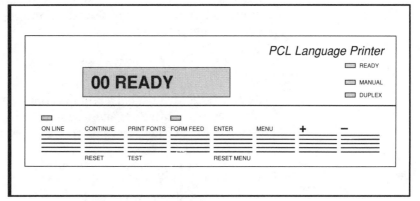

• Figure 2.12: *LaserJet IID control panel*

that the printer is on and ready. All the possible displays are listed in Tables 2.2, 2.3, and 2.4.

Table 2.2 shows status messages, which tell you about the condition of the printer. Table 2.3 lists conditions that require some action from the operator. Table 2.4 lists error conditions that require special action or repair. Call for repair if any of these conditions occur repeatedly.

In Tables 2.3 and 2.4, the conditions marked with an asterisk can be cleared with the Continue button, as discussed shortly.

The On Line Button and Indicator

When the printer is on line, the indicator light above the On Line button is lit and the printer is ready to accept characters from the computer. When the On Line indicator is off, the printer is called off line, and the computer will not transmit any characters. To switch between on and off line, press and release the On Line button.

To use any of the other controls on the panel, the printer must first be off line.

The Continue/Reset Button

You can continue printing after you remedy any of the conditions marked with an asterisk in Tables 2.3 and 2.4. Press and release the Continue/Reset button to clear the error and continue printing.

Hold down the Continue/Reset button to reset the printer, returning it to the settings contained in its control panel. Any formatting or orientation settings and any temporary softfonts set previously will be erased. After about three seconds, the display will show 07 RESET, and then the printer will return to the ready state. Softfonts loaded as permanent will remain in the printer's memory.

The Print Fonts/Test Button

Press and release the Print Fonts/Test button to print a report listing the name, size, and symbol sets of the printer's internal fonts; any installed cartridges and softfonts; and a sample of each. Figure 2.13 shows an example of a portrait fonts report. The message 06 FONT PRINTOUT appears during this process.

If you hold down the Print Fonts/Test button too long, 04 SELF TEST will appear and the printer will continue making test prints until you press the On Line button. Several sheets may print before the LaserJet responds.

Hold the Print Fonts/Test button down about three seconds to perform a two-part test. During the first phase, 05 SELF TEST appears in the display as the printer tests its controller circuitry. Then 06 PRINTING TEST appears as a full-page test pattern is printed listing the Printing and Configuration menu settings. Figure 2.14 shows an example of a test pattern. The complete test takes only a few seconds. When it's completed, the display shows 00 READY again, indicating the printer is in ready condition.

If any other messages appear during the test, refer to Tables 2.2, 2.3, and 2.4 to see what's wrong and how it can be corrected.

The Form Feed Button and Indicator

The indicator on the Form Feed button lights when data is being received from the computer. When the page becomes full or a form-feed command is received from your software, the page is ejected and the Form Feed indicator light goes off.

```
                -------- PORTRAIT FONTS --------

FONT                              POINT SYMBOL
 ID          NAME          PITCH  SIZE  SET      PRINT SAMPLE
----  ------------------   -----  ----- ------   ------------------------

"PERMANENT" SOFT FONTS


LEFT FONT CARTRIDGE


RIGHT FONT CARTRIDGE


INTERNAL FONTS

 I00  COURIER              10     12       8U   ABCDEfghij#$@[\]^`(|)~123
                                                ÀÂ°ÇÑ¡¿£§êéàèëòÀØåæÄÜßÅÐÒ
 I01  COURIER              10     12      10U   ABCDEfghij#$@[\]`'(|)`123
                                                íó|┤╡╣╗╝┘┐└┴┬├─┼╞╟╚╔╩╦╠║╪╫┐│απΦ
 I02  COURIER              10     12      11U   ABCDEfghij#$@[\]`'(|)`123
                                                íó|┤╡╣╗╝┘┐└┴┬├─┼╞╟╚╔╩╦╠║╪╫┐│απΦ
 I03  COURIER              10     12       0N   ABCDEfghij#$@[\]`'(|)`123
                                                ¡¢³´¶.¹»½ÃÅÈÉÍÎÐÓÕ×ØÚÞàãè
 I04  COURIER BOLD         10     12       8U   ABCDEfghij#$@[\]^`(|)~123
                                                ÀÂ°ÇÑ¡¿£§êéàèëòÀØåæÄÜßÅÐÒ
 I05  COURIER BOLD         10     12      10U   ABCDEfghij#$@[\]`'(|)`123
                                                íó|┤╡╣╗╝┘┐└┴┬├─┼╞╟╚╔╩╦╠║╪╫┐│απΦ
 I06  COURIER BOLD         10     12      11U   ABCDEfghij#$@[\]`'(|)`123
                                                íó|┤╡╣╗╝┘┐└┴┬├─┼╞╟╚╔╩╦╠║╪╫┐│απΦ
 I07  COURIER BOLD         10     12       0N   ABCDEfghij#$@[\]`'(|)`123
                                                ¡¢³´¶.¹»½ÃÅÈÉÍÎÐÓÕ×ØÚÞàãè
 I08  LINE_PRINTER         16.6   8.5      8U   ABCDEfghij#$@[\]^`(|)~123
                                                ÀÂ°ÇÑ¡¿£§êéàèëòÀØåæÄÜßÅÐÒ
 I09  LINE_PRINTER         16.6   8.5     10U   ABCDEfghij#$@[\]`'(|)`123
                                                íó|┤╡╣╗╝┘┐└┴┬├─┼╞╟╚╔╩╦╠║╪╫┐│απΦ
 I10  LINE_PRINTER         16.6   8.5     11U   ABCDEfghij#$@[\]`'(|)`123
                                                íó|┤╡╣╗╝┘┐└┴┬├─┼╞╟╚╔╩╦╠║╪╫┐│απΦ
 I11  LINE_PRINTER         16.6   8.5      0N   ABCDEfghij#$@[\]`'(|)`123
                                                ¡¢³´¶.¹»½ÃÅÈÉÍÎÐÓÕ×ØÚÞàãè
```

• Figure 2.13: *Sample portrait fonts report*

If you've printed less than a full page and no form-feed command is sent by your software, you have to eject the page yourself after it is printed. Press the On Line button to place the printer off line, press the Form Feed button to eject the paper, and then press the On Line button to return the printer to the ready condition.

Pressing the Form Feed button also clears the LaserJet's internal buffer, which is the memory area where your document is stored after being received from the computer. So don't press the Form Feed button unless you're sure all the data has been transmitted and the page won't eject by itself. If you press the Form Feed button in the middle of a printing function, some of your text may be lost.

```
Page Count=15464
Program ROM Datecode=19861203, Internal Font ROM Datecode=19860611
Auto Continue=OFF
Installed Memory=512 Kbytes
Symbol Set=ROMAN-8
Menu Items:
   Copies=1, Manual Feed=OFF, Font Source=I, Font Number=00,
   Form=66 Lines
Parallel I/O


 !"#$%&'()*+,-./0123456789:;<=>?@ABCDEFGHIJKLMNOPQRSTUVWXYZ[\]^_`abcdefghijklmno
!"#$%&'()*+,-./0123456789:;<=>?@ABCDEFGHIJKLMNOPQRSTUVWXYZ[\]^_`abcdefghijklmnop
"#$%&'()*+,-./0123456789:;<=>?@ABCDEFGHIJKLMNOPQRSTUVWXYZ[\]^_`abcdefghijklmnopq
#$%&'()*+,-./0123456789:;<=>?@ABCDEFGHIJKLMNOPQRSTUVWXYZ[\]^_`abcdefghijklmnopqr
$%&'()*+,-./0123456789:;<=>?@ABCDEFGHIJKLMNOPQRSTUVWXYZ[\]^_`abcdefghijklmnopqrs
%&'()*+,-./0123456789:;<=>?@ABCDEFGHIJKLMNOPQRSTUVWXYZ[\]^_`abcdefghijklmnopqrst
&'()*+,-./0123456789:;<=>?@ABCDEFGHIJKLMNOPQRSTUVWXYZ[\]^_`abcdefghijklmnopqrstu
'()*+,-./0123456789:;<=>?@ABCDEFGHIJKLMNOPQRSTUVWXYZ[\]^_`abcdefghijklmnopqrstuv
()*+,-./0123456789:;<=>?@ABCDEFGHIJKLMNOPQRSTUVWXYZ[\]^_`abcdefghijklmnopqrstuvw
)*+,-./0123456789:;<=>?@ABCDEFGHIJKLMNOPQRSTUVWXYZ[\]^_`abcdefghijklmnopqrstuvwx
*+,-./0123456789:;<=>?@ABCDEFGHIJKLMNOPQRSTUVWXYZ[\]^_`abcdefghijklmnopqrstuvwxy
+,-./0123456789:;<=>?@ABCDEFGHIJKLMNOPQRSTUVWXYZ[\]^_`abcdefghijklmnopqrstuvwxyz
,-./0123456789:;<=>?@ABCDEFGHIJKLMNOPQRSTUVWXYZ[\]^_`abcdefghijklmnopqrstuvwxyz{
-./0123456789:;<=>?@ABCDEFGHIJKLMNOPQRSTUVWXYZ[\]^_`abcdefghijklmnopqrstuvwxyz{|
./0123456789:;<=>?@ABCDEFGHIJKLMNOPQRSTUVWXYZ[\]^_`abcdefghijklmnopqrstuvwxyz{|}
/0123456789:;<=>?@ABCDEFGHIJKLMNOPQRSTUVWXYZ[\]^_`abcdefghijklmnopqrstuvwxyz{|}~
0123456789:;<=>?@ABCDEFGHIJKLMNOPQRSTUVWXYZ[\]^_`abcdefghijklmnopqrstuvwxyz{|}~▒
123456789:;<=>?@ABCDEFGHIJKLMNOPQRSTUVWXYZ[\]^_`abcdefghijklmnopqrstuvwxyz{|}~▒ 
23456789:;<=>?@ABCDEFGHIJKLMNOPQRSTUVWXYZ[\]^_`abcdefghijklmnopqrstuvwxyz{|}~▒ !
3456789:;<=>?@ABCDEFGHIJKLMNOPQRSTUVWXYZ[\]^_`abcdefghijklmnopqrstuvwxyz{|}~▒ !"
456789:;<=>?@ABCDEFGHIJKLMNOPQRSTUVWXYZ[\]^_`abcdefghijklmnopqrstuvwxyz{|}~▒ !"#
56789:;<=>?@ABCDEFGHIJKLMNOPQRSTUVWXYZ[\]^_`abcdefghijklmnopqrstuvwxyz{|}~▒ !"#$
6789:;<=>?@ABCDEFGHIJKLMNOPQRSTUVWXYZ[\]^_`abcdefghijklmnopqrstuvwxyz{|}~▒ !"#$%
789:;<=>?@ABCDEFGHIJKLMNOPQRSTUVWXYZ[\]^_`abcdefghijklmnopqrstuvwxyz{|}~▒ !"#$%&
89:;<=>?@ABCDEFGHIJKLMNOPQRSTUVWXYZ[\]^_`abcdefghijklmnopqrstuvwxyz{|}~▒ !"#$%&'
9:;<=>?@ABCDEFGHIJKLMNOPQRSTUVWXYZ[\]^_`abcdefghijklmnopqrstuvwxyz{|}~▒ !"#$%&'(
:;<=>?@ABCDEFGHIJKLMNOPQRSTUVWXYZ[\]^_`abcdefghijklmnopqrstuvwxyz{|}~▒ !"#$%&'()
;<=>?@ABCDEFGHIJKLMNOPQRSTUVWXYZ[\]^_`abcdefghijklmnopqrstuvwxyz{|}~▒ !"#$%&'()*
<=>?@ABCDEFGHIJKLMNOPQRSTUVWXYZ[\]^_`abcdefghijklmnopqrstuvwxyz{|}~▒ !"#$%&'()*+
 ÀÂÈÊËÎÏ´`ˆ¨˜ÙÛ£¯Ýý°ÇçÑñ¡¿¤£¥§ƒ¢âêôûáéóúàèòùäëöüÅîØÆåíøæÄìÖÜÉïßÔÁÃãÐðÍÌÓÒÕõŠšÚŸÿ
ÀÂÈÊËÎÏ´`ˆ¨˜ÙÛ£¯Ýý°ÇçÑñ¡¿¤£¥§ƒ¢âêôûáéóúàèòùäëöüÅîØÆåíøæÄìÖÜÉïßÔÁÃãÐðÍÌÓÒÕõŠšÚŸÿÞ
ÂÈÊËÎÏ´`ˆ¨˜ÙÛ£¯Ýý°ÇçÑñ¡¿¤£¥§ƒ¢âêôûáéóúàèòùäëöüÅîØÆåíøæÄìÖÜÉïßÔÁÃãÐðÍÌÓÒÕõŠšÚŸÿÞþ
ÈÊËÎÏ´`ˆ¨˜ÙÛ£¯Ýý°ÇçÑñ¡¿¤£¥§ƒ¢âêôûáéóúàèòùäëöüÅîØÆåíøæÄìÖÜÉïßÔÁÃãÐðÍÌÓÒÕõŠšÚŸÿÞþ·
ÊËÎÏ´`ˆ¨˜ÙÛ£¯Ýý°ÇçÑñ¡¿¤£¥§ƒ¢âêôûáéóúàèòùäëöüÅîØÆåíøæÄìÖÜÉïßÔÁÃãÐðÍÌÓÒÕõŠšÚŸÿÞþ·µ
ËÎÏ´`ˆ¨˜ÙÛ£¯Ýý°ÇçÑñ¡¿¤£¥§ƒ¢âêôûáéóúàèòùäëöüÅîØÆåíøæÄìÖÜÉïßÔÁÃãÐðÍÌÓÒÕõŠšÚŸÿÞþ·µ¶
ÎÏ´`ˆ¨˜ÙÛ£¯Ýý°ÇçÑñ¡¿¤£¥§ƒ¢âêôûáéóúàèòùäëöüÅîØÆåíøæÄìÖÜÉïßÔÁÃãÐðÍÌÓÒÕõŠšÚŸÿÞþ·µ¶¾
Ï´`ˆ¨˜ÙÛ£¯Ýý°ÇçÑñ¡¿¤£¥§ƒ¢âêôûáéóúàèòùäëöüÅîØÆåíøæÄìÖÜÉïßÔÁÃãÐðÍÌÓÒÕõŠšÚŸÿÞþ·µ¶¾-
´`ˆ¨˜ÙÛ£¯Ýý°ÇçÑñ¡¿¤£¥§ƒ¢âêôûáéóúàèòùäëöüÅîØÆåíøæÄìÖÜÉïßÔÁÃãÐðÍÌÓÒÕõŠšÚŸÿÞþ·µ¶¾-¼
`ˆ¨˜ÙÛ£¯Ýý°ÇçÑñ¡¿¤£¥§ƒ¢âêôûáéóúàèòùäëöüÅîØÆåíøæÄìÖÜÉïßÔÁÃãÐðÍÌÓÒÕõŠšÚŸÿÞþ·µ¶¾-¼½
ˆ¨˜ÙÛ£¯Ýý°ÇçÑñ¡¿¤£¥§ƒ¢âêôûáéóúàèòùäëöüÅîØÆåíøæÄìÖÜÉïßÔÁÃãÐðÍÌÓÒÕõŠšÚŸÿÞþ·µ¶¾-¼½ª
¨˜ÙÛ£¯Ýý°ÇçÑñ¡¿¤£¥§ƒ¢âêôûáéóúàèòùäëöüÅîØÆåíøæÄìÖÜÉïßÔÁÃãÐðÍÌÓÒÕõŠšÚŸÿÞþ·µ¶¾-¼½ªº
˜ÙÛ£¯Ýý°ÇçÑñ¡¿¤£¥§ƒ¢âêôûáéóúàèòùäëöüÅîØÆåíøæÄìÖÜÉïßÔÁÃãÐðÍÌÓÒÕõŠšÚŸÿÞþ·µ¶¾-¼½ªº«
ÙÛ£¯Ýý°ÇçÑñ¡¿¤£¥§ƒ¢âêôûáéóúàèòùäëöüÅîØÆåíøæÄìÖÜÉïßÔÁÃãÐðÍÌÓÒÕõŠšÚŸÿÞþ·µ¶¾-¼½ªº«■
Û£¯Ýý°ÇçÑñ¡¿¤£¥§ƒ¢âêôûáéóúàèòùäëöüÅîØÆåíøæÄìÖÜÉïßÔÁÃãÐðÍÌÓÒÕõŠšÚŸÿÞþ·µ¶¾-¼½ªº«■»
£¯Ýý°ÇçÑñ¡¿¤£¥§ƒ¢âêôûáéóúàèòùäëöüÅîØÆåíøæÄìÖÜÉïßÔÁÃãÐðÍÌÓÒÕõŠšÚŸÿÞþ·µ¶¾-¼½ªº«■»±
¯Ýý°ÇçÑñ¡¿¤£¥§ƒ¢âêôûáéóúàèòùäëöüÅîØÆåíøæÄìÖÜÉïßÔÁÃãÐðÍÌÓÒÕõŠšÚŸÿÞþ·µ¶¾-¼½ªº«■»± 
Ýý°ÇçÑñ¡¿¤£¥§ƒ¢âêôûáéóúàèòùäëöüÅîØÆåíøæÄìÖÜÉïßÔÁÃãÐðÍÌÓÒÕõŠšÚŸÿÞþ·µ¶¾-¼½ªº«■»±  
ý°ÇçÑñ¡¿¤£¥§ƒ¢âêôûáéóúàèòùäëöüÅîØÆåíøæÄìÖÜÉïßÔÁÃãÐðÍÌÓÒÕõŠšÚŸÿÞþ·µ¶¾-¼½ªº«■»±  À
°ÇçÑñ¡¿¤£¥§ƒ¢âêôûáéóúàèòùäëöüÅîØÆåíøæÄìÖÜÉïßÔÁÃãÐðÍÌÓÒÕõŠšÚŸÿÞþ·µ¶¾-¼½ªº«■»±  ÀÂ
```

• Figure 2.14: ***Sample test pattern***

Never turn off your printer when the Form Feed indicator light is on because this means that there is data in the printer. Place the printer off line, and then press the Form Feed button to print whatever is there. You can then turn off the printer without losing any data.

Changing the LaserJet II and LaserJet IID Settings

The last four buttons on the control panel of the LaserJet II and IID let you change the printer's default settings and, as you learned earlier, the configuration.

The Menu button allows you to change settings in two menus: Printing and Configuration. You use the + and − buttons to display selections for the menu options, and the Enter/Reset Menu button to save them. To return to the default settings, press the Enter/Reset Menu button and hold it down. The message 09 MENU RESET will appear on the display.

Now let's take a look at these menus in detail and see how to select options.

Changing Printing Menu Settings

Press and release the Menu key to change any of the settings on the Printing menu. Through this menu you can perform the following functions:

- Change the number of copies
- Switch between manual and continuous feed
- Select the source of fonts
- Select the font number
- Set the number of lines per inch

With the LaserJet IID, the Printing menu also allows you to make other selections:

- Turn on duplex printing
- Select a binding edge
- Select the paper tray
- Set the paper size
- Select landscape or portrait orientation
- Select the symbol set

To change any of the Printing menu settings, follow this general procedure:

1. Press and release the Menu button to display the message COPIES = 01∗, the first Printing menu option.

2. Press and release the Menu button to display the option you wish to change.

3. Press the + or − button to display your specific selection.

4. Press and release the Enter/Reset Menu button to accept your setting. An asterisk will appear next to your selection, indicating it is the new default value.

To make other changes, repeat steps 2 through 4; then follow step 5 to reset the printer and save your changes.

5. With the LaserJet II: You *must* return the printer to the ready condition and reset the printer to save your changes. Press the Menu button to display the message 00 READY. Then press and hold down the Continue/Reset button until the message 07 RESET appears.

With the LaserJet IID: Just press the On Line button. The LaserJet IID automatically resets itself when you press the Enter/Reset Menu button after making a menu selection. However, if you have characters in the buffer or fonts loaded, you'll see the message 10 RESET TO SAVE, warning you something will be lost if you reset the printer. If this occurs, take one of these actions: Press and release the Continue/Reset button to save your menu changes but clear the buffer, press and hold down the Continue/Reset button to remain off line without saving your changes, or press the On Line button to go back on line without saving your changes.

Printing Menu Options

The Printing menu on both the LaserJet II and IID contains the following options:

The LaserJet II and IID display the Printing menu options in a different order. Here they are listed in the LaserJet II order. For both models, press the Menu button until you see the option you want to change.

- **Copies**: Press the Menu button to display COPIES = 01∗, then press the + or − button to display the number of copies you want to print.

- **Manual Feed**: Press the Menu button to display the message MANUAL FEED = OFF∗. Press the + or − button to display MANUAL FEED = ON. In this mode, the PF message will flash on the display when you have to insert paper. The message alternates with a code indicating the type of paper expected: L for letter, LL for legal, A4 for A4, or B5 for B5. It's your responsibility to insert the correct size. You might lose some characters if the sheet is smaller than the size requested. When you see these codes flashing, it means that your text has been transmitted and is ready to print. Do not turn off or reset the computer until you load the paper and print the page, or your data will be lost.

- **Font Source**: Press the Menu button to display FONT SOURCE = I∗, then the + or − button to make your selection. The options are I for internal fonts, L for left cartridge, R for right cartridge, and S for softfonts.

- **Font Number**: Press the Menu button to display FONT NUM- BER = 00∗, then the + or − button to make your selection. Valid font numbers range from 0 to 99. The report generated when you press and release the Print Fonts/Test button will list the number of all internal fonts.

- **Form Length**: Press the Menu button to display FORM = 060 LINES∗, then the + or − button to make your selection. This sets the number of lines that print on the page, not the length of the page. Valid settings are from 5 to 128. For example, on 8½- by 11- inch paper, set FORM = 080 LINES to print eight lines per inch.

The LaserJet IID Printing menu lists the following additional items:

- **Duplex**: Press the Menu button to display DUPLEX = OFF∗. Press the + or − button to display DUPLEX = ON, and then press and release the Enter/Reset Menu button. The Duplex indicator will light when the LaserJet IID is in duplex mode. You'll learn more about duplex printing in Chapter 3.

- **Binding Edge**: Press the Menu button to display BIND = LONG- EDGE∗. Press the + or − button to display your selection, and then press the Enter/Reset Menu button. Binding edge choices are also discussed in Chapter 3.

- **Paper Tray**: Press the Menu button to display TRAY = BOTH∗. Press the + or − button to select from Upper and Lower, and then press the Enter/Reset Menu button.

- **Paper Size**: Press the Menu button to display PAPER = LET- TER∗. Depending on the tray or envelope feeder being used, press the + or − button to display your selection. The choices for paper are Letter (8½ by 11 inches), Legal (8½ by 14 inches), Executive (7¼ by 10½ inches), and A4 (210 by 297 mm). The choices for envelopes are Commercial-10 (4 $\frac{1}{8}$ by 9$\frac{1}{2}$ inches), Monarch (3 $\frac{7}{8}$ by 7$\frac{1}{2}$ inches), DL (110 by 220 mm), and C5 (162 by 229 mm). Make your selection, and then press the Enter/Reset Menu button.

- **Orientation**: Press the Menu button to display the message ORIEN-TATION = P∗. Press the + or − button to display ORIENTA-TION = L∗, and then press the Enter/Reset Menu button.

- **Symbol Set**: Press the Menu button to display SYM SET = Roman-8∗. Press the + or − button to select the desired symbol set, and then press the Enter/Reset Menu button. If you select a new symbol set, check the font number setting to confirm it hasn't changed.

Changing Configuration Menu Settings

To access the Configuration menu, press and hold down the Menu key. Through this menu, you can perform the following functions:

- Change the symbol set (on LaserJet II only)

- Switch auto-continue off and on

- Select the serial or parallel interface

- Select the baud rate

- Select Robust on or off

- Change the DTR polarity

To change any of the Configuration menu settings, follow this general procedure:

1. Press and hold down the Menu button to display SYM SET = ROMAN-8∗, the first menu option on the LaserJet II, or AUTO CONT = OFF∗, the first one on the LaserJet IID.

2. Press and release the Menu button to display the option you wish to change.

3. Press the + or − button to display your specific selection.

4. Press and release the Enter/Reset Menu button to accept your setting. An asterisk will appear next to your selection, indicating it is the new default value.

5. To make other changes, repeat steps 2 through 4. Then press the On Line button to save your changes. (You do not have to reset the computer when selecting from the Configuration menu.)

Configuration Menu Options

The Configuration menu on the LaserJet II and IID contains the following options:

The LaserJet II and IID display the Configuration menu options in a different order. Here they are listed in LaserJet II order.

- **Symbol Set** (LaserJet II only): As you learned in Chapter 1, each font can contain up to 255 different letters, numbers, symbols, and other characters, grouped into symbol sets. To change from the default Roman-8 symbol set, hold down the Menu button until SYM SET = ROMAN-8∗ is displayed. Press the + or − button to display the symbol set desired, and then press the Enter/Reset Menu button. If you select a new symbol set, check the font number setting to confirm it hasn't changed.

- **Auto Continue**: Normally when an error occurs, the message flashes on the display until you press Continue and correct the error condition. If you turn auto-continue on, error messages will flash about ten seconds, and then the printer will automatically go back on line. To change this mode on the LaserJet II, hold down the Menu button until you see SYM SET = ROMAN-8∗, and then press the Menu button to display AUTO CONT = OFF∗. (With the LaserJet IID, just hold down the Menu button until you see AUTO CONT = OFF∗.) After the option is displayed, press the + or − button to display AUTO CONT = ON, and then press the Enter/Reset Menu button.

- **I/O**: This option, as you've already learned, lets you change between serial and parallel interfaces. If you installed an optional interface into the I/O slot on the LaserJet, the I/O selections will include Optional. If you change this setting, make sure you have the appropriate cable attached to the corresponding port on the printer.

These last four options will not be displayed if the interface is set for parallel.

- **Serial Card**: (LaserJet IID only): Select the RS-232 or RS-422 interface.

- **Baud Rate**: After selecting serial I/O, press the Menu button to display BAUD RATE = 9600. Press the + or − button to display your selected baud rate, and then press the Enter/Reset Menu button.

- **Robust XON**: Press the Menu button to display the message ROBUST XON = ON∗. Press the + or − button to display ROBUST = OFF, and then press the Enter/Reset Menu button.

- **DTR Polarity**: Press the Menu button to display the message DTR POLARITY = HI∗. Press the + or − button to display DTR POLARITY = LO, and then press the Enter/Reset Menu button.

Adjusting Print Density

Appendix A explains how to select and install toner cartridges.

The density dial, located underneath the toner rack, controls the darkness of the printed image. Turn it clockwise (to a higher number) for a lighter image, or counter-clockwise (to a lower number) for a darker one.

You won't see much difference between the two end positions, but the printer will use less toner at the lighter side. Start with the dial at the center position, then lower it for a few test sheets. To extend toner cartridge life, keep the dial as low as possible. As your toner starts to run out, you'll have to turn the dial up to main printing quality.

Operating the LaserJet 2000

The "industrial strength" LaserJet 2000 is certainly the most powerful of them all. It's a special printer designed for large organizations with high-volume, high-speed needs. Yet it is compatible with the remaining LaserJet line.

Chances are, if you have a LaserJet 2000 in your office, there's an operator assigned to maintain it. Even so, you should know what its indicators mean and how the controls work.

The Display Window

The display window on the left of the control panel reports status and error conditions. It's larger than the displays on the other models and can display fuller, more complete, messages such as

11.1- ADD PAPER
UPPER TRAY

The messages are self explanatory.

The Indicator Lights

There are three indicator lights next to the display window:

- The On Line indicator, when lit, means that the printer is ready to accept characters from the computer.

- The Attention indicator, when lit, means that the printer requires attention. The specific condition is indicated in the display window.

- The Data indicator light flashes when data is being received.

The Control Buttons

Most actions can be performed using the following control buttons:

- The On Line button turns the printer on and off line. The printer must be off line for any of the other buttons to function.

- The Form Feed button ejects a page from the printer.

- The Shift button allows you to use the functions printed on top of the buttons that are labeled with two functions. A small s appears in the display window when you press this button.

- The Menu/Enter button, unshifted, steps through menu items. Shifted, it accepts selections you've made in the menu.

- The Up/Down button steps through menu options.

- The Self Test/Reset button, unshifted, performs a self test. Shifted, it resets the printer and clears the buffer.

Changing Menu Settings

Press the On Line button to place the printer off line, and then press the Menu button to step through menu options. When the option you want to change is displayed, press Up or Down until the desired setting appears. Press Shift, then Enter to make the selection the default, and an asterisk appears on the display. Press the Menu button to display other options or the On Line button to begin printing.

The LaserJet 2000 menu options include the following:

- **Paper Size**: Paper up to 11 by 17 inches can be selected.

- **Secure Source**: When off, the printer will switch paper trays when one becomes empty. When on, the printer will not use the second tray.

- **Orientation**: Select portrait or landscape.

- **Form Length**: Select the number of lines per page.

- **Primary Font**: Select the font number.

- **Attendance Bell**: Turn off or on an electronic bell that rings when error conditions occur.

- **Auto Continue**: When off, the printer waits until you press the On Line button when an error condition occurs. When on, the printer goes on line automatically after ten seconds.

- **Job Separation**: Select to insert a blank separator sheet between print jobs.

Adjusting Print Density

You can control the density of the printed image using the dial on the inside of the upper-right printer door. To print darker images, turn the dial counter-clockwise toward a lower number. Turn the dial clockwise to a higher number to print lighter images.

Selecting an Interface

The LaserJet 2000 can use a serial (RS-232 or RS-422), parallel, or Dataproducts interface, purchased separately. The selected interface is controlled by switches located under an access door on the right side of the printer.

Now that your printer is connected and ready and you know how to operate the control panel, you can start using your LaserJet. The next chapter covers common printing tasks that you might perform every day.

H·P L·A·S·E·R·J·E·T

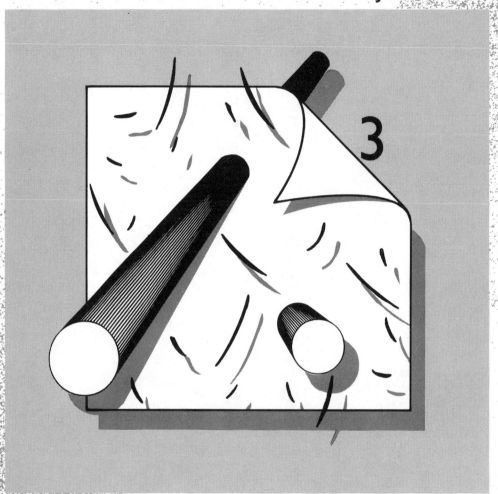

Using the LaserJet
for Everyday Tasks

- This chapter explains how to accomplish common printing chores:

  - Printing screens

  - Printing on the full page

  - Printing envelopes

  - Printing in special formats

  - Printing output designed for a dot-matrix printer

In some cases—when you're working from DOS or with an application that isn't designed for use with the LaserJet—you'll need to use a special program. Along with commercial software, you can obtain public domain and shareware programs that will get the job done.

• *Using Public Domain and Shareware Programs*

Public domain software refers to computer programs contributed by their authors to the greater computer-user community. You can buy a disk full of these programs for $3 to $6 from a number of public domain libraries, or get them free from bulletin board services. You can use, copy, or trade these programs freely.

Shareware programs are slightly different. These are copyrighted programs that the author makes available through public domain sources at the same low cost. You can look at, copy, and give away the programs, just like those in the public domain. But if you decide to use a shareware program, you must register the software and, in many cases, pay a fee, usually from $10 to $60. Registering entitles you to receive some additional support, which could include extras such as more powerful versions of the program, a detailed manual, update notices, and telephone or bulletin board support.

Both public domain and shareware software usually include basic documentation on the program disk. How good are public domain and shareware programs? You'll have to evaluate each individually. For a few dollars, you're not going to buy a Ventura Publisher or WordPerfect. I've tested all the programs mentioned in the book and found them to work. But keep in mind that you sometimes get what you pay for.

Throughout the book, I'll suggest specific public domain and shareware programs, as well as commercial products, to help you achieve the task at hand. Appendix C lists sources for the public domain, shareware, and commercial programs discussed in the book.

Consider the problem of a computer virus. All reputable public domain libraries and bulletin boards take every possible step to keep their software clean and healthy. To play it safe, purchase or download software only from nationally recognized libraries or services.

• *Sending the Next Screen to the Printer*

Ctrl-P works the same as Ctrl-PrtSc.

When you press the Ctrl-PrtSc key on your computer keyboard, everything that next appears on your screen will also go to the printer. Ctrl-PrtSc won't print what's already on your screen (we'll cover that next) but just what you type or display after you press it. After you have pressed Ctrl-PrtSc, you must explicitly turn off the function by pressing Ctrl-PrtSc again.

As an example, suppose that you want to print a listing of a directory. You would follow these steps:

1. Make sure the printer is on line and type **DIR**.

2. Press the Ctrl-PrtSc key.

3. Press the ⟵ key.

4. When the listing is complete, press Ctrl-PrtSc again.

While the directory is on the screen, you'll see your printer's On Line indicator blinking, letting you know that it is accepting data.

The LaserJet only prints and ejects a page when the page becomes full, when a form-feed command is received from the computer, or when certain format codes are received.

However, since the LaserJet is a page printer, it will not automatically eject any listing less than one page (or the second page of a long printout). You could leave the paper in there if you plan to print something else, like a second disk directory. It will eject when the page becomes full. Otherwise, you have to manually eject the page using the Form Feed button on the control panel. Here's a review of how that's done:

1. Press the On Line button until its indicator light goes out.

2. Press the Form Feed button to eject the page.

3. Press the On Line button to turn its indicator light back on.

Use this same technique to manually eject pages from the DeskJet + .

Before you turn off your printer, make sure the Form Feed indicator light is off. If not, the printer is holding some data that you'll lose when you turn it off. Eject the page first, then turn off the printer.

• *Printing the Screen Image*

Pressing the Shift-PrtSc key on your computer keyboard prints whatever is currently displayed on your screen (called a *screen dump*). Unlike the Ctrl-PrtSc function, this function doesn't have to be turned off since it just gives a quick printed "picture" of whatever you see on the monitor at the time.

What the LaserJet prints when you press Shift-PrtSc depends on whether you're in a text or graphics mode, and what characters are displayed on the screen.

When your computer is in text mode, the laser printer has no trouble printing the letter, number, and punctuation characters that you see on the keyboard. But that's not the case with graphic characters, such as lines and boxes. If you tried to print the screen shown at the top of Figure 3.1, for instance, you'd probably get the output shown at the bottom of the figure.

This brings us back to the subject of symbol sets. Remember that each LaserJet model has certain internal symbol sets available to it. By default, the LaserJet starts with the Roman-8 symbol set that contains the first 127 ASCII characters and certain foreign-language characters. But the Roman-8 set does not include line-draw and other graphic symbols needed to reproduce all the characters that can be displayed on the computer's monitor. These are found in the PC symbol set.

Printing Screens in Text Mode with the LaserJet II and LaserJet IID

With the LaserJet II and IID, you can select the PC symbol set, or any other, from the control panel menu. If you want to print a screen that contains

The DeskJet + is set to use the PC-8 symbol set, which matches the characters on your screen. Screen dumps in text mode should print correctly. You can select other symbol sets by using switches on the printer or by issuing PCL commands. See Appendix D for details.

Please Pay All Charges Before Leaving

• Figure 3.1: *Printing a text screen with graphic characters using the default Roman-8 symbol set*

graphics characters, follow these steps to switch to the PC symbol set:

1. Press the On Line button to turn the indicator light off.

2. With the LaserJet II: Press and hold down the Menu button until you see SYM SET = ROMAN-8* in the display window.

   With the LaserJet IID: Press the Menu button 10 times (11 if you're in duplex mode) until you see SYM SET = ROMAN-8*.

3. Press the + or − button (on the printer, not on your keyboard) until the display shows SYM SET = IBM-US.

4. Press the Enter/Reset Menu button. An asterisk will appear after the symbol set name.

5. Press the On Line button to turn the indicator light back on.

When you want to switch back to the default symbol set, follow the same steps to display and set SYM SET = ROMAN-8.

DISPPS is a public domain program for printing text mode screen dumps on PostScript-equipped printers.

Printing Screens in Text Mode with the LaserJet, LaserJet +, and LaserJet 500 +

Printing screens with graphics characters is more complicated with the earlier LaserJet models. These models don't have the PC symbol set built in, but you can print text screens with graphic characters by using cartridge fonts, filtering programs or, with the LaserJet + and 500 +, a soft-font. Or you can capture the screen image in a text file and print it after making the necessary adjustments.

Using Cartridge Fonts

Chapter 4 describes how to install a font cartridge.

Some plug-in font cartridges contain symbol sets that are not provided internally. For instance, cartridges 92290S1 and 92290S2 contain the PC-8 symbol set that matches your computer's characters, and cartridges 92286G, H, and T have line-draw symbol sets. But since the early LaserJet models don't have a built-in control panel menu from which to select features, you have to choose symbol sets using PCL commands or a program that provides these capabilities.

There are a number of both public domain and commercial programs that you can use to select printing options. All of them either present a menu of options or let you enter your selection on the DOS command line.

For example, the shareware program SU is a TSR (terminate and stay resident) program that lets you select any LaserJet option before printing the screen. Here's how to use it to print a screen that contains graphic characters:

1. Load SU and display the screen you want to print.

2. Press Shift-PrtSc to activate SU and display the menu illustrated in Figure 3.2. The menu will appear at the bottom of your screen. To use the line-draw symbol set of cartridge H, press F to select Fonts. You'll see the menu shown at the top of Figure 3.3.

4. Press ◄─┘ twice to display the menu shown at the bottom of Figure 3.3.

5. Press the ─► key to select 92286H.

6. Press ◄─┘ to return to the main menu.

```
===============================Setup v3.1===============================
Select : :
   F-ont Select   V-ert & Horz Pitch   P-age Length      A-dditional Utils
   M-argin Setup  S-kip Perf Region    N-umber of Copies T-ray Select

F1 = Exit  F2 = Reset LJ  F3 = Show SETUP  F4 = PrtSC  F10 = Setup LaserJet
```

- Figure 3.2: *SU main menu*

```
===============================Setup v3.1===============================
Select ==> Goto Pg 2    Orient   92286-A    92286-B    92286-C

<esc> to exit function menu


===============================Setup v3.1===============================
Select ==> Goto Pg 4  92286-H  92286-J  92286-L  92286-M

<esc> to exit function menu
```

- Figure 3.3: *SU Fonts menu*

7. Press F10 to send the PCL commands that activate that symbol set.

8. Press F4 to print the screen. The SU menu will disappear, and the original screen will be printed.

Version 4.4 of LaserJet, another shareware program, only controls cartridges A, B, D, E, F, and L, but it lets you "manually" eject a page from your computer and send custom PCL commands. It comes with a label and envelope printing feature and even a built-in notepad.

An inexpensive commercial alternative is E-Z-Set. It allows you to select from all available cartridges, set margins and orientation, and manage softfonts.

Using Filtering Programs

A filter is a small memory-resident program that intercepts all characters going to the printer. When it receives a graphics character, it substitutes the appropriate LaserJet PCL command that will produce the character correctly.

HPFILTER is a filtering program that's available in the public domain. Figure 3.4 shows how HPFILTER handled the screen shown at the top of Figure 3.1. It printed the double-line border, but it used a single line in place of the wide graphic character.

Using Softfonts

Another way to print a screen with graphics characters is to download a softfont that contains the PC symbol set.

For example, FT10.SFP, placed in the public domain by Orbit Enterprises, is a 12-point portrait softfont that contains all the characters shown in Figure 3.5. As you can see, the font contains most of the PC symbol set. When you download this softfont and print a text mode screen dump, the line, graphic, and other symbols will be reproduced correctly.

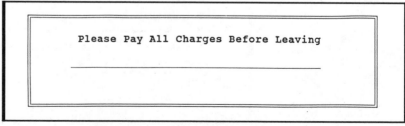

Please Pay All Charges Before Leaving

• Figure 3.4: *HPFILTER output for sample text screen with graphic characters*

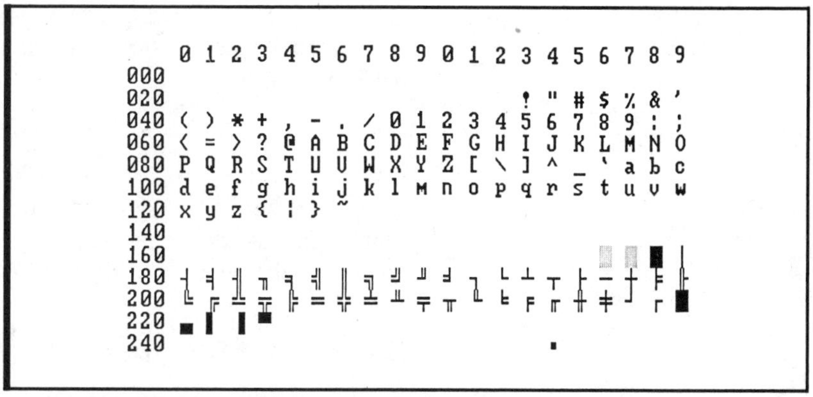

```
     0 1 2 3 4 5 6 7 8 9 0 1 2 3 4 5 6 7 8 9
000
020                                  ! " # $ % & '
040 ( ) * + , - . / 0 1 2 3 4 5 6 7 8 9 : ;
060 < = > ? @ A B C D E F G H I J K L M N O
080 P Q R S T U V W X Y Z [ \ ] ^ _ ` a b c
100 d e f g h i j k l m n o p q r s t u v w
120 x y z { | } ~
140
160
180
200
220
240
```

• Figure 3.5: *FT10.SFP softfont characters*

You can download the FT10.SFP softfont by using the DOS Copy command:

```
copy /b ft10.sfp lpt1:
```

However, not all softfonts can be downloaded this way; some require the use of a special utility program. See Chapter 4 for a detailed discussion of softfonts.

A number of commercial softfonts contain the PC symbol set, usually with the Courier typeface. Elfring Soft Fonts, for example, has fixed-width Courier fonts in 8, 9, and 10 points, as well as 5- and 6-point fonts with line-draw characters (useful for printing spreadsheets).

Capturing the Screen to a File

As an alternative to printing directly from the screen, you can capture the screen image to a text file, and then edit or print it using any word processing program. This way, you can delete the graphic characters that are not in your symbol set or replace them with a similar character your word processor supports. WordPerfect and Word, for example, have a line-drawing feature that works well with the LaserJet, even if the lines won't print from the screen dump. WordPerfect, by the way, can print many graphics characters on the LaserJet + using the Line Draw font, as discussed in Chapter 5.

A good public domain program to use for this purpose is Snapshot. Here's how to use it to save a screen and then print it:

1. Load Snapshot and display the screen you want to save.

2. Press Alt-Shift-P. The screen image is saved as plain ASCII characters. Screen images are stored and numbered consecutively, such as SNAPSHOT.01.

3. Load the file into your word processor.

4. Print the document as is or replace the graphic characters with line-draw characters. If your word processor doesn't have line-draw characters, just delete the symbols that won't print, realign the remaining characters, and then print the document.

Printing Screens in Graphics Mode

Some utility programs for printing graphic screens will work with both LaserJet and DeskJet printers. Check the documentation that came with the software. Resources for the DeskJet are listed in Appendix D.

Printing your screen in graphics mode is more complicated than printing it in text mode. No matter what type of printer you have, you'll need a special program to accomplish this. Most versions of DOS come with a program called Graphics that will print your graphic screen on a standard dot-matrix printer. But so far, there is no DOS program that works with laser printers. If you tried to print a graphic screen on your laser printer, you would get something that looks like Figure 3.6.

I've tested several public domain programs using both CGA (color graphics adapter) and EGA (extended graphics adapter) monitors, but I haven't found one that works with VGA (video graphics array) monitors.

LG and LJSP, available from bulletin boards or their creators, are shareware programs that work with CGA graphics. Both print a reverse

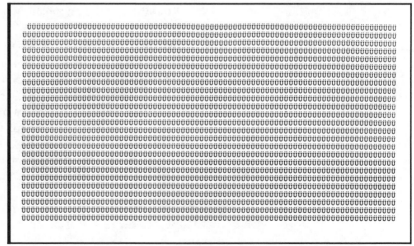

• Figure 3.6: *Graphic screen printed without a special program*

image of what you see on the screen, but LJSP lets you select from 75, 100, 150, and 300 dpi. (At 300 dpi, the printout will be just about 2¹/₄ by 1¹/₄ inches.) Figure 3.7 shows a CGA screen printed at 150 dpi with LJSP.

HPPS is for EGA displays and has options for printing in reverse with either the LaserJet + or LaserJet II. You can get HPPS from Genie, several public domain libraries, or the creator's own bulletin board.

Color printing is discussed in Chapters 10 and 14.

More expensive but complete solutions to the graphics problem come in commercial packages. E-Z-Dump works only with CGA monitors and comes free with E-Z-Set, the setup utility mentioned earlier. Pizazz Plus, on the other hand, can handle CGA, EGA, VGA, and MCGA (microchannel graphics adapter) graphics. You can convert color screen images into black and white with up to 256 shades of gray, or print them in color on color printers. Pizazz Plus is a memory-resident program that you activate when you want to print or save the screen image. Screens can be scaled, rotated, smoothed, and even transferred to use with programs such as Ventura Publisher, Aldus Pagemaker, and Microsoft Word. Figure 3.8 shows a cropped printout of the Windows Paint screen, captured using Pizazz Plus from a color monitor.

There are many utility programs that capture the image into a graphic file format that can be imported into and printed by programs such as Ventura Publisher, WordPerfect, and Word. These are similar to Grab, which comes free with WordPerfect, and Capture, which is provided with Word. Other programs that convert files from one format to another are discussed in Chapter 14.

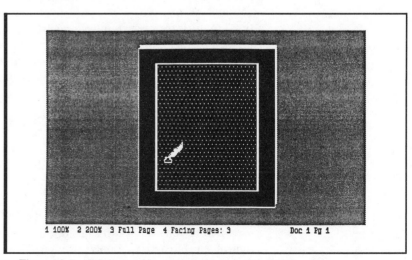

• Figure 3.7: *CGA graphic screen printed with LJSP*

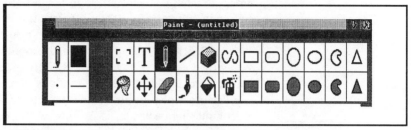

• Figure 3.8: *Window Paint screen captured with Pizazz Plus*

• *Printing on the Full Page*

Programs designed to use the LaserJet will compensate for the non-printing areas on all sides. WordPerfect 5.0, for example, won't let you enter any margins less than 1/4 inch. It will automatically reset smaller margins to .25" when you attempt to leave the Format Page menu.

If you want to print something within one of the default margins and are using a program designed for the LaserJet, you may be able to do this by setting up a larger page size. For example, suppose that you are using WordPerfect and want to add a line to the very bottom of an 8 1/2- by 1-inch flyer. To get around the default bottom margin, set up WordPerfect for an 8 1/2- by 14-inch legal-sized page. This will fool the LaserJet into thinking that it can print a full 13 1/2 inches. Then type your text just before the 11-inch position, and the line will print at the bottom of the page, inside the usual default margin.

Software designed to work with a generic printer, however, is not so accommodating—you can only print 60 lines on each page. The best solution I found is the use of public domain programs such as Laser66. This sets up the LaserJet to print 66 lines on the page, leaving only 1/4-inch top and bottom margins. For some applications, the extra six lines aren't important, but they can come in handy if you're using DOS, a word processor, or another program with page breaks set every 60 or more lines.

• *Printing on Both Sides of the Page*

While the LaserJet IID and 2000 can automatically print duplex (on both sides of the page), you can manually print duplex on all models. (With the LaserJet 2000, you'll need the D option installed.)

Duplex Printing with the LaserJet IID

Before you print a two-sided document with the LaserJet IID, use the control panel to activate duplex printing. Follow these steps:

1. Press the On Line button to turn the indicator light off.

2. Press the Menu button four times to display DUPLEX = OFF∗.

3. Press the + or − button to change the display to DUPLEX = ON.

4. Press the Enter/Reset Menu button.

5. Press the Menu button again to display BIND = LONG-EDGE∗.

The binding edge options are Long-Edge and Short-Edge, depending on where you plan to hole-punch or otherwise bind the pages together. For long-edge binding, the LaserJet IID will print the pages head to head; for short-edge binding, it prints them head-to-tail, as illustrated in Figure 3.9. When you select Long-Edge, the top margin is on the same edge of the paper for both sides. The Short-Edge selection prints the top margin of one side opposite the bottom margin of the other.

6. Press the + or − button to select the binding edge.

7. Press the Enter/Reset Menu button.

8. Press the On Line button to turn the indicator light on.

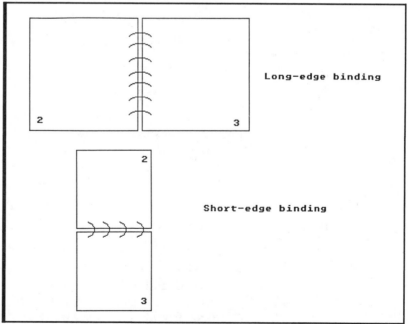

• Figure 3.9: *Long-edge and short-edge binding*

Duplex Printing with the LaserJet, LaserJet +, LaserJet 500 +, and LaserJet II

With the other LaserJet models, you can print on both sides of the page by printing pages individually or feeding the paper in manually.

Using the Page-By-Page Method

You can use the procedure described here if your application allows you to print individual pages. As an example, suppose that you want to print multiple copies of a two-sided flyer. Follow these steps:

1. Set up your word processor to print just the first page, in as many copies as you'll need.

2. Print the first page.

3. Remove the printed first pages and reinsert them into the paper cassette. With the LaserJet, LaserJet +, and LaserJet 500 +, insert the paper printed side up, blank side down. With the LaserJet II, insert the paper printed side down, blank side up.

4. Set up your word processor to print the second page.

5. Print the second page.

Load paper with the printed side up.

Manually Feeding Pages

If you can't print a page at a time (perhaps your application doesn't provide for it or you're printing from DOS), you have to feed the paper in manually. Follow these steps:

1. Press the On Line button to turn the indicator light off.

2. With the LaserJet and LaserJet +: Press the Manual Feed button.

   With the LaserJet 500 +: Press the Paper Select button until the Manual Feed indicator light goes on.

   With the LaserJet II: Press the Menu button twice to display MANUAL FEED = OFF*, press the + or − button to turn manual feed on, and then press the Enter/Reset Menu button. Press the Menu button four times to display 00 READY, and then press the Continue/Reset button until the display shows 07 RESET.

3. Press the On Line button to turn the indicator light on.

4. Start printing your document. You'll see a PF message on the control panel display, indicating that you should feed a sheet of paper through the manual tray.

5. Insert the page into the tray, keeping it against the feed guide on the right side of the slot. The sheet will be picked up, printed, and ejected. The PF message will appear when the printer is ready for the next page.

6. Feed the same sheet back into the manual feed tray with the printed side down, the blank side up (when printing from the manual feed tray, the LaserJet prints on the *top*).

7. Repeat this procedure until the entire document is printed.

• *Printing Envelopes*

Printing envelopes can be tricky, even with a word processing program. The printer has to be set for landscape mode, and the text must have the proper margins and spacing.

You'll learn how to print envelopes from specific applications in later chapters. The following sections explain how to feed envelopes and ways to print them without an application that supports the LaserJet.

Feeding Envelopes

Hewlett-Packard does not recommend printing envelopes on the LaserJet 2000.

Unless you have the optional envelope feeder, you'll have to manually insert envelopes into the feed tray.

With the original LaserJet, LaserJet +, and LaserJet 500 +, feed envelopes in printing side up, the bottom of the envelope (the edge opposite your return address) against the right paper-feed guide, as shown in Figure 3.10. If your application doesn't support the LaserJet, you will have to manually set the printer to manual feed, set a landscape font, and select the paper size. You'll also have to set the margins by using PCL commands or a utility program.

See Appendix D for information about printing envelopes.

With the LaserJet II and LaserJet IID, adjust the paper-feed guides on the manual paper tray to match the size of the envelope. Feed the envelope printing side up, the bottom against the right feed guide. Use the control panel to select manual feed, a landscape font, and paper size; then use PCL commands or a utility program to adjust the margins.

Details for using PCL commands to print envelopes will be given in Chapter 17.

If you have trouble feeding your envelopes through the printer, you can purchase special laser printer envelopes. Look for envelopes that are as

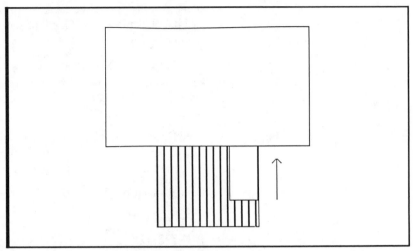

● Figure 3.10: *Feeding envelopes in a LaserJet, LaserJet+, and Laser-Jet 500+*

thin as possible. If they jam or wrinkle, consult your stationery store or supplier. Details on paper and envelope selections are in Appendix A.

Programs for Printing Envelopes

If your application is not designed for the LaserJet, you can use a special program to print envelopes from DOS.

For example, ENVLJ is a shareware program that uses a graphic approach. It displays a facsimile of an envelope on the screen, as shown in Figure 3.11. You can enter a return and mailing address or use a data file to store the addresses of up to 128 recipients. The program also lets you select the font to use, as well as define five envelope sizes by entering the row and column coordinates of the return and mailing addresses. Using the menu bar at the top of the screen, select the envelope size and the class of printer: LJ or LJII. The margins are set to match the feeding position, as described in the previous section.

The HPLZLAB shareware program uses a simpler approach. It lets you enter up to seven lines for the address, confirm your entry, and then print the envelope using the internal Courier landscape font. The margins are set to print on the LaserJet, LaserJet+, and LaserJet 500+.

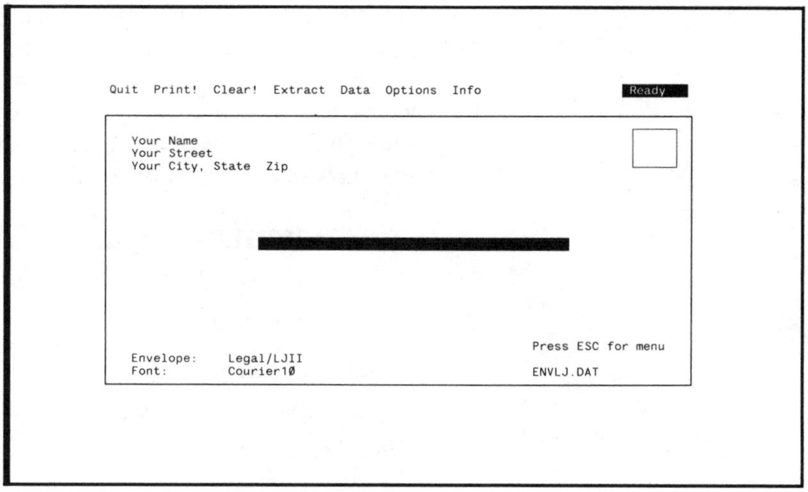

```
       Quit  Print!  Clear!  Extract  Data  Options  Info          Ready

       Your Name
       Your Street
       Your City, State  Zip




                                                           Press ESC for menu
       Envelope:      Legal/LJII
       Font:          Courier1Ø                            ENVLJ.DAT
```

• Figure 3.11: *ENVLJ screen display*

• *Printing in Special Formats*

You can print text files in a variety of special formats, such as in a pamphlet layout or with two to eight pages on a single sheet of paper. For example, suppose you used dBASE V to write a large text file listing database records, or PFS: First Choice to create an unformatted ASCII file. Why not print two, four, or even eight pages on each sheet of paper? Or maybe you want to print copies of your program listings in 5½-by-8½-inch booklets.

The methods discussed here work for plain text files. These may be documentation files for programs you've purchased or ASCII files created by a word processing or other program. In later chapters, you learn how your word processor can save documents in ASCII files for printing in these alternate formats.

Printing in Pamphlet Format

A document printed in pamphlet format is ready to be assembled and folded into a booklet. One program that you can use for this type of printing is Pamphlet, a shareware program written by Martin Beattie. It requires an internal Line Printer font or the Y cartridge, and the text must be in plain ASCII code.

Pamphlet sets the LaserJet to the Line Printer font, then divides the text file named into pages of 66 lines, each line a maximum of 80 characters each. Any form-feed commands in the file will end the page at that point. The pages are separated into front and back pages so when printed, placed together, and folded, the text is in proper sequence, as shown in Figure 3.12.

Here's how to use Pamphlet to print in pamphlet format:

1. Type **PAMPHLET**, and then press ◄─┘ to start the program. You will see the menu shown in Figure 3.13.

2. Complete the menu.

3. Press F2. The fronts of the pages will be printed and ejected.

4. Remove the pages and reinsert them, without turning them over, into the paper cassette. The backs of the pages will be printed.

Pamphlet also has options for setting the printer to any of its internal fonts, installed cartridge fonts, or softfonts before printing the document. You can also change fonts within the document by using embedded commands.

Printing Two or Four Pages Per Side

Some programs can print two pages side by side on one side of a sheet of paper, and others can print four pages on a single sheet.

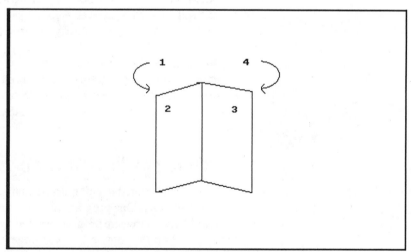

• Figure 3.12: *Sequence of text printed with Pamphlet*

For example, the public domain program LJ2 prints files two-up, like Pamphlet, but only on one side of the page. Odd-numbered pages are on the left, even ones on the right, separated by a vertical line. Pages are printed consecutively, so you can't fold them into a booklet. The file name, page number, and current date and time are printed on the top of each page.

The public domain disk with LJ2 even contains the C language source code for the program, which shows how PCL commands can be controlled by that language.

The shareware program 4UP squeezes the most out of a single sheet of paper. It prints four 60-line pages on one side of the page. It contains a special 3.8-point font (21.4 characters per inch) that's first downloaded to the printer. The file is then divided into pages and printed. You can arrange your pages as shown in Figure 3.14. The print is readable but small, so reserve this for archiving hard copies of little-used files.

If you want to see a similar program in assembly language, look up the April 11, 1989 issue of *PC Magazine*.

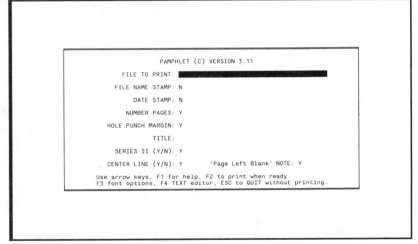

• Figure 3.13: *Pamphlet menu*

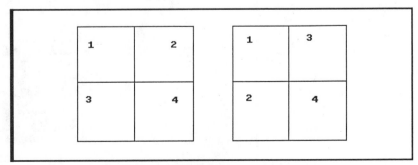

• Figure 3.14: *4UP page arrangement*

• *Emulating a Dot-Matrix Printer*

Believe it or not, you may want to turn your sophisticated laser printer into a dot-matrix clone. This will allow you to print documents designed to be printed on a dot-matrix printer.

A number of programs are specifically designed to print graphics on dot-matrix printers, not laser ones. You might have an older version of a program that you purchased before getting your laser printer. If you don't use the program often enough to update to a version that supports the LaserJet, a public domain or shareware solution may be an economical alternative.

For example, EP2HP is a public domain program that prints output designed for the Epson family of printers. To use EP2HP, you must first capture printed output into a disk file using another utility or your application's print-to-file feature. Figure 3.15 shows a Printshop creation saved to disk using a program called LPTX, then printed by EP2HP. The resolution

• Figure 3.15: *Graphic printed using a dot-matrix emulator*

mimics the dot-matrix printer, but the entire operation, including saving the file and printing it with EP2HP, is faster than using many dot-matrix printers.

Claser uses a different approach. It is a TSR program that lets you install a dot-matrix emulation filter. When you print text designed for a dot-matrix printer, Claser attempts to convert it for the LaserJet. This approach is particularly useful with word processing programs that do not have LaserJet drivers. Dot-matrix printer features that cannot be emulated are "captured" and not passed on, providing a useful way of printing basic text from your word processor. You can use Claser within graphic-based programs such as Printmaster and Printshop. Some of your borders may not print, but text and graphics will. Claser also provides font and cartridge control and CGA screen dumps.

H·P L·A·S·E·R·J·E·T

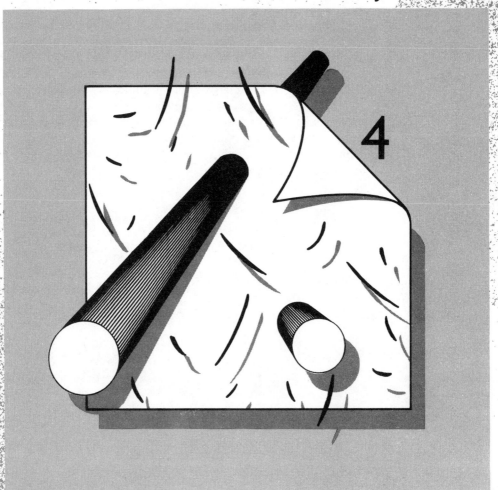

4

Printing Fonts with Your LaserJet

• The ability of the LaserJet to print a variety of high-quality type styles and sizes is one of its most attractive features. But fonts can be confusing, even if you're only using the printer's internal ones. If you want to take advantage of all the printer's capabilities, fonts can be a complex subject.

This chapter will take the mystery out of fonts. You'll learn the basics of typography, the sources of fonts, and details about softfonts, which provide the most variety and flexibility.

• *Typography Basics*

Before you make any decisions about fonts, you should have at least a basic understanding of typography. As explained in Chapter 1, a font is a specific size and style within the more general classification of typeface.

Every typeface has been given a name by its designer, who is the individual or company that created the shape and characteristics of the fonts. Most fonts are copyrighted, and the rights to convert and sell the designs as LaserJet PCL bit maps have been granted to the softfont manufacturer. Times Roman and Helvetica, for example, are trademarks of the Linotype Corporation.

However, some fonts look very similar to others but were created by another designer. For example, the Century Schoolbook and Dutch fonts look like Times Roman, and the Swiss fonts look like Helvetica. Except for public domain fonts, these type styles are also usually copyrighted.

The next sections describe the characteristics of fonts and the other elements of type that affect its appearance on the page.

In only some cases does the typeface name tell you something about its shape or design, so be sure to look at a sample before selecting a font. Most font manufacturers will supply a sample printout showing each of their fonts.

Characteristics of Fonts

The appearance of individual characters in a font depends on the following elements:

- **Baseline**: As a reference point, every font has a baseline where the bottom of most characters rest, as shown in Figure 4.1. Most letters and numbers sit squarely on the line. The distance from one baseline to the next is called *line spacing*.

Abcdefghijklmnopqrstuvwxyz ——— Baseline

• Figure 4.1: *Characters align on an invisible baseline*

- **Ascenders and descenders**: Some characters, such as *j*, *p*, and *y*, have descenders that go below the baseline. Depending on the typeface, other letters, even capital ones, may also have descenders. Most lowercase letters extend above the baseline to a specific level, sometimes called the *x-height*, the height of the lowercase letter *x*. Ascenders are strokes on lowercase letters that go above that level, usually to the full height of an uppercase character.

- **Serifs**: Some people feel that fonts with serifs (small strokes at the ends of lines) are easier to read than those without them. The LaserJet can recognize nine different serif styles, including line, triangular, block, and round.

- **Style**: The character's style refers to its angle in relation to the vertical axis of the page. Upright characters (nonitalic) are parallel to the axis; italic characters (also called oblique) slant to the right. In PCL printers such as the LaserJet, the angle is fixed by the font design. (PostScript printers can print characters at any angle, converting upright to any oblique angle.)

- **Stroke weight**: The thickness of the lines used to create each character, called the stroke weight, determines how light or dark the font is. Most softfonts, for example, can be purchased in four weights: light, regular (or medium), bold, and extra bold. The LaserJet can handle up to 14 different stroke weights.

- **Orientation**: You already know that the LaserJet can print in portrait and landscape orientation. However, with all models but the LaserJet IID and 2000, you must have separate fonts for each orientation. Most fonts are sold just in portrait orientation, but you can use utility programs (such as Port2lan) to convert them to landscape.

- **Kerning**: Each character is in an imaginary box that encloses the height and width of its particular font. Normally, the characters are put together so the left edge of one box meets the right edge of the next box. In kerning, the boxes overlap, reducing the amount of white space between characters, as shown in Figure 4.2. Kerning takes advantage of the opposing slants of the letters and generally gives a more pleasing visual effect.

Type Size and Spacing

The size of a font and its spacing on a line are important considerations when you are selecting fonts.

Roman is sometimes used as a synonym for upright. Swiss Roman, for instance, is an upright Helvetica-type font.

Very light stroke weights might not reproduce properly at high resolution.

Fixed and Proportional Spacing

Fonts can either be fixed (also called monospaced) or proportionally spaced, as illustrated in Figure 4.3.

In a fixed-width font, each character is assigned the same horizontal space, as with the characters on standard typewriters. There will be extra white space around smaller characters, such as *i*, less around large characters like *W*.

Characters in a proportionally-spaced font take up just enough space for the character itself; the space assigned is proportional to the size of the character. These fonts have a more professional look, as if commercially typeset and printed.

Working with fixed-width fonts is relatively simple. Since all the characters occupy the same space, an application can underline or justify text by counting characters. For instance, twenty 10-pitch characters can be underlined by twenty 10-pitch underline symbols because they occupy the same amount of space. To compute the number of characters that will fit on a line, the program simply counts each character because only sixty 10-pitch characters can be placed across a six-inch line.

Underlining or justifying is more complex with proportionally-spaced fonts. For each proportionally-spaced font, the program must maintain a width table, which contains the exact space occupied by each character. To fit text on a line, the program adds the individual widths instead of counting

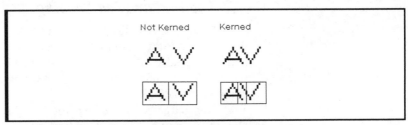

• Figure 4.2: *Kerned and unkerned characters*

Use fixed-width fonts when you want to ensure that characters listed in columns are aligned under each other. Proportionally-spaced fonts do not work well in printed spreadsheets and other documents with columns of numbers.

We hold these truths to be self-evident, that all men are created equal, that they are endowed by their Creator with certain unalienable Rights, that among these are Life, Liberty, and the pursuit of happiness.

We hold these truths to be self-evident, that all men are created equal, that they are endowed by their Creator with certain unalienable Rights, that among these are Life, Liberty, and the pursuit of happiness.

• Figure 4.3: *Fixed-width and proportionally-spaced fonts*

characters. Many programs can automatically generate width tables from the bit-map font file.

Pitch and Points

The pitch of a font is the number of characters that will fit in each horizontal inch of space, abbreviated as cpi for characters per inch. Pitch only has real meaning with fixed-width fonts—the actual characters per inch with a proportionally-spaced font will vary with the specific characters. The two most common pitches are 10 and 12, meaning that 10 and 12 characters will fit in every inch of space.

Point size is the vertical measurement of the font: the height measured from the bottom of the lowest descender to the top of the highest ascender. You can't measure any one character to get its point size, as Figure 4.4 illustrates. The 36-point character shown in the figure doesn't take up a full $1/2$ inch—it's sitting in an invisible box that encompasses the font's lowest descender and highest ascender.

Fonts in 10 or 12 points are considered "normal," which means that they are easy to read while taking up the minimum amount of room. Larger fonts are used for headlines or where readability is important. Use smaller fonts for superscripts and subscripts, or when trying to squeeze as much text onto a page as possible. Fonts less than 6 points should only be used for special purposes.

Leading or Line Spacing

Leading is extra line spacing, in points, added to the point size of the font. It gives extra room between the descenders of characters on one line and the ascenders of characters on the line below. A printer or typesetter might refer to a line as "10 on 12," meaning a 10-point font with an extra 2 points of leading.

Normally, with no leading, you would be able to print just over seven lines of 10-point type on each vertical inch on the page. With 10 on 12 spacing, you would have to compute spacing as if you were using a 12-point font—six lines per inch.

While there are not exactly 72 points to an inch, most people round it to 72. This could lead to problems in a tightly composed page.

• Figure 4.4: *Measuring point size*

In most word processing software, the term line spacing is used instead of leading. Some programs, such as Microsoft Word, let you specify line spacing in points, so you can set line spacing for a 10-point font at 12 points, giving the effect of 2-point leading.

• *Selecting Fonts*

In general, the methods for selecting fonts can be classified into these areas:

- **Application programs**: Many programs, mostly word processors and desktop publishers, are designed to work with the LaserJet printer. The manufacturers supply drivers that contain the appropriate commands for selecting various types of fonts.

- **PCL commands**: If your application doesn't have a LaserJet driver, you might be able to issue Hewlett-Packard PCL commands from within the program. You can also use PCL commands from within your own programs written in Pascal, Basic, C, or any other language that lets you send control codes directly to the printer.

- **Control panel**: If you want to use one font for the entire document or print job, you can select fonts directly from the control panel menu (if your model has one). You'll only be able to use one font for the whole job, but you don't have to know anything about PCL.

- **Utility programs**: Using a utility program is very much like selecting fonts from the control panel. Programs such as E-Z-Set from Orbit Enterprises allow you to access fonts directly from the keyboard. Before printing a document, you can call up the utility and select the font or symbol set desired. As with control panel selections, you can have only one font active at a time, so the entire document will print in the selected font. However, even LaserJet II users may find using a utility more convenient than walking over to the control panel.

- **Filtering programs**: As discussed in Chapter 3, a filtering program intercepts characters on their way to the printer. If your application doesn't support the LaserJet, a filtering program can select any available font and even print multiple fonts on the same page.

You'll learn how to use specific applications and PCL commands to select fonts in later chapters, and the use of the control panel and utility programs has been explained in earlier chapters. Filtering programs will be discussed in more detail later in this chapter.

DeskJet and LaserJet cartridges are not interchangeable. See Appendix D for details.

• *Installing and Using Cartridges*

Cartridges give you the ability to select from a wider range of fonts and symbol sets than those stored internally. Hewlett-Packard and other vendors market a number of cartridges, each of which contain from 3 to more than 200 fonts. The 92286PC cartridge, for example, contains 16 Courier, 12 Prestige Elite, 12 Letter Gothic, 14 Times Roman, and 9 Helvetica fonts.

One end of the cartridge slides into the slot on the printer. That's the end with the "card edge," the end of a circuit board with metallic contacts on the top and bottom. These contacts fit into a complementary connector within the printer.

On top of the cartridge, near the other end, is a label showing the cartridge number, its name, and a list of fonts it contains. For example, the label on cartridge 92286A (usually just called the A cartridge) shows it is called COURIER 1 and displays the font information illustrated in Figure 4.5. As you can see from the label shown in the figure, this cartridge contains three fonts: Courier in bold and light italic, in portrait orientation, and in 12 points, 10 pitch; and a landscape Line Printer font that's 8.5 point, 16.66 pitch. All the fonts in this case use the Roman-8 symbol set.

Once installed, cartridge fonts are considered to be in ROM. Like internal fonts, they are available immediately upon selection and don't take up any RAM or disk space (as do softfonts).

There is a limit, however, to the number of times you can remove and insert a cartridge. After about 500 insertions, the metal contacts wear down and may not make a solid electrical connection in the printer. If you get erratic results with an old cartridge, you'll have to replace it. To avoid replacing cartridges, select one that you'll use most of the time. If you have a LaserJet II or IID which accepts two cartridges, plan on installing the one you use more often as "permanent." Leave that one in place and use the other slot for your other font cartridges.

Before installing a cartridge, turn the printer off or place if off line. Turn off the LaserJet 2000.

ROMAN8 symbol set		ORIENT	PITCH	POINT
COURIER	**bold**	portrait	10	12
COURIER	*light*	portrait	10	12
Line Printer	light	landscape	16.66	8.5

• Figure 4.5: *The label on the Hewlett-Packard 92286A (A) cartridge*

• *Installing and Using Softfonts*

A softfont is actually the bit-map information for an entire font that's stored on your disk. When you want to use the font, the bit-map data must

Although not all softfonts are designed for use with the LaserJet, those that are LaserJet compatible can be used with any computer. A LaserJet softfont on Macintosh media is the same softfont sold on an IBM disk. Fonts designed for the LaserJet are called PCL fonts.

be transferred to the printer's memory in a process called *downloading*.

Softfonts provide the fullest range of type styles and sizes, but they have disadvantages. For all practical purposes, you need a hard disk to use any number of softfonts, and since they take up the printer's memory, they limit the amount of text you can print at the highest resolution. When you use just internal and cartridge fonts, all your printer's memory can be devoted to page information. Downloaded softfonts use some of that memory for the bit-map information—enough memory to store the entire font, even if you're using just a single character from it.

In addition, a font with more defined symbols requires more memory in your printer. The PC symbol set, for instance, has all 255 characters defined by ASCII codes, while the USASCII set contains only 127. If your printer has limited memory, use the USASCII set when you know you don't need the extra characters in your document. You won't be able to print foreign-language characters and graphic symbols, but you'll have a wider range of fonts and sizes to select from. Look at this comparison of the memory requirements for the same fonts but with different symbol sets:

Font Size	USASCII	PC
8	8K	15K
10	10K	20K
12	13K	27K
14	17K	35K
18	25K	53K
24	42K	88K

The PC set requires twice the memory as the USASCII set. By downloading the fonts with the smaller symbol set, you'll have an extra 123,000 bytes of printer memory to store your document and graphics.

In the following sections, you'll learn the details of downloading and using softfonts. Then we'll take a look at three popular programs that install font support directly in your application and some programs for editing fonts.

Downloading Softfonts

Fonts can be downloaded as either temporary or permanent. A temporary font will be erased when you reset the printer and can be overwritten by another downloaded font. Permanent softfonts remain even after the

LaserJet and DeskJet softfonts are not interchangeable.
To use softfonts on DeskJet
printers, you must install an
optional RAM cartridge and
the font must be in DeskJet
format. (See Appendix D for
details.) The downloading
programs discussed here work
with either type of printer, but
the utilities and installation
programs are for use with the
LaserJet only.

printer is reset. You can only erase them by turning off the computer or issuing a PCL command that clears all fonts.

To get the most from your printer's memory, plan your font usage
carefully. Load as permanent any softfonts that you plan to use all day or
for a number of documents. Load fonts that you're using just for headlines
or special effects as temporary.

During the downloading process, the printer assigns an ID number to
the font. This is a number from 0 to 65,535, which can be used later to select
fonts to use for specific characters.

Fonts can also be given primary or secondary status when they are
downloaded. Unlike an ID number or having permanent or temporary status, this classification is optional. When a font is loaded as primary, it is
immediately available for use. A font downloaded as secondary can be
selected for use by PCL commands.

There are a variety of ways to download fonts:

• Through integrated downloaders

• Through manual downloaders

• With the DOS Copy command

These methods are summarized in the following sections.

Downloading Through an Application

Most application programs designed to work with the LaserJet
include an integrated downloader. This means that the application will be
able to download the softfonts as it needs them. WordPerfect, Word, Ventura Publisher, and Pagemaker, for example, can download the fonts during the printing process because the font name and width table are stored in
the printer driver.

Some programs will download the fonts with each job. So if you print
two documents in a row using the same font, the font will actually be
downloaded twice. Other applications give you the option of loading a font
with each document or using fonts that have already been downloaded.

Applications that have a printer driver for the LaserJet expect to find
fonts using Hewlett-Packard's naming conventions. Hewlett-Packard
names its font using the pattern *NNPPPSWW.CSO*. The elements represent the following information:

If you have a choice and
you're using just a few fonts
for every document, you
can download them once at
the start of the day, and
then have your application
access those needed for
specific documents. But
download fonts used for
headlines and other special
purposes only when they are
needed. This keeps as much
memory clear as possible
for your documents.

• *NN* is the font name. Some common names are TR for Times
Roman, HV for Helvetica, CO for Courier, and OE or OD for Old
English.

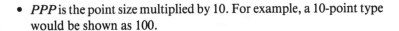

- *PPP* is the point size multiplied by 10. For example, a 10-point type would be shown as 100.

- *S* is the stroke weight. It can be R for regular, B for bold, I for italic, or X for bold italic.

- *WW* is the spacing. This is the pitch in cpi for fixed-width fonts. Proportionally-spaced fonts, which aren't measured in pitch, end with the letters PN, PX, or PY.

- *CS* is the character set. It can be US for USASCII, PC for IBM PC, or R8 for Roman 8.

- *O* is the orientation. It's either P for portrait or L for landscape.

Some DeskJet softfonts use DJ as the character set abbreviation.

Using these conventions, for example, you should be able to tell that the font TR120IPN.USL is Times Roman, 12 points, italic, and proportionally spaced. It contains the ASCII character set and is in landscape orientation.

Some applications, such as Word, also refer to fonts by a two-letter classification, as listed in Table 4.1. Word's documentation, for example, lists drivers by font name and by set. So if a driver is listed for AC, it is configured to use the Times Roman/Helvetica font set.

Not all softfont vendors, however, use the same naming conventions. You might see a font called CNT10.SFP or OLDENG.SFP. If the application is already set for the Hewlett-Packard name, it won't recognize these names, so it won't be able to download the fonts.

Hewlett-Packard's Type Director program also modifies some application drivers to handle softfonts, as discussed shortly. Glyphix 3.0, from Swfte International, installs scalable outline fonts in WordPerfect and Word, similar to PostScript (see Chapter 15).

A number of font suppliers package special programs to take care of this problem. Bitstream, for instance, supplies fonts with a program called Fontware that, among other things, modifies the application's driver to recognize names of Bitstream fonts. Softcraft uses a different approach. Its Font Solution Pack can change the Bitstream names to match Hewlett-Packard conventions, as well as add other fonts directly into the application's print driver. We'll discuss these packages in detail later in the chapter.

If your font vendor doesn't offer this type of program, you could try changing the name yourself with the DOS REN command. However, this often does not work because other driver information is incompatible with the third-party font. For example, the width of characters in the font may not match the measurements in the width table. You may be able to modify the program's driver to accept the name and font information for the softfont you want to use, but this can be a complicated process.

Table 4.1: *Two-Letter Classifications for Fonts*

FONT SET	CONTENTS
AC, AD	TMSRMN
	HELV
AE, AF	TMSRMN
	HELV
AG	HELV Headlines
DA	Letter Gothic
	Presentation
EA	Prestige Elite
RA, RB	ITC Garamond
SA, SB	Century Schoolbook
TA, TB	Zapf Humanist 601
UA, UB	Bauer Bodoni Black
	Broadway
	Cooper Black
	Coronet
	University Roman

Downloading with a Utility

If your application doesn't have an integrated downloader, you can download softfonts independently by using a utility program. Once you manually download fonts, you can still use them from applications with compatible LaserJet drivers—just don't bother downloading them again from within the program.

Usually, however, you'll need to manually download fonts when you're using programs without any LaserJet support. Then to access the fonts, you'll need to issue PCL commands, use a separate utility program, or use the control panel.

Some manual downloaders let you select from a list of fonts it finds on your disk. Others load one font named on the command line. There are commercial and shareware downloaders, and even memory-resident versions that you can pop up from within applications.

For example, Download, the manual downloader that is packaged with Softcraft's version of Fontware, asks you to enter the name of the font, its ID number, whether you want to make it permanent or temporary, if it should be the current font immediately ready for use, and if you want to print a sample. It only loads one font at a time. So to load several fonts, you have to repeat the process for each one.

Hewlett-Packard's Type Director takes a different approach. It has a download option that lets you download several fonts at one time. It will display a list of fonts it finds on your directory, showing the name, size, orientation, symbol set, and amount of printer memory required to hold it. It automatically assigns default ID numbers and permanent status, which you can override. If you load the same set of fonts often, you can save your selections through the File Setup option. You'll then be able to download the entire set in a few keystrokes. You'll learn more about this program a little later in the chapter.

Using DOS to Download Fonts

There are some fonts, such as the FT10.SFP font discussed in Chapter 3, that can be downloaded with the DOS Copy command. In addition to the character bit-map information, this type of font contains the PCL commands that load it in the printer's memory, set it as permanent, and designate it as primary, so it is immediately available without any further selection. Some public domain fonts that can be loaded from the DOS command line have an LOD extension.

Unfortunately, you can't use the Copy command with all softfonts, just those designed to be downloaded that way.

Using Outline Fonts

Most softfonts are sold as individual files, each font in the size and orientation in which you'll use it. If you want to use a typeface in five different sizes, you'll need five separate files.

Other fonts are sold as outlines, a generic file from which fonts of any size and orientation can be generated. You can't use these outlines directly in an application or load them into the printer. They must first be used to generate the bit map for a font of a specific size and orientation. Using the outline file for Times Roman Normal, for example, you can generate Times Roman Normal files of almost any size, in either portrait or landscape orientation.

This type of font generation allows you to create fonts in almost any size—you're not locked into a fixed point size determined by the vendor.

While you can create fonts of almost any size, don't generate fonts larger than your LaserJet can handle. See Chapter 1 for the maximum point sizes each model can print.

You'll learn how to install Hewlett-Packard and Bitstream outline fonts later in the chapter. We'll also cover Publisher's Type Foundry, which includes a program for editing outline fonts.

Using PostScript Fonts

Using Publisher's Type Foundry, as you'll learn later, you can convert PostScript outline fonts to PCL bit-map fonts.

All PostScript fonts are in outline form. But unlike PCL outline fonts, PostScript fonts do not have to be made into individually sized font files before being installed in the application. PostScript printers (or PostScript add-ons to your LaserJet) create the font characters directly from the outline "on the fly"—as needed at the time of printing. Characters can be scaled, rotated, and otherwise manipulated to create special effects.

While this provides a greater variety of fonts and styles, the process can take a great deal of time. PCL fonts have the advantage of being available immediately after they are downloaded to the printer.

In Chapter 15, you'll see how to add PostScript capabilities to the LaserJet, as well as how to duplicate PostScript special effects.

Using Public Domain Softfonts

Public domain and shareware fonts are available for the DeskJet. See Appendix D for details.

With the popularity of laser printers, a number of softfonts are now available from public domain and shareware vendors. Some even come with downloading utilities or in a format that can be downloaded with the DOS Copy command. In many cases, the fonts are samples placed in the public domain by a commercial firm who wants to gain recognition. Other times, they've been developed by talented LaserJet users with special needs and interests.

In most cases, the fonts emulate popular type styles such as Times, Helvetica, and Old English. Some fonts, like those shown in Figure 4.6, were designed for other purposes. The Impaired font was created for the visually impaired (notice that the characters become clear if you squint). Teacher, on the other hand, seems to have been created just for fun.

You can find fonts like this in public domain libraries and bulletin boards. Just be aware that they will take a long time to download directly over your modem.

IMPAIRED.SFP IS FOR THE VISUALLY IMPAIRED

teacher is just for fun!

• Figure 4.6: *The Impaired and Teacher public domain fonts*

Adding Fonts with Bitstream Fontware

Bitstream has taken a bold marketing stance by offering Fontware, an installation program, and a collection of fonts free or at low cost with a growing number of applications. The Fontware program is customized for the application it is supplied with, so there are separate Bitstream packages for WordPerfect, Word, WordStar, Pagemaker, Gem applications such as Presentation Team, Ventura Publisher, and many others. Each installs fonts only in the specific application.

Included with Fontware is a sampler of outline fonts, usually Dutch, Swiss, and Charter. The installation program lets you select the font sizes you want, and then it installs them in the application's printer driver in the appropriate form. Fontware for WordPerfect, for example, adds support to WPRINT1.ALL, the Ventura Publisher version creates a WID file, and the Word version constructs a PRD file.

Note that Bitstream uses different font-naming conventions than Hewlett-Packard. The names even vary slightly between different applications, but the typical font name has the form *NNPPPCDO.HPF*. These elements represent the following information:

- *NN* is the font name. Some common font names are aa for Swiss Roman (like Helvetica Normal), ab for Swiss Italic, ai for Dutch Roman (like Times Roman Normal), and aj for Dutch Italic.

- *PPP* is the point size. A 10-point type would be shown as 010.

- *C* is the character set code.

- *D* is the device code, normally h for LaserJet printers.

- *O* is the orientation: P for portrait or L for landscape.

The process of installing fonts with Bitstream is a simple one but can be very time consuming. Extracting a single 12-point font can take up to 15 minutes on a standard PC. Creating a full range of sizes and styles can take an entire day. The advantage is that you can install fonts of any size, up to the maximum size allowed by your printer.

As an example, we'll go through the steps for installing Swiss Bitstream fonts in WordPerfect. The process is similar for most applications.

Installing the Fontware Control Panel

You can't use Bitstream Fontware with a floppy-disk system.

The first task is to install the Fontware Control Panel on your hard disk. Before you begin, make sure that the WPRINT1.ALL file is on your WordPerfect directory.

1. Insert the disk called Fontware Installation for WordPerfect Disk 1 in drive A.

2. Type **run_fw**, and then press ←. (Use run_fw only to install the program for the first time—after it's on the hard disk, start the program by entering **FONTWARE**.) Next you'll see the Fontware logo and the prompt

   Do you see more than two colors?
   Press Y -Yes or press N -No

3. Press Y or N to display the Fontware Main menu. Before installing fonts, you must first set up the program.

4. Press ← to select the Set Up Fontware option, which is already highlighted. In a series of prompts, you'll be asked to enter the directory in which to place Fontware, the path for WordPerfect, and where you want to place the fonts.

5. Respond to the prompts, pressing ← after you enter each item. You'll see the prompt

   Accept your choices and continue Fontware installation?
   Press Y -Yes or press N -No

6. Press Y. You'll be prompted to insert disks as Fontware copies itself to the hard disk. When all the files have been copied, you'll see a list of supported printers.

7. Highlight the model of your printer, and then press ← to display orientation options.

8. Select to make either portrait, landscape, or both fonts, and then press ← to display possible symbol sets.

9. Select a character set that contains the characters you want, keeping in mind the memory limitations of your printer (discussed earlier in the chapter), and then press ← to complete the installation process. Figure 4.7 shows an example of a completed Fontware Control Panel screen.

10. Press F10 to display the Typefaces menu.

Fontware gets the printer names from the WPRINT#-.ALL files on your Word-Perfect directory. LaserJet printers are supported by WPRINT1.ALL, so make sure that you have that file loaded. If not, you'll have to exit Fontware, copy WPRINT1.ALL from your floppy disk, and then restart the program.

No typefaces are listed because none have been copied from floppy disks to the hard drive. We'll take care of that in the next section.

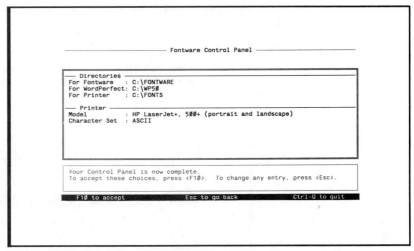

- Figure 4.7: *Completed Fontware Control Panel screen*

Installing Outline Fonts

Your next task is to copy outline fonts onto the hard disk.

1. To install Swiss fonts, press F3 to add a new typeface. You'll be asked to install one of the Font disks in drive A.

2. Install the disk, and then press ⏎ to see the typefaces available on that disk. You now have to select each outline that you want copied to the hard disk. Remember, the fonts listed are outlines that can be used to generate fonts of almost any size.

3. Press ⏎ four times to select all the fonts, and then press F10 to copy them to the hard drive. The Typefaces menu will appear with the four fonts listed.

4. Press F10 to select Make Fonts and display the Point Size Selection window on the right side of the screen. The first font, Swiss Roman in this case, is highlighted.

5. Press ⏎, and the cursor will move to the right window.

6. Enter the sizes of Swiss Roman that you want to create. Type each size, in ascending numeric order, with one space between each size. Figure 4.8 shows an example.

7. Press ⏎ to complete the selection.

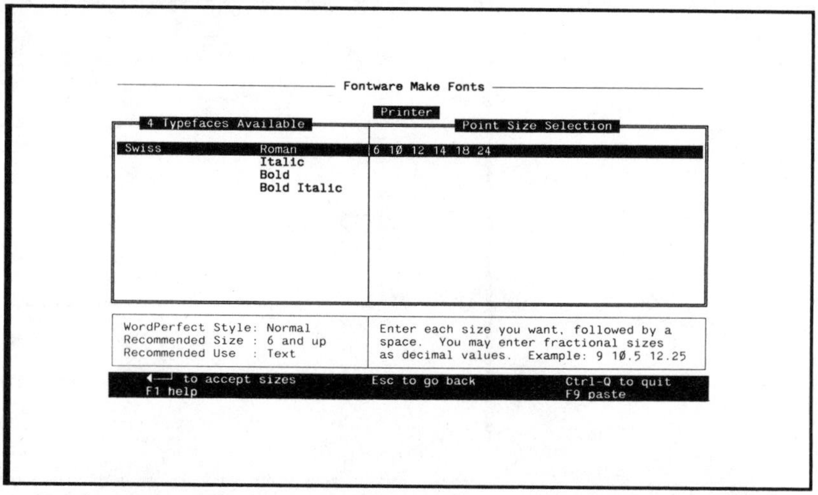

● Figure 4.8: *Sample point sizes entered for the Swiss Roman typeface*

8. Enter sizes for the other fonts in the same manner: Highlight the font name, and then press ◄—┘ to enter sizes.

9. Press F10 to create the fonts. The Time and Space Estimates box appears, showing how long it will take to make the fonts on your system and if you have sufficient hard disk space.

10. Press Y to make the fonts. Fontware will extract the fonts of the sizes specified. During the process, it will display messages like this on the screen:

    Font 1 of 6
    Swiss Roman   6.0 Point
    ASCII Character Set
    HP LaserJet + , 500 +

    When the process is complete, you should see the message

    Bitstream Fontware Installation Completed.
    No warnings or errors reported

If the final message reports a number of warnings or errors, return to DOS and display the file FONTWARE.LOG by using the Type command. A list of errors will appear. Consult the Fontware manual, and then try to install the fonts again.

Using Bitstream Fonts

Before you can actually print with the fonts, you have to select or update your printer driver from the WPRINT1.ALL file, as explained in Chapter 5. Mark the Fontware fonts on the softfont list with an * (Present) or + (Can Be Downloaded), as appropriate, and then complete the setup procedure described in that chapter. These fonts will now be available for use from within WordPerfect.

Adding More Fonts

If you want to install more Bitstream fonts in WordPerfect, follow these steps:

1. Log onto the Fontware directory, type **FONTWARE**, and then press ↵.

2. When the Fontware Main menu appears, select the Make Fonts option to create fonts from typefaces already on your hard disk, or choose the Add/Delete Fontware Typefaces option to copy additional outlines from floppy disks.

Versions of Fontware for Pagemaker and Ventura Publisher can also create matching screen fonts. The procedure will take longer, but it installs both printer and screen fonts in your application.

Adding Softfonts with Type Director

Like Bitstream Fontware, Hewlett-Packard's Type Director makes PCL fonts from font outlines and installs them directly into your application. However, instead of a separate version for each application, Type Director 1.0 supports Ventura Publisher, Microsoft Windows (and Windows applications such as Pagemaker), and Microsoft Word versions 4 and 5. If you have another application, Type Director can still extract the PCL fonts and even download them for you.

The Premier Collection package, for example, is packaged with Type Director and 12 fonts: CG Times and Univers in Normal, Bold, Italic, and Bold Italic; and the decorative fonts Brush, Dom Casual, Park Avenue, and Uncial. After the fonts are extracted from the outlines in designated sizes, they can be used by any program that reads LaserJet softfonts.

In addition to creating fonts and modifying drivers, Type Director can create width tables for fonts you already have. This is particularly useful if you have third-party softfonts that were not supplied with width tables. The program will create PRD (Word), WID (Ventura), or PFM (Windows) files that can be used with your application.

Both printer and screen fonts can be generated for Windows and Ventura Publisher.

Installing Type Director

The Install program on Disk 1 will copy the necessary files to your hard disk. You'll be prompted to confirm creation of the td directory and asked if you have a color or monochrome monitor. Then follow the directions on the screen, inserting the Type Director disks when requested.

Install does not copy the fonts to the hard disk. This must be done from within Type Director. As an example, let's see how the Uncial font can be created and used in Microsoft Word.

Setting the Environment

Before making fonts, you have to set up Type Director for your system and applications.

1. Log onto the td directory, type **td**, and then press ←. The Main menu will appear with the Fonts option already selected. First you should make sure that the program is set correctly for your system.

2. Use the arrow keys or cursor to select the Environment option, and then press ← to display the Set Environment/Defaults menu.

3. Highlight Printer, and then press ← to select it and list supported printers.

4. Select your model, and then press ←.

5. Designate the printer port, and press ←. Next you must indicate the application you want to use with generated fonts. This lets Type Director know the format of the width table and where to place the font and driver files.

6. Highlight Application, and then press ← to list supported programs.

7. Highlight your application, and then press ←.

8. Select Symbol Set to designate the symbol set you want to create. Although all the options will be listed, not all sets are supported by all Hewlett-Packard outline fonts. The four decorative fonts in Premier Collection, for instance, are not compatible with the Math, Math-8, and Ventura Math sets. So select a symbol set that corresponds to the outline.

Select Unlisted Application to generate fonts without creating application-specific width tables.

9. Enter the correct paths for the Application and Printer Fonts directories. Figure 4.9 shows an example of a completed screen.

10. Press the F8 function key to return to the Main menu.

Installing Typefaces

The next task is to copy font outlines from the floppy disk to the hard drive.

1. Select the Typefaces option to see the options

   Install Typefaces
   List/Delete Typefaces

2. Select Install Typefaces, insert a font disk in drive A, and then press F3. The fonts on that disk will be listed on the screen.

3. Highlight a font you want to copy, and then press F2.

4. When all the fonts you want are selected, press F1. The files will be copied to the hard disk, and you'll see the prompt

   Typeface installation complete.
   <Press ESCAPE to continue>

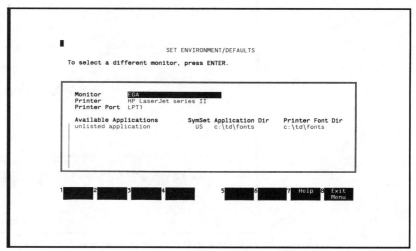

• Figure 4.9: *Completed Type Director Set Environment/Defaults screen*

5. Press Esc twice, and then select the Fonts option from the Main menu.

6. Select the Make Fonts option from the Fonts menu, and the Make Fonts menu will appear. You use this menu to select the typeface and sizes you want created.

7. Highlight the Typefaces option to display available outline fonts.

8. Select the font, and then press ⏎.

9. Under Point Sizes, type the sizes you want in ascending order, with a space between each, as shown in Figure 4.10. The remaining options will fill in automatically.

10. Change the other options as necessary. For Device, the options are P for printer fonts, S for screen fonts, and P&S for both. Screen fonts can only be made for Ventura Publisher and Windows applications. The Ori (orientation) options are P for portrait or L for landscape. For SymSet, the symbol set selected in the Environment menu will be displayed.

11. Press F1 when you're finished with the Make Fonts menu. The PCL fonts and the appropriate driver or width table will be created

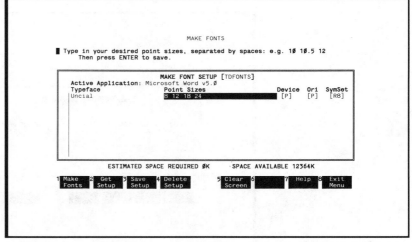

• Figure 4.10: *Point sizes entered in Type Director's Make Fonts menu*

or modified. (The driver is not actually saved on disk until you exit Type Director.) When the process is done, you'll see the prompt:

Font making was completed successfully
<Press ESCAPE to continue>

12. Press Esc twice to return to the Main menu; then press F8 Y ◄┘ to exit the program.

Using Hewlett-Packard Fonts

After the fonts and drivers have been created, you can use the softfont as explained in the chapter that discusses the particular application. With Word, for example, use the Print Options menu to select TDFONTS.PRD, and then use the Format Character menu to select the font and size. If you created a WID file for Ventura Publisher, select the TDFONTS.WID width table. Figure 4.11 illustrates the Uncial font printed by Word.

Downloading Fonts

To download fonts in a directory not associated with a supported application, use the Environment menu. Select the Unlisted Application option, and then enter the paths in the Application and Printer Fonts fields. In the Download menu, select Unlisted Application. You can override the default ID# and Status options.

If your application doesn't have an integrated downloader you can use Type Director to download fonts as follows:

1. Select the Download option from the Main menu to display the Download menu.

2. To download fonts from another application, press F5 to clear the list.

3. Select the Active Application field, and then press ◄┘. You will see a list of applications set in the Environment menu.

4. Select the application, and then press ◄┘.

5. Highlight the field under Typefaces, and then press ◄┘ to list the fonts available.

6. Highlight the font you want, and then press F1.

Uncial is a decorative font

• Figure 4.11: *Uncial font printed with Word*

7. To save your Download menu selections as a Font Setup (for quick recall), after setting all the options, press F3. Enter a file name, and then press ◀─┘.

When you later want to download the same fonts, select F2, enter the Font Setup file name, and then press ◀─┘. Press F1 to download the fonts.

Installing Third-Party Fonts

If you already have some softfonts, Type Director can add these to the supported applications. Copy the fonts you want to install to the application's directory.

When you create and save the new driver, any existing one called TDFONTS will be overwritten. For example, suppose that you already used Type Director to create TDFONTS.PRD holding the Uncial font. If you now use the program to install some third-party font, the original TDFONTS.PRD will be erased, and Uncial will no longer be available.

One way to avoid this is to first rename TDFONTS.PRD something like UNCIAL.PRD. You'll then have a separate driver for the Uncial font and the new ones you install. If you then want one driver to hold all the fonts, run MergePRD to combine both drivers.

When you're ready to install the fonts, follow these steps:

1. Start Type Director, and then select the Utility option from the Main menu.

2. Select Application Utility from the Utilities menu to see the Application Utility menu.

3. If the application is selected in the Environment menu, the font you want to install will be listed on the screen. If you want to install fonts in another support application, press F5 to clear the font list, highlight the Active Application option, then press ◀─┘ to list programs in your environment. Select the application, and then press ◀─┘. Now highlight the Typefaces option and press ◀─┘ to list available fonts.

4. Highlight the font you want to install, press ◀─┘ to list it in the menu, and then press F1. Type Director will analyze the font and create the appropriate driver or width table.

When you exit Type Director, the driver will be saved on the disk. You'll be prompted to confirm overwriting any existing TDFONTS driver. If you select N, you will exit Type Director without installing your fonts.

Adding Fonts with Softcraft Programs

Softcraft Inc. distributes a number of programs for installing and manipulating softfonts. The programs can be purchased separately or combined in the Font Solution Pack, a special package that includes all the Softcraft programs discussed here and in Chapter 15.

Using Softcraft Fontware

Softcraft's version of Fontware can create several different types of fonts from Bitstream outlines, as well as condense, expand, and slant the fonts to any dimension.

SC LASER fonts are designed for Softcraft's Fancy Font and Fancy Word programs.

Separate fonts can be made for the LaserJet + and later models. As listed on the installation menu, shown in Figure 4.12, each type of font is given a unique name by Softcraft. HP PORT fonts don't include symbols in the ASCII ranges from 0 to 31 and 128 to 159, which cannot be accepted by the LaserJet +. Since more recent LaserJet models can handle those characters, HP 2PORT fonts can include all 255 ASCII symbols. Similar fonts can be made in landscape orientation.

By varying the horizontal resolution of the fonts, you can condense or expand characters, making some unique special-purpose fonts. Condensed fonts, for example, are useful for squeezing extra characters in headlines. A horizontal resolution of 200 would make characters two-thirds the normal width.

The program can also create custom symbol sets from the 560 characters that are in the Bitstream International character set. By creating a reduced

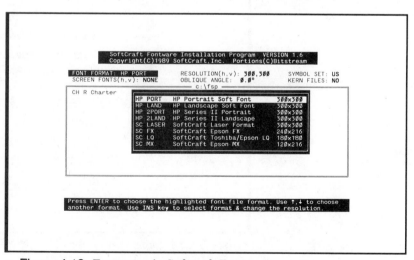

• Figure 4.12: *Font types in Softcraft Fontware*

character set, you can make maximum use of printer memory. For example, you might have a font for which you only use uppercase characters in headlines. Instead of downloading uppercase and lowercase characters, create an uppercase-only font that requires less than half the memory.

Installing Fonts

Softcraft's font installation program comes in several versions. Laser Fonts installs PCL fonts (both Hewlett-Packard and third-party) in Microsoft Word (version 2.0 or later), WordPerfect (version 4.1 and 4.2), Office Writer, WordStar 2000 (release 2.0), and Softcraft's Fancy Font and Fancy Word. A sample Laser Fonts Setup Utility screen is shown in Figure 4.13.

Laser Fonts can also generate outline and shadow fonts, rename Bitstream fonts to Hewlett-Packard conventions, and create landscape fonts from portrait fonts. A separate downloading facility and a printer-control menu, shown in Figure 4.14, make it an all-around utility.

WPIP is a special version of Laser Fonts for WordPerfect 5.0. It too can generate outline and shadow fonts accessible from WordPerfect's Font Appearance prompt line (Ctrl-F8 2) and build kern tables. A sample WPIP screen is shown in Figure 4.15. If you have a nonstandard font that WordPerfect doesn't handle correctly, you can use WPIP to set its attributes, using the menu shown in Figure 4.16. Once you describe the font's features, WordPerfect's PTR program can deal with it correctly.

• Figure 4.13: *Laser Fonts screen*

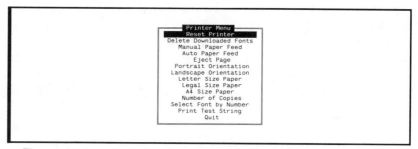

• Figure 4.14: *Laser Fonts Printer menu*

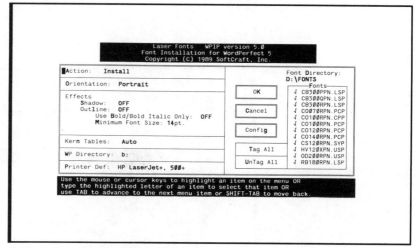

• Figure 4.15: *WPIP menu for installing fonts in WordPerfect*

If you have Pagemaker or Ventura Publisher, WYSIfonts! installs printer fonts and also creates and installs matching screen fonts. By installing both at the same time, you get a perfect match of printer and screen fonts. Figure 4.17 shows the WYSIfonts! menu for Ventura Publisher. The Pagemaker version is similar.

Installing fonts from this menu is simple. Select the Action desired: Install, Reinstall, Remove, or Width Table Only. At the Font Directory prompt, designate the directory where your fonts are stored. WYSIfonts! will search the directory and list the appropriate fonts in the right window.

To install all the fonts shown, select Tag All, or highlight individual fonts, and then press ←┘. Select an orientation, then set the other menu options. Finally, select OK.

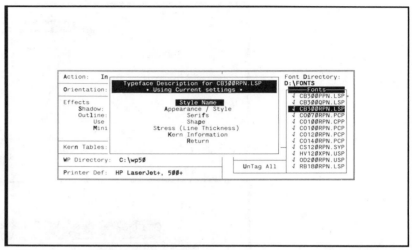

• Figure 4.16: *WPIP font attribute menu*

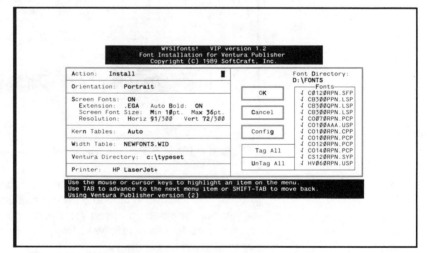

• Figure 4.17: *WYSIfonts! menu for Ventura Publisher*

The Ventura Publisher version creates the width table NEW-FONTS.WID; the Pagemaker version modifies the WIN.INI file. Both versions create matching screen fonts.

As I mentioned before, a collection of Softcraft products is available in the Font Solution Pack. This package also includes a central menu that lets you set up the environment and select functions, as shown in Figure 4.18. When you run a Softcraft program from this menu, the available fonts will be listed.

Editing Softfonts

If you need to print a character that isn't in an available symbol set, such as a slashed zero (Ø) or some other special character, you may be able to create it with a special program.

Using Font Editors

A font-editing program lets you change each dot that makes up the character's bit map. You don't necessarily have to be an artist or designer to edit fonts, but you do need a good eye for detail and a steady hand. All font editors require a graphic display—CGA, EGA, VGA, or Hercules—and are easier to use if you have a mouse.

Figure 4.19, for example, shows two custom-made characters created using the Softcraft Font Editor. They were created from a 24-point Helvetica font that was copied to LO240BPN.USP (leaving the original intact on disk), then loaded into the font editor. One character is an enlarged O with a smiling face added by using the mouse pointer as a drawing tool. The other shows how custom logos can be designed. Figure 4.20 shows the Softcraft Font Editor screen.

Using a font editor, you could create and use an entirely new font, not just a character or two. It wouldn't be difficult, for example, to create a semaphore font for budding sailors, or a sign language font to help the hearing impaired.

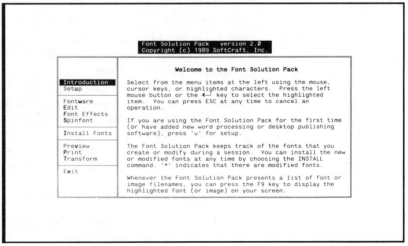

• Figure 4.18: *Font Solution Pack menu*

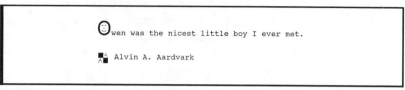

- Figure 4.19: *Edited font characters*

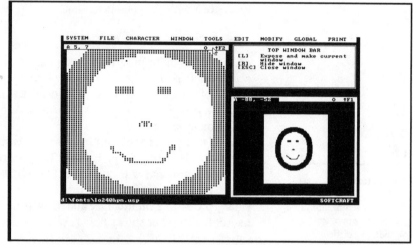

- Figure 4.20: *The letter O enlarged and edited in Softcraft Font Editor*

After you create and save the font, use a font installation program to install it in your application. When you want to print the character, type the character you started with, such as an O for the sample character, and select the proper typeface and size.

Other program options let you invert, rotate, slant, and combine characters. You can even import a drawing made with another program.

Qfont is a shareware font editor that offers many of the same features as the Softcraft program. It requires an EGA color system. Along with the graphic display of each character, it fully describes the character's size and style. A sample display is shown in Figure 4.21.

Using Other Font Utility Programs

Programs that let you examine but not change character bit maps are also available. These are useful when you just want to see how characters are formed and fonts are described. The shareware program Fontview displays font and character data, as illustrated in Figure 4.22.

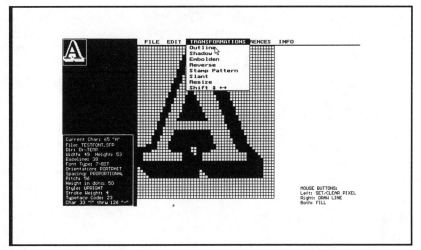

• Figure 4.21: *Qfont screen*

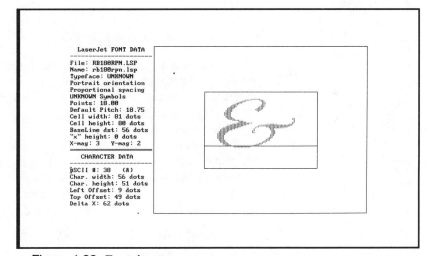

• Figure 4.22: *Fontview screen*

MAKEHOLL and MAKESHAD are shareware programs that will make outline and shadow fonts from standard PCL fonts. These are particularly useful if you're using softfonts with WordPerfect 5.0, which has options for these attributes in the Font Appearance menu. Create the fonts, then use the PTR program to modify the driver. Designate the new fonts names in the Automatic Font Selection menu, as described in Chapter 5. Both of the programs, by the way, are supplied with the C source code.

Theme, from Theme Software Company, prints musical notation on LaserJet printers. This program is like a word processor for music. It allows you to copy or transpose notes within the score, keeping track of the beats per measure.

Manipulating Fonts with Publisher's Type Foundry

Publisher's Type Foundry is actually a collection of programs designed to manipulate fonts and scanned images.

Scanning and scanning programs are discussed in detail in Chapter 14.

It includes a bit-map editor for editing fonts, an outline editor for manipulating outline fonts, PC Paintbrush Plus, and a scanning program, PB/Scan. Because the system runs under Windows, the four programs combine to form a powerful utility system that can share information via the clipboard.

Using the Bit-Map Editor

US Software markets a similar program for manipulating fonts and scanned images.

Like other font-editing programs, the editor lets you change individual dots that make up characters and symbols. A sample screen is shown in Figure 4.23. Using drawing tools, you can quickly add lines, dots, and geometric shapes to a character, and even enlarge the display to work in close detail, as illustrated in Figure 4.24.

The editor works only with files in a special XFR format, but options are provided for converting back and forth between XFR and LaserJet, Ventura, Pagemaker, Paintbrush, Gem, and Windows formats. Fonts can also be saved for use with the outline editor.

Using the Outline Editor

You can use the Windows option to create screen fonts.

The outline editor lets you display and edit characters from font outlines. The files must be in a special OTL format, but utilities are provided for converting bit-map fonts into this format. From OTL files, you can create fonts of other sizes.

For example, suppose you have a bit-map font in only 12 points. To create any other size font, use the bit-map editor to convert the file to an outline, load it into the outline editor, and then save it as a bit-map font in the new

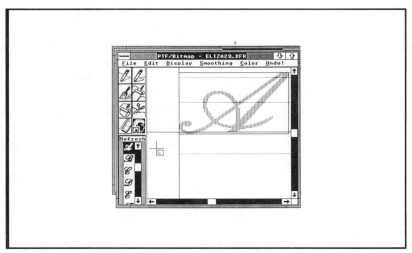

• Figure 4.23: *Publisher's Type Foundry bit-map editor screen*

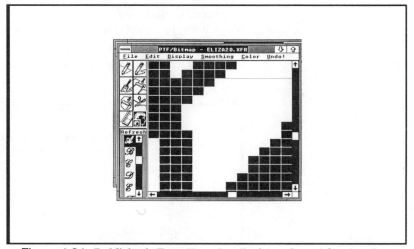

• Figure 4.24: *Publisher's Type Foundry display enlarged for detail*

You can even convert Post-Script outline fonts to Laser-Jet bit maps. Use the outline editor to convert the Post-Script outline font to OTL format. Load the new OTL files into the editor, set the bit-map parameters to the point size desired, and then save the font in HP format.

size. Load it back into the bit-map editor to make minor dot-by-dot changes to clean up any rough edges. Save the final bit-map font in the correct format for your application, and then use the font as you would any other.

A separate utility is provided for downloading files to LaserJet printers. Outline fonts can also be made in PostScript format or downloaded directly to a PostScript printer.

The ability to edit an outline font and convert it to a bit-map font gives you complete control over font design and style. Unlike a bit-map font, which is a series of dots in a fixed size and shape, an outline font is a series of descriptions of the lines and arcs that make up the general shape of each character. When you create a bit-map font from an outline, the segments are made larger or smaller to create the finished font size.

Figure 4.25, for example, shows the character D from one of the sample outline fonts provided with the Publisher's Type Foundry software (several OTL outline and bit-map fonts are supplied). In the enlarged display, you can see the segments that form the letter. Each of the small boxes and dots is a juncture point of a line or arc segment.

By using the outline editor, you can change any or all of the individual segments, and even add new ones. For example, Figure 4.26 shows the sample character D with the single straight line on the left divided into two line segments.

You can also use the outline editor's drawing tools to add lines and geometric shapes, reshape the proportions, and rotate sections of the character. Menu options allow you to move, scale, angle, or slant individual characters or the entire font.

When you are finished with your design, you can use the clipboard to store the results. Figure 4.27 shows the results of using the outline editor to slant and extend a letter, and then copying it as a bit map to the clipboard for display.

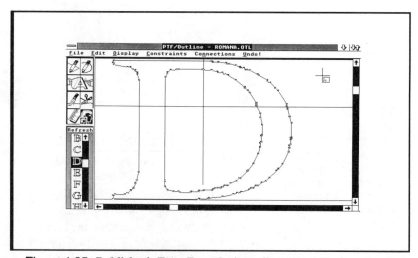

• Figure 4.25: *Publisher's Type Foundry's outline editor displays the character's line and arc segments*

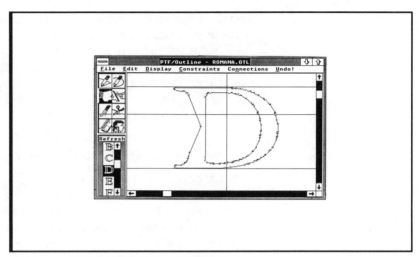

• Figure 4.26: *Modifying an outline font*

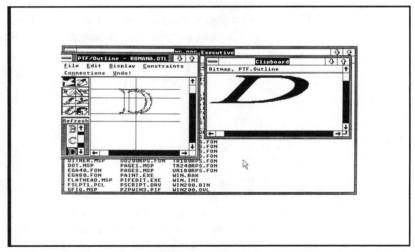

• Figure 4.27: *Using the Publisher's Type Foundry clipboard, the character can be shown in both outline and bit-map form*

• *Using Filtering Programs to Print ASCII Files*

What's the worst case? You have a laser printer with terrific capabilities but want to use an application that doesn't support it and won't let you

insert PCL commands. You could use a utility to print the entire document in one of your fancy fonts, but you want to use several different fonts.

In this case, a filtering program may provide the solution. These programs handle plain ASCII text—documents that have no formatting commands inserted by the application itself. You insert the special codes that the filtering program uses to control the LaserJet.

Let's briefly look at two examples.

Controlling Fonts with LJFonts

LJFonts, by Keller Software, is a memory-resident filtering program that can select and change fonts from 18 different font cartridges. It works directly from within word processors, spreadsheets, and other programs as they send characters to the printer. SFont, also by Keller Software, does the same for softfonts that have already been downloaded.

LJFonts intercepts the stream of characters going to the printer, looking for font ID numbers and other commands within brackets, such as [074], and then translates them into PCL commands. The program comes with a table showing the numbers assigned to each supported font and function.

For example, your document may start something like this:

```
[416][427]
   [006]Resume[007]

   Alvin A. Aardvark
```

This sets the printer to 66 lines per page (416) with a three-line top margin (427). The title will be printed in 14.4-point Helvetica Bold (006), and the remainder will be in 10-point Times Roman Medium (007), both from the B cartridge.

This program is powerful, but you have to control the spacing yourself. For example, you would have to insert the correct spacing for the word *Resume* in the example above to appear centered when printed in 14.4-point type.

Using Pamphlet to Control Fonts

The Pamphlet program discussed in Chapter 3 can also control fonts within a document, but only when it's printing a pamphlet from DOS. You have to first save the document as an ASCII file, and then print it from the Pamphlet menu. All fonts must be loaded before you print the document.

Special commands are entered following an escape character, which signals Pamphlet to send the following characters as PCL commands, not normal text to be printed. For example, the command

/t41h10

would set the LaserJet to print in 10-point Helvetica.

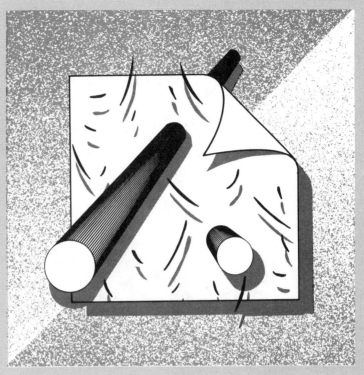

·Using the LaserJet
with Your Applications

Here are nine chapters that explain in detail how to use your LaserJet with popular software applications. More than a general guide, these chapters present inside information on printer drivers and how to utilize them with all LaserJet models.

Additional information for DeskJet users can be found in Appendix D.

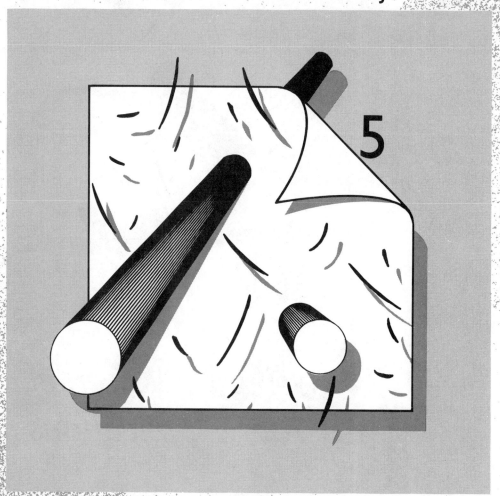

H·P L·A·S·E·R·J·E·T

5

Printing with WordPerfect

- WordPerfect 5.0 provides excellent support for LaserJet printers. It has the following resources:

  - Integrated downloading

  - Installable support for Hewlett-Packard cartridges and softfonts

  - Bitstream Fontware available at no charge

  - Resolution options

  - Graphic file printing

  - Portrait and landscape orientation support

  - Printer driver modification program included with the package

  - DeskJet printer support

In this chapter, you'll learn how to use the full capabilities of the LaserJet with WordPerfect.

• *Accessing Printer Drivers*

DeskJet drivers are in WPRINT2.ALL. Install your printer, fonts, and cartridges as discussed here, but use the printer disk with the WPRINT2.ALL file.

The LaserJet printer drivers are in a file called WPRINT1.ALL on the Printer 1 disk. Before printing for the first time, you must extract the driver you want to use. Drivers are supplied for all six LaserJet models. (If the LaserJet 2000 driver isn't listed when you install drivers, contact Word-Perfect Corporation for a copy.)

Although only Hewlett-Packard cartridges and softfonts are supported by the drivers, registered WordPerfect owners can get the Bitstream Fontware package free. This creates Bitstream fonts and adds their support to the library file WPRINT1.ALL. Softcraft also markets a softfont installation package called Laser Fonts, which not only modifies the Word-Perfect driver but can create outline and shadow fonts that are directly accessible from WordPerfect.

• *Installing Printers*

The printer installation process extracts the appropriate driver information from the WPRINT1.ALL file, creating a separate file with the extension PRS. Once this file is created, you can select to use the driver for your documents.

Here's the procedure for installing your printer:

1. Start WordPerfect.

2. Press Shift-F7 to see the Print menu, shown in Figure 5.1.

3. Press S to select a printer. You'll see the Select Printer menu, shown in Figure 5.2. It will not list any printers if you haven't installed one yet.

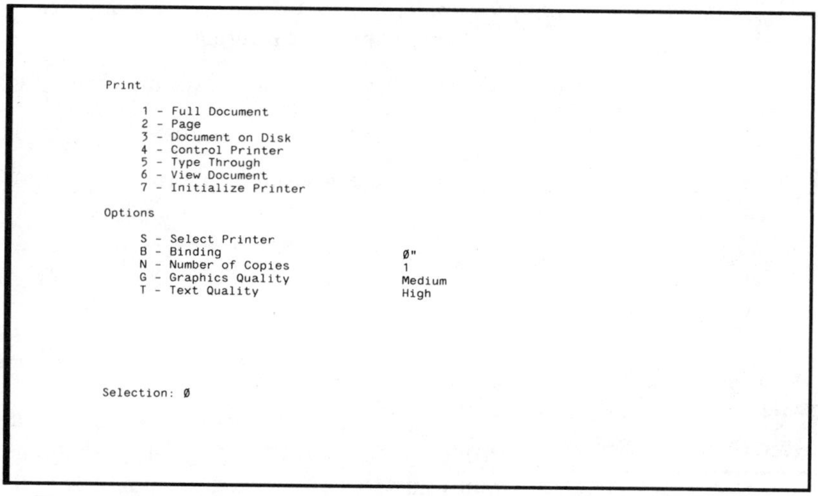

```
        Print

            1 - Full Document
            2 - Page
            3 - Document on Disk
            4 - Control Printer
            5 - Type Through
            6 - View Document
            7 - Initialize Printer

        Options

            S - Select Printer
            B - Binding                    Ø"
            N - Number of Copies           1
            G - Graphics Quality           Medium
            T - Text Quality               High




        Selection: Ø
```

• Figure 5.1: *WordPerfect Print menu*

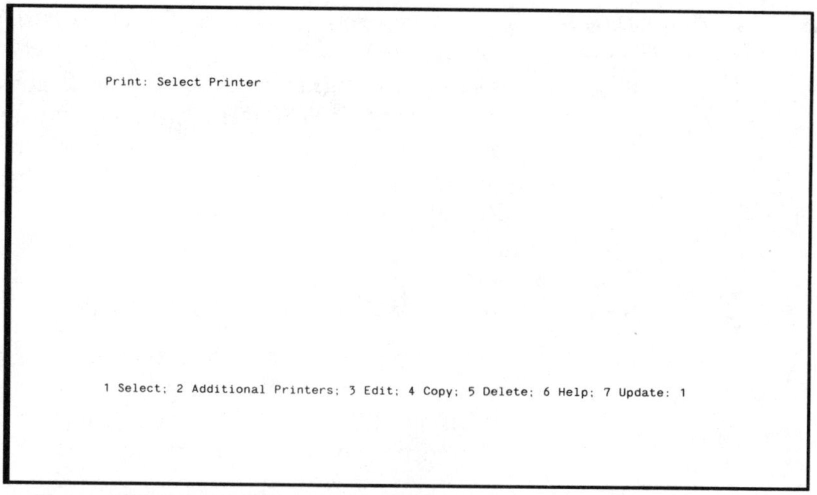

```
        Print: Select Printer













    1 Select; 2 Additional Printers; 3 Edit; 4 Copy; 5 Delete; 6 Help; 7 Update: 1
```

• Figure 5.2: *WordPerfect Select Printer menu*

4. Press 2 or A to select Additional Printers.

If you haven't copied the WPRINT1.ALL file onto a hard disk, WordPerfect will report that the printer files were not found. If the WPRINT1.ALL is on your hard disk, skip steps 5 and 6. A full list of printers will appear on your screen. As you press the ↓ key to move through the printers, the list will scroll off the top to display more printers at the bottom. You can press the ↑ key to redisplay any names that have scrolled off the top of the screen.

5. Place the Printer 1 disk in drive A (drive B if you have a floppy-disk system).

6. Press 2 or O to select Other Disk, type **A:** or **B:**, and then press ⏎. You'll see the Additional Printers screen, which lists the printers WordPerfect works with, as shown in Figure 5.3.

7. To select your printer from the list, press ↓ to highlight its name, and then press ⏎. At the bottom of the screen, you'll see the prompt

   Printer Filename: (your printer's name).PRS

8. Press ⏎. You'll see the message

   Updating font:

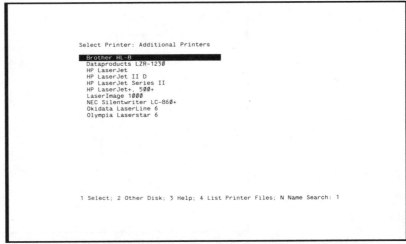

• Figure 5.3: *WordPerfect Additional Printers list*

at the prompt line, followed by a font number, as WordPerfect transfers the driver information from WPRINT1.ALL to the PRS file. Next, the Printer Helps and Hints screen will appear. Figure 5.4 shows the information displayed for the LaserJet IID.

9. Read the screen, and then press F7. After the file is loaded, you'll see the Edit menu, as shown in Figure 5.5.

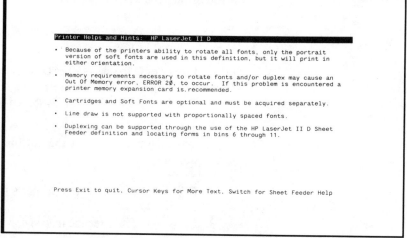

• Figure 5.4: *WordPerfect Printer Helps and Hints screen*

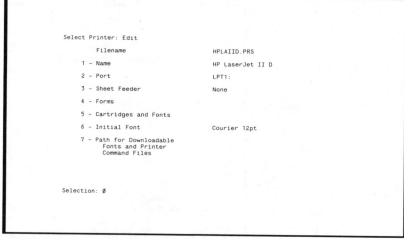

• Figure 5.5: *WordPerfect Select Printer: Edit menu*

10. Press 2 or P to select the Port option to designate the port where your printer is attached to your computer. This displays the prompt line

    Port: 1 LPT 1; 2 LPT 2; 3 LPT 3; 4 COM 1; 5 COM 2; 6
    COM 3; 7 COM 4; 8 Other: 0

Chapter 15 explains how you can use the Other option, along with the PostScript driver, to use a PostScript interpreter such as GoScript.

11. Press the number corresponding to your printer's port. LPT refers to parallel ports, COM to serial. The Other option is used to send the printer output to a disk file. You can use this if you want to later print the file using the DOS Print command. If you are using a parallel port, skip the next step.

12. If you selected a serial (COM) port, you will see a menu for setting the interface protocol, as shown in Figure 5.6. The values listed match the default settings for the LaserJet, so just press ← if you haven't changed the printer's serial configuration. If you did change any of these settings, you must reset the values in this menu. Press 1 to change the baud rate, or 2 to reset the parity. Make your selection from the choices listed at the bottom of the screen, and then press ←. To change stop bits, character length, or XON settings, select the appropriate menu item, type your new setting, then press ←. Press ← after you've made your selections.

13. Press F7 to display the Printer Selection menu, which now lists the printer you just selected. If this is the first printer you've installed,

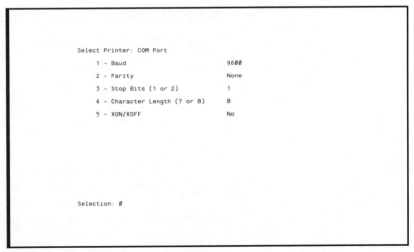

```
Select Printer: COM Port

    1 - Baud                            9600

    2 - Parity                          None

    3 - Stop Bits (1 or 2)              1

    4 - Character Length (7 or 8)       8

    5 - XON/XOFF                        No




    Selection: 0
```

• Figure 5.6: *WordPerfect serial interface menu*

there will be an asterisk next to it, indicating it is already selected for use. Otherwise, highlight the printer, type an asterisk, and press ⏎.

14. Press F7 to return to the document.

The printer driver is now a separate file on your disk. If you later modify WPRINT1.ALL, or add softfont support such as Bitstream, you must update the PRS file, or extract it again, to include the new data. To update the driver, press Shift-F7 S, highlight the printer's name, and then press U to select Update. Any new functions or modifications to the WPRINT1.ALL file will be added to the driver.

• *Adding Support for Cartridges and Softfonts*

You can purchase a special Hewlett-Packard Word-Perfect cartridge that contains CG Times from 6 to 24 points, and Univers in 14, 18, and 24 points.

If you purchased cartridges or softfonts, you must tell WordPerfect what and where they are before you use them for the first time.

Designating Cartridges and Softfonts

First, make a note of the cartridge number or the name, set, and directory of your downloadable fonts. Then follow these steps:

1. Press Shift-F7 S to display the Select Printer menu.

2. Highlight the name of your printer.

3. Press 3 or E to see the Edit menu.

4. Press 5 or C to display the Cartridges and Fonts menu, shown in Figure 5.7. (With the LaserJet 2000, the Duplex option, which is used to print on both sides of the paper, will also be listed on this menu.)

This menu indicates how many cartridge slots you have and the amount of memory your printer has available to hold downloaded fonts. If you've added extra memory to your printer, you can change the amount shown in the Quantity column: Select Softfonts, press 2 or Q, and enter the new value.

Selecting Cartridges

To use internal landscape fonts with the DeskJet +, select *DeskJet + Internal Fonts* from the Cartridges and Fonts menu. Mark Courier Landscape Internal as Present (∗).

Your LaserJet may have one, two, or three cartridge slots. Now you will mark the cartridge (or cartridges) you will be using.

1. The Cartridge Fonts category should be highlighted. Press ↵ to display a list of cartridges available for your printer, as shown in Figure 5.8.

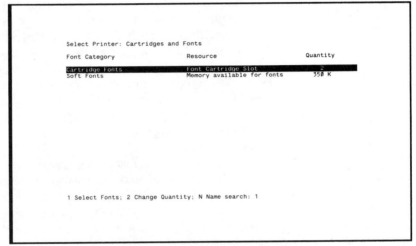

• Figure 5.7: *WordPerfect Cartridges and Fonts menu*

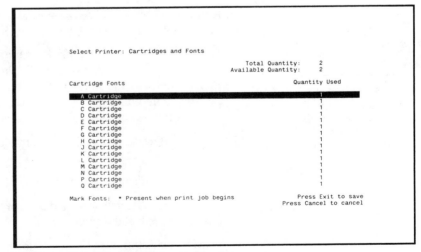

• Figure 5.8: *WordPerfect cartridge list*

2. Use the arrow keys to highlight the cartridge you will be using and type *. Repeat this step if your printer accepts more than one cartridge at a time.

3. Press F7 to return to the previous menu.

Selecting Softfonts

You can designate softfonts as Present or Can Be Loaded. WordPerfect assumes that all fonts marked Present (with an asterisk) will have already been downloaded when you start to print a document. (You can download them yourself or have WordPerfect download them for you.) Fonts marked Can Be Loaded (with a plus sign) will be downloaded by WordPerfect when you start to print a document that uses them.

When you use WordPerfect to download your Present fonts, it will try to download all of them, even if they are not being used in the current document. Therefore, before you begin to mark fonts, you should plan a font-management strategy, particularly if you have many softfonts you want to make available.

One strategy is to mark a small set of softfonts that you will use all the time as Present. Then mark the remaining infrequently used fonts as Can Be Loaded. Another option is to mark some fonts as both Present and Can Be Loaded. If you just want to use a few of them, let WordPerfect download them as needed. When you want to use the entire set, have WordPerfect download them all.

1. Highlight the Soft Fonts option on the Cartridges and Fonts menu, and press ⏎ to see a list of available softfonts, as shown in Figure 5.9. It might take a few seconds for this list to appear.

2. Scroll through the list and mark each of your fonts with either * (Present) or + (Can Be Loaded). When you mark a font, WordPerfect subtracts the amount of printer memory it requires from the Available Quantity amount listed at the top of the menu. Remember, you can't use all of this memory for softfonts.

3. Press F7 after you finish marking fonts. The Edit menu will appear again.

4. Press 7 or D to enter the path for downloadable fonts.

5. Type the complete path (disk and directory) where the downloadable fonts are stored, and then press ⏎.

6. Press F7 twice to return to the document.

Except with the LaserJet IID and LaserJet 2000, if you plan on printing in landscape mode, you must select landscape fonts.

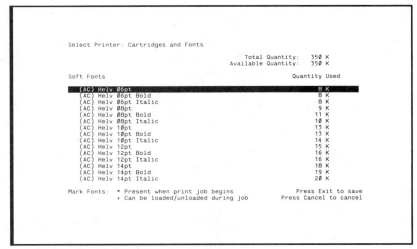

• Figure 5.9: *WordPerfect Softfont list*

Changing the Default Font

WordPerfect will use the printer's default Courier font with each document. You can change this to use a different internal font, one from a cartridge, or a softfont as the default. Note that this only changes the default font used for WordPerfect documents—other programs will still use the printer's default font.

Only select a softfont as the initial font if you plan to use it all the time. Otherwise, select an internal or cartridge font (that's going to be installed), which won't take up the printer's memory.

To change the default font, return to the Select Printer: Edit menu, and then press 6 or I to select the Initial Font option. WordPerfect will display a list of available fonts. Highlight the font you want to use as the default when you start WordPerfect, and then press ◄─┘.

Downloading Fonts

To have WordPerfect download the fonts you marked as Present, press Shift-F7 7 to select the Initialize Printer option from the Print menu. Note that this will erase any softfonts currently in the LaserJet's memory. WordPerfect will download every font marked with ∗, and those fonts will remain in the printer's memory until you turn your printer off. Fonts marked with + will be downloaded during printing as necessary.

• *Using Fonts*

Through WordPerfect, you can temporarily change the font and its size, position, and appearance.

Changing Fonts

You can change to another available font at any time. Just keep in mind that the number of fonts you can print per page is limited by your printer and its memory.

To temporarily change fonts, press Ctrl-F8 F to list the available fonts. The currently selected font is the *base font*. WordPerfect uses the base font as a reference for the font size and style selections you make, as explained in the following sections. Highlight the font you want to use as the base font and press ←. A font code will be inserted in the document, and text you enter from that point on—for that document only—will be in that font until you select another base font.

If you want to use a new default font with every document, set it through the Initial Font option on the Select Printer: Edit menu, as explained earlier.

Changing the Font Size and Position

When you want to change the font's size or position, press Ctrl-F8 1 to display the prompt line

1 Suprscpt; 2 Subscpt; 3 Fine; 4 Small; 5 Large; 6 Vry
Large; 7 Ext Large:0

These options represent sizes that are relative to the base font. For example, if the base font is 12-point Times and 6-, 10-, 12-, 14-, 18-, and 24-point sizes are available, WordPerfect will match up the fonts and sizes as follows:

Fine	6
Small	10
Normal	12 (the base font)
Large	14
Very Large	18
Extra Large	24

If you changed the base font to 10-point Times, the relative sizes would shift down: Large would be 12 points, Very Large 14 points, and Extra Large 18 points.

Figure 5.10 shows a test printout of different fonts in various sizes and styles. The first line is printed in the default Courier font. The second line is in a new base font, 12-point Dutch. The next three lines show samples of the sizes and appearances available in that base font (the outline and shadow fonts were created and installed using Softcraft's Font Solution Pack). The last line is in another base font, 12-point Helvetica.

From the Ctrl-F8 1 prompt line, press the number or letter for the font size or position, and then type the text you want in that format. Press the → key or Ctrl-F8 3 to return to the normal position and size.

To change the size or appearance of text (discussed below) you've already typed, highlight it as a block (using Alt-F4), and then press Ctrl-F8.

Changing the Font Appearance

To change the appearance of a font, press Ctrl-F8 2 to display the prompt line

> 1 Bold 2 Undrln 3 Dbl Und 4 Italc 5 Outln 6 Shadw 7 Sm
> Cap 8 Redln 9 Stkout: 0

As with font sizes, the style selections are based on your base font. For example, if the base font is 12-point Times, WordPerfect will use 12-point Times Italic if you press 4, or 12-point Times Bold if you press 1.

From the prompt line, press the number or letter for the style you want, and then type the text. Press → or Ctrl-F8 3 to return to the normal style.

Testing Your Printer's Font Support

Now let's test the printer driver to see what font features it supports. If you installed softfont support, use Ctrl-F8 F to select a typeface that you have in a variety of sizes. Then follow these steps:

1. Type **H**.

2. Press Ctrl-F8 1 to select a size.

DEFAULT FONT

NEW BASE FONT

WPWP WPWP WPWP WPWP WPWP WPWP WPWP **WPWP** WPWP

BOLD   *ITALIC*

OUTLINE   SHADOW

NEW BASE FONT

• Figure 5.10: *Sample printout showing multiple fonts and sizes*

3. Press 2 to select a subscript character.

4. Type **2**.

5. Press → or Ctrl-F8 3 to return to the normal position and size, and then type **0**.

6. Press ←, and type **Footnote goes here**.

7. Press Ctrl-F8 1 1 to select superscript.

8. Type **1**, and then press → to move the cursor beyond the superscript code.

9. Press ←.

10. Press Ctrl-F8 1 3 for fine printing.

11. Type **Fine**, press →, and then press ←.

12. Press Ctrl-F8 1 4 to select small printing.

13. Type **Small**, press →, and then press ←.

14. Type **Normal,** and then press ←.

15. Press Ctrl-F8 1 5 to select large printing.

16. Type **Large**, press →, and then press ←.

17. Press Ctrl-F8 1 6 to select very large printing.

18. Type **Very large**, press →, and then press ←.

19. Press Ctrl-F8 1 7 to select extra large printing.

20. Type **Extra large**, press →, and then press ←.

21. Press Ctrl-F8 2 to display the appearance options.

22. Press 3 to select double underlining. (The position indicator will change color or appearance depending on your computer hardware.)

23. Type **Double underline**.

24. Press → or Ctrl-F8 3 to select Normal and turn off the double-underline style.

25. Press ←.

26. Press Ctrl-F8 2 4 to select italic printing.

27. Type **Italic,** press the → key once, and then press ←. (The text may change color or appear in reverse, depending on your system.)

Remember, the text may not appear underlined on the screen.

28. Press Ctrl-F8 2 5 to select outline printing.

29. Type **Outline**, press →, and then press ↵.

30. Press Ctrl-F8 2 6 to select shadow printing.

31. Type **Shadow**, press →, and then press ↵.

32. Press Ctrl-F8 2 7 to select small cap printing.

33. Type **Small caps**, press →, and then press ↵.

34. Press Ctrl-F8 2 8 to select redline printing.

35. Type **Redline**, press →, and then press ↵.

36. Press Ctrl-F8 2 9 to select strikeout printing.

37. Type **Strikeout**, press →, and then press ↵.

38. Press Shift-F7 1 to print a copy of the test document.

Controlling the Line Spacing

By default, WordPerfect adjusts the line spacing (leading) to accommodate whatever size type your printer is using. If you want to set the line height yourself, press Shift-F8 1 to display the Format Line menu. Then press 4 or H to see the prompt

    1 Auto; 2 Fixed: 0

Now press 2 or F. The cursor moves to the Line Height option on the Format Line menu, and the word Auto is replaced by a measurement in inches for the type size you're currently using. (Standard six lines per inch is spaced 0.17 inches.) Type the line height you want, in points or inches, and then press ↵. For example, to print 12-point type using 14-point leading, you would enter 14pt. WordPerfect will convert 12 points to .19″. Press ↵ twice to return to the document.

Printing Graphic Characters

Line Draw is supported with cartridges A, B, and C. For ASCII line draw or screen dumps, use the PC-8 symbol set.

Line Draw is a special font that contains the definitions for the box and graphic characters that make up the PC symbol set. If you have a LaserJet that doesn't have the symbol set built in, you can use Line Draw to print graphic boxes and lines. For example, use it to print text screens captured with programs like Snapshot. Figure 5.11, which shows the supported characters, was printed on a LaserJet + .

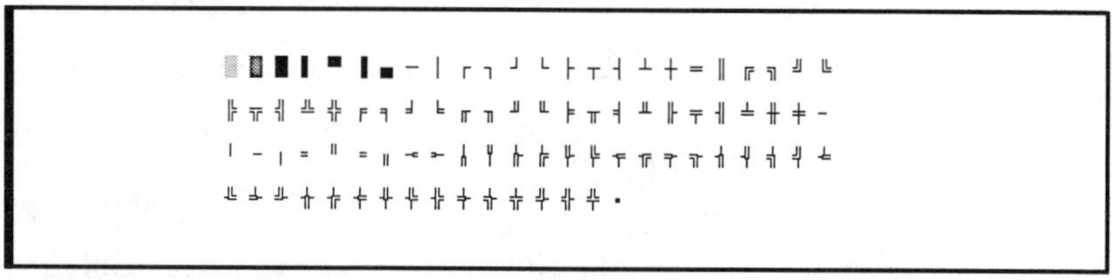

• Figure 5.11: *Graphic characters in WordPerfect's Line Draw font*

• *Controlling Paper Size, Feed, and Orientation*

The WordPerfect printer driver stores information about the types of paper you're using in a series of forms. Each form contains the size, type, orientation, and source for one category of paper. All printers come with a predefined Standard form, which is on plain 8½- by 11-inch paper. Other printers also have envelope, legal-size paper, or other forms defined already. When you want to print on one of these types of paper, you only have to tell WordPerfect what form you're using—you do not have to change the margins or other settings. Table 5.1 lists the predefined forms for LaserJet printers.

You can add new forms to the printer's file. However, if the size you want to print on is neither wider nor longer than the Standard form, you can just enter the new page length or width, without defining a new form.

Using Predefined Forms

All LaserJet models use the Standard form by default. To see the list of forms that are already defined for your printer, press Shift-F7 S to choose the Select Printer option. The driver you're currently using will be selected. Press 3 or E to edit the printer definition, and then press 4 or F to select the Forms option. You will see the Select Printer: Forms menu, as shown in Figure 5.12.

As shown on this menu, in addition to paper type and size, each form is classified by the following:

- **Orientation**: Forms can be portrait (P), landscape (L), or both. A Y under the letter shows the orientation.

- **Initially Present**: If a form is marked as initially present (with a Y), WordPerfect expects the first sheet of paper to be ready when you start printing.

Table 5.1: *WordPerfect Predefined Forms*

FORM TYPE	SIZE	ORIENT P L	INIT PRES	LOCATION	OFFSET TOP SIDE
LaserJet, LaserJet + , and LaserJet 500 +					
Envelope	4" × 9.5"	N Y	N	Manual	1.5" 4.5"
Standard	8.5" × 11"	Y Y	Y	Contin	0" 0"
[All Others]	Width < 8.5"		N	Manual	0" 0"
LaserJet II and LaserJet IID					
Envelope	4" × 9.5"	N Y	Y	Manual	0" 0"
Standard	8.5" × 11"	Y Y	Y	Contin	0" 0"
[All Others]	Width < 8.5"		N	Manual	0" 0"
LaserJet 2000					
Standard	8.5" × 11"	Y Y	Y	Contin	0" 0"
[All Others]	Width < 11"		N	Contin	0" 0"

- **Location**: If the location is set as Contin, WordPerfect assumes you're using the paper cassette, and it won't stop between pages to let you manually insert individual sheets. You can set this to Manual or enter a bin number (as discussed shortly).

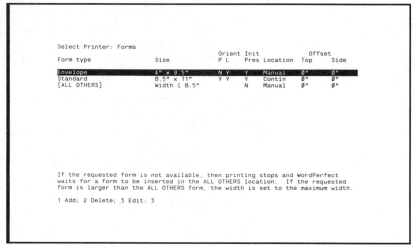

• Figure 5.12: *WordPerfect Select Printer: Forms menu*

• **Offset:** An offset is additional margin space at the top or left side of the form. For example, multipart 8½-by 11-inch forms often have a narrow area before the perforation at the top margin. The total form length is actually 8½ by 11½ inches. A top page offset of ½ and a top margin of 1 inch would advance the form 1½ inches before printing. Left offsets can be used with continuous form paper to accommodate the tractor holes.

The Standard form is either portrait or landscape, uses continuous paper from the cassette, and is initially present. The [All Others] form is used when you select a form type that's not defined. Its size is limited by the maximum width that can feed through the printer: 8½ inches for all models except the LaserJet 2000.

The other predefined form for all models but the LaserJet 2000 is for envelopes. The original LaserJet and LaserJet + assume the envelope is not initially present and has top and side offsets of 1.5 and 4.5 inches (because envelopes are fed aligned at the right paper guide). All the Envelope forms are listed as landscape only.

The envelope form is not predefined. See Appendix D for details.

To select a predefined form, make sure the cursor is at the start of the document (or at the beginning of a page), and then press Shift-F8 2 to display the Format Page menu. Press 8 or F to display the paper size options, as shown in Figure 5.13. Press the number or letter corresponding to the page size you want, and WordPerfect will list paper types, as shown in Figure 5.14.

```
Format: Paper Size                    Width  Height

    1 - Standard                      (8.5" x 11")

    2 - Standard Landscape            (11" x 8.5")

    3 - Legal                         (8.5" x 14")

    4 - Legal Landscape               (14" x 8.5")

    5 - Envelope                      (9.5" x 4")

    6 - Half Sheet                    (5.5" x 8.5")

    7 - US Government                 (8" x 11")

    8 - A4                            (210mm x 297mm)

    9 - A4 Landscape                  (297mm x 210mm)

    o - Other


Selection: 1
```

• Figure 5.13: *WordPerfect paper size options*

```
Format: Paper Type

    1 - Standard

    2 - Bond

    3 - Letterhead

    4 - Labels

    5 - Envelope

    6 - Transparency

    7 - Cardstock

    8 - Other




Selection: 1
```

• Figure 5.14: *WordPerfect paper type options*

Press the number or letter corresponding to the paper type you want. If you select a form size and type that hasn't been defined, WordPerfect will use Standard in its place and display the message

*requested form is unavailable

Press ◄─┘ twice to accept the page size change.

The code

[Paper Sz/Typ: (*size and type*)]

is inserted into the text. To return to the default form, delete the code.

When you select a landscape form, WordPerfect will automatically use the default Courier landscape font. If you press Ctrl-F8 F to select a new base font, only landscape fonts will be listed.

Adding Sheet Feeder Support

If you want to designate bin locations for various forms, you must first add support for a sheet feeder.

Press Shift-F7 S, then 3 or E to edit the printer definition. Next press 3 or S for the Sheet Feeder option, and you'll see a list of sheet feeders supported by the printer driver:

Printing in duplex with the LaserJet 2000 is discussed in the next section.

BDT MF 830 (6 Bin)
BDT MF 850 (3 Bin)
Build Your Own
Dataproducts LZR-1230 Multi-Bin
HP LaserJet
HP LaserJet 500 +
HP LaserJet IID
Mechanical
NEC LC-860 +
Ziyad PaperJet 400

Highlight your sheet feeder or printer's name, and then press ←. You'll see the Sheet Feeder Helps and Hints screen. Figure 5.15 shows the information displayed for the LaserJet IID. Press F7 four times to return to the document.

Now when you define a form, you'll be able to designate one of the 11 bin numbers as the location. The first five bins are used to select the feed for one-sided printing (bin 1 is the upper cassette, 2 the lower cassette, etc.). To print in duplex, enter bin number 6, 7, or 8 for long-edge binding; or bin 9, 10, or 11 for short-edge binding. WordPerfect will take care of the rest.

Printing Duplex on the LaserJet 2000

To print duplex on the LaserJet 2000, follow these steps:

1. Press Shift-F7 S E C to display the Cartridges and Fonts menu.

```
Sheet Feeder Helps and Hints:  HP LaserJet II D

Note: Be sure to use the Forms option on the Printer Select
      Edit menu to indicate the location of available forms.

 • Simplex
     Bin 1 =  Upper Cassette
     Bin 2 =  Lower Cassette
     Bin 3 =  Manual Paper Feed
     Bin 4 =  Manual Envelope Feed
     Bin 5 =  Auto Envelope Feeder

 • Vertically Bound Duplex
     Bin 6 =  Upper Cassette
     Bin 7 =  Lower Cassette
     Bin 8 =  Manual Paper Feed

 • Horizontally Bound Duplex
     Bin 9 =  Upper Cassette
     Bin 10 = Lower Cassette
     Bin 11 = Manual Paper Feed



Press Exit when done                    (Use Cursor Keys for more text)
```

• Figure 5.15: *WordPerfect Sheet Feeder Helps and Hint screen*

2. Highlight Duplex and press ←. You'll see another menu with only Duplex listed.

3. Type * (an asterisk), and then press ← to update the font list. This might take a few minutes, depending on your system.

4. Press F7 three times to return to the Print menu.

5. Press 7 or I to initialize the printer.

When you want to print single sides again, repeat the process but press the ← key to remove the asterisk from the Duplex option. Initialize the printer again to turn Duplex off.

Defining New Forms

If you want to use a paper size that's not defined for your printer, you must first create a new form for it. Follow these steps:

1. Press Shift-F7 S to choose the Select Printer function.

2. Make sure your printer is selected, and then press 3 or E to edit the printer definition. The Change Settings menu appears.

3. Press 4 or F to display a list of forms defined for your printer.

4. Press 1 or A to add a new form definition. You'll see a list of form

To modify a predefined
form, press 3 or E from the
Forms menu.

types:

1 - Standard
2 - Bond
3 - Letterhead
4 - Labels
5 - Envelope
6 - Transparency
7 - Cardstock
8 - [ALL OTHERS]
9 - Other

5. Press the number or letter corresponding to the type of form or select Other to name your own type. You will see a menu for modifying the form. Figure 5.16 shows the menu for the Standard form type.

6. Press 1 or S to set the form size. You'll see the page size selection menu, as shown in Figure 5.17.

7. Press the number or letter for the size of the form. The Forms menu will reappear.

8. Press 4 or L if the paper location (feed) is incorrect. You'll see the prompt line

Location: 1 Continuous; 2 Bin Number; 3 Manual: 0

```
Select Printer: Forms

        Filename              HPLAIID.PRS

        Form Type             Standard

    1 - Form Size             8.5" x 11"

    2 - Orientation           Portrait

    3 - Initially Present     Yes

    4 - Location              Continuous

    5 - Page Offsets - Top    Ø"
                      Side    Ø"




    Selection: Ø
```

• Figure 5.16: *WordPerfect menu for editing the Standard form*

```
Select Printer: Form Size
                                    Inserted
                                      Edge

           1 - Standard            8.5"   x   11"

           2 - Standard Wide        11"   x   8.5"

           3 - Legal               8.5"   x   14"

           4 - Legal Wide           14"   x   8.5"

           5 - Envelope            9.5"   x   4"

           6 - Half Sheet          5.5"   x   8.5"

           7 - US Government         8"   x   11"

           8 - A4                  210mm  x   297mm

           9 - A4 Wide             297mm  x   210mm

           o - Other

       Selection: 1
```

• Figure 5.17: *WordPerfect page size selection menu*

9. Press 1 for continuous, press 3 for manual, or press 2 and then enter the bin number to use a sheet feeder definition.

10. Press 3 then Y to set the form as Initially Present. Check the settings for orientation and page offset. Change either of these settings if necessary.

11. Press ←. The new form will be added to the list of those already defined.

12. Press F7 four times to return to the typing window.

Now that you've created the form, it will be listed with forms. Press Shift-F8 2, then 8 or F, and select the form when you want to use this paper size.

Printing on Smaller Paper

You can use a page size that's not defined as a form, as long as it is no wider than the printer can handle: 11 inches for the LaserJet 2000, 8½ inches for the other models. This is convenient when working with smaller forms, such as 3- by 5-inch index cards. Follow these steps:

1. Press Shift-F8 2 to display the Format Page menu.

2. Press 8 or S to display the form size options.

3. Press O to select Other. You'll see the prompt

   Width: 8.5″

4. Type the width of the form (not larger than 8.5), and then press ↵ to see the prompt

   Height: 11

5. Type the height, or length, of the form (not larger than 11), and then press ↵ to display the paper type list.

6. Press 1 for Standard, and then press ↵ twice to return to the document.

Changing the page size does not change the default 1-inch top and bottom margins. If you're using a small sheet, these margins might be too large. For example, a 3- by 5-inch index card would have only 1 inch, or six lines, of typing space available. To fit more on the page, change the top and bottom margins.

Using Multibin LaserJets

If you're using the LaserJet 500+, LaserJet IID, or LaserJet 2000, you can streamline printing by creating new forms and designating various bins as their location. If you use both plain and letterhead paper, for example, define the standard size and type form for tray 1, the standard size/letterhead type form for tray 2.

For duplex printing with the LaserJet IID, select Other for the type, and then name it Duplex. Enter one of the duplex bin numbers listed for your sheet feeder.

When you want to print, select the form. Choose Other for the Duplex form, and then select it from the list of your custom forms.

Printing Envelopes

When you print envelopes, WordPerfect automatically uses the 10-point Courier landscape font. It also sets the printer for manual feed unless you've defined the location as the auto envelope feeder bin.

Follow these steps to print envelopes:

1. Press Shift-F8 P S to display the form types.

Print envelopes in portrait orientation using the Standard form. See Appendix D for details.

2. Press 5 twice (for the envelope type and size), and then press ◄—┘.

3. With the LaserJet, LaserJet +, and LaserJet 500 +: Set the top margin to 1.5 inches and the left margin to 4 inches. The envelope form already has 4½ and 1½ inch offsets.

   With the LaserJet II and LaserJet IID: Set the top margin to 4.5 inches and the left margin to 5.5 inches.

4. Press Shift-F7 1 to print the envelope. With the LaserJet, Laser-Jet +, and LaserJet 500 +, you'll also have to press Shift-F7 4 G because the form is defined as not initially present.

Printing Multiple Orientations

Because WordPerfect uses forms to control page size, you can easily print a document containing both portrait and landscape pages. The most useful application of this technique is to print a letter and its envelope at the same time. This way you can just type the address once, and then copy it from the letter to the envelope.

If you don't have an envelope feeder, you'll have to manually insert the envelope. But if you have an optional envelope tray, the entire process will be automatic.

Here's the general procedure for printing a letter and envelope together:

1. Type the letter as usual.

2. When you complete the letter, press Ctrl-◄—┘ to insert a page break line.

3. Select the envelope form.

4. Set the top and left margins as explained in the previous section.

5. Copy the address from the letter and insert it on the second page.

6. Press Shift-F7 1 to print the document.

• *Printing Graphics*

WordPerfect 5.0 documents can include graphic files in a number of popular formats. You simply press Alt-F9 to insert the file. But before you print the document, check the Graphics Quality setting on the Print menu.

The options correspond to the following printer resolutions:

- **None**: Graphics will not print
- **Draft**: 75 dpi
- **Medium**: 150 dpi
- **High**: 300 dpi

Remember that most LaserJet models require extra memory to print a full page at high resolution. Try it at the High setting anyway. If the graphic images are small enough, you'll probably get away with it. If not, you'll see the 20 error message flashing on the printer's control panel display. Press the Continue button, and then try one of these techniques:

- **Print the graphics and text separately**. If you're using softfonts, the fonts and graphics are competing for the same memory. Delete all the fonts from the printer's memory (turn it off then on again if you have to). Then use the Print menu to select Do Not Print for Text Quality, and High for Graphics Quality. Print the page, and only the graphics will print. Insert the same sheet back into the tray, printed side up (down with the LaserJet, LaserJet +, and LaserJet 500 +). Use the Print menu to select High for Text Quality and Do Not Print for Graphics Quality, then print the page again. This time the text will print.

- **Change the fonts**. Again, if you're using softfonts, try using ones with a smaller symbol set, such as USASCII instead of IBM-PC. If that doesn't help, use less fonts, such as underlining instead of italic and boldface. (WordPerfect doesn't have to download a special font to underline.) To save even more memory, use smaller fonts. Reduce the size of headlines or body text; use underlined titles instead of a larger size.

- **Modify the graphics**. As a last resort, print the document in a lower graphics quality, Medium instead of High, or reduce the size of the graphics using the Size option on the Graphics menu.

WordPerfect and PostScript

Chapter 15 covers PostScript solutions for the LaserJet. But generally, using the PostScript driver in WordPerfect isn't much different than using the HP drivers. When you select a base font, however, you'll be prompted to enter its point size. All sizes will then be scaled from that point.

Capturing Graphic Screens with Grab

Grab is WordPerfect's screen-capture utility, which saves any screen image in graphics mode to a WPG formatted graphics file. You can then insert the screen image in a WordPerfect document as a figure (using the Alt-F9 key).

Follow these steps to use Grab:

1. To load the utility from DOS, type **GRAB**, and then press ⏎. You'll see the message

   ```
   Screen capture utility successfully installed
   Activation (hot key) sequence is
   "<ALT><SHIFT><F9>"
   Output goes to active directory at time of capture
   Output file name is "GRAB.WPG"
   For help, type "grab /h"
   ```

Type **GRAB/H** to see several screens of information explaining how the program operates.

2. When you want to capture a screen, just press Alt-Shift-F9. If your screen is not in graphics mode, you'll hear a beep. Otherwise, you'll hear a two-tone beep, and a box will appear over the image on your screen. You adjust this box to enclose the area that you want to capture.

3. Press any of the directional arrow keys to move the box, or Shift and any arrow key to resize it. When resizing, only the bottom and right sides of the box move. So if you want to capture the entire screen, use the arrow keys to place the box in the upper-left corner, then press Shift-↓ and Shift-→ to expand the box to cover the whole screen.

4. Press ⏎, and the image in the box will be saved to a WPG file. (Press Esc if you decide not to capture the screen.)

The first image you capture is saved under the name GRAB.WPG. Subsequent images will be numbered consecutively as GRAB1.WPG to GRAB999.WPG.

To remove the resident program from memory, type **GRAB/T** from the DOS prompt.

• *Modifying the Printer Driver*

Chances are, you'll find the built-in printer driver suitable for your needs. If you decide to add other, non-Hewlett-Packard softfonts, try to

Chapter 4 explains how to install Bitstream fonts.

select those that come packaged with a installation program, such as Bitstream or Softcraft. Hewlett-Packard might even release new fonts that aren't supported by your version of WPRINT1.ALL. If that happens, check with WordPerfect Corporation to see if they have additional drivers available.

There may be occasions, however, when you want to customize the way the printer driver works. You can make changes by using WordPerfect's PTR program to modify the driver. It's a challenging process but one that could be well worth it. Even if you don't want to modify the driver, you may want to use PTR to look at the inner workings of printer drivers.

Using PTR to Arrange Font Sizes

As an example, suppose that you want to use specific fonts when changing sizes. The SA series of Century Schoolbook includes fonts in 6 through 12, 14, 18, and 24 points. (The SA series uses the ASCII symbol set; the SB series uses Roman-8.) To save printer memory, you plan on using normal, bold, and italic for the 12-point size, but just normal for all the others.

You want to arrange your font sizes this way:

Superscript	6 points
Subscript	6 points
Fine	7 points
Small	10 points
Normal	12 points
Large	14 points
Very Large	18 points
Extra Large	24 points

As you work your way through the driver using PTR, don't worry if you make some changes you're not sure about. Before leaving the program, you'll be asked to confirm the changes or not. If you're not absolutely sure, just say No.

You can use PTR whether you have softfonts or not. But since we're using softfonts for this example, we'll assume you have PTR on the WordPerfect directory of your hard disk.

Follow these steps to modify the driver:

1. Copy the file WPRINT1.ALL from the Printer 1 disk to the WordPerfect directory.

2. Type **PTR WPRINT1.ALL**, and then press ←┘. In a moment, you'll see the opening screen listing the printers included in that library, as shown in Figure 5.18.

3. Use the arrow keys to highlight the name of your printer, and then press ←┘. You'll see a new menu, which lists the options available for viewing or modifying the driver, as shown in Figure 5.19.

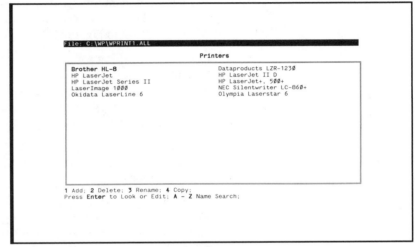

• Figure 5.18: *Printers in WPRINT1.ALL*

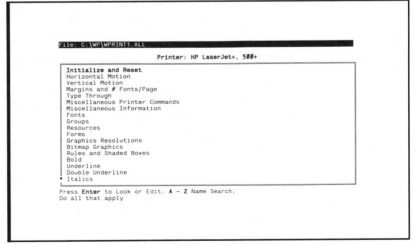

• Figure 5.19: *Options for modifying the WordPerfect printer driver*

4. Highlight an option you want to look at and press ←. You can work through any number of menus the same way. When you want to return to the options screen, press F7 until it appears.

5. Select Fonts, and then press ←. In a few moments, the list of fonts supported by the driver will appear on the screen.

6. Use the arrow keys to scroll through the list until you see the base font you want to modify, (SA) Century Schoolbook 12pt, and then press ←. PTR displays a new menu listing actions you can take on that font, shown in Figure 5.20.

7. To specify which fonts are used when this is the base font, select Automatic Font Changes, and then press ←. You'll see a screen showing the size and appearance options for that font on the left side under the heading Feature, as shown in Figure 5.21. Your goal is to insert the appropriate font names on the right.

8. Extra Large Print is already selected. Press ←, and the list of supported fonts will appear. Scroll through the list to select (SA) Century Schoolbook 24pt.

9. Type *, and then press F7. The previous screen appears with your selection opposite the Extra Large Print feature. When you later update the printer driver and select Very Large Print, WordPerfect will use 24-point Century Schoolbook.

10. Highlight Very Large Print, and then press ←.

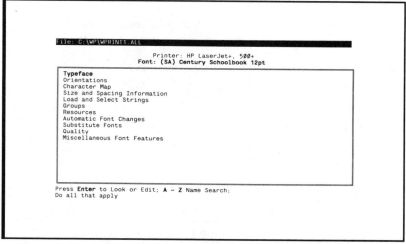

File: C:\WP\WPRINT1.ALL

```
                    Printer: HP LaserJet+, 500+
                 Font: (SA) Century Schoolbook 12pt

Typeface
Orientations
Character Map
Size and Spacing Information
Load and Select Strings
Groups
Resources
Automatic Font Changes
Substitute Fonts
Quality
Miscellaneous Font Features




Press Enter to Look or Edit; A - Z Name Search;
Do all that apply
```

• Figure 5.20: *Options for modifying WordPerfect printer driver fonts*

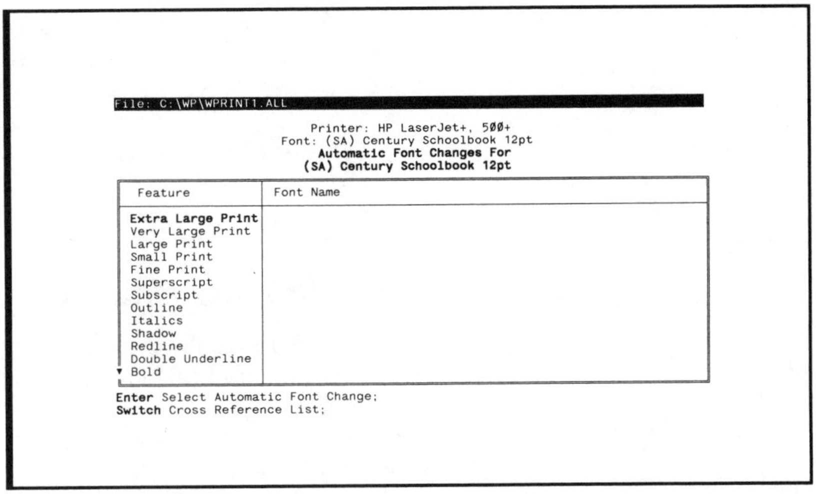

- Figure 5.21: *Options for modifying WordPerfect printer driver automatic fonts*

11. Scroll through the fonts to highlight (SA) Century Schoolbook 18pt, type *, and then press F7.

12. In the same manner, select the (SA) Century Schoolbook fonts for each of the sizes and attributes:

Large	14pt
Small	10pt
Fine	7pt
Superscript	6pt
Subscript	6pt
Italics	12pt Italic
Bold	12pt Bold
Small Caps	10pt

13. Press F7 five times to display the PTR opening screen. You'll see the prompt

   Save File? (Y/N) Y

You can select any of the softfonts you have available for the features listed. If you don't have an outline or shadow font, for instance, you can select an entirely different typeface of the correct point size. (You could do the same thing by changing base fonts in the middle of a sentence, but designating the fonts as a feature makes them easier to enter.)

14. Press Y. (Press N to cancel the changes.) It may take a few minutes while PTR rewrites the library file to the disk. After the changes are made, you'll see the message

Exit Printer Program? (Y/N) N

15. Press Y.

Recording the Changes

After you modify the driver information in WPRINT1.ALL, you must record these changes in the PRS file that was extracted when you installed your printer. Follow these steps:

1. Start WordPerfect.

2. Press Shift-F7 S.

3. Highlight the name of the printer and press U.

4. Press F7 to display the Edit menu.

5. Press 5 or C to display the Cartridges and Fonts menu.

6. Press ↓ to highlight Soft Fonts, and then press ←⅃.

7. Scroll through the list and mark each of the Century Schoolbook fonts you selected as either * (Present) or + (Can Be Loaded).

8. Press F7.

9. Press 7 or D to enter the path for downloadable fonts.

10. Enter the complete path (disk and directory) where the downloadable fonts are stored, and then press ←⅃.

11. Press F7 twice to return to the document.

Now whenever you select 12-point Century Schoolbook as the base font, the fonts you designated will automatically be used when you change size or appearance. You can use similar techniques to modify the printer driver in other ways. For example, you can build support for new font cartridges or softfonts, or insert PCL commands directly into the driver for features not currently supported.

H·P L·A·S·E·R·J·E·T

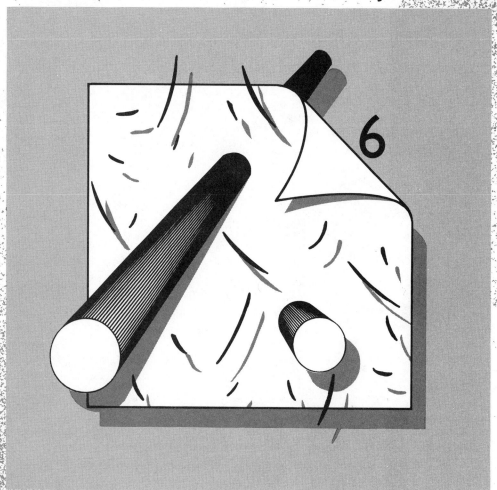

6

Printing with Microsoft Word

- Microsoft Word 5.0 was one of the first word processing programs to easily accommodate fonts in a variety of sizes. It has the following LaserJet resources:

  - Integrated downloading

  - Installable support for Hewlett-Packard cartridges and softfonts

  - Resolution options

  - Graphic file printing

  - Portrait and landscape orientation support

  - Layout options in points or inches

  - Printer driver modification possible

  - Bitstream Fontware available at low cost

  - DeskJet printer support

You can easily select different type styles and Word will automatically adjust the character, line, and paragraph spacing to the font's size. Version 5.0 of Word also includes additional design tools traditionally provided by desktop publishing programs: merging and scaling graphic images, manipulating text and graphic placement using frames, and displaying multiple columns while editing.

All these features, combined with a variety of printer drivers, allow you to take full advantage of your LaserJet's capabilities.

• *Accessing Printer Drivers*

All the internal and cartridge drivers are supplied with Word, but the package only contains the AC and AD softfont PRD files. Contact Microsoft for additional softfont drivers.

The printer drivers for Word are supplied in a series of files with the PRD extension, as listed in Table 6.1. One PRD file supports all the internal fonts; the others support 12-point Courier, Line Printer, and specific Hewlett-Packard cartridge or softfonts. Separate files are provided for portrait and landscape fonts.

To access the printer driver, you must have the PRD file for your fonts in the Word directory. Additional files with a DAT extension are needed to use softfonts. (These files contain the font names and PCL commands for downloading softfonts to the printer.) If you have a PostScript option installed in your LaserJet or you're using a PostScript software interpreter, you'll also need the INI files. In Word, you use the Print Options menu to select the PRD file you want to use for the document, the computer port to use, and your LaserJet model.

• Table 6.1: *Word PRD Files*

PRD FILE	FONTS SUPPORTED
Internal Fonts	
HPLASER.PRD	Internal fonts, all models
Cartridge Portrait	
HPLASER1.PRD	A,B,C,D,E,G,H,J,L,Q,W,X
HPLASER2.PRD	F,K,P,R,U
HPLASER3.PRD	J,R,Z
HPLASPS.PRD	B (USACSII symbol set)
HPLASRMN.PRD	F (Roman-8 symbol set)
HPLAS2S1.PRD	S1 (PC-8 symbol set)
HPLAS2S2.PRD	S2 (PC-8 symbol set)
HPLASTAX.PRD	T (ASCII and Line Draw sets)
HPPCCOUR.PRD	Y (PS Set 1)
HPLASMS.PRD	Z, MICROSOFT 1 (ECMA symbol set)
HPLASMS2.PRD	Z, MICROSOFT 1A (Roman-8 symbol set)
HPLASMSA.PRD	Z, MICROSOFT 1A (ASCII symbol set)
HPPRO.PRD	Pro Collection
Cartridge Landscape	
HPLASLAN.PRD	A,B,C,G,H,L,M,N,P,O,R,U,V
HPLASMSL.PRD	Z (Roman-8 symbol set)
HPPROL.PRD	Pro Collection

Table 6.1: *Word PRD Files (Continued)*

PRD FILE	FONTS SUPPORTED
Softfont Portrait	
HPDWNACP.PRD	AC (ASCII symbol set)
HPDWNADP.PRD	AD (Roman-8 symbol set)
HPDWNSFP.PRD	AC and AE (ASCII symbol set)
HPDWNR8P.PRD	AD and AF (Roman-8 symbol set)
HPDWNHHP.PRD	AG (Roman-8 symbol set)
HPDWNLGP.PRD	DA (several symbol sets included)
HPDWNPRP.PRD	EA (several symbol sets included)
HPDWNGAP.PRD	RA (ASCII symbol set)
HPDWNGA8.PRD	RB (Roman-8 symbol set)
HPDWNCNP.PRD	SA (ASCII symbol set)
HPDWNCN8.PRD	SB (Roman-8 symbol set)
HPDWNZHP.PRD	TA (ASCII symbol set)
HPDWNZH8.PRD	TB (Roman-8 symbol set)
HPDWNHLP.PRD	UA (ASCII symbol set)
HPDWNHL8.PRD	UB (Roman-8 symbol set)
Softfont Landscape	
HPDWNACL.PRD	AC (ASCII symbol set)
HPDWNADL.PRD	AD (Roman-8 symbol set)
HPDWNSFL.PRD	AC and AE (ASCII symbol set)
HPDWNR8L.PRD	AD and AF (Roman-8 symbol set)
HPDWNLGL.PRD	DA (several symbol sets included)
HPDWNPRL.PRD	EA (several symbol sets included)

Note: Each PRD file also supports internal Courier and Line Printer fonts.

See Chapter 4 for details on
softfont utility packages.

You can add support for other softfonts by using Hewlett-Packard's
Type Director; Softcraft's Laser Fonts; or Bitstream Fontware, which is
available at low cost from Microsoft. These products create fonts from outlines and modify the appropriate PRD file.

You can have as many PRD files on your disk as you want but you can
use only one per document. However, you can merge PRD files to build
support for combinations of cartridges and softfonts. This is particularly
useful if your LaserJet can accept several cartridges or if you use both cartridge and softfonts at the same time. You'll learn how to select PRD files
and merge them later in this chapter.

• *Setting Up Your System*

When you run the Setup program supplied with Word, you'll be asked to
indicate the printer model and fonts you'll be using. Setup will then copy the
appropriate files to your disk. However, you don't have to use Setup again to
later add support for additional fonts. You just need to copy the appropriate
PRD, DAT, and INI (if your LaserJet is equipped for PostScript) files from the
Word Printer disk to your Word directory. Each of the drivers contains the data
required for all the LaserJet models, so select the printer driver by the fonts it
supports.

Even though the following steps are for initially setting up Word on a
hard disk, the procedures for selecting display interfaces and printers are
the same as those for floppy-disk systems. So even floppy-disk users should
read through the steps.

1. Start your computer and insert the Word Utilities 1 disk in drive A.

2. Type **A:SETUP**. The Welcome to Setup screen will appear.

3. Press ◄┘, and you'll see a screen listing the possible types of setup
   for your computer.

4. Press the key corresponding to the disk where you want to copy the
   Word files: H for a hard disk, F for high capacity floppy disks, or P
   for 360K floppy disks.

5. Next you'll be prompted to enter the directory where you want
   Word placed. Type the directory name, such as WORD5, and press
   ◄┘. Then press C to continue with Setup.

6. Press W to copy Word to your hard disk.

7. Now in a series of steps, you'll be asked to insert the Word disks in drive A. Follow the prompts on the screen and insert the disk requested. At one point, you'll see the screen listing computer types, as shown in Figure 6.1.

8. Type the number corresponding to your computer, and then press ←.

9. When you see the video adapter menu, type the number corresponding to your video adapter, and then press ←. If your adapter isn't listed, press PgDn to see more.

10. Continue inserting the disks as you are prompted until the main Setup menu appears again.

11. Use the S, T, and L options on the menu to copy the Speller, Thesaurus, and Learning Word programs onto your hard disk. Follow the prompts as they appear. Now you're ready to select the proper printer files.

12. From the main Setup menu, press P. A partial list of supported printers will appear.

13. Press PgDn five times to display the Hewlett-Packard printers, as shown in Figure 6.2.

14. Type the number to the left of your printer, and then press ←. You'll see a list of fonts, as shown in Figure 6.3. You can display additional

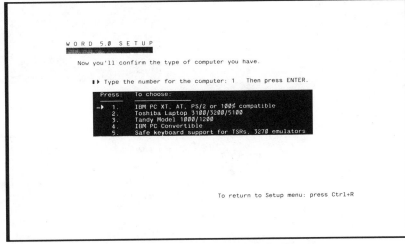

• Figure 6.1: *Computer type menu for setting up Word*

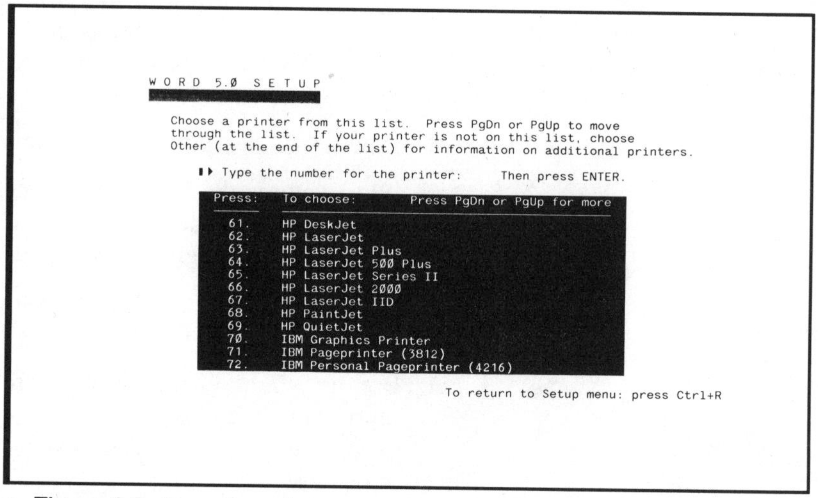

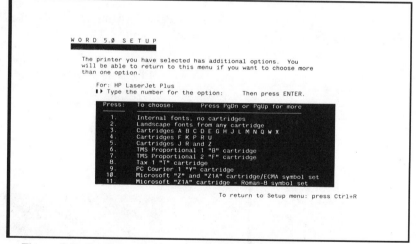

• Figure 6.2: *LaserJet printers supported by Word*

• Figure 6.3: *Partial list of fonts supported by Word*

fonts by pressing PgDn, but it's best to start by installing support for the internal fonts, and then add cartridge and softfont support.

15. Press 1, then ⏎ to select the Internal Fonts option. You'll be prompted to enter S to select additional fonts, F to finish printer installation, or U to cancel your last selection. If you want to use more than one cartridge or softfont set, press S, repeat this step

until each of the appropriate PRD files have been selected, and then press F. A similar prompt appears.

16. Press F to finish the installation, and you'll see a list of printer ports:

    1. LPT1:
    2. LPT2:
    3. LPT3:
    4. COM1:
    5. COM2:

17. Press the number corresponding to your port. You will be prompted to insert the appropriate printer disk, Printer Disk 2, in drive A. Follow the instructions on the screen to copy the correct PRD file onto your hard disk.

18. If you have a mouse, press M from the main Setup menu and follow the prompts on the screen. The mouse driver program MOUSE.SYS will be copied onto your hard disk.

19. The Customize Word Settings option on the Setup menu allows you to change the default page size, graphics mode, and screen display. If you're new to Word, skip this option for now. You can change these settings within Word itself later.

20. Press Q to finish the setup procedure. You'll see a screen asking if you want to modify the DOS configuration files.

21. If you need to configure your DOS disk to work with Word and the mouse—your system has not been specially set up for another program or this is your only program that uses the mouse—press M and follow the remaining prompts.

22. You'll be asked if you want to view README.DOC, a file that contains any last-minute documentation not included in the Word manual. Press V to see the file on the screen, then follow the instructions given, or press Q to end Setup.

Remember, you can manually add font support by copying the driver files to your Word directory.

• *Selecting the PRD File for Printing Your Document*

You're now ready to start Word and, if you have more than one driver installed, select the PRD file to use for printing. Remember, you can only use one PRD file for each document.

Follow these steps to selecting printing options:

1. Type **WORD,** and then press ⟵.

2. Press Esc P O to display the Print Options menu, shown in Figure 6.4. If you set up more than one PRD file, you have to select three critical printer driver options from this menu: the PRD file, the computer port being used, and your LaserJet model.

3. The Printer option should be selected. Press F1 to display a list of PRD files on your directory.

4. If necessary, press the arrow keys to highlight the PRD file you want to select.

5. If the Setup option is not correct, press Tab to select it, and then press F1 to display possible selections. Highlight the port you're using to communicate with the printer.

6. If the Model option is not correct, press Tab to select it, and then press F1 to display supported models. Highlight your model.

7. Select from the other options on the Print Options menu to customize your printing operation. These options are described in Table 6.2.

8. When all the Print Option menu settings are correct, press ⟵ to return to the Print command line. Then press Esc and type your document. To print the document, press Ctrl-F8.

All the fonts supported by the selected PRD file are now available, and you can use as many different fonts from the driver as your LaserJet can print.

To print in landscape orientation, you must select a landscape PRD file.

```
PRINT OPTIONS printer: █                    setup: LPT1:
       model:                               graphics resolution:
       copies: 1                            draft: Yes(No)
       hidden text: Yes(No)                 summary sheet: Yes(No)
       range:(All)Selection Pages           page numbers:
       widow/orphan control:(Yes)No         queued: Yes(No)
       paper feed: Continuous               duplex: Yes(No)
Enter printer name or press F1 to select from list
Pg1 Col          ()                    ?
                                                       Microsoft Word
```

• Figure 6.4: *Word Print Options menu*

- Table 6.2: *Word Printing Options*

OPTION	FUNCTION
Graphics Resolution	Sets the dot-per-inch resolution of graphic images: 75, 150, or 300 dpi. Keep in mind that most laser printers may not have enough memory to print a whole page of text and graphics at high resolution.
Copies	Determines the number of copies to be printed.
Draft	Prints the document in draft mode, without special character formats.
Hidden Text	Indicates whether or not text designated as hidden (not normally displayed on the screen) will be printed.
Summary Sheet	Determines whether or not the summary sheet is printed with the document.
Range	Indicates if you want to print the entire document, specific pages, or just selected text.
Page Numbers	If you selected Pages as the range, indicates the pages to be printed.
Widow/Orphan Control	If active, prevents widows (the first line of a paragraph appearing by itself at the bottom of the page) and orphans (the last line of a paragraph appearing by itself on the top of a page).
Queued	Prints documents while you edit or create another (if you select Yes).
Paper Feed	Determines the source of paper. Select this option, then press F1 to display alternatives. Possible alternatives include Manual (the manual tray), Continuous (the default cassette), Bin1, (the top tray), Bin2 (the bottom tray), Bin3 (the third drawer of multidrawer printer), Mixed (the first sheet from Bin 1, the remainder from Bin 2), and Envelope (an envelope feeder).
Duplex	Select Yes to print text on both sides of the page with the LaserJet IID or if you have the D option installed in the LaserJet 2000.

• *Using Fonts*

When you want to change fonts or sizes, follow these steps.

1. To select a font for text you are about to type, make sure that the cursor is not on the endmark. To change the fonts of existing text, highlight the characters with either the function keys or by dragging the mouse.

2. Press Alt-F8. The Format Character menu appears with the Font Name option already selected, as shown in Figure 6.5. Values may already be specified for the Font Name and Font Size options, or they may be blank.

3. Press F1. A list of fonts available in the printer driver appears at the top of the screen. The names in the parentheses are Word's own way of referring to different fonts.

4. Use the arrow keys to highlight the font you want.

5. Press Tab to select the Font Size option.

6. Press F1. A list of possible font sizes will appear at the top of the screen. In many cases, you might see only one size listed.

7. Highlight the size desired and press ←⏎.

The text size will not change on the screen, but the font and size you selected will be printed.

You can get an indication of how the document looks using the Print Preview command.

Controlling Line Spacing

Normally, Word prints six lines of text per inch, the setting for 12-point type. If you choose a larger font without changing line spacing, the text may overlap. Fortunately, Word lets you set line spacing in a variety of ways.

```
FORMAT CHARACTER bold: Yes(No)        italic: Yes(No)        underline: Yes(No)
        strikethrough: Yes(No)        uppercase: Yes(No)        small caps: Yes(No)
        double underline: Yes(No)     position:(Normal)Superscript Subscript
        font name: Courier            font size: 12              font color: Black
        hidden: Yes(No)
Enter font name or press F1 to select from list
Pg1 Co1                  {}                 ?                     Microsoft Word
```

• Figure 6.5: *Word's Format Character menu*

To adjust line spacing, place the cursor in the paragraph or highlight the text you want to format, and then press Esc F P to display the Format Paragraph menu. Press ↓ to reach the Line Spacing option. Enter the spacing in lines or points (such as 12pt), or type AUTO to have Word automatically adjust the line spacing for the point size. For extra leading, enter spacing a few points larger than the font size, such as 14pt for a 12-point font.

Downloading Fonts

When you print a document using a PRD file that contains softfonts, even if your document does not contain any of these fonts, you'll see the message

> Enter Y to download New Fonts, A to download All Fonts, N to skip

From this prompt, you can press Y to download any softfonts not previously downloaded, press A to download all the softfonts used in the document, or press N if the document doesn't use softfonts or the softfonts were previously downloaded.

Turning On the Graphics Display

Start Word by typing **WORD/G** to place your system in graphics mode. You can switch modes once you've started the program.

To display the character styles that Word can produce, your system must be in graphics mode. Follow these steps to see which mode you are in and switch to graphics mode if necessary:

1. Press Esc O to display the Options menu.

2. Press ↓ five times, then → to reach the Display Mode option. The number displayed as the default will depend on your computer's display card.

3. Press F1 to see the possible modes available for your system. For example, with an EGA card, you'll see these options (mode 1 is the default):

   1 Text, 25 lines, 16 colors
   2 Text, 43 lines, 16 colors
   3 Graphics, 25 lines, 16 colors
   4 Graphics, 43 lines, 16 colors

4. Press 3, then ←┘. You are now in graphics mode.

To quickly toggle back and forth between graphics and text mode, press Alt-F9.

Selecting Character Styles

You can select specific character styles through Word's Format Character menu or by using speed keys. If you format characters as bold or italic, Word will attempt to use the correct font for the type and size you've selected. If the font is not available, the normal style will be used.

As an example, suppose that you're using the AD softfont PRD file, which supports TmsRmn and Helv fonts (Hewlett-Packard's versions of Times Roman and Helvetica). Fonts 18 points and larger, however, are only in bold, not medium or italic. If you format a character in 30-point Helv Italic, the 30-point Helv Bold font will be used instead.

To format characters, press the speed key for the character format you want. Table 6.3 lists the speed keys and styles they produce. Next type the text you want formatted. Finally, press Alt-spacebar to return to the normal character style.

• Table 6.3: *Word Speed Keys for Formatting Characters*

SPEED KEY	STYLE
Alt-U	Underline
Alt-D	Double underline
Alt-B	Boldface
Alt-I	Italics
Alt-K	Small capital letters
Alt-S	Strikethrough
Alt-+	Superscript letters and numbers
Alt--	Subscript letters and numbers
Alt-E	Hidden text (characters that can optionally be displayed and printed)
Alt-spacebar	Normal character style (cancels all other styles)
Alt-Z	Cancels all characters styles except for font and font size

To format characters you've already typed, select them first with the function keys or by dragging the mouse, then use the appropriate speed key. Combine styles by pressing two or more speed keys. To print in bold italic, for example, press Alt-B then Alt-I.

As an alternative to using the speed key, you can format characters by choosing options from the Format Character menu.

• *Controlling Page Divisions*

The paper source and duplex printing are controlled by the settings on the Print Options menu.

The default page used by Word is 8½ by 11 inches, single column, with 1-inch top and bottom margins and 1¼-inch left and right margins. To use any other paper size or margins, you have to make division changes.

To change the page format, press Esc F D to see the command line

FORMAT DIVISION: Margins Page-numbers Layout
line-Numbers

Press M to select Margins and display a menu for setting the following divisions:

- Top and bottom margins

- Left and right margins

- Page length and width

- Gutter width

- Running head (header and footer) position

- Mirror margins

- New defaults

To set page numbering options, press P. Press L to set the footnote position, the number and spacing of columns, and the type of division break. Press N to print line numbers down the left margin of the document.

After you've made your selections from the Format Division menu, press ↵ to return to the document. Two dotted lines, called the *division mark*, will appear across the screen. All the text above the division mark will have the page formats you just selected.

You can change division formats before or after you've typed the document. The cursor does not have to be at the end of the document when you change division settings. Wherever it is located, a division mark will be added to the end of your document. The text above the division mark will print according to your division changes.

• *Printing Envelopes*

You can print envelopes using a portrait font and orientation. See Appendix D for details.

As long as you have a landscape font—internal or otherwise—printing envelopes is no problem. You can print an individual envelope or a number of them from a mailing list. If you don't have an optional envelope feeder, however, you have to manually insert the envelopes one at a time.

To print envelopes in landscape orientation, follow these steps:

1. Press Esc P O to display the Print Options menu.

2. Select a landscape PRD file for the Printer option.

3. Set the paper feed to Manual, or set it to Envelope if you have an envelope feeder.

4. Press ◄— to exit the menu. Press Esc to return to the document.

5. Press Esc F D M, then change the page size and margins. To print a number 10 commercial envelope on a LaserJet, LaserJet +, or LaserJet 500 +, set a top margin of 6, a left margin of 5.5, a length of 8.5, and a width of 11. For a LaserJet II or IID, set a top margin of 4.5, a left margin of 5.5, a length of 8.5, and a width of 11.

6. Press ◄— to return to the document.

7. Type the address, or a series of addresses separated with page break lines (press Ctrl-Shift-◄— for page breaks).

8. Press Esc P P to start printing. Word will set the LaserJet to manual feeding, so insert an envelope into the paper tray.

• *Combining Orientations In One Document*

You can only use one PRD file per document, and you can't combine portrait and landscape fonts in the same driver. So using normal Word techniques, your entire document must either be in landscape or portrait orientation. However, you can combine orientations in a document by inserting PCL commands directly into the document.

In typing PCL commands, make sure you correctly distinguish between the lowercase letter l and the number 1; and the upper-case letter O and the number 0.

As an example, suppose that you want to print a letter and its envelope in the same document. Follow these steps to insert the PCL commands in your document:

1. Select the appropriate portrait PRD file from the Print Options menu and set paper feed to Continuous.

2. Before typing the letter, enter the codes to ensure that it will print in portrait orientation using the paper cassette (the printer could still be in landscape mode from a previous job). Press and hold down the Alt key while you type **27** using the numeric keypad.

3. Release the Alt key. You'll see a small left-pointing arrow on the screen. This arrow represents the Escape code, the special character that starts all PCL commands. (You can't use the Esc key to enter the code because Word uses it for its own purposes.)

4. Type **&l0O**. Make sure you enter a lowercase L, not a one, then a zero, followed by a capital O. This code is the PCL command for using portrait orientation.

5. Type the letter.

6. Press Ctrl-Enter to insert a division mark.

Now you'll enter the codes for printing the envelope. The code is rather long because you have to set the paper type, manual feed, and top and left margins. (You set the margins here because you won't be using Word's division formats.)

7. Press Alt-27 and type **&l1O**.

8. Press Alt-27 and type **&l2H**.

9. Press Alt-27 and type **&l81A**.

10. Press Alt-27.

11. With the LaserJet, LaserJet +, and LaserJet 500+: Type **&l38E**.

    With the LaserJet II and IID: Type **&l27E**.

12. Press Alt-27 and type **&a0R**.

13. Press Alt-27 and type **&a50L**.

14. Press Enter. Figure 6.6 shows the commands entered after a sample letter.

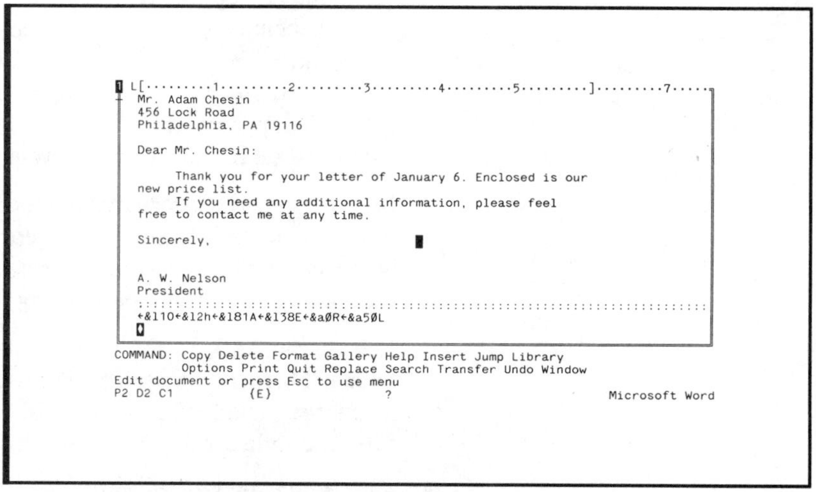

```
 L[········1·········2·········3·········4·········5·······]·········7·····
  Mr. Adam Chesin
  456 Lock Road
  Philadelphia, PA 19116

  Dear Mr. Chesin:

      Thank you for your letter of January 6. Enclosed is our
  new price list.
      If you need any additional information, please feel
  free to contact me at any time.

  Sincerely,


  A. W. Nelson
  President
  ::::::::::::::::::::::::::::::::::::::::::::::::::::::::::::::::::::::::::::
  +&l1O+&l2h+&l81A+&l38E+&a0R+&a50L



COMMAND: Copy Delete Format Gallery Help Insert Jump Library
         Options Print Quit Replace Search Transfer Undo Window
Edit document or press Esc to use menu
P2 D2 C1          (E)              ?                        Microsoft Word
```

• Figure 6.6: *PCL commands for landscape orientation and envelope feed in the manual tray*

15. Copy the address from the first page onto the new division, following the codes.

16. Press Esc P P.

After the page is printed, a blank page will eject from the printer. You'll see the PF message flashing on the printer's control panel, indicating that you should feed paper in the manual tray. Adjust the tray and insert an envelope, as explained in Chapter 3. The address will print in landscape orientation using the default Courier font.

Just in case you have to adjust the margins for your own envelopes, here's what each of the codes do:

&l1O	Sets landscape orientation
&l2H	Sets manual feed
&l81A	Sets the paper size
&l38E or &l27E	Sets the top margin
&a0R	Activates the top margin
&a50L	Sets the left margin at 50 characters; adjust if necessary

You'll learn more about PCL commands in later chapters. Just remember that with Word, press Alt-27 to enter an Escape code before the command.

• *Collating Pages With Earlier LaserJet Models*

Older LaserJet printers ejected paper in reverse order—the first page on the bottom, the last page on the top. You can't change the way the printer works, but you can use a macro to deliver the pages collated correctly.

The macro described here determines how many pages are in the document, then starts at the end, printing the document page by page. This way, the last page out of the printer—and on top of the stack—will be the first.

To create the macro, type exactly what you see listed. (Enter the codes for « and » by pressing Ctrl-[and Ctrl-], respectively.) Then select it, press Esc D, enter a macro name, and press ←⎯.

```
<esc>pr<enter>
<ctrl pgdn>
<esc>jp«SET size = field»<esc>
«WHILE size > 0»
<esc>po<down 4>p<tab>«size»<enter>p
«SET size = size -1»
«ENDWHILE»
```

When you want to print a document, type the macro name, and then press F3.

• *Printing Graphics*

You can import graphic files in the following formats directly into a Word document:

- CAPTURE.COM files

- Hewlett-Packard HPGL files

- Lotus PIC files

- Microsoft Pageview files

- PC Paintbrush PCX and PCC files

Scanned files should be captured in one of these formats. See Chapter 14 for details on using scanners.

- PostScript printer files

- TIFF (tag image file format) files

- Windows Clipboard files

Once imported, an image can be scaled, surrounded in a box, and placed anywhere on the page.

Like many desktop publishing programs, Word uses the "frame" concept for positioning text as well as graphics. Visualize the frame as an invisible box around every paragraph. Using all the default settings, the frame extends from the left to right margins—the full 6 inches across the page—for the depth of the paragraph, the selected text, or graphic. You can place a box around a frame with the Format Border command, but frames do not have to be boxed. The frame exists whether or not you see an actual box around it.

You control the size and position of the frame on the page through the Format Position command. The size and position of graphic images that can be put into frames are controlled by the Library Link Graphics command.

Figure 6.7 shows a sample document that includes graphics. It was printed on a Hewlett-Packard LaserJet + with standard memory.

The masthead is a graphic image created using Spinfont, a program that creates curved and rotated graphic files from softfont outline files. All the text was printed in various type styles supplied with the Font Solution Pack.

The first "paragraph" actually contains two frames. One holds the large initial capital (called a *drop capital*) formatted in 30-point Cooper Black; the other contains text in a proportionally-spaced 12-point Times.

The rest of the text, mostly single-line paragraphs, is in separate frames. The box with small print (8.5-point Line Printer) is in a boxed paragraph with a frame width 1¼ inches wide. Since the frame is smaller than the column width, the other text in the document "wraps" around it.

To import a graphic image, press Esc L L G to see the Library Link menu, shown in Figure 6.8. Table 6.4 summarizes these options.

Type the full path and name of your graphic file, and then press ⏎. Word checks for the presence of the file and determines its format. The file name appears at the File Format option, and then the document appears with the graphic code inserted. For example, if you were importing a Lotus PIC file named FACULTY, the code would look like this:

\FACULTY.PIC;3″;2.165″;Lotus PIC

This code tells Word to merge the file into the document when you print or preview it. The size is automatically set at the column width and scaled for the proper length.

The characters .G. are entered as hidden text before the graphic code.

LASERJET NEWS

For Hewlett-Packard Printers

This special issue contains the full list of PRD files now available with Microsoft Word. Contact Microsoft for files not shipped with Word.

```
All PRD's
support
internal
Courier and
Line Printer
```

These Hewlett-Packard PRD files contain driver information for all LaserJet models. Transfer the appropriate PRD files to your Word directory, then use Print Options to select the printer and model options. Check the Setup and Graphics Resolution settings before printing.

Internal Fonts
HPLASER.PRD   Internal Fonts, all models

Cartridge Portrait
HPLASER1.PRD   A,B,C,D,E,G,H,J,L,Q,W,X
HPLASER2.PRD   F,K,P,R,U
HPLASER3.PRD   J,R,Z
HPLASPS.PRD   B (USACSII symbol set)
HPLASRMN.PRD   F (Roman-8 symbol set)
HPLAS2S1.PRD   S1 (PC-8 symbol set)
HPLAS2S2.PRD   S2 (PC-8 symbol set)
HPLASTAX.PRD   T (ASCII and Line Draw sets)
HPPCCOUR.PRD   Y (PS Set 1)
HPLASMS.PRD   Z, MICROSOFT 1 (ECMA symbol set)
HPLASMS2.PRD   Z, MICROSOFT 1A (Roman-8 symbol set)
HPLASMSA.PRD   Z, MICROSOFT 1A (ASCII symbol set)
HPPRO.PRD   Pro Collection

Cartridge Landscape
HPLASLAN.PRD   A,B,C,G,H,L,M,N,P,O,R,U,V
HPLASMSL.PRD   Z (Roman-8 symbol set)
HPPROL.PRD   Pro Collection

Softfont Portrait
HPDWNACP.PRD   AC (ASCII symbol set)
HPDWNADP.PRD   AD (Roman-8 symbol set)
HPDWNSFP.PRD   AC and AE (ASCII symbol set)
HPDWNR8P.PRD   AD and AF (Roman-8 symbol set)
HPDWNHHP.PRD   AG (Roman-8 symbol set)
HPDWNLGP.PRD   DA (several symbol sets included)
HPDWNPRP.PRD   EA (several symbol sets included)
HPDWNGAP.PRD   RA (ASCII symbol set)
HPDWNGA8.PRD   RB (Roman-8 symbol set)
HPDWNCNP.PRD   SA (ASCII symbol sedt)
HPDWNCN8.PRD   SB (Roman-8 symbol set)
```

• Figure 6.7: *Sample Word document with graphics*

If Word can't locate the graphic file on your disk, you will hear a beep and see the message

file does not exist

Reenter the file name and the complete path, or press Esc to cancel the operation.
```

```
LIBRARY LINK GRAPHICS filename: █
             file format:                    alignment in frame: Centered
             graphics width: 6"              graphics height: 6"
             space before: 0"                space after: 0"
Enter filename or press F1 to select from list
Pg1 Col              {}                  ?                        Microsoft Word
```

- Figure 6.8: *Word Library Link Graphics menu*

- Table 6.4: *Word Library Link Graphic Menu Options*

OPTION	FUNCTION
Filename	The name of the graphic file to be merged, including its full path and extension.
File Format	After reading the graphic file, Word will display its format type. If none appears, select this option and press F1 to see a list of possible formats.
Alignment in Frame	Positions the graphic in relation to the left edge of the frame.
Graphics Width	Changes the default graphic width. Press F1 to see suggested alternatives.
Graphics Height	Changes the default graphic height. Press F1 to see suggested alternatives.
Space Before	Sets the amount of blank space between the graphic frame and preceding text.
Space After	Sets the amount of blank space between the graphic frame and the following text.

To print a quick draft copy of graphic documents, select the lowest Graphics Resolution setting on the Print Options menu. Once the layout is finalized, change the setting to a higher resolution for the final copy.

Adjusting the Frame

The Library Link Graphics menu options control the size and position of the contents of a frame. The Format Position menu, shown in Figure 6.9, controls the frame itself. Table 6.5 summarizes the options on this menu.

Adjusting the size and position of a graphic image and frame affects the placement of other elements on the page. Text and graphics will be

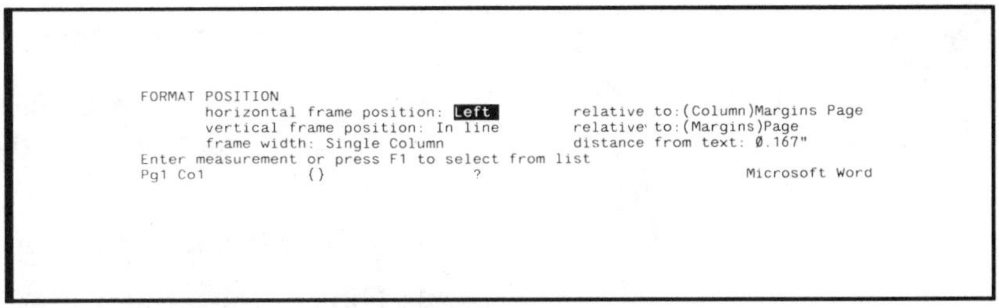

```
FORMAT POSITION
      horizontal frame position: Left           relative to:(Column)Margins Page
      vertical frame position: In line          relative to:(Margins)Page
      frame width: Single Column                distance from text: 0.167"
Enter measurement or press F1 to select from list
Pg1 Col              {}                 ?                        Microsoft Word
```

• Figure 6.9: *Word Format Position menu*

• Table 6.5: *Word Format Position Menu Options*

OPTION	FUNCTION
Horizontal Frame Position	Sets the alignment of the frame in relation to the column, area between the margins, or left and right edges of the page.
Relative To	Sets columns, margins, or page for horizontal positioning.
Vertical Frame Position	Sets the alignment of the frame in relation to the margins or top and bottom edges of the page.
Relative To	Sets margins or page for vertical positioning.
Frame Width	Adjusts the width of the frame.
Distance From Text	Sets the amount of white space between the frame and surrounding text.

pushed up or down as necessary to adjust to the changes. If you make a frame too large, however, it might be pushed onto the next page. Experiment with the various settings in the Library Link Graphics and Format Position menus, and then use the Print Preview command to see how your adjustments affected the layout.

Creating Drop Capitals

It takes a little trial and error to properly align drop capitals, and the exact settings depend on the point size used. The 30-point letter *T* in Figure 6.7, for instance, is in a frame 0.3 inches wide, with the Distance From Text option set at 0.15. The line spacing (in the Format Paragraph menu) is set at 2 lines.

To create your own drop capitals, follow this general procedure:

1. Place the letter in its own paragraph directly above the remaining text in the "paragraph." Just place the cursor on the character next to it and press ←⎯.

2. Format the letter in the type style and size desired.

3. Use the Format Position menu to adjust the letter's frame width to the size of the character. Keep checking the appearance in preview mode (use the Print Preview command) until the remaining text is as close to the drop character as you like like. Make sure you set the Distance From Text option to zero.

4. Print a sample to see how the character aligns with the rest of the text. If the letter is too high, reduce the Line Spacing setting in the Format Paragraph menu, using a point size slightly smaller than the point size of the letter. Again, review the alignment in preview mode and adjust the line spacing and frame size until the character is properly spaced.

Printer Memory Limitations

If your printer does not have enough memory to hold all the fonts and graphics, you'll see error number 20 on its control panel display. If that happens, consider taking one of the following actions to reduce the amount of memory required:

Set the resolution of printed graphics through the Graphics Resolution option on the Print Options menu.

- **Select internal or cartridge fonts over softfonts.** For example, use an internal or cartridge font for the body text instead of a softfont of the same size.

- **Change the fonts.** Select softfonts with the smallest symbol set you can use, such as USASCII instead of IBM PC. If that doesn't help, use fewer fonts. Use the Format Replace command to replace bold or italic formats, which require separate softfonts, with underlining. If you still need more space, reduce the size of headlines or body text.

- **Modify the graphics.** As a last resort, select a lower graphics resolution from the Print Options menu. Changing from 300 dpi to 150 dpi will usually do the trick. You could also use the Library Link Graphics menu options to reduce the size of the graphics.

Using Capture to Import Screens

The Capture program that is supplied on the Word Utilities disk captures graphic screen images into a disk file. You can then merge the image and print it along with your Word document. To use Capture, return to the DOS prompt, type **Capture**, and then press ←┘. Press Shift-PrtScr to capture the screen.

Capturing Text Mode Screens

When you capture a text image, you'll be prompted to accept Word's suggested file name or enter your own. If you press ←┘, the screen will be saved under the name CAPT0001.LST. Capture will automatically increment the number in the file name to avoid overwriting existing files.

Capturing Graphic Screens

When you capture a graphic screen, you can clip, or crop, the image before saving it. Word surrounds the screen with clipping lines. You position these lines to enclose just the part of the screen you want to save. Clip the image as desired, and then press ←┘.

Use these keystrokes to clip the image:

- Press the arrow keys to move the top and left lines.

- Press Tab to activate the bottom and left lines.

- Press Ins to move both the top and bottom lines toward each other simultaneously.

- Press Del to return to single-line control.

- Press the + or − key on the keypad to increase or decrease the distance the lines move each time you press an arrow key.

Merging PRD Files

Merging PRD files allows you to use softfonts from several sets or mix cartridge and softfonts on the same page. By using the MergePRD utility supplied with Word, you can create a new PRD file (and a DAT file if it contains softfonts) from others.

Creating a New PRD File

As an example, suppose that you want to be able to use internal fonts along with Courier fonts from the S1 cartridge and softfonts in the AD set.

To do this, you have to combine fonts from HPLASER.PRD, HPLAS-2S1.PRD, and HPDWNADP.PRD. Follow this procedure:

1. Make sure that the PRD files you want to use are on the same disk or directory. Make a note of their names.

2. Type **MERGEPRD**, and then press ←⎯. You'll see the screen shown in Figure 6.10.

3. Press 1 to display the Main menu, shown in Figure 6.11.

In order to create a new PRD file, you must go though at least three steps on this menu: enter the PRD files you want to use, select fonts and font sizes from the files, and create the output PRD file.

4. Press 1 to see the prompt

   Enter .PRD filename (or press Enter to return to menu):

5. Type **HPLASER**, and then press ←⎯. You'll be prompted to enter the printer model, as shown in Figure 6.12.

6. Press the number corresponding to your printer.

7. Repeat steps 5 and 6, entering **HPLAS2S1** and **HPDWNACP**. Then, when you're prompted for the PRD file, just press ←⎯ to display the Main menu again.

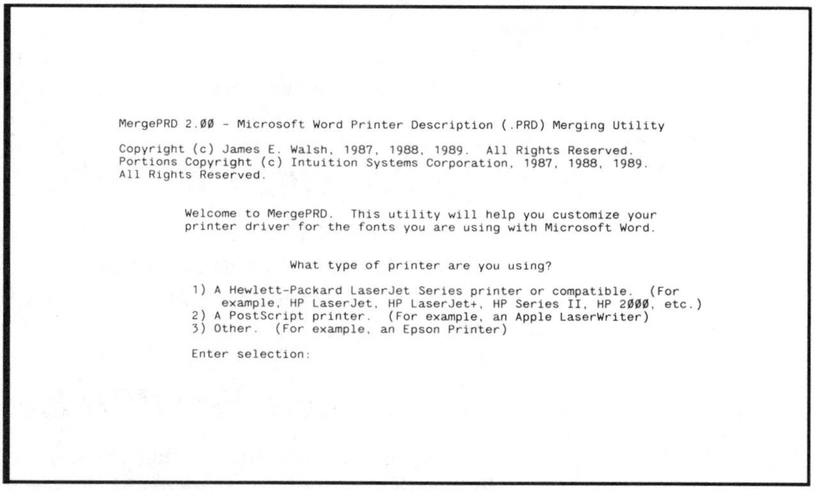

```
MergePRD 2.00 - Microsoft Word Printer Description (.PRD) Merging Utility

Copyright (c) James E. Walsh, 1987, 1988, 1989.  All Rights Reserved.
Portions Copyright (c) Intuition Systems Corporation, 1987, 1988, 1989.
All Rights Reserved.

         Welcome to MergePRD.  This utility will help you customize your
         printer driver for the fonts you are using with Microsoft Word.

                  What type of printer are you using?

         1) A Hewlett-Packard LaserJet Series printer or compatible.  (For
            example, HP LaserJet, HP LaserJet+, HP Series II, HP 2000, etc.)
         2) A PostScript printer.  (For example, an Apple LaserWriter)
         3) Other.  (For example, an Epson Printer)

         Enter selection:
```

• Figure 6.10: *Initial MergePRD menu*

```
           MergePRD - Microsoft Word .PRD Merging Utility

                             Main Menu

           1) Enter input .PRD list
           2) Display the list of available fonts and font sizes
           3) Print the list of available fonts and font sizes
           4) Select fonts and font sizes
           5) Display selected fonts and font size entries
           6) Change bin support
           7) Create the output .PRD file with the fonts you have selected
           8) Quit program

           Enter selection:
```

- Figure 6.11: *Main MergePRD menu*

```
    Enter .PRD filename (or press Enter to return to menu): HPLASER

    Testing .PRD file HPLASER.PRD

             Which model from this .PRD?  (Should match previous selections)

                 1) LaserJet Series II
                 2) LaserJet 500+
                 3) LaserJet+
                 4) LaserJet (Original)
                 5) LaserJet 2000
                 6) LaserJet IID

                 Enter selection:
```

- Figure 6.12: *Select the printer model for the new PRD file*

8. Press 2 to display the available fonts and sizes, as shown in Figure 6.13. When you create a new PRD file from these fonts, you can include only one set from each generic family. For example, you can only include one Modern a font in the new file, so you won't be able to choose both fonts 3 and 5.

9. Make a note of the fonts you'd like to incorporate in the new PRD file (1, 2, 3, 8, and 9), and then press ◄┘.

10. Press 4 from the Main menu, and you'll see the font selection menu, as shown in Figure 6.14.

11. Press 1 to add fonts. You'll see another list of fonts to select from, as shown in Figure 6.15.

```
                1) Enter input .PRD list
                2) Display the list of available fonts and font sizes
                3) Print the list of available fonts and font sizes
                4) Select fonts and font sizes
                5) Display selected fonts and font size entries
                6) Change bin support
                7) Create the output .PRD file with the fonts you have selected
                8) Quit program

                Enter selection: 2


    Font    PRD File    Generic     Font Name      Sizes
    #
    Ø       HPLASER     Modern a    Courier        10 12
    1       HPLASER     Modern b    CourierPC      10 12
    2       HPLASER     Modern h    LinePrinter     8.5
    3       HPLAS2S1    Modern a    Courier        10 12
    4       HPLAS2S1    Modern h    LinePrinter     8.5
    5       HPDWNACP    Modern a    Courier        12
    6       HPDWNACP    Modern b    CourierPC      12
    7       HPDWNACP    Modern h    LinePrinter     8.5
    8       HPDWNACP    Modern i    HELV            6   8 10 12 14 18 24 30
    9       HPDWNACP    Roman a     TMSRMN          6   8 10 12 14 18 24 30
    Press a key to continue...
```

• Figure 6.13: *Fonts available in the loaded PRD files*

```
                        Select Fonts and Font Sizes

                1) Add font/size from .PRDs already entered
                2) Change symbol set for font
                3) Delete existing font/size entry
                4) Display current font/size entries
                5) Change linedraw font
                6) Return to main menu

                Enter selection:
```

• Figure 6.14: *Font selection menu*

```
        Font    PRD File    Font Name      Set
        Ø       HPLASER     Courier        R8
        1       HPLASER     CourierPC      P8
        2       HPLASER     LinePrinter    R8
        3       HPLAS2S1    Courier        P8
        4       HPLAS2S1    LinePrinter    P8
        5       HPDWNACP    Courier        R8
        6       HPDWNACP    CourierPC      P8
        7       HPDWNACP    LinePrinter    R8
        8       HPDWNACP    HELV           US
        9       HPDWNACP    TMSRMN         US




        Add - Enter Font # (Ø-9):
```

• Figure 6.15: *Adding fonts to the new PRD file*

12. Press 1. You'll see a description of the font, along with a request to indicate the sizes desired, as shown in Figure 6.16.

13. Type **ALL**, and then press ↵ to include all the available sizes in that font. An asterisk will appear next to the font in the list.

14. Repeat steps 12 and 13 until you've selected all the fonts, then press ↵ when you are prompted for a new font number.

15. From the Main menu, press 7 to create a new font. You'll see the prompt

    Enter Output .PRD filename (Enter to return to menu):

16. Type **NEW**, or some other PRD file name, and then press ↵. MergePRD will display status messages as it reads and creates the files, and then return you to the DOS prompt.

You can use the same general procedure to merge any fonts from PRD files. You just can't have portrait and landscape fonts in the same PRD file, except with the LaserJet IID and LaserJet 2000.

Using Your Custom PRD File

When you want to use the new PRD file, select its name from the list of PRD files displayed on Word's Print Options menu. Be sure to select the same model that you chose in MergePRD. When you format characters, all the fonts and sizes you selected for the new PRD file will be available, and the newly created DAT file will properly download the softfonts.

```
Add - Enter Font # (0-9): 1

  1   HPLASER    Modern b    CourierPC      10 12
Enter Sizes desired, separated by spaces, then press Enter
(ALL = All Sizes):
```

• Figure 6.16: *Indicate the sizes desired*

• *Modifying the Printer Driver*

Changing a PRD file is more complicated than merging fonts from existing ones. Microsoft provides a utility called MakePRD, but you need an indepth understanding of your printer and Word's PRD format to use it.

Because there are so many PRD files available and you can use other programs to install additional softfont support, you shouldn't ever have to delve into the mysteries of PRD files. But if you want to examine a PRD file, you can use MakePRD to convert the file into a readable form. Follow these steps:

1. Type **MAKEPRD**, and then press ⏎. You'll be prompted

   Name of PRD file:

2. Type the name of the PRD file, including the PRD extension, and then press ⏎. You'll see the prompt

   Name of Text file:

3. Type a file name to hold the PRD information, and then press ⏎ to see the prompt

   Select PRD to Text conversion (Press T)
   or Text to PRD conversion (Press P):

4. Press T, then ⏎. The PRD file will be converted into an ASCII text file.

5. Use the DOS Type or Print command to take a look at it, or use the Transfer Load command to bring it into Word. (Since it doesn't have the DOC extension, press Esc T L, type the name followed by a period, then press ⏎.)

6. If you modify the file, save it as Text Only, and then convert it back to a PRD file by selecting P for the Text to PRD Conversion option.

If you use a font-installation program (discussed in Chapter 4), print the ASCII version of the new and original PRD files. Compare the files to see how new fonts and character sets were added. Then, if you purchase a cartridge that isn't supported by your version of Word, use those techniques as a guide. Just make a backup copy of the original before starting.

H•P L•A•S•E•R•J•E•T

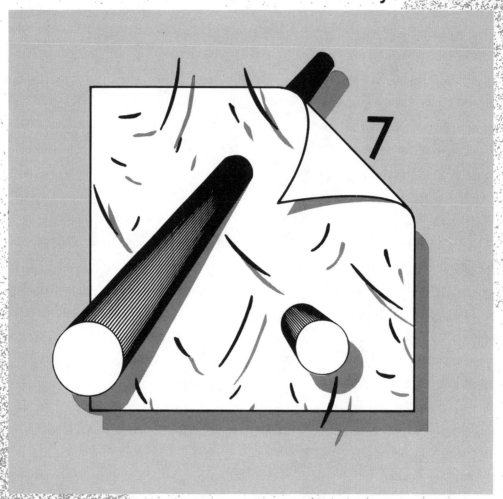

Printing with Microsoft Windows

• Windows, like the disk operating system, is an environment in which you work with other programs. It provides a graphic interface that includes pull-down menus, icons, and mouse support—similar to the Apple Macintosh computer interface. Windows provides the following LaserJet resources:

Newer releases of Windows support DeskJet printers. Follow the instructions in this chapter, but select DeskJet when installing printers. Contact Microsoft or the manufacturer of your application if your version does not have a DeskJet driver.

- Integrated downloading

- Installable device drivers

- Softfont support

- Resolution options

- Screen fonts

- DeskJet support

Some programs, such as Ami and Aldus Pagemaker, have been specifically designed to work within Windows; they get much of their power and versatility from Windows itself. Rather than have their own printer and screen drivers, for example, they use the drivers installed in Windows. Since they must be used with Windows, they're sold with a special run-time version in case you don't have Windows already. The run-time version includes the basic interface and screen and printer drivers needed to run the application.

• *Accessing the Printer Driver*

The HPPCL printer driver supports a number of PCL printers, including some that are not manufactured by Hewlett-Packard.

Windows contains the HPPCL.DRV driver for use with LaserJet printers. You select the driver by using the Setup program or by adding a printer through the Windows Control Panel. Within Windows, you add font support and customize the printer driver settings to your own needs, including the graphics resolution, paper size and source, and orientation.

The driver works in tandem with a configuration file called WIN.INI. Windows checks this file every time it starts, obtaining settings and default values that it needs to operate. Among other items, the file includes a list of ports, the names of printers and printer drivers, and names and sizes of available fonts. Having the printer driver on your disk is not enough—the appropriate entry for the driver must be in the WIN.INI file.

How softfont support is added depends on your version of Windows and the driver. In earlier releases of Windows, softfonts must be installed through a series of utility programs that modify the driver and WIN.INI file. Newer versions of the driver include a softfont installation option. This new driver is also packaged with certain Windows-based applications, such as Aldus Pagemaker. So if you don't have the driver with your version of Windows, you may get it with some other application.

After you've made all your settings and additions to the driver, its features are available to all Windows-based programs the next time you start Windows. If you added softfont support, for example, those softfonts can be used by any program designed for the Window's environment. DOS programs not specifically designed for Windows cannot access the full features of the driver.

• *Installing Printers*

When you set up Windows, the appropriate files are transferred to your hard disk, and you designate the printer and port you'll be using. Additional drivers can be added later from within Windows itself.

The figures shown in this chapter are from Windows version 386.

Setting Up Your Printer

Follow these steps to install your printer when you set up Windows:

1. Insert the Windows Setup/Build disk in drive A. Depending on your version, the disk may be labeled Setup Build Displays 1 or Setup Build Utilities 1.

2. Log onto drive A, type **SETUP**, and then press ↵.

3. In a series of screens, you'll be asked to confirm the type of computer, video adapter, keyboard, and mouse you're using. Respond to the prompts displayed.

4. When you see the screen shown in Figure 7.1, press I to install a printer. A list of supported printers will appear.

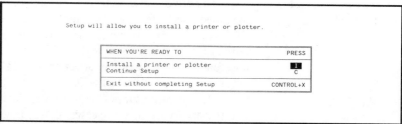

• Figure 7.1: *Windows printer setup screen*

If your LaserJet is PostScript-equipped, check your manual for compatible printers. Select the appropriate driver. See the section about setting up for PostScript later in this chapter for details.

5. Press the arrow keys to scroll through the list until your printer is highlighted, and then press ←. (If your driver does not support the LaserJet IID, select the LaserJet 2000 instead.) Next you will see a screen listing possible ports:

LPT1:
LPT2:
LPT3:
COM1:
COM2:
EPT:
None

6. Press the arrow keys to highlight the port you are using, and then press ←. The next menu gives you the option of repeating the process to install another printer.

7. If you want to install another printer driver at this time, repeat steps 4 through 6. Otherwise, press C to continue. Setup will prompt you to install the appropriate disk in drive A. Follow the prompts and menus to complete the setup process.

If you installed more than one printer, the first one will be the default printer used when you start Windows. You can change printers or designate a new default from within Windows, as explained later in the chapter.

Installing Drivers within Windows

If you want to add another printer after you've set up Windows, you can install it from within Windows. This is accomplished by using the control panel, which lets you change many of the settings and default values in the WIN.INI file.

With full versions of Windows, you access the control panel by running the program CONTROL.EXE. If you have a run-time version, when an instruction in this chapter says to use CONTROL.EXE, pull down the System menu and click on Control Panel.

Follow this procedure to add a printer from within Windows:

1. Start Windows according to the instructions packaged with your version. If you have a run-time version, start your application.

2. Double-click on the program name CONTROL.EXE listed on the screen. You will see the Control Panel window, as shown in Figure 7.2.

3. Click on the Installation option to pull down the menu, and then on the Add New Printer option to display the dialog box shown in Figure 7.3.

4. Insert the disk containing the printer drivers in drive A, then press ◄─┘. The Available Printers dialog box will appear, as shown in Figure 7.4. (If you insert the incorrect disk, you'll see a warning message—insert another disk, click OK, then try again.)

5. Scroll through the list until you see your printer's name, and then double-click on it.

6. When you are asked to confirm copying the driver to your Windows directory, click on Yes.

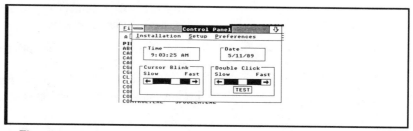

• Figure 7.2: *Windows Control Panel window*

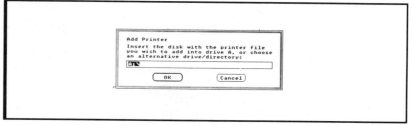

• Figure 7.3: *Windows Add Printer dialog box*

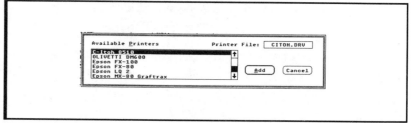

• Figure 7.4: *Windows Available Printers dialog box*

When you add a printer from the Control Panel, you are not asked to specify the port. But you can't have more than one printer connected to the same port. So, next you must use the Setup option to choose a port for this printer.

7. From the Control Panel window, click on Setup to pull down the menu, and then click on the Connection option to display the dialog box shown in Figure 7.5.

8. Click on the printer's name on the left side, click on a port listed on the right, and then click on OK.

Finally, if you selected a serial (COM) port, you should make sure the communications settings match those set in the LaserJet.

9. Click on Setup; then click on the Communications Port option to see the dialog box shown in Figure 7.6. Change the settings to match those of your LaserJet, and then click on OK.

Leave the Control Panel on the screen if you plan to change the default printer settings or install font support.

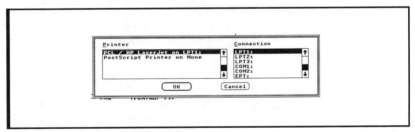

• Figure 7.5: *Windows Connection dialog box*

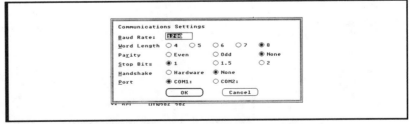

• Figure 7.6: *Windows Communications Settings dialog box*

• *Customizing Printer Settings*

After the drivers are on your disk and added to the WIN.INI file, you can change the default printer and specify printer settings, including paper size and source, graphics resolution, and cartridges. These options are controlled through the Control Panel. Start Windows and double-click on CONTROL.EXE to display the screen shown in Figure 7.2.

From the Control Panel screen, click on Setup, and then click on the Printer option. You'll see the dialog box shown in Figure 7.7. Select the printer you want to use. If you choose a printer that is different from the one you selected when you set up Windows, it will now be the default printer.

Make sure that the port for the selected printer is listed correctly. For example, if your LaserJet is attached to parallel port number one, make sure the menu includes

PCL / HP LaserJet on LPT1:

If your printer connection is listed incorrectly, click on Cancel, and then select Setup. Choose the Connection option to display the dialog box shown in Figure 7.5. Select your printer and the correct port, and then click on OK.

Changing Timeout Settings

The bottom of the Default Printer dialog box shows the Printer Timeout settings. These determine how many seconds Windows will wait before reporting a printer problem. Device Not Selected shows the seconds Windows will wait if the printer is turned off or off line when you start to print. The default setting (15 seconds) gives you some time to turn the printer on or place it on line.

The Transmission Retry setting shows the seconds Windows will wait to report an error, such as running out of paper or a paper jam, after the

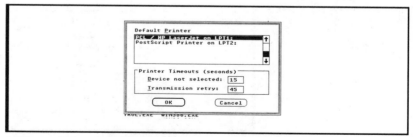

• Figure 7.7: *Windows Default Printer dialog box*

document has begun printing. The default setting (45 seconds) is long enough for you to see the error message on the LaserJet's control panel display and correct the problem. If you're paying attention to the printer, you will probably be able to fix the problem and continue printing without it affecting the program.

You can change either of the timeout settings to give yourself more or less time. Click on the option, enter a new value, and click on OK.

Changing Printing Options

From the Control Panel's Default Printer dialog box (choose Setup, then Printer), click on OK to display the printer driver setup menu. Figure 7.8 shows the menu for the LaserJet 500+.

Before you change any of these settings, make sure the correct printer name is selected; click on the correct one if necessary. Then you can select new settings for the options as follows:

Notice that some of the selections are displayed in a lighter shade. These settings are not available to your printer. Using the original LaserJet, for instance, Fonts, several of the paper sources, and all the duplex options are unavailable.

- **Uncollated copies**: If you want to change the number of copies for each print job, enter the new number here.

- **Paper**: Select the paper size you're using.

- **Orientation**: Click on either Portrait or Landscape.

- **Graphics resolution**: Click on 75, 150, or 300 as the dpi setting. Just keep your printer's memory limitations in mind.

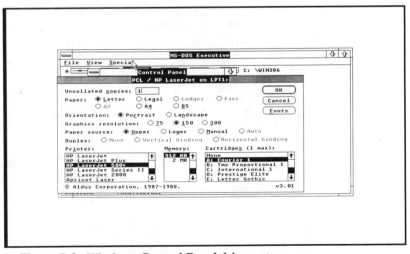

- Figure 7.8: *Windows Control Panel driver setup menu*

- **Paper source**: Select one of the available options.

- **Duplex**: If you have a duplex printer, select None or the binding desired.

- **Memory**: If your printer can accept additional memory, there may be several options listed under Memory. Click on the amount of memory in your printer.

- **Cartridges**: Select None if you're using just internal fonts. Otherwise, select the cartridges you have installed. The number of cartridges you can select for your printer is listed above the box. (If you have a LaserJet IID but are using the LaserJet 2000 driver, select only two cartridges.) To select more than one cartridge, click on the first one and then hold down the Shift key while you click on the others.

The menu may also include the Fonts option, which is used to add softfont support, as explained in the next section.

Click on the option and select the new setting as described above. When you are finished making changes, click on OK to record your settings in the printer driver file. (Click on Cancel to return to the Control Panel screen without making the changes.)

• *Adding and Using Softfonts*

If you have softfonts available, you have to add them to the printer driver before using them in an application. As I mentioned before, the newer drivers have this ability built in, and you can add fonts through the Control Panel. To add font support to earlier versions, you use a utility program supplied with Windows.

Adding Fonts through the Control Panel

If you have a newer version of the driver, Fonts is listed as an option on the Control Panel's driver setup menu. Follow these steps to add your softfonts:

1. Display the printer driver setup menu as described in the previous section: Run CONTROL.EXE, select Setup, select Printer, and then click on OK.

To quickly install the same fonts on another printer, pull down the System menu, then select Copy Between Ports.

2. Click on the Fonts option (on the right side of the screen) to display the Soft Font Installer dialog box, as shown in Figure 7.9. This screen contains two boxes. The one on the right lists the softfonts you have available to install; the one on the left displays the fonts Windows already recognizes. If this is the first time you've installed softfonts, the message

No soft fonts installed

will appear in the left box.

3. Click on Add Fonts to display the Add Fonts dialog box.

4. Type the drive and directory where your softfonts are stored, and then click on OK. Windows will list in the right box all the softfonts it finds and display a message beneath the box indicating how many softfonts are available.

5. Click on the name of the font you want to install. To install more than one, hold down the Shift key as you click.

6. Click on Add, and you'll be prompted to enter the drive on which to store the fonts. The drive c:\PCLFONTS will be listed as the default.

7. Press ⏎ to accept the default, or enter your own directory, and then press ⏎. As each font is copied to the designated directory, its name appears in the left box.

8. Click on Close Drive, and the font names will disappear from the right box.

You now have to give the fonts a download status by designating each as either permanent or temporary. Windows will download temporary fonts

A special PFM file for each font is added to the designated directory. The PFM file name is a modified version of the font file name to designate the font's orientation. For example, font HV120BPN.USP (a 12-point bold Helvetica font) will be matched with the file HVPB0120.PFM.

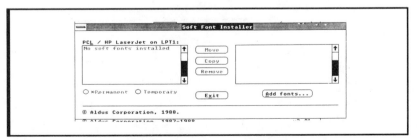

• Figure 7.9: *Windows Soft Font Installer dialog box*

when they are called for in a document, but it assumes that all permanent fonts have already been downloaded. You can either download permanent fonts yourself or have Windows change your AUTOEXEC.BAT file to do it for you. By default, all fonts are initially considered temporary.

9. Click on the fonts you want to make permanent.

10. Click on Permanent for the download status. If this is the first font you're changing to permanent, you'll see a dialog box asking you to confirm your choice. Click on OK.

11. Click on Exit.

12. If you marked fonts as permanent, you'll see the dialog box shown in Figure 7.10. Select Download Now to download the fonts immediately. Select Download at Startup to modify your AUTOEXEC.BAT file to download the fonts when you start up your computer. If you want to manually download the fonts, make sure neither option is selected. Click on OK.

13. Click on OK on the printer driver setup menu, and then close the Control Panel.

This procedure creates a new file, which contains the information Windows needs to download the fonts, and places it in the Windows directory. It will be consulted when you print a document requiring softfonts.

Reverse the selections to change the status from permanent to temporary.

The last four characters of the file name will designate your own printer port.

Changing Font Settings through the Control Panel

After you install a font, its download status, name, and family are recorded in the WIN.INI file. To change these settings, you run CONTROL.EXE and use the Soft Font Installer's editing options.

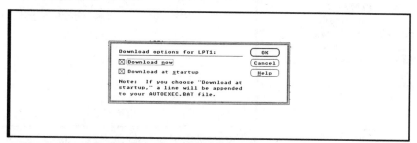

• Figure 7.10: *Windows permanent font download options*

To access the editing options, pull down the Control menu from the Soft Font Installer dialog box, and then click on Enable Edit Button. An Edit option will appear under the Remove option.

Select the font you want to edit, and then click on Edit to display the dialog box shown in Figure 7.11. Change the name, font ID, download status, or family, and then click on OK.

Adding Font Support to Older Drivers

The older Windows printer drivers do not have the Soft Font Installer option. Instead, Windows contains a number of utility programs that allow you to add softfont support. The READMEHP.TXT file supplied with Windows explains how to use these programs.

Here's a review of the procedure for adding softfont support:

If your READMEHP.TXT file doesn't include this procedure, your driver has the Soft Font Installer.

1. Create a subdirectory on your disk named PCLPFM. For example, you might use the command MD\WIN286\PCLPFM.

2. Log onto that directory (CD\WIN286\PCLPFM).

3. Copy the program PCLPFM.EXE (on the Fonts disk) to the new directory.

4. Type **PCLPFM**, and then press ←┘. You'll be prompted to enter the name of the softfont you want to install. To process several, use the ? or ∗ wildcards. For example, enter HELV∗.USP to install all HELV fonts with the USP extension.

The program will create a new file with the PFM extension for every font being installed. The name will be the same as the font file, except the last character will be replaced with a P or L (for portrait or landscape).

• Figure 7.11: *Windows Soft Font Installer editing options*

5. When you are asked if you want to create the file APPNDWIN.INI, press Y. The program creates and saves this file.

6. Start Windows, and then double-click on APPNDWIN.INI. The contents of the file will appear in the Notepad. You want to add this information to the WIN.INI file.

7. Pull down the Edit menu, click on Select All, and then click on Copy to copy the file to the Windows Clipboard.

8. Close the Notepad, then double-click on WIN.INI to bring that file into the Notepad.

9. Scroll through the file to find the name of the printer driver and port you are using. For example, look for [HPPCL,LPT1] if you're using the HPPCL driver for the first parallel port.

10. Place the cursor at the end of that line or directly under it, pull down the Edit menu, and then click on Paste. The contents of APPNDWIN.INI will appear.

11. Scroll down and delete the small end-of-file box.

12. Pull down the File menu, and then click on Save.

The softfonts you added will be available the next time you start Windows.

Using Softfonts

Remember, while Windows contains a Notepad and other desktop utilities, it is really just a platform for running other applications. Selecting fonts, controlling pages, printing in duplex, etc., are controlled through a Windows application that can perform those tasks.

In order to use softfonts, you need an application designed to work with Windows that allows you to change fonts and sizes. Two such programs, Write and Paint, are packaged with Windows, and a number of other software products are available as well.

The Ami word processor is one example of a program designed to take full advantage of the Windows graphic environment. It includes many features provided in desktop publishing programs. Ami can use any of the softfonts you've already installed. Furthermore, you can even access the driver from within Ami by selecting Change Printer from the Options menu, and then following the procedure for installing softfonts (as explained earlier). Ami is also available in a Professional version, which is designed for power users and departmental word processors.

As an example of using softfonts with a Windows application, here is the procedure for importing a file from WordPerfect into Ami, then adding headlines and graphics, to produce the printout shown in Figure 7.12.

Faculty News and Notes

William Watson College

This past year has been a productive one for our faculty. Twenty-one faculty members participated in funded research projects representing over $120,000. Twelve of the projects have been published in professional journals.

Included in this newsletter are summaries of all twenty-one projects.

- Factors Involved in French Language Word Processing Utilizing the Standard English Language Keyboard, Dr. Renee Voltaire, French Department.

Dr. Voltaire analyzed several popular word processing programs for their capacity to display and print French language characters. Dr. Voltaire then studied the difficulties encountered in typing French documents using the standard QWERTY keyboard.

- The Possible Contributions of Computers to the Creative Writing Process, Dr. Leslie Van Mot, English Department.

Dr. Van Mot tested the effects of using word processing programs on the creative output of students. The writing of student volunteers was measured using several criteria. These included sentence complexity, character development, and grammatical accuracy. The students were divided into test and control groups. The test group was trained in using a word processing program, while the control group was given standard writing practice exercises. The report studies the results of the training.

- The Economic Impact of Computer Technology on the Gross National Product, Dr. William Duke, Economics Department.

Dr. Duke abstracted data from the past 10 years supplied by the National Economics Institute. He concludes that starting in 1984 there has been a direct relationship between the GNP and the fortunes of the computer industry.

- Art Education and the Computer, Dr. Wilma Stephens, Art Department.

Dr. Stephens has been researching the use of computer technology in the design process. Her primary interest is in the use of simulated graphics to project light patterns on angular objects and the effects of the projections on color density as observed by the human eye.

• Figure 7.12: *Sample page created with Ami*

1. From Ami, pull down the File menu and select Import File to display a dialog box listing compatible formats.

2. Scroll through the list to select the format of your file, then enter the drive and directory at the Import File prompt. A list of files in the directory will appear in the right box. Select the file you want, and then click on Import. The file will appear on the screen.

3. To add text using softfonts, pull down the Text menu and click on Font, as shown in Figure 7.13. You will see the font selection dialog box, which shows a sample of the currently selected font on the right.

4. Click on the name of the font in the Face box and its size in the Size box. Figure 7.14 shows 30-point Cooper Black selected for the headline. (The black and white figure doesn't show it, but the Color option displays eight text colors from which you can select.)

5. Click on OK.

6. Type your text, selecting the face and size as you go along. You can also select existing text and change its font using the same menu. Figure 7.15 shows the document with text in Cooper Black, Collegette (for the second headline), and Times Roman (for body text).

7. To add emphasis to the document, import a graphic file and use another style for selected paragraphs. The example shown in Figure 7.12 includes a TIFF file and a paragraph using the Second Bullet format defined for that stylesheet.

8. Finally, print the document by selecting Print from the File pulldown menu. Select options from the Print dialog box, shown in Figure 7.16, and then click on Print. The example was printed at 150 dpi on a LaserJet + .

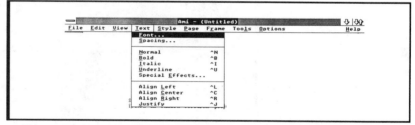

• Figure 7.13: *Ami Text menu*

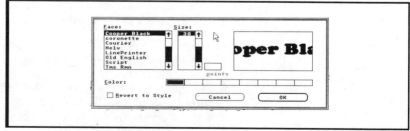

• Figure 7.14: *Ami font selection dialog box*

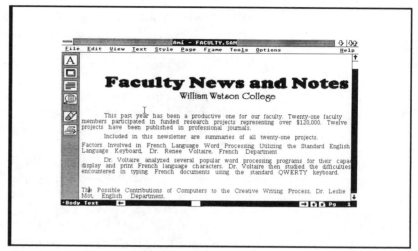

• Figure 7.15: *Ami document with three fonts*

• Figure 7.16: *Ami Print dialog box*

In Chapter 10, you'll learn
how to control the LaserJet
through another popular
Window's application,
Aldus Pagemaker.

All Windows graphic-based programs provide similar options for changing text font and size. And as you'll learn in the next section, with screen fonts installed as well, the screen display shows exactly how the printed document will appear.

• *Screen Fonts Versus Printer Fonts*

Designing a printed page is much easier when you know the final output will match the display on the screen. If you are using softfonts or cartridge fonts, the fonts on the Windows screen may not look like the fonts in the printed version. This depends on which screen fonts are installed.

Screen fonts are files of binary data with the FON extension. Like softfont files, each file contains the data necessary to describe each character and symbol. But in this case, the file is used to reproduce the font on the screen, not on the printer. These font files are totally independent of the printer softfonts—you can't download them to the printer and, as supplied, they have no relation to softfonts.

Windows comes with a number of screen fonts already installed. These include both stroke and raster fonts in several typefaces and sizes. *Stroke fonts* are used for displaying text on the screen, printing to a plotter or printer in a graphics mode. *Raster fonts* are device-specific; that is, the fonts used depend on the resolution of your screen and your particular printer.

Windows comes with three stroke fonts—Roman, Modern, and Script—and five raster fonts—Helv, Courier, Tms Rmn, System, and Terminal. The System and Terminal fonts are built into the Windows environment and are not separate FON files.

The way that these screen fonts are used depends on the particular application. With Windows Paint, for example, you can use the System and Terminal screen fonts in your drawings. When you print your creation on the LaserJet, Windows will convert the screen fonts into bit-map data that will be printed as graphics, not as high-resolution text. Aldus Pagemaker does the same for all the screen fonts if matching softfonts are not available.

Windows Write, on the other hand, can't access most of the screen fonts unless you have related cartridge fonts or softfonts. Using just internal fonts, Write's only font option will be 12-point Courier. When you do add cartridge fonts or softfonts, however, Windows will use one of the screen fonts to represent it on the screen, selecting the font that most closely resembles it. This means that when your font is Helvetica, Times, or Script, the screen display will be very close to the printed version. However, if you're using Cooper Black, Broadway, or some other ornamental font, Windows will display the Tms Rmn screen font, which is not an accurate representation.

You can install more screen fonts by adding FON files, which are available from public domain sources such as Compuserve and Genie. You can also use a screen font installation program. For example, the screens shown in Figures 7.13 through 7.16 display fonts installed with Softcraft's WYSIfonts program. Bitstream Fontware will create similar screen fonts, as described in Chapter 4.

To add support for a new FON file, use the Control Panel's Installation option to add fonts, as described earlier in the section about adding softfonts.

• *Setting Up For PostScript*

In Chapter 15, you'll learn how to equip your LaserJet for PostScript. If you plan to do this, you should install or add the PostScript driver to the Windows environment. Select the PostScript driver compatible with your upgrade from the list of available printers, then set the port and communications parameters using the Setup Connection and Setup Communications Port dialog boxes (Figure 7.5 and 7.6), as explained in the section about installing drivers within Windows.

To adjust the driver, select Printer from the Control Panel's Setup Printer dialog box (Figure 7.7) to display the dialog box shown in Figure 7.17. Click on your printer at the bottom of the screen; then select the number of copies, orientation, paper size and source, and resolution. Some LaserJet upgrades allow resolutions higher than 300 dpi; check with the manual that came with your hardware for the maximum dpi setting.

Before saving the settings, click on Options to display the dialog box shown in Figure 7.18. This lists the following settings for a PostScript printer:

- **Job Timeout:** Determines how many seconds Windows waits before reporting a timeout error.

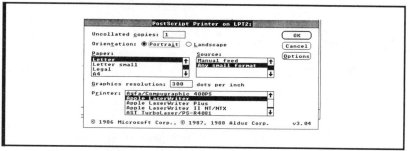

• Figure 7.17: *Windows PostScript printing options*

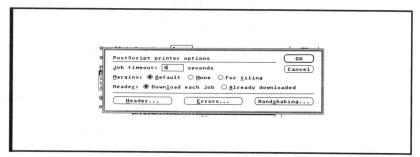

• Figure 7.18: *Windows PostScript printer settings*

- **Margins:** The Default setting avoids printing in the LaserJet's non-printable region. If you set Margins at None, the PostScript interpreter may attempt to print in this area, losing some of your text or graphics. The Tiling option prints a large document over a number of sheets.

- **Header:** Each time a PostScript file is printed, a header containing setup information is first transmitted. When Header is set at Already Downloaded, the driver assumes the header has already been received. You can only select this option if you create a special header file and add a command in your AUTOEXEC.BAT file to copy it to the printer when you start your computer.

The three selections at the bottom of the screen perform these functions:

- **Header...:** You can select to send the header immediately to the printer or to a disk file. To use the Already Downloaded option discussed above, select to write the header to the disk, then enter a file name such as POST.TXT. The header will be written to the disk at this time. When you exit Windows, add the command COPY POST.TXT LPT1: (or whatever port you're using) to the AUTOEXEC.BAT file.

- **Errors...:** The PostScript interpreter can create an error message when it encounters some problem in the PostScript file. Click on Errors, then select to have these messages sent to the printer or to a disk file.

- **Handshaking...:** You can select to use hardware or software handshaking for the communications between the computer and printer. In most cases, the spooler will handle handshaking, so you can leave this at the default Software. Some PostScript adapters, however, have their own handshaking built in and using the spooler is not recommended. In this case, select Hardware handshaking.

Whether your LaserJet is equipped with PostScript or not, the Windows environment provides complete support for fonts and graphics. Keep in mind that the full support is only provided for applications designed to run under Windows. When you purchase a Windows application, see if it includes new versions of the printer drivers. Newer applications will include updated drivers.

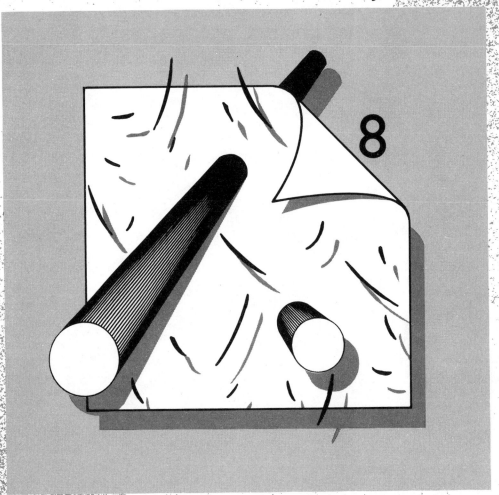

8

Printing with WordStar

Bitstream fonts are discussed in Chapter 4.

• The word processor that started it all back in the "old days" has kept pace with its competitors. WordStar Professional 5.5 is packaged with a speller, thesaurus, form-document generator, and even a telecommunications module. As with other word processors in its class, WordStar offers excellent support for laser printers. It provides the following LaserJet resources:

- Installable printer drivers
- Softfont support with manual downloading
- Hewlett-Packard softfont and cartridge support
- Third-party softfont support
- Print preview mode with screen fonts
- Bitstream Fontware included with the package
- DeskJet support

In this chapter, you'll learn how to install your printer for WordStar and create and use LaserJet printer drivers.

• *Accessing Printer Drivers*

WordStar is packaged with the following five printer databases:

New versions of the DTF printer database support cartridges and softfonts. See Appendix D for details.

File Extension	Supported Printers
DTB	Nonlaser printers, A to I
DTC	Nonlaser printers, J to Z
DTD	HP laser printers with HP cartridges
DTE	HP compatible laser printers with non-HP cartridges
DTF	Other laser printers and DeskJet printers

The DTD database does not include specific support for the LaserJet 2000—select LaserJet IID instead.

Each database contains five files: DB00, DB01, DB02, DB04, and Index. (The numbering is correct—there's no DB03).

The package also contains a number of utility programs that you can use to create your own printer drivers. You create as many drivers as you need and switch to the appropriate one just before printing. You can have more than one driver for the same printer, each supporting different cartridges and fonts.

The printer drivers supplied with the package only include the basic Hewlett-Packard and PostScript fonts available when your version of WordStar was manufactured. Table 8.1 shows the fonts supported by WordStar Professional 5.5. If you have third-party fonts or Hewlett-Packard fonts released after your version of WordStar, you must create a "user database" of font information before installing them.

Before installing WordStar and adding softfont support, consider which fonts you want to use and how many will be included in a single document. WordStar doesn't have an integrated downloader, but it can create a batch file to download fonts manually from DOS. The file will download

• Table 8.1: *Fonts Supported by WordStar Professional 5.5*

CARTRIDGES			
S1	S2	A	B
C	D	E	F
G	H	J	K
L	M	N	P
Q	R	T	U
V	W1	X	Y
Z1	Z1a	Pro Collection	Pro Collection
SOFTFONTS			
AA	AB	AC	AD
AE	AF	AG	DA
EA			
Zapf (Ta, TB) Century Schoolbook (SA, SB) Garamond (RA, RB) Headlines 1 (UA, UB)			

all the softfonts you install in the printer driver as permanent fonts. So if you add support for 30 softfonts to one driver, the file will download all 30, using up quite a bit of your printer's memory.

There are two ways to avoid this problem:

All the fonts in a driver do not have to come from the same set. For example, you could combine several text fonts from the AD set with a few headlines from AG.

- Create several drivers, each with a small group of softfonts that you will probably use in a single document. For example, create a driver called TMSHELV to use the AC softfont set, another called HPSCHOOL for the SA set. Then use the supplied utility programs to create two download batch files, one for each of the drivers. When you want to use the AC set, download the files from DOS, start WordStar, then select the TMSHELV driver before printing.

- Install all your fonts in one driver, then manually divide the download batch file into several smaller files. You'll still have to use the batch file for the fonts you want to include, but you won't have to bother changing drivers. See the section about modifying the download batch file for more details.

• *Using the Installation Utilities*

The WordStar package includes a number of programs that install WordStar and printer support. Several of the programs perform similar functions. Table 8.2 lists the programs and their functions.

The installation utilities should be used in the following order to provide the fullest support for your LaserJet:

The PDFEDIT initial screen warns that Micropro offers support for this program only on a "fee basis," although a help disk is available from Micropro's technical support group.

1. Use WSSETUP to copy the program to the hard disk and create an initial printer driver.

2. Use WINSTALL (or LSRFONTS and PRCHANGE individually) to install third-party fonts.

3. Run WSCHANGE to customize WordStar's default settings.

4. If you purchase another printer, create the printer driver with WINSTALL or PRCHANGE.

5. Run PDFEDIT if you need to make very specific changes to the printer driver. (Make a copy of your driver before starting.)

• Table 8.2: *WordStar Installation Utilities*

UTILITY	FUNCTION
WSSETUP	The main setup utility. It copies the program to your hard disk and establishes your hardware configuration, including the monitor and printer. Use it to create your first printer driver and install font support. Note that you can't use the option for installing third-party softfonts until you create a DTU database using the WINSTALL or LSRFONTS program.
WINSTALL	Modifies your working copy of WordStar and the printer driver. Like WSSETUP, it can create printer drivers from printer database files—building support for internal fonts, cartridges, and HP softfonts. It can also modify drivers you already have by calling PRCHANGE and build support for third-party fonts by calling LSRFONTS.
LSRFONTS	Adds support for softfonts not included in the standard LaserJet and PostScript drivers. The file created is called printer database 0.
PRCHANGE	Creates additional printer drivers or modifies ones you've already created, so you can add newly purchased softfonts or cartridges. Softfonts not supported by the standard driver must first be processed with LSRFONTS.
PDFEDIT	Allows direct customization of the printer driver. Lets you change the actual PCL commands transmitted to the printer. You can use it (if you are an advanced or adventurous user with a knowledge of PCL) to print with a LaserJet "compatible" printer that doesn't respond properly to standard HP PCL commands.
WSCHANGE	Customizes the way WordStar operates after it's installed. Use this utility to change layout, editing, printing, and other default settings.

Installing WordStar

Follow these steps to initially install WordStar and create a printer driver:

1. Insert the Initialization Customization disk in drive A.

2. Log onto drive A, type **WSSETUP**, and then press ↵.

3. Press F10 when you see the initial screen. You'll be asked to confirm the source drive (A) and the hard-disk directory on which to install the program. The default is c:/WS5.

4. Press F10 to accept the default values, or enter new drive paths, and then press F10. The main installation menu will appear, as shown in Figure 8.1.

5. Use the arrow keys to highlight each feature you want on your hard disk and mark it with a + (plus). To cancel a feature, enter a - (hyphen). As you scroll through each item, the required disk space will be listed at the Description line.

6. Press PgDn to see another list of features. To return to the original screen, press PgUp.

7. Press F10 when you have finished marking features. In a series of screens, you'll be asked to insert disks in drive A. Insert the disks and press F10 to continue.

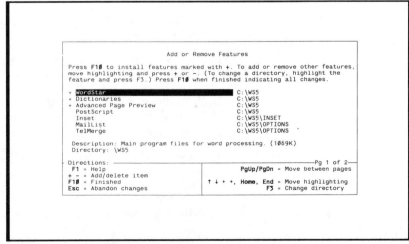

• Figure 8.1: *WSSETUP main menu*

8. When you're asked to designate your monitor and screen type, follow the directions on the screen. You'll then be prompted to install a printer by inserting the Initialization Customization disk in drive A. Next you'll see the Installed Printer menu.

9. Type **HPLASER** (or some other name with no more than eight characters), and then press ←⎯. You'll see the Printer Type menu with the following options:

HP LaserJet or compat—HP cart
HP LaserJet compat—no HP cart
Other lasers and HP DeskJet
Others A-I (incl. generic)
Others J-Z

10. Highlight your choice, and then press ←⎯. Insert a printer disk in drive A when you are prompted to, type **A:**, and then press F10. (If you copied the printer files to the hard disk, type **c:\WS5** and press F10.) You'll see the Printer Selection menu with these choices:

Brother HL-8 Laser (HPLJ + mode)
Hewlett-Packard LaserJet
Hewlett-Packard LaserJet IID
Hewlett-Packard LaserJet Plus
Hewlett-Packard LaserJet Series II
Olivetti PG108 Laser

11. Highlight your model, and then press ←⎯. The Additional Installation menu, shown in Figure 8.2, will appear.

12. Press the up arrow four times to highlight the Select Printer Adapter Port option, and then press ←⎯ to display port options.

13. Select the port your LaserJet is attached to, and then press ←⎯ to return to the previous menu. The Install Sheet Feeder option will be highlighted when the menu appears.

14. Press ←⎯ to display feed options. If you're using a printer with several different options, highlight your selection.

15. Press ←⎯ to return to the previous menu. The Go to Printer Information Menu option will be highlighted.

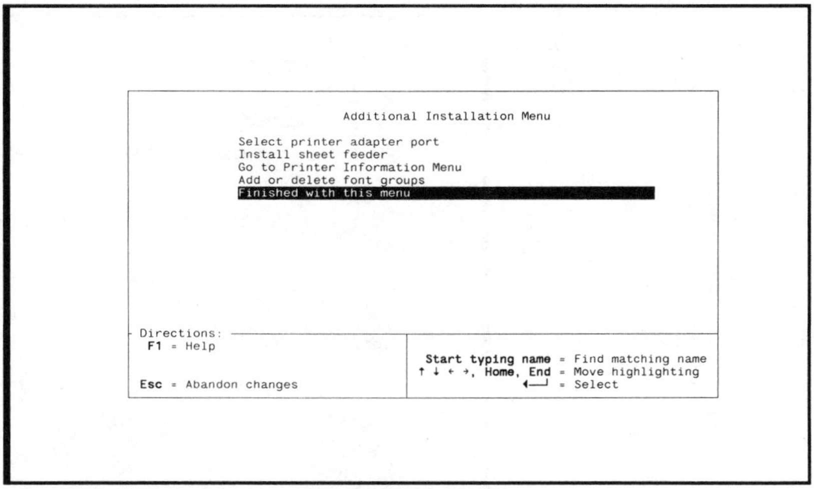

```
                        Additional Installation Menu

               Select printer adapter port
               Install sheet feeder
               Go to Printer Information Menu
               Add or delete font groups
               Finished with this menu




   Directions:
     F1 = Help
                                        Start typing name = Find matching name
                                        ↑ ↓ ← →, Home, End = Move highlighting
     Esc = Abandon changes                           ←┘ = Select
```

• Figure 8.2: *WordStar Additional Installation menu*

16. Press ←┘ to see four options:

    View printer information
    Print printer information
    Save printer information to a disk file
    Return to Additional Installation Menu

    The first option will be highlighted.

17. Press ←┘ to display a screen containing useful information about the printer driver. Press PgUp or PgDn to see the remaining screens.

18. Press Esc twice to return to the Additional Installation menu; then press ↓ to select the Add or Delete Font Groups option.

19. Press ←┘ to display the Current Fonts in PDF menu. As you install cartridges and softfonts, their names will be added to this screen.

20. Press Y to display the menu shown in Figure 8.3.

21. Press ←┘ to select the Add Cartridge Fonts option, which is already highlighted. You'll see a list of cartridges supported by the printer database. You can press PgDn to display a second list of cartridges. Press PgUp to return to the first list.

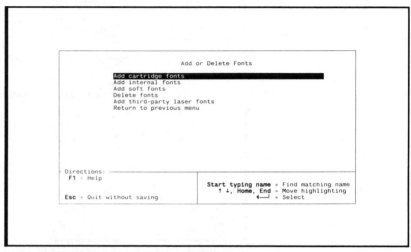

● Figure 8.3: *WordStar Add or Delete Fonts menu*

22. Select each of the cartridges you have available. A small box will appear next to the chosen cartridges. You can include as many cartridges as you want, even if your printer only has one cartridge slot. It will be your responsibility to make sure the proper cartridge is installed for the fonts in the document being printed.

23. Press F10 to save the selected cartridges and return to the Add or Delete Fonts menu.

24. Select Add Internal Fonts, and then press ◄─┘ to display a list of supported internal fonts.

25. Highlight each of the groups you want to use, and then press ◄─┘.

26. Press F10 to save the changes and return to the previous menu.

27. If you have any of the softfonts listed in Table 8.1, select the Add Soft Fonts option to see the menu shown in Figure 8.4.

28. Use the arrow keys to highlight each font you want in the driver, and then press ◄─┘. A small box will appear to the left of the file name. To select all the fonts, press F4.

29. Press F10 after you've selected all the fonts. The Available Typefaces menu appears.

30. Use the arrow keys to highlight each typeface you want in the driver, and then press ◄─┘. Press F4 to select them all.

In installing softfonts in the next steps, consider how you want to download and use them. As discussed earlier, you might want to create several drivers with a few softfonts each.

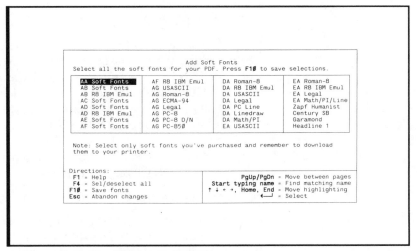

• Figure 8.4: *WordStar Add Soft Fonts menu*

31. Press F10 after you've selected all the typefaces. The Available Type Sizes menu appears.

32. Select the sizes you want and press ↵, or press F4 to select them all. Then press F10 to save the fonts and return to the Add or Delete Fonts menu.

33. Select Return to Previous Menu, and then press ↵. If you installed softfonts, you'll be asked if you want to create screen fonts for the Preview feature.

34. Press Y. You'll be prompted to enter the path for the WordStar program and the location of your fonts.

35. Enter the paths, and then press F10. After the fonts have been created, the main WSSETUP menu will appear.

36. Select Finished with this Menu, and then press F10. You'll be prompted to insert the Initialization Customization disk in drive A.

37. Insert the disk, and then press F10. Next you'll be asked if you want to modify the AUTOEXEC.BAT file to include the WordStar paths.

38. Press Y. When you see the Installation Summary screen, press F10 to complete the setup and return to the DOS prompt.

Adding Third-Party Softfonts

If you have third-party softfonts, you must create a user database before adding them to the driver. You can do this from either WINSTALL or LSRFONTS. You must then add the fonts to the driver using PRCHANGE, another option on the WINSTALL menu.

Follow these steps to install third-party or unsupported Hewlett-Packard softfonts through WINSTALL:

1. Copy your PCL softfonts to a separate directory (for example, PCLFONTS) on your hard disk.

2. Run WINSTALL. You'll see the opening screen shown in Figure 8.5.

3. Select the Use Third-Party Laser Fonts (LSRFONTS) option, and then press ←┘. The Add Third-Party Laser Fonts menu will appear.

4. Press ←┘ to select the Add Hewlett-Packard or Compatible Fonts to Database option. You'll be prompted to enter the path of the softfonts.

5. Type the path, and then press ←┘. A list of fonts in that path will appear, as shown in Figure 8.6.

6. Use the arrow keys to highlight each font you want in the database, and then press ←┘. As you select fonts, look at the font information beneath the listing to see if the Menu name is listed as Unknown.

As an alternative to selecting fonts individually, you can press F4 to select them all. (Deselect them by pressing F4 again.) However, you should use the arrow keys to highlight each one separately to check for unknown font names.

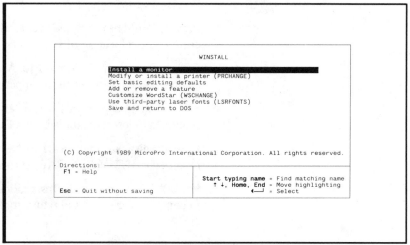

Figure 8.5: *WINSTALL opening screen*

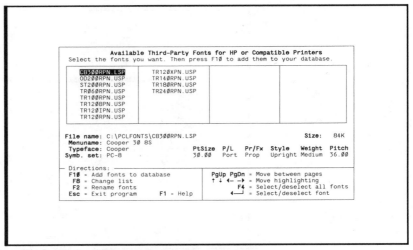

● Figure 8.6: *Softfonts available for WordStar*

7. When you see an Unknown font, press F2, enter a name for it, and press ◄─┘. If you don't name the font, it will be listed as Unknown on WordStar's Font menu.

8. Press F10 after you've selected all the fonts. LSRFONTS will ask for the directory in which to place the database.

9. Press ◄─┘ to accept the current directory or enter a new one, and then press ◄─┘. The user database will be created and each of the fonts added. When LSRFONTS reaches an Unknown font, you'll be asked to select a typeface name, as shown in Figure 8.7.

10. Press PgDn and PgUp until you see an appropriate typeface name listed, select it with the arrow keys, and press ◄─┘.

If you plan on adding several different groups of fonts to the database, use more descriptive names.

11. After you've added all the fonts, you must enter their group name at the prompt shown in Figure 8.8. Press ◄─┘ to accept the default group name, which is a combination of the current system time and date. The fonts will be added to the database, and then the Add Third-Party Laser Fonts menu will reappear.

12. Select the Return to WINSTALL Menu option, and then press F10. Your own printer database, with the DTU extension, is now on the directory. The next step is to add the third-party fonts to the driver.

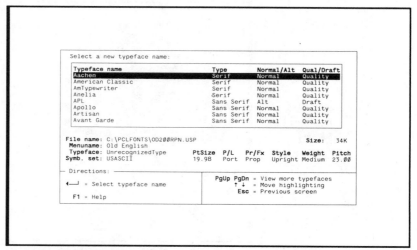

• Figure 8.7: *Naming an unknown typeface for WordStar*

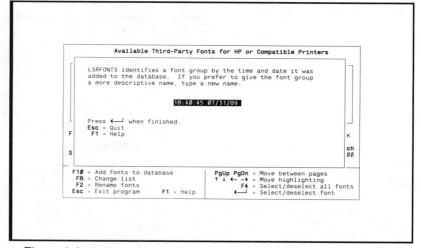

• Figure 8.8: *Each group of newly supported fonts must be given a name
in the database*

13. From the main WINSTALL menu, select the Modify or Install a
Printer (PRCHANGE) option. You'll see the Installed Printer
menu, listing the driver files on your WordStar directory, as shown
in Figure 8.9.

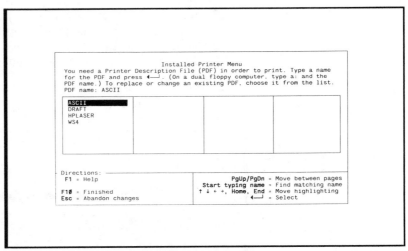

• Figure 8.9: *WordStar driver files on the disk*

To create a new driver, type its name, and then press ←⎯.

14. Select the driver you want and press ←⎯. You'll be asked if you want to modify that driver or create an entirely new one with the same name.

15. Press Y to modify the driver. You'll be prompted to enter the drive and path of the printer files.

16. Type **C:/WS5** if you copied the files to the hard disk, or insert the disk in drive A and type **A:**. Press F10 to see the PDF Modification menu, shown in Figure 8.10.

17. Select Add or Delete Fonts, and then press ←⎯. The Current Fonts menu appears. Press Y to display the Add or Delete Fonts menu.

18. Select Add Third-Party Laser Fonts, and then press ←⎯. You'll be asked for the path of printer data 0.

19. Type **c:\WS5** (or whatever directory you've placed WordStar in), and then press F10. A list of group names included in your database appears.

20. Select the font, and then press F10 to display a list of fonts in the database.

21. Select typefaces and sizes and create screen fonts, just as you did when installing Hewlett-Packard softfonts. When you're finished, follow the menu prompts to return to the PDF Modification menu.

22. Select the Change Custom Print Control option, and then press ←┘. This option displays the Custom Print Control menu, which lets you specify what PCL commands are sent to the printer for the user-defined printer commands ^PF, ^PG, ^PQ, ^PW, and ^PE.

23. Press + (plus) to display the custom control definition screen, shown in Figure 8.11.

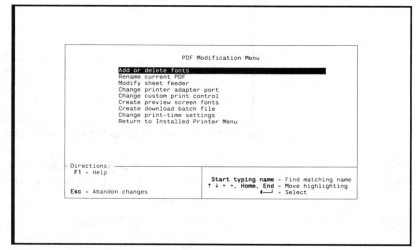

• Figure 8.10: *WordStar PDF Modification menu*

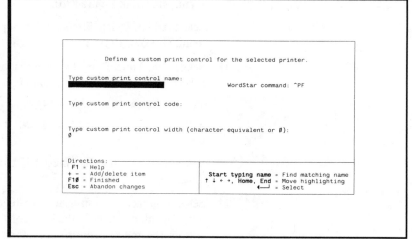

• Figure 8.11: *WordStar custom control definition menu*

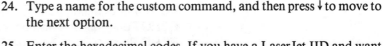

If you have a LaserJet IID but don't want to define a custom code, print in duplex by selecting one of the duplex feed options when you create the driver, and then choosing that driver before printing.

24. Type a name for the custom command, and then press ↓ to move to the next option.

25. Enter the hexadecimal codes. If you have a LaserJet IID and want to use several feed options, you could define one of the custom print codes to turn on duplex printing rather than creating three different drivers. The PCL command for duplex with long-edge binding is 1B 26 6C 31 53. This allows you to activate duplex printing by pressing Ctrl-PF.

26. Press F10 twice to return to the PDF Modification menu.

27. If you don't have your own downloading utility, select Create Download Batch File to be able to download fonts from DOS.

28. Press ↵ to display the Batch File menu.

29. Type **DOWN**, then press ↵. You'll be prompted to enter the path of the WordStar program and font files.

30. Enter the two paths, and then press F10. In a moment, you'll see the prompt:

    The installation program has finished creating the
    requested file(s)

31. Press any key to return the PDF Modification menu. The Change Print-Time Settings option will be highlighted. This lets you change the use of form feeds or the pause between pages setting.

32. Press ↵, change either of the settings, and then return to the PDF Modification menu.

Press Esc to quit without saving the changes at this point.

33. Follow the menu prompts to return to the WINSTALL menu, and then select the Save and Return to DOS option.

Modifying the Download Batch File

The download batch file that you created is on your WordStar directory and looks something like this:

    ECHO OFF
    ECHO Batch file to download fonts to an HP LaserJet
    page printer.
    ECHO Created by MicroPro's PRCHANGE.

```
ECHO Fonts will be downloaded to printer device: LPT1:
ECHO Fonts will be downloaded as permanent.
ECHO Press ^C (Ctrl key and C) to quit.
PAUSE
PECHO *c0D
ECHO ON
COPY /B \pclfonts\CO120RPN.PCP LPT1:
ECHO OFF
PECHO *c5F
PECHO *c1D
ECHO ON
COPY /B \pclfonts\CO070RPN.PCP LPT1:
ECHO OFF
PECHO *c5F
PECHO *c2D
ECHO ON
COPY /B \pclfonts\CO100RPN.PCP LPT1:
ECHO OFF
PECHO *c5F
ECHO ON
            .
            .
            .
```

The real work for downloading each font is done in three lines:

```
PECHO *c0D
```

The PECHO program supplied with WordStar transmits the PCL codes that indicate the ID for the font about to be sent to the printer.

```
COPY /B \pclfonts\CO120RPN.PCP LPT1:
```

The bit-map information for the font is copied to the printer's memory.

```
PECHO *c5F
```

The PCL codes that make the font permanent are transmitted.

If you included more fonts in the driver than you want to (or can) download at one time, divide the batch file into smaller files with sets of fonts you plan to use in a single document. You do this from within WordStar by loading the batch file as a nondocument file, blocking off sections, and then writing smaller files to the disk (using Ctrl-KW). Just be sure to include the PECHO command line before and after each font name.

• *Modifying WordStar Printer Defaults*

The WSCHANGE utility supplied with the software package lets you modify WordStar's default settings and "patch" the program with custom changes to the WordStar code itself. Patching is a very technical process that should be left to the experts. It was most commonly done to older versions of WordStar to add printer and other support that the program didn't normally allow. Fortunately, because of the wide range of options available in the utility programs provided with WordStar Professional, you probably won't have to patch WordStar.

However, there are several default settings that you might want to change, and these modifications are not difficult to make. For example, because of the LaserJet's nonprinting region, WordStar recommends that you set the top margin at 1.6 inches. This is particularly important if you plan to use large type sizes on the first line of the page. Although you can change the setting for each document from within WordStar, it's too easy to forget and lose some text. Instead, you can make that margin the new default value.

Follow these steps to change WordStar's default settings for printing:

If you're uncertain about the changes you're about to make, enter WS as the current file name and WS1 as the new one. This way, your original WordStar program file will remain unchanged.

1. Type **WSCHANGE**, and then press ⏎. You'll be prompted to enter the name and path of the WordStar program you want to change, and the name and path of the program you want to create. The WSCHANGE Main menu will appear, as shown in Figure 8.12.

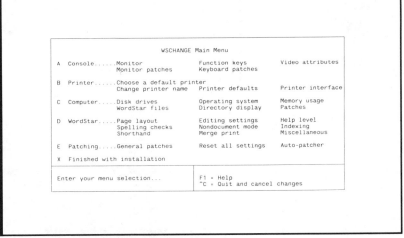

• Figure 8.12: *WSCHANGE Main menu*

2. Press B to display the Printer menu, as shown in Figure 8.13. The first menu option lets you select the default printer, which is the driver file to be used automatically when you start WordStar.

3. Press A to set the default printer. The PDF files on your disk are listed, along with a short description of each file. Press the number corresponding to the printer you want to use as the default.

4. Press X to return to the Printer menu.

5. Press C to display the Printing Defaults menu, as shown in Figure 8.14. The list shows the settings you can change and their current status. The setting DIS stands for discretionary, meaning that several options are available from within WordStar.

6. To change a setting, press the letter at the left of the option, then respond to the prompt displayed on the screen. The normal character font (option G) is the default font used with that driver. In WordStar, switch to the alternate character font (option H) by pressing Ctrl-PA; change back to the normal font by pressing Ctrl-PN.

7. Press X twice to return to the WSCHANGE Main menu.

8. Press D to select the WordStar option. You'll see the WordStar menu, as shown in Figure 8.15.

9. Press A to display the Page Layout menu, then A again to display the Page Sizing and Margins menu, as shown in Figure 8.16.

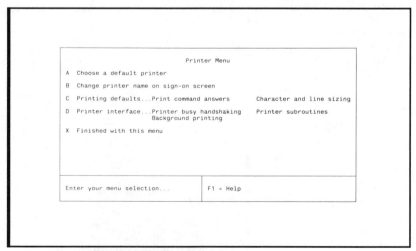

• Figure 8.13: *WSCHANGE Printer menu*

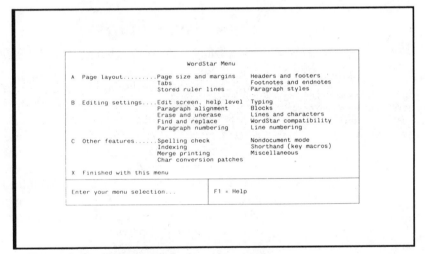

```
                    Printing Defaults Menu

A   Print nondocument as default................OFF      PNODOC
B   Bidirectional printing......................ON       .bp
C   Letter quality printing (NLQ)...............DIS      .lq
D   Microjustification..........................DIS      .uj
E   Underline blanks............................OFF      .ul
F   Proportional spacing........................DIS      .ps
G   Normal character font.......................No font name
H   Alternate character font....................No font name
I   Strikeout character.........................."-"      STKCHR
J   Line height (1440ths/inch)..................240      INIEDT+40
K   Sub/superscript roll (1440ths/inch).........90       .sr
L   Print page numbers..........................ON       .op
M   Load Inset at print-time....................ON       IINSET

X   Finished with this menu


Enter your menu selection...        F1 = Help
```

• Figure 8.14: *WordStar Printing Defaults menu*

```
                    WordStar Menu

A   Page layout........Page size and margins      Headers and footers
                       Tabs                       Footnotes and endnotes
                       Stored ruler lines         Paragraph styles

B   Editing settings....Edit screen, help level   Typing
                        Paragraph alignment       Blocks
                        Erase and unerase         Lines and characters
                        Find and replace          WordStar compatibility
                        Paragraph numbering       Line numbering

C   Other features......Spelling check            Nondocument mode
                        Indexing                  Shorthand (key macros)
                        Merge printing            Miscellaneous
                        Char conversion patches

X   Finished with this menu


Enter your menu selection...        F1 = Help
```

• Figure 8.15: *WordStar default settings menu*

10. To avoid losing text in the nonprinting region, press B, type **1.6**, and then press ⏎.

11. Press X three times to return to the Main menu.

12. Press X to save the changes and exit WSCHANGE. Press Y when you are asked if you are through making changes.

```
                     Page Sizing and Margins Menu
A   Page length.......................11.00"        INIEDT+18  .pl
B   Top margin........................00.50"        INIEDT+14  .mt
C   Bottom margin.....................01.33"        INIEDT+16  .mb
D   Header margin.....................00.33"        INIEDT+1F  .hm
E   Footer margin.....................00.33"        INIEDT+21  .fm
F   Page offset on even page..........00.80"        INIEDT+24  .poe
G   Page offset on odd page...........00.80"        INIEDT+26  .poo
H   Left margin.......................00.00"        RLRINI     .lm
I   Right margin......................06.50"        RLRINI+2   .rm
J   Paragraph margin (-1 for none).....(none)       RLRINI+4   .pm

X   Finished with this menu



   Enter your menu selection...             F1 = Help
```

• Figure 8.16: *WordStar Page Sizing and Margins menu*

• *Using Fonts*

When you want to select a font for a WordStar document, press Alt-S
to pull down the Style menu, select Choose Font, and press ◄─┘. A list of
available fonts will be displayed, as shown in Figure 8.17. Highlight the font
you want to use, and then press ◄─┘. The code for the font will be inserted in
the document. To toggle the display of codes off and on, press Ctrl-OD.

Type your document, using the Style menu to change fonts or select
other attributes. Figure 8.18 shows a short document that includes several
fonts. To see how the document will appear when printed, press Ctrl-OP (or
select Page Preview from the Layout pull-down menu) to activate preview
mode. In this mode, select Options to display the document enlarged or to
show a multipage document in thumbnail display. Figure 8.19 shows the
sample document in preview mode.

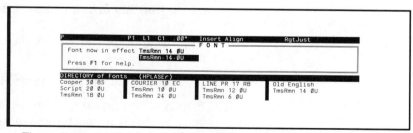

• Figure 8.17: *Available fonts in WordStar*

• Figure 8.18: *WordStar document with several fonts*

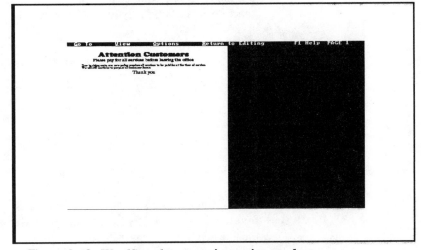

• Figure 8.19: *WordStar document in preview mode*

The selected font becomes the reference point for attributes such as bold-face and italic. If you select a 12-point Helvetica softfont, then press Ctrl-PY for italic, WordStar will expect the 12-point Helvetica Italic font to be available. As a recap, here are the speed keys used for formatting characters:

Ctrl-PB	Boldface
Ctrl-PS	Underlining
Ctrl-PY	Italic
Ctrl-PV	Subscript
Ctrl-PT	Superscript
Ctrl-PX	Strikeout
Ctrl-P =	Select font
Ctrl-P?	Select driver

Controlling Leading or Line Height

Line spacing, such as single or double spacing, is controlled by the Ctrl-OS command. However, line height is set with the dot command .lh. By default, each line is placed in $^{8}/_{48}$ of an inch, or six lines per inch, the best setting for standard 12-point type.

When you're using a much larger font size, WordStar still uses the same line height, running the lines together, as shown on the top of Figure 8.20. The two lines at the bottom of the figure, however, were printed by adding the dot command to set the line spacing at $^{16}/_{48}$ inch, print the 12-point line, and then space down appropriately for the 24-point text:

```
.lh 16
<TmsRmn 12 0U>Times 12-point
<TmsRmn 24 0U>Times 24-point
```

If you placed the line height dot command like this:

```
<Helv 12 0U>Times 12-point
.lh 16
<Helv 24 0U>Times 24-point
```

the two lines would still run together because you are going from a small font to a larger one. If you're using two different font sizes in one line, set the line height for the largest font.

Because softfonts are measured in points ($^{1}/_{72}$ of an inch), you have to convert points into 48ths for the line height command. For a quick conversion, use a line height about two-thirds of the point size, such as $^{16}/_{48}$ths of an inch for a 24-point type.

Helvetica 12-point
Helvetica 24-point

Helvetica 12-point
Helvetica 24-point

• Figure 8.20: ***The line height must be set correctly to avoid overlapping***

• *Controlling Paper Size, Orientation, and Feed*

To change page size and margins, press Ctrl-OL to pull down the Margins and Tabs menu, as shown in Figure 8.21. Make your adjustments, and then press F10. The corresponding dot commands will be inserted in your text. Of course, you could also enter the dot commands manually.

To change page orientation, use the dot command .pr or =l for landscape, or .pr or =p for portrait. To use a softfont, press Ctrl-P =, highlight the name of a landscape softfont you've downloaded, and press ←.

As an example, here are the commands to print envelopes in the landscape mode using the default Courier font on the LaserJet II (the comments in parentheses explain the purpose of each command):

Print envelopes using portrait orientation. See Appendix D for details.

For the LaserJet + and similar models, use .mt 41 for the top margin.

> .pr or = l   (landscape mode)
> .bn 3   (manual envelope feed)
> .po 56   (page offset of 56 characters—like a left margin)
> .pl = 51   (page length of 51 lines)
> .mt 26   (top margin of 26 lines)
> .mb 0   (no bottom margin)
> .op   (omit page numbers)

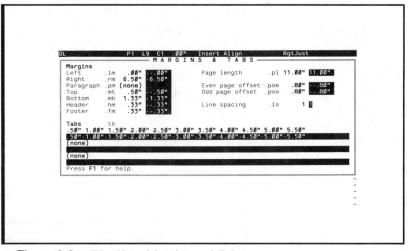

• Figure 8.21: *WordStar Margins and Tabs menu*

Setting Duplex Printing and Other Special Features

If you need to use a PCL command that isn't supported by a dot command, you can either insert a custom code or associate the PCL command with a user-defined printer code. To insert a custom code in the document, press Ctrl-P! to display the screen shown in Figure 8.22. The codes for the Characters to Send to Printer option can be entered in two ways: as Escape characters or hexadecimal codes.

To use Escape characters, enter the Escape code by holding down the Alt key and then typing 27 on the keypad. Release the Alt key, then type the remainder of the code. Press ⏎ to move to the next prompt, then type the characters you want displayed on the screen for this code. If the PCL command requires any space on the page, such as for a top margin or graphic macro, enter the measurement at the final prompt. Press F10 to return to the document.

For example, set duplex printing by typing Alt-27 &l1S for the characters to send to the printer and DUPLEX for the characters to display on the screen. When you press F10, your screen will look like this:

　　　<^[&l1S>

The characters ^[represent the Escape code. If you turn off the display of codes by pressing Ctrl-OD, the word DUPLEX will appear.

If you plan to use the command more than once, instead of defining a custom code, associate the PCL code with one of the user-defined printer commands: ^PQ, ^PG, ^PW, ^PE, or ^PF. Use the dot command .x followed by the second letter of the command, then the hexadecimal code for the command. For example, the command for setting ^PQ to send the codes for duplex printing is

　　　.xq 1B 26 6C 31 53

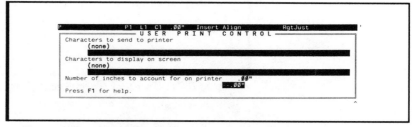

• Figure 8.22: *WordStar custom code screen*

Press Ctrl-PQ before you print the document to activate the command.

Selecting the Paper Source

Feed options are .bn1 for letter size and .bn2 for legal-size.

For all models except the LaserJet IID, set the paper source using the following .bn dot commands:

.bn1   Cassette

.bn2   Manual feed—letter size

.bn3   Manual feed—envelope

.bn4   Manual feed—legal size (LaserJet II)

For the LaserJet IID, use these commands:

.bn1   Upper tray, letter size

.bn2   Lower tray, letter size

.bn3   Upper tray, legal size

.bn4   Lower tray, legal size

.bn5   Envelope feeder

.bn6   Manual feed, letter size

.bn7   Manual feed, legal size

.bn8   Manual feed, envelope

• *Printing WordStar Documents*

Before printing your document, make sure the correct printer driver is selected. While editing a document, press Ctrl-P? to display the screen shown in Figure 8.23. If the incorrect driver is listed, press ↓, highlight the proper driver, and then press ←.

As an alternative, press Ctrl-KD to save your document, then Alt-FP to display the Print menu, shown in Figure 8.24. Use the arrow keys to select the document name, or press ← if its name appears at the File prompt. When you move to the Printer Name option, the list of available PDF files will be shown at the bottom of the screen. Type the driver you want to use, and then press F10 to print the document.

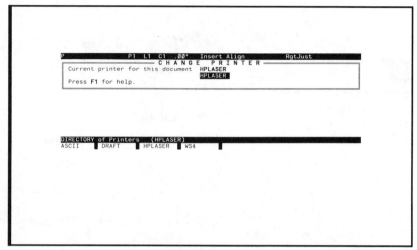

• Figure 8.23: *Drivers can be changed from within the document*

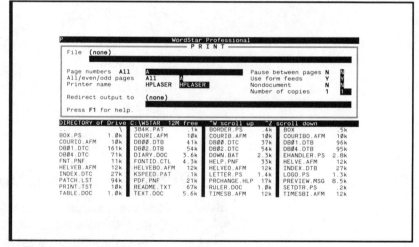

• Figure 8.24: *WordStar Print menu*

• *Printing Envelopes with Merge Print*

Micropro supplies a number of files to streamline envelope and label printing, as listed in Table 8.3. The files contain the merge print codes to automate the process of formatting, data entry, and printing.

Table 8.3: *Merge Files for Printing Envelopes and Labels with WordStar*

FILE	FUNCTION
HP-ENV.LST	Prints envelopes on the LaserJet, LaserJet +, and LaserJet 500 +. Addresses are manually entered.
HP2-ENV.LST	Prints envelopes on the LaserJet II and LaserJet IID. Addresses are manually entered.
HP-ENVMM.LST	Prints envelopes on the LaserJet, LaserJet +, and LaserJet 500 + from addresses in the merge file WSLIST.DTA.
HP2-ENVMM.LST	Prints envelopes on the LaserJet II and LaserJet IID from addresses in the merge file WSLIST.DTA.
HP-LAB3.LST	Prints $1 \times 2^{3/4}$ inch labels 3-up on $8^{1/2} \times 11$ inch label stock, 33 labels per page.
LSRLABL3.LST	Prints $1 \times 2^{5/8}$ inch labels 3-up on $8^{1/2} \times 11$ inch label stock, 30 labels per page.

You can also merge print a document while editing. Press Ctrl-KPM or Alt-F, then select Merge Print from the File pull-down menu.

To use any of the files, press Alt-FM from the opening menu to display the Merge Print pull-down menu, shown in Figure 8.25. Select the file to print and any other options desired, and then press F10.

If you're manually entering envelope addresses, you'll hear a beep. Press Alt-FM again to display the screen shown in Figure 8.26. Enter each of the address items, insert an envelope into the manual tray, and then press ←.

• *PostScript Printing with WordStar*

If your LaserJet is equipped for PostScript printing, follow the installation procedure described for the LaserJet models. After you've designated which fonts to install, you'll be prompted to enter the point sizes for each. Type the point size, and then press ←. Repeat the process, then press Esc after you've entered all the point sizes for that font.

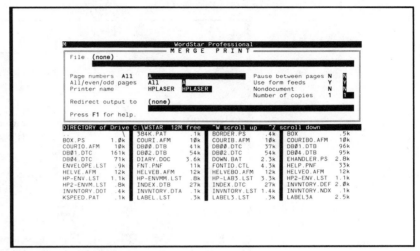

• Figure 8.25: *WordStar Merge Print menu*

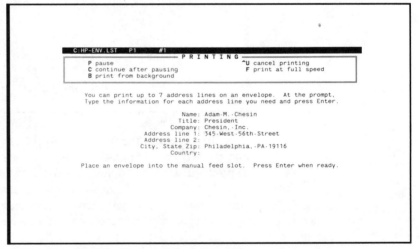

• Figure 8.26: *WordStar envelope merging screen*

When installing the printer, select PostScript Generic, or choose Post-Script Generic (Two-up) to print two pages on a single page in landscape mode, with fonts reduced to 65 percent.

Before starting WordStar and printing a document, make sure the files DRIVERS.OVR, WSPROL.PS, and WPROL2.PS are on the Word-Star directory. See Chapter 15 for details on PostScript printing with your LaserJet.

The other PS files on the PostScript disk are demonstration script files.

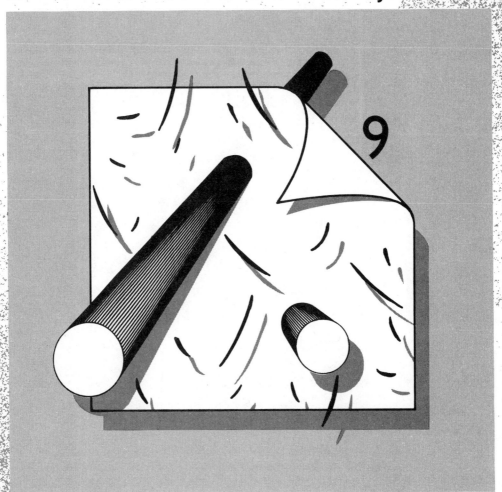

9

Using Other Word Processors

• Word processing programs that support the LaserJet have their own ways of dealing with laser printers and fonts. Each provides some method for selecting or creating printer drivers and designating the types of fonts being used.

This chapter describes two popular word processing programs, Multi-Mate and XyWrite III Plus, which demonstrate alternative approaches to printer drivers. Although they aren't covered in the same amount of detail as the word processors discussed in the previous chapters, they are powerful programs with a solid reputation for excellence.

Read this chapter even if you're not using either of these programs. The discussions will help you understand how your application's printer driver can be used and modified.

See Appendix D for details on using MultiMate with DeskJet printers.

• *Printing with MultiMate*

MultiMate gained prominence some years ago as a "Wang-like" word processor. The menu system and interface resembled that of Wang dedicated word processing machines, allowing Wang-trained operators to move onto PCs with fewer reservations.

Today, MultiMate Advantage II is a full-featured program with complete LaserJet support, including integrated downloading and facilities for customizing printer drivers and width tables.

An add-on package for MultiMate, called the Printer Enhancement Pack, provides WYSIWYG document preview, Bitstream Fontware, and a pull-down menu to easily select fonts within a document.

Accessing MultiMate Printer Drivers

Unlike other programs, MultiMate stores printer driver information and character width tables in separate files. The Printer Table disk contains printer drivers (PAT files) and width tables (CWT files) for all Hewlett-Packard internal and cartridge fonts, as listed in Table 9.1. A single PAT file can include up to 26 fonts, the maximum number of fonts you can include in any one document.

The Printer Table disk also contains LJETENV.PAT, a driver to print envelopes in landscape orientation, and sheet feeder files (with an SAT extension) for printers with multiple bins.

You can manually copy the files to your MultiMate disk or have the Printer program on the Printer Table disk do it for you. Follow these steps to use the Printer program:

1. Run Printer to see the menu shown in Figure 9.1.

2. Type the disk and directory path for your MultiMate program.

3. Press F9 to switch to the list of printers.

• Table 9.1: *MultiMate Printer Drivers (Printer Table Disk)*

FILE NAME	SUPPORTED FONTS
LJETFS1	Internal fonts for the original LaserJet, LaserJet +, and LaserJet 500 +; cartridges A, C, D, E, G, and H
LJETPS1	Cartridges B, F, and K
LJETFS2	Cartridges J, L, M, N, and Q
LJETPS2	Cartridges P, T, U, and V
LJETFS3	Cartridges R, W, X, and Y

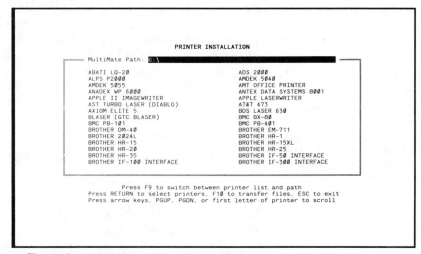

• Figure 9.1: *MultiMate Printer Installation menu*

4. Press the arrow keys to display the list of LaserJet options. They will be listed according to the cartridges they support, such as H-P LASERJET (FS: A-H) for fixed-space fonts in cartridges A to H.

5. Highlight a driver, then press ←┘. The name will appear in boldface and the highlighting will move to the next driver on the list.

6. Repeat the procedure until all the drivers you want to access are selected.

7. Press F10 to copy the appropriate files onto the named directory.

Additional driver and width tables are in the LJETPLUS directory of the Conversion 2 disk. These include four printer drivers, a number of width tables supporting popular softfonts (listed in Table 9.2), and LJIIS1 for the S1 cartridge. To access this support, copy the appropriate files to your MultiMate directory.

• Table 9.2: *Additional MultiMate Printer Drivers (Conversion 2 Disk)*

FILE NAME	SUPPORTED FONTS	CWT FILE	ID LETTER	ID NUMBER
LJETTMS.PAT	TR100RPN.USP	LJETTMSA	A	1
	TR100BPN.USP	LJETTMSB	B	2
	TR100IPN.USP	LJETTMSC	C	3
	TR080RPN.USP	LJETTMSD	D	4
	TR080BPN.USP	LJETTMSE	E	5
	TR080IPN.USP	LJETTMSF	F	6
	TR060RPN.USP	LJETTMSG	G	7
	TR140RPN.USP	LJETTMSH	H	8
	TR180BPN.USP	LJETTMSI	I	9
LJETHLV.PAT	HV100RPN.USP	LJETHLVA	A	11
	HV100BPN.USP	LJETHLVB	B	12
	HV100IPN.USP	LJETHLVC	C	13
	HV080RPN.USP	LJETHLVD	D	14
	HV080BPN.USP	LJETHLVE	E	15
	HV080IPN.USP	LJETHLVF	F	16
	HV060RPN.USP	LJETHLVG	G	17
	HV140RPN.USP	LJETHLVH	H	18
	HV180BPN.USP	LJETHLVI	I	19
LJETGTH.PAT	LG120R12.USP	LJETGTHD	A	21
	LG120B12.USP		B	22
	LG120I12.USP		C	23
	LP120R12.USP		D	24
	LG140R10.USP		E	25

Table 9.2: *Additional MultiMate Printer Drivers (Conversion 2 Disk)* *(Continued)*

FILE NAME	SUPPORTED FONTS	CWT FILE	ID LETTER	ID NUMBER
LJETGTH.PAT	LG140B10.USP		F	26
	PS160B08.USP		G	27
	PS180B06.USP		H	28
	LG095R16.USP		I	29
LJETPRE.PAT	PR100R12.USP	LJETPRED	A	31
	PR100B12.USP		B	32
	PR100I12.USP		C	33
	LP120R12.PLP		D	34
	PR070R16.USP		E	35

Each font in a driver is associated with a font ID number and a special ID letter. The ID numbers are the standard ones assigned to all LaserJet fonts. The ID letters are used within your MultiMate document to switch fonts. If you download softfonts manually, you must assign them the same ID numbers used in the driver.

After you've copied the appropriate PAT and CWT files to your MultiMate directory, you can select the printer driver you want to use for your document through MultiMate's Document Print Options menu, as explained in the next section.

Using Fonts with MultiMate

To use fonts within MultiMate, you have to know the following information about each font:

- Its PAT file name
- The designated ID letter
- The pitch of fixed-width fonts
- The corresponding CWT file name

If you want to use one font for the entire document, you can just name the CWT file and default font ID letter in the Document Print Options menu.

Appendix D of the MultiMate *Printer Guide* (supplied with the software) lists this information, as well as suggested pitch (in MultiMate's own numbering scheme), margin, and line-length settings for each font.

If you want to use softfonts, place the font files on the MultiMate directory so they can be downloaded when you print a document.

To use a font in a document, you enter one or more Alt-C commands to change the font ID letter and/or pitch. Then enter the driver name (PAT file) in the Document Print Options menu before printing the document. When you print the document, MultiMate will select whatever fonts are associated with those font ID letters in the current PAT file.

Figure 9.2 shows a short document with two font and pitch settings. The *Pt* characters show where Alt-C was entered to insert a font or pitch change. The document uses font ID letter H in MultiMate's pitch code 1 and font ID letter G in pitch code 9. The right and left margins were adjusted to accommodate the smaller type size.

Using the LJETTMS driver, for which the sample document was designed, the printed fonts will be 14-point and 6-point Times Roman. If you accidentally selected the LJTGTHD driver, MultiMate would try to download and use Presentation 16-point Regular and 18-point Bold, the fonts associated with that driver's G and H font ID letters.

Figure 9.3 shows the Document Print Options menu settings for the sample document. Draft printing and proportional spacing have been set at Y, and LJETTMS selected as the Printer Action Table. No CWT file is named because the font ID letters in the document will specify the proper character width table when the font is downloaded.

```
DOCUMENT: UNIFORMS              PAGE:   1 LINE:   1 COL:   5
 1--[----»----»------------------------------------------------------------------
    «
    «
    «
    RHR1«
    PLEASE TAKE THIS HOME TO YOUR PARENTS«
    «
    RGR9«
    Dear Parents:«
    «
    Beginning next week, all students will be required to have two gym uniforms
    Please contact the Athletic Director if you have any questions.«
    «
    «
    Thank you.«
    «
    «
    Alvin Aardvark«
    Principal


                                                            S:↓ N:↓
```

• Figure 9.2: *MultiMate document using different font and pitch settings*

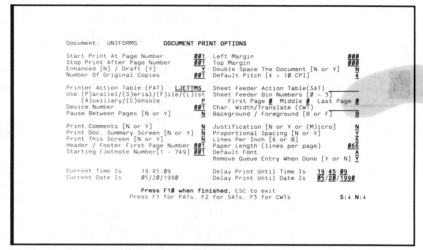

```
Document:  UNIFORMS       DOCUMENT PRINT OPTIONS

Start Print At Page Number          ØØ1    Left Margin                          ØØØ
Stop Print After Page Number        ØØ1    Top Margin                          ØØØ
Enhanced [N] / Draft [Y]              Y    Double Space The Document [N or Y]    N
Number Of Original Copies           ØØ1    Default Pitch [4 = 1Ø CPI]            4

Printer Action Table (PAT)    LJETTMS    Sheet Feeder Action Table(SAT)
Use.(P)arallel/(S)erial/(F)ile/(L)ist    Sheet Feeder Bin Numbers [Ø - 3]
     (A)uxiliary/(C)onsole         P         First Page Ø  Middle Ø  Last Page Ø
Device Number                     ØØ1    Char. Width/Translate (CWT)
Pause Between Pages [N or Y]         N    Background / Foreground [B or F]       B

Print Comments [N or Y]             N    Justification [N or Y or (M)icro]     N
Print Doc. Summary Screen [N or Y]  N    Proportional Spacing [N or Y]         Y
Print This Screen [N or Y]          N    Lines Per Inch [6 or 8]               6
Header / Footer First Page Number  ØØ1   Paper Length (lines per page)        Ø66
Starting Footnote Number[1 - 749]  ØØ1   Default Font                          A
                                         Remove Queue Entry When Done [Y or N] Y

Current Time Is    19:45:Ø9   Delay Print Until Time Is   19:45:Ø9
Current Date Is    Ø5/2Ø/199Ø   Delay Print Until Date Is   Ø5/2Ø/199Ø

            Press F1Ø when finished, ESC to exit
        Press F1 for PATs, F2 for SATs, F3 for CWTs              S:↓ N:↓
```

• Figure 9.3: *MultiMate Document Print Options menu for sample document*

Customizing and Creating MultiMate Printer Drivers

Along with the LaserJet printer drivers, the MultiMate package also includes four generic laser printer action tables: LJDNPSP.PAT and LJDNPSL.PAT, for portrait and landscape proportionally-spaced fonts; and LJDNFSP.PAT and LJDNFSL.PAT, for fixed-width portrait and landscape fonts. You can customize these or any of the other drivers, or create a new one, using the UTIL program on the MultiMate Utilities disk. For example, you can combine several typefaces in one driver or change the font information to support third-party fonts.

Before modifying a driver, make a copy of it under a different name. Then make your changes to the new copy. This keeps the original intact in case you make a mistake.

Make sure you thoroughly understand PCL programming, and carefully read Chapter 3 in the MultiMate *Printer Guide* before starting. When you're ready, follow these steps:

1. Access the Utilities disk and type **UTIL**. If you're running the program from a directory other than the one holding the MultiMate program, you will then be prompted to enter the path for the

WPSYSD.SYS file, then press F10. Next you'll see the main UTIL menu, as shown in Figure 9.4.

2. Press F10 to select Printer Tables Editor, which is already highlighted. The Printer Tables Editor menu will appear, as shown in Figure 9.5.

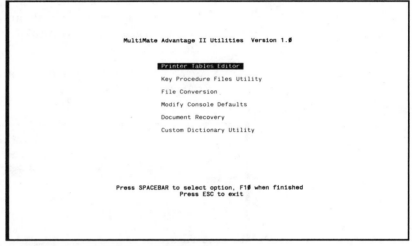

• Figure 9.4: *MultiMate utilities menu*

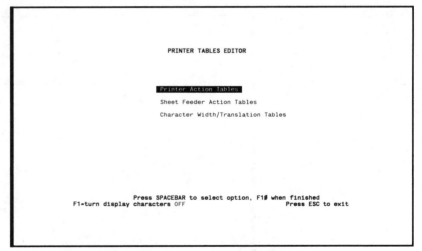

• Figure 9.5: *MultiMate Printer Tables Editor menu*

3. Press F10 again to display three options:

   Edit An Old File
   Create A New File
   Delete A File

4. To edit or customize a file, select the first option, and then press F10. If your drivers are on a floppy disk, you'll be asked to enter the path. Then you will see a list of printer drivers, as shown in Figure 9.6.

5. Select the driver, and then press F10 to see the editing options, as shown in Figure 9.7.

• Figure 9.6: *MultiMate printer drivers listed for editing*

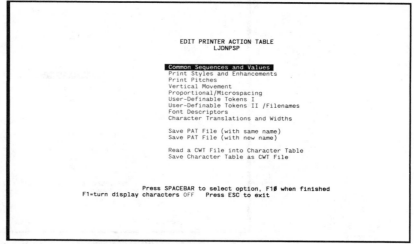

• Figure 9.7: *MultiMate printer driver editing options*

6. To change any of the softfont specifics, select the Font Descriptors option. This displays the menu shown in Figure 9.8. From here, assign the font ID letter and ID number (in hex code) and specify the font file to he downloaded. The selection at the prompt

Soft Font Y or N

should be set at N.

7. Select the other options you want to change from the driver editing options menu, make your modifications, and then select one of the Save PAT File options.

8. Press F10 to exit the program, returning to the DOS prompt.

Printing MultiMate Documents in Landscape Orientation

MultiMate cartridge PAT files support both portrait and landscape orientation, but the four softfont drivers are just for portrait. To print in landscape orientation with a cartridge font, use the proper cartridge and its associated PAT file; then select the font ID letter for the landscape font.

To print softfonts in landscape, however, you have to either customize one of the generic drivers for your landscape fonts or use the LJETENV PAT file, which supports the internal Courier landscape font.

```
EDIT PRINTER ACTION TABLE        LJETTMS                    Font Descriptor
F2 will change input mode to ASCII              Soft Font Y or N? N
Fonts Currently Used:   ABCDEFGHI................
CWT Letter: A
             Font Name: TIMES ROMAN 1ØPT REGULAR
             ← ( 1 X
           1  1B28315800000000          5  ................


           2  ................          6  ................


           3  ................          7  ................


           4  ................          8  ................

          Keys: F1=Goto Font, PGUP=Previous Font, PGDN=Next Font
                F4=List Fonts
                SHIFT-F7=Delete Font, SHIFT-F9=Clear All Fields

   F1Ø = save this screen in memory                    ESC to PAT menu
```

• Figure 9.8: *MultiMate font descriptors options*

To print envelopes with the LJETENV file, follow these steps:

1. Press ⏎ 24 times (35 with the LaserJet, LaserJet +, and Laser-Jet 500 +), and then type the address at the left margin.

2. Press Alt-F2 and type **45** to set the page length.

3. Press F10 to return to the document.

4. Press Alt-3, and then save the document and display the Document Print Options menu.

5. Make these settings on the menu:

Enhance/Draft	Y
Printer Action Table	LJETENV
Left Margin	050
Top Margin	000
Pitch	4
Paper Length	45

6. Press F10 to start printing, and insert the blank envelope into the manual feed tray—printing side up, top of the envelope to the left.

Adding Duplex Support to MultiMate

Sheet-feeder information is provided in files with the SAT extension. If your version of MultiMate doesn't have a SAT file for the LaserJet IID, look for one called LPLUS500.SAT on the Printer Table disk. You can use this SAT file from the Document Print Options menu to select the upper tray (bin 1), lower tray (bin 2), or manual feed (bin 3).

To print in duplex, however, you must create a custom SAT file using the UTIL program on the Utilities disk. Follow these steps:

1. Run UTIL and select Sheet Feeder Action Tables from the Printer Tables Editor menu (Figure 9.5).

2. Select to create a new file, then enter **DUPLEX** as the name. You'll see the menu shown in Figure 9.9.

```
Edit Sheet Feeder Table           DUPLEX
    F2 will change input mode to ASCII


                              BIN 1           BIN 2           BIN 3

 Eject current sheet         ..............   ..............   ..............

 Select bin                  ..............   ..............   ..............

 Load sheet from bin         ..............   ..............   ..............
          OR

 Eject sheet & load sheet    ..............   ..............   ..............


 F10 to save this screen in memory                      Press ESC to exit
```

• Figure 9.9: *MultiMate options for editing the sheet feeder table*

3. Next to the last option, Eject Sheet & Load Sheet, enter the appropriate PCL commands:

Bin	PCL Code to Enter	Purpose
1	1B 26 6C 31 48	Upper tray
2	1B 26 6C 31 53	Duplex, long-edge
3	1B 26 6C 32 53	Duplex, short-edge

4. Save the file and exit UTIL.

5. When you want to print in duplex, display the Document Print Options menu, and enter **DUPLEX** for the Sheet Feeder Action Table option. Enter bin number 2 or 3 for all the Page options.

• *Printing with XyWrite III Plus*

XyWrite III Plus is a word processing program known for its speed. It uses a different approach for printer drivers. Drivers are stored in text files that include specifications for your printer and, optionally, display characteristics. The XyWrite drivers do not download fonts, so you must manually download the ones you want to use.

You don't need a special driver modification program to customize the printer drivers. Because they are text files, you can recall them to the screen and edit them as you would any document. However, you must know how to use PCL commands and thoroughly understand the format of printer drivers.

Accessing XyWrite Printer Drivers

Use 3DJET.PRN to support DeskJet internal fonts, or use a LaserJet driver for compatible cartridge or softfonts. Contact XyQuest, Inc., for information about updated DeskJet drivers.

Two printer drivers are supplied with the software: 3HP-CART.PRN supports all cartridge fonts, and 3HP-SOFT.PRN supports softfont sets AC, AD, AE, AF. Two additional drivers (3HP-SOFT1.PRN and 3HP-SOFT2.PRN) that support the other Hewlett-Packard fonts are available free from the manufacturer. All these drivers support the LaserJet's internal fonts.

When you first install XyWrite III Plus, you'll be asked to select a default driver to use, as shown in Figure 9.10. This is the driver that will be loaded automatically whenever you start the program.

You can change to any other printer driver from within XyWrite by loading the PRN file into memory. Before printing the document, load the printer driver with the command

load *driver-name*.prn

All the fonts included in that file, and installed for the printer, are now available for use.

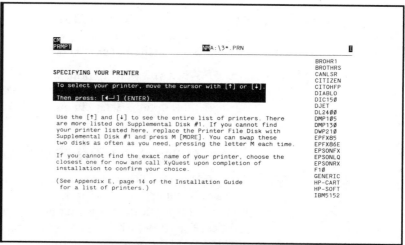

• Figure 9.10: *XyWrite printer installation menu*

Editing the XyWrite Printer Driver Files

Even though a driver is said to "support" all cartridges or a series of softfonts, only a few preselected fonts are immediately available. To use any other supported font, you have to edit the printer driver.

Each driver can consist of nine parts:

- **Terminator characters:** Define the codes to send to your printer to end paragraphs and word-wrap lines, to start and end files, and for page breaks.

- **Print type (PT) tables:** List the font families available using XyWrite PT and attribute commands.

- **Attribute tables:** Contain the PCL commands for formats such as underline, double underline, subscript, superscript, reverse, and italic printing.

- **Font tables:** Contain the PCL commands for orientation and font selection, the leading value, and the width and substitution tables to use.

- **Width tables:** Specify the width of all characters in XyWrite width units.

- **Substitution tables:** Define the symbol set and support foreign-language and graphic characters.

- **Vertical spacing:** PCL codes for leading and vertical spacing.

- **Microjustification:** Information for high-quality justification.

- **Printer control tables:** Contain miscellaneous printer commands.

Although all the fonts described by the font tables are supported by the driver, only those listed in the PT tables can actually be used. For example, 3HP-SOFT.PRN contains 114 font tables, but only nine fonts are in the PT tables and available. In order to use any of the other 105 fonts, you must add them to a PT table.

PT Tables

Figure 9.11 shows the PT tables listing in the driver 3HP-SOFT.PRN. By default, only four font groups can be used: the internal Courier and Line Printer fonts and the 10-point Times and 14-point Helvetica softfonts. The four PT tables (PT = 1, PT = 2, PT = 3, and PT = 4) define the font groups.

```
PT=1
MD NM+MED-COURIER
MD BO+BOLD-COURIER
MD UL+MED-COURIER+UNDERLINE
MD RV+MED-COURIER+FORMS
MD BU+BOLD-COURIER+UNDERLINE
MD BR+MED-COURIER
MD SU+MED-COURIER+SUPERSCRIPT
MD SD+MED-COURIER+SUBSCRIPT
;
PT=2
MD NM+LT-LINEPTR
MD BO+LT-LINEPTR+BOLD
MD UL+LT-LINEPTR+UNDERLINE
MD RV+LT-LINEPTR+FORMS
MD BU+LT-LINEPTR+BOLD+UNDERLINE
MD BR+LT-LINEPTR
MD SU+LT-LINEPTR+SUPERSCRIPT
MD SD+LT-LINEPTR+SUBSCRIPT
;
PT=3
MD NM+10TIMES
MD BO+10TIMES-BOLD
MD UL+10TIMES+UNDERLINE
MD RV+10TIMES+FORMS
MD BU+10TIMES-BOLD+UNDERLINE
MD BR+10TIMES-ITALIC
MD SU+10TIMES+SUPERSCRIPT
MD SD+10TIMES+SUBSCRIPT
;
PT=4
MD NM+14HELV
MD BO+14HELV-BOLD
MD UL+14HELV+UNDERLINE
MD RV+14HELV+FORMS
MD BU+14HELV-BOLD+UNDERLINE
MD BR+14HELV-ITALIC
MD SU+14HELV+SUPERSCRIPT
MD SD+14HELV+SUBSCRIPT
```

- Figure 9.11: *The PT tables listing in the XyWrite 3HP-SOFT.PRN file*

Each font group includes eight different attribute modes:

- NM (normal)

- BO (bold)

- UL (underline)

- RV (reverse—used for italic on the LaserJet)

- BU (bold underline)

- BR (bold reverse—usually used for bold italic)

- SU (superscript)

- SD (subscript)

Attribute Tables

In some cases, a character attribute uses a specific softfont file, such as 10-point Times, 10-point Times Bold, or 10-point Times Italic. Those softfonts are defined in the driver's font and width tables. The other attributes combine a softfont with the PCL commands found in the driver's attribute tables. Figure 9.12 shows the attribute tables for 10-point Times (the PT = 3 font group) in the 3HP-SOFT.PRN driver.

The following codes are listed for each attribute table (AT:Bold, AT: Underline, AT: Double-Underline, etc.):

- AT<, followed by the PCL commands for the attribute, turns the attribute on.

- AT>, followed by the PCL commands for the attribute, turns the attribute off.

- AT# is the code sent after each character.

- ET ends each table.

- ; precedes a comment.

- ► represents the Escape code.

- ← is a carriage return.

- Figure 9.12: *Attribute tables in the XyWrite 3HP-SOFT.PRN file*

Your HP LaserJet Handbook

Font Tables

The fonts themselves are selected by commands in the font tables. Figure 9.13 shows the font tables for 10-point Times in the 3HP-SOFT.PRN driver.

The following codes are listed for each font table (FO:10Times, FO:10Times-Bold, etc.):

- FO<, followed by the PCL commands describing its attributes, selects the font.

- VL shows the leading value used if you select automatic leading. With the LaserJet, vertical leading is measured in dots. VL 50 represents 50-dot spacing, about six lines per inch.

- UW names the width table to use.

- US represents the substitution table (symbol set) for using line-draw and graphic characters.

Any font listed in a font table can be added to a PT table and used in your document.

Width Tables

A width table defines the character widths for a font. Figure 9.14 shows the width table for 10-point Times in the 3HP-SOFT.PRN driver.

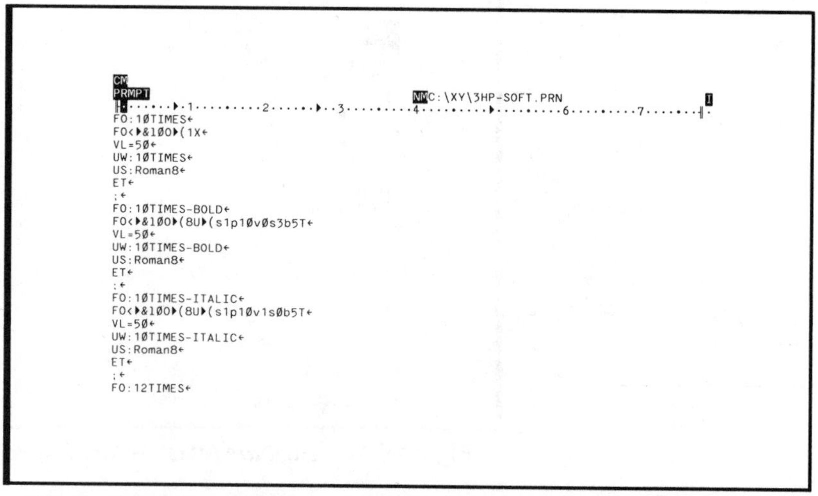

• Figure 9.13: *Font tables in the XyWrite 3HP-SOFT.PRN file*

- Figure 9.14: *Width tables for 10-point Times in the XyWrite 3HP-SOFT.PRN file*

The SW code at the beginning of the table indicates the standard width of characters not specifically listed in the table; in this example, the standard width is 20 units. Characters that take up less or more room than the standard width are listed below the SW line. The 10-point Times table, for example, shows that the colon and semicolon occupy 11 width units, the capital I is 15 units, the capital J is 18 units, and so on.

Adding Supported Fonts

You can make any font that is supported by the driver's font tables available by adding its description to the PT tables. For example, suppose that you want to use 8-point Times softfonts. You would recall the driver with the command **ca 3HP-SOFT.PRN**, and then add this entry to the end of the PT tables:

```
PT = 5
MD NM + 8TIMES
MD BO + 8TIMES-BOLD
MD UL + 8TIMES + UNDERLINE
MD RV + 8TIMES + FORMS
MD BU + 8TIMES-BOLD + UNDERLINE
MD BR + 8TIMES-ITALIC
MD SU + 8TIMES + SUPERSCRIPT
MD SD + 8TIMES + SUBSCRIPT
;
```

Using similar techniques, you can make any of the supported fonts available, or even combine cartridge fonts from the 3HP-CART.PRN file with softfonts in 3HP-SOFT.PRN.

Adding Third-Party Softfont Support

If you don't have width table information, try to match your font with a similar supported one. Use the 10-Point Times width table, for example, with a 10-point Century School-book font.

To add fonts that are not listed in the font tables, you must create custom PT, font, and width tables. However, you don't have to enter the long PCL commands for font specification. Since you have to manually download your fonts, you can also use the font ID number for font selection.

For example, suppose that you want to add 10-point Century School-book fonts. Download them with these ID numbers:

10-point Normal	0
10-point Bold	1
10-point Italic	2

Then add these sections to the softfont driver (enter the Escape code ► by pressing Esc):

```
PT = 6
MD NM + 10SCHOOLBOOK
MD BO + 10SCHOOLBOOK-BOLD
MD UL + 10SCHOOLBOOK + UNDERLINE
MD RV + 10SCHOOLBOOK + FORMS
MD BU + 10SCHOOLBOOK-BOLD + UNDERLINE
MD BR + 10SCHOOLBOOK-ITALIC
MD SU + 10SCHOOLBOOK + SUPERSCRIPT
MD SD + 10SCHOOLBOOK + SUBSCRIPT
;
```

The first part of the FO< command (►&l0O) activates the portrait mode; the second part selects the font by its downloaded ID number.

```
FO:10SCHOOLBOOK
FO < ►&l0O ►(0X
VL = 50
UW:10TIMES
US:Roman8
ET
;
FO:10SCHOOLBOOK-BOLD
FO < ►&l0O ►(1X
VL = 50
```

```
UW:10TIMES-BOLD
US:Roman8
ET
;
FO:10SCHOOLBOOK-ITALIC
FO< ►&l0O►(2X
VL = 50
UW:10TIMES-ITALIC
US:Roman8
ET
;
```

Be sure to store the edited table back on disk; then load it before printing.

Using Fonts with XyWrite

All softfonts must be manually downloaded and all cartridges installed before starting XyWrite.

In XyWrite, you select the font type and size by entering a PT command on the command line. First, make sure you're on the command line (press F10 if not), then load the driver that you want to use. If you plan on using fonts of different sizes, enter the command AL 1 to activate automatic leading (line spacing). Then, to select a font, enter the PT command. For example, using the 3HP-SOFT.PRN PT tables, with the addition of 8-point Times and10-point Century Schoolbook, these commands would select fonts:

You must include a space between the command and font number. However, when you turn on the display of codes using Ctrl-F9, the space will not appear on the screen.

- **PT 1**: Internal Courier Medium

- **PT 2**: Internal Line Printer

- **PT 3**: 10-point Times

- **PT 4**: 14-point Helvetica

- **PT 5**: 8-point Times

- **PT 6**: 10-point Century Schoolbook

Unlike other word processing programs, XyWrite doesn't have separate commands for font type and size. A specific size is associated with each PT command number.

To specify an attribute for the font (underline, reverse, etc.), enter the attribute command after you select the font. You can use either the mode command from the command line or the built-in control codes, as follows:

Mode Command (Press F5)	Control-Key Combination	Attribute
	Ctrl-0	Reset to default
MD NM	Ctrl-1	Normal
MD BO	Ctrl-2	Bold
MD UL	Ctrl-3	Underline
MD RU	Ctrl-4	Reverse
MD BU	Ctrl-5	Bold underline
MD BR	Ctrl-6	Bold reverse
MD SU	Ctrl-7	Superscript
MD SD	Ctrl-8	Subscript

Figure 9.15 shows a sample XyWrite document set at automatic leading (AL1) and using two fonts, PT 3 (10-point Times) and PT 4 (14-point Helvetica). One word in the first sentence is formatted with the reverse attribute, set as italic with LaserJet drivers.

Printing XyWrite Documents in Landscape Orientation

To print in landscape orientation, make sure one of the landscape fonts is listed in a PT table, and then change the page margins as necessary.

• Figure 9.15: *XyWrite document using several fonts and automatic leading*

The font name begins with L-, and the FO< command switches the printer into landscape mode with the PCL command ►&l1O.

Font tables for landscape fonts look like this:

```
FO:L-7 TIMES-ITALIC
FO< ►&l1O ►(8U ►(s1p7v1s0b5T
VL = 33
UW:7 TIMES-ITALIC
US:Roman8
ET
```

Adding Paper Feed and Duplex Support to XyWrite

So far, we've discussed the parts of the driver that provide font support. But the driver can also include a printer control table to take advantage of all your printer's features, such as multiple bins, manual feeding, and duplex printing.

The printer control table is just a list of PCL codes. To issue the command to the printer, you enter a PC command followed by the row number of the code you want to activate.

Figure 9.16 shows an example of a printer control table for the Laser-Jet IID. The line PC:10 indicates that the table contains ten codes. The commands, by row number, are for the following features:

Row	Purpose
1	Upper tray feed
2	Lower tray feed
3	Manual paper feed
4	Manual envelope feed
5	Envelope feeder
6	Landscape mode
7	Portrait mode
8	Simplex (one-side) printing
9	Duplex, long-edge
10	Duplex, short-edge

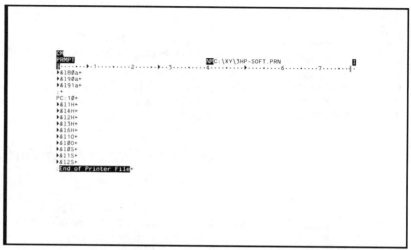

• Figure 9.16: *Sample printer control table for XyWrite driver*

To issue any of these commands from within XyWrite, place the cursor at the start of the document or page, press F10 to enter the command line, then type **PC**, a space, then the row number of the code. PC 9, for example, would set the printer for long-edge duplex printing.

If your word processor was not covered here, refer to your software manual to see how drivers are selected and modified. Become familiar with PCL commands, the format of your driver files, and any utility programs supplied for customizing the driver. Make sure you work with a *copy* of your driver, with the original stored in a safe location.

H•P L•A•S•E•R•J•E•T

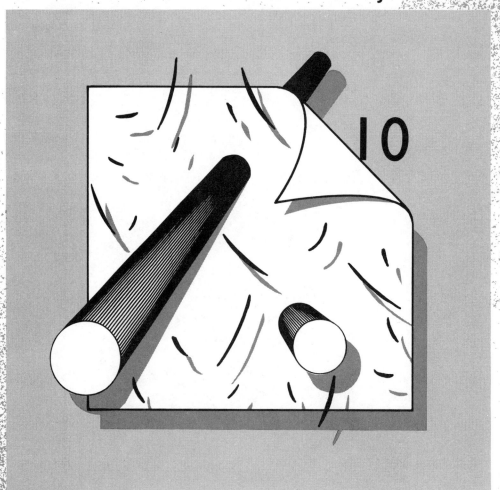

10

Desktop Publishing

- By combining text and graphics functions with sophisticated layout tools, desktop publishing applications provide complete control over the design and production process. Your LaserJet can generate the high-quality output your publications deserve.

In this chapter, we'll cover describe several approaches to desktop publishing with your LaserJet: full-featured Ventura Publisher; Aldus Pagemaker, which takes advantage of the Windows environment; and PFS: First Choice, a modestly priced alternative. These applications include integrated downloaders and installable softfont support.

• *Printing with Ventura Publisher*

Ventura does not have a separate DeskJet driver. Contact the software manufacturer for recent developments.

Xerox's Ventura Publisher is a popular desktop publishing program suitable for documents of all sizes. It uses the Gem graphic interface, which provides a Windows-like environment with pull-down menus, mouse support, and WYSIWYG capabilities. Here, we'll cover Ventura Publisher version 2.0, which has the following LaserJet resources:

- Integrated downloading

- Starter set of printer and screen fonts

- Utility programs to add additional font support

- 150- or 300-dpi resolution

- Cartridge F support

- International symbol set

- Drawing tools and graphics file importing capabilities

The starter set of softfonts and matching screen fonts includes Ventura's own international symbol set, as well as the special Symbol Font set. Table 10.1 lists the fonts in the starter set, and Figure 10.1 shows the symbol sets included.

Accessing Ventura Printer Drivers

Drivers are also included for PostScript, dot-matrix, and Xerox laser printers.

Ventura Publisher is shipped with two drivers for LaserJet printers: PD_HPLM5.SYS for PCL printers at 150 dpi and PD_HPLH5.SYS for PCL printers at 300 dpi.

Separate character width tables are provided for the Hewlett-Packard F cartridge (the only supported cartridge) and the PCL softfonts supplied with Ventura. The width tables for F cartridge fonts are in the HPF.WID

- Table 10.1: *Ventura Printer and Screen Fonts*

TYPE STYLE	POINTS	ATTRIBUTES
Dutch (like Times)	2	Normal
	6	Normal
	8	Normal, Bold
	10	Normal, Bold, Italic
	12	Normal, Bold, Italic
	14	Bold
	18	Bold
	24	Bold
Swiss (like Helvetica)	2	Normal
	6	Normal
	8	Normal, Bold
	10	Normal, Bold, Italic
	12	Normal, Bold, Italic
	14	Bold
	18	Bold
	24	Bold
Courier	10	Normal
Symbol	10	Normal

file, and those for Ventura PCL softfonts are in HPLJPLUS.WID.

In addition, during installation Ventura creates a special text file with a CNF extension, which includes path, download, and ID information for each softfont. This file is only needed if you want to manually download PCL fonts or PostScript softfonts.

When you install Ventura, the appropriate driver, width tables, and CNF file are copied onto your hard-disk directory. The WID table is also copied to a file called OUTPUT.WID, the default width table used by the program. After you select either 150- or 300-dpi printing, the printer and screen fonts are created.

You can add more fonts to the driver or to their own WID file by using utility programs included with the Ventura package. As with other desktop

Standard Fonts		Symbol Font		Standard Fonts		Symbol Font	
32	space	32	space	79	O	79	O
33	!	33	!	80	P	80	Π
34	"	34	∀	81	Q	81	Θ
35	#	35	#	82	R	82	P
36	$	36	∃	83	S	83	Σ
37	%	37	%	84	T	84	T
38	&	38	&	85	U	85	Y
39	'	39	∋	86	V	86	ς
40	(	40	(	87	W	87	Ω
41	)	41	)	88	X	88	Ξ
42	*	42	*	89	Y	89	Ψ
43	+	43	+	90	Z	90	Z
44	,	44	,	91	[	91	[
45	-	45	−	92	\	92	∴
46	.	46	.	93	]	93	]
47	/	47	/	94	^	94	⊥
48	0	48	0	95	_	95	_
49	1	49	1	96	`	96	
50	2	50	2	97	a	97	α
51	3	51	3	98	b	98	β
52	4	52	4	99	c	99	χ
53	5	53	5	100	d	100	δ
54	6	54	6	101	e	101	ε
55	7	55	7	102	f	102	ϕ
56	8	56	8	103	g	103	γ
57	9	57	9	104	h	104	η
58	:	58	:	105	i	105	ι
59	;	59	;	106	j	106	φ
60	<	60	<	107	k	107	κ
61	=	61	=	108	l	108	λ
61	>	61	>	109	m	109	μ
63	?	63	?	110	n	110	ν
64	@	64	≅	111	o	111	o
65	A	65	A	112	p	112	π
66	B	66	B	113	q	113	θ
67	C	67	X	114	r	114	ρ
68	D	68	Δ	115	s	115	σ
69	E	69	E	116	t	116	τ
70	F	70	Φ	117	u	117	υ
71	G	71	Γ	118	v	118	ϖ
72	H	72	H	119	w	119	ω
73	I	73	I	120	x	120	ξ
74	J	74	ϑ	121	y	121	ψ
75	K	75	K	122	z	122	ζ
76	L	76	Λ	123	{	123	{
77	M	77	M	124	|	124	|
78	N	78	N	125	}	125	}

• Figure 10.1: *Ventura symbol sets*

Standard Fonts		Symbol Font		Standard Fonts		Symbol Font	
126	~	126	~	173	¡	173	⊆
127		127		174	«	174	∈
128	Ç	128		175	»	175	∉
129	ü	129	Υ	176	ã	176	∠
130	é	130	′	177	õ	177	∇
131	â	131	≤	178	Ø	178	®
132	ä	132	∕	179	ø	179	©
133	à	133	∞	180	œ	180	™
134	å	134	ƒ	181	Œ	181	∏
135	ç	135	♣	182	À	182	√
136	ê	136	♦	183	Ã	183	·
137	ë	137	♥	184	Õ	184	¬
138	è	138	♠	185	§	185	∧
139	ï	139	↔	186	‡	186	∨
140	î	140	←	187	†	187	⇔
141	ì	141	↑	188	¶	188	⇐
142	Ä	142	→	189	©	189	⇑
143	Å	143	↓	190	®	190	⇒
144	É	144	°	191	™	191	⇓
145	æ	145	±	192	"	192	◊
146	Æ	146	″	193	…	193	⟨
147	ô	147	≥	194	‰	194	®
148	ö	148	×	195	•	195	©
149	ò	149	∝	196	–	196	™
150	û	150	∂	197	—	197	Σ
151	ù	151	•	198	°	198	⎛
152	ÿ	152	÷	199	Á	199	⎜
153	Ö	153	≠	200	Â	200	⎝
154	Ü	154	≡	201	È	201	⎡
155	¢	155	≈	202	Ê	202	⎢
156	£	156	…	203	Ë	203	⎣
157	¥	157			204	Ì	204	⎧
158	¤	158	—	205	Í	205	⎨
159	ƒ	159	↵	206	Î	206	⎩
160	á	160	ℵ	207	Ï	207	⎪
161	í	161	ℑ	208	Ò	208	
162	ó	162	ℜ	209	Ó	209	⎞
163	ú	163	℘	210	Ô	210	⎟
164	ñ	164	⊗	211	Š	211	⎡
165	Ñ	165	⊕	212	š	212	⎢
166	ª	166	∅	213	Ù	213	⎣
167	º	167	∩	214	Ú	214	⎫
168	¿	168	∪	215	Û	215	⎬
169	"	169	⊃	216	Ÿ	216	⎭
170	"	170	⊇	217	ß	217	⎪
171	‹	171	⊄				
172	›	172	⊂				

• Figure 10.1: *Ventura symbol sets (Continued)*

publishing programs, you can't modify the driver beyond adding or deleting support for additional fonts and selecting printing options.

Installing Ventura

Depending on the speed of your system and hard-disk drive, the installation process can take anywhere from a few minutes to a half an hour or more. To start with, the main Ventura program is more than 400,000 bytes and is divided between two floppy disks. You must combine the program into one file on the hard-disk drive, then copy all the associated files and utilities.

The PCL printer fonts are stored in a special compressed format so that they fit on two disk drives. The most time-consuming task of the installation process is to copy and expand these files to their normal state, make screen fonts for each, and then create matching landscape fonts for all the portrait fonts.

Once the program is installed the first time, you can easily add support for additional printers or change your system's configuration.

Here's a review of the installation process:

1. Insert Application Disk #1 into drive A.

2. Type **A:VPPREP**, and then press ◄┘.

3. You'll be asked to confirm the drive letter of your hard disk and indicate if you're installing Ventura for the first time. Respond to these prompts as required.

4. In a series of screens, you'll be prompted to insert a series of disks, then to indicate your display system, the type of mouse and, if appropriate, the port to which it is attached. Next you'll see a list of supported printers, as shown in Figure 10.2.

5. Enter the letter corresponding to your printer. For all models except the original LaserJet, you can select either C or D. (Remember, you must have extra memory to print a full page of graphics at 300 dpi.) If you have the original LaserJet, select B to use internal fonts and the F cartridge.

6. Press ◄┘, and you'll then be asked to enter the interface port.

7. Type the letter corresponding to the port, and then press ◄┘. You'll see the prompt

   Do you want to select another printer? N

All Hewlett-Packard drivers support the internal Courier font.

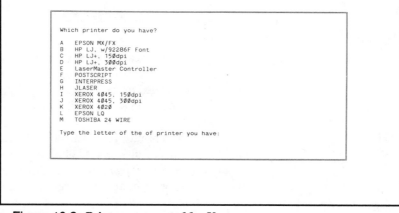

```
Which printer do you have?

A    EPSON MX/FX
B    HP LJ, w/92286F Font
C    HP LJ+, 150dpi
D    HP LJ+, 300dpi
E    LaserMaster Controller
F    POSTSCRIPT
G    INTERPRESS
H    JLASER
I    XEROX 4045, 150dpi
J    XEROX 4045, 300dpi
K    XEROX 4020
L    EPSON LQ
M    TOSHIBA 24 WIRE

Type the letter of the of printer you have:
```

• Figure 10.2: *Printers supported by Ventura*

The first printer you select will be used as the default when you start Ventura, but you can have more than one driver available. Select both the 150- and 300- dpi drivers. Try printing your document at 300 dpi. If you find you don't have enough memory, switch to 150 dpi and try again.

8. Press Y, then repeat steps 5, 6, and 7 for each printer you want to install; or press N to continue with the installation.

9. Follow the instructions given on the screen, inserting the disks requested and responding to the prompts that appear. Finally, you'll see the C: > prompt.

During installation, screen fonts are created matching the printer fonts listed in Table 10.1. The file names indicate the type style and size; their extensions match your display adapter. IBMET08.EGA, for instance, is an 8-point Times screen font for an EGA display.

Adding Softfonts to Ventura

If you want to use softfonts other than those provided, you must have width tables for them. Some softfont manufacturers provide a Ventura width table with their fonts. Look for a file with the WID extension, copy it and the fonts to your Ventura directory, then refer to the section about selecting width tables later in this chapter.

Other suppliers, like Bitstream and Softcraft, provide programs that automatically install the fonts in the driver and create matching screen fonts. These are discussed in Chapter 4.

If you purchased fonts without a width table, you must first create one using the utility programs supplied with Ventura. This is a three-step process:

- Change the font names to match Ventura's naming conventions.
- Create a VFM (Ventura font matrix) file for each softfont.
- Convert the VFM file to a width table.

You use the HPLTOVFM program to create the VFM file and the VFMTOWID program to convert that file to a width table. If you want to create a landscape font from a portrait font, you'll also need to use the PORTOLAN utility. However, you only need to build width tables for portrait fonts because their landscape equivalents use the same table.

As an example, we will go through the procedure for adding SC100RPN.USP, a 10-point script font placed in the public domain by Gary Elfring.

Copying the Files

You begin by copying the appropriate files to your Ventura directory on the hard disk:

This procedure does not create matching screen fonts; it only produces Ventura-compatible printer fonts and tables.

- The softfonts, but rename them, if you have to, with the SFP or SFL extension. In this example, you would rename the file to **SC100RPN.SFP**.
- The HPLTOVFM.EXE file from the HPLJPLUS directory of Ventura Utilities Disk #5.
- The VFMTOWID.EXE file, and PORTOLAN.EXE if you want to create a landscape font from a portrait font, from the root directory of Ventura Utilities Disk #5.

These files may be on different disks in earlier versions of Ventura.

Landscape to Portrait

Use the command PORTOLAN, followed by the name of the portrait font, to convert it to landscape. For our example, entering

        PORTOLAN SC100RPN.SFP

will create a font called SC100RPN.SFL.

Creating a Font Matrix File

Creating a VFM file for each of the portrait fonts is the most complex step because you have to give specific information about each font to the HPLTOVFM program.

The general format is:

```
HPLTOVFM
font-name.SFP/F = typeface-name/N = font-number
ID/P = point-size/W = weight
```

The /F = *typeface-name* switch specifies the name of the font you want to appear on the Font pull-down menu.

The /N = *font-number* ID switch specifies the font's unique ID number. Appendix K of the Ventura manual lists the ID numbers that have already been assigned to certain fonts. Here are some common ones:

ID Number	Font
1	Courier
2	Helvetica
14	Times
20	Century Schoolbook
21	Palatino
22	Garamond
23	Bookman

Font ID numbers 1 through 14 are reserved for Ventura's own fonts. If you're installing another font that has an assigned ID number, use that number in the command line. Otherwise, select a font ID that has not yet been assigned using these rules:

ID Number	Font Type
40 to 49	Serif fonts
61 to 99	Sans serif fonts
106 to 127	Monospaced fonts
131 to 255	All others

Ventura recommends starting with the higher numbers in the range when installing new fonts.

The /P = *point-size* switch specifies the point size of the font in two numbers. For example, enter 06 for a 6-point font.

The /W = *weight* switch uses N for normal, B for bold, I for italic, or T for bold italic.

To create a VFM file for the new font SC100RPN, the command line would look like this:

```
HPLTOVFM  SC100RPN.SFP/F = Script /N = 99
ID/P = 10/W = N
```

Creating a Width Table

The VFMTOWID program gets its input from a text file listing the VFM files to convert. Before you use the program to create a width table, you must create the text file. Follow these steps:

To create a width table with several fonts, include their VFM file names in the text file.

1. Type **COPY CON: SCRIPT.LST**, and then press ↵.

2. Type the font's VFM file name, and then press ↵. For our example, enter **SC100RPN.VFM**.

3. Press Ctrl-Z, then ↵. The file SCRIPT.LST is now on your disk, so you can create the width table.

4. Type **VFMTOWID SCRIPT.LST**, and then press ↵. You'll see the prompt

   Creating width table (script.wid)

   The word Finished will appear when the width table named SCRIPT.WID is completed.

This completes the procedure for adding the softfont. It is now available for use in Ventura documents.

Selecting Ventura Width Tables and Printer Drivers

Within Ventura, you can change from the default width table (OUT-PUT.WID) to any font width table you have available. You can also switch to a different driver. These changes are made through the Set Printer Info option on Ventura's Options menu. Select this option to display the dialog box shown in Figure 10.3. It contains the following options:

You can also merge tables to combine your own fonts with those provided by Ventura, as explained in the next section.

- **Device Name:** The printer drivers available. Figure 10.3 includes drivers for 150 and 300 dpi on the LaserJet, PostScript printers, and the LaserMaster interface card.

- **Screen Fonts**: The file extension for screen font files.

- **Output To**: The communications port. Select Filename to save the printer file to disk.

- **Width Table**: The active width table.

- **Command**: The option for changing to another width table.

To select a different width table, click on the box following the Command option to display a list of available width tables. Figure 10.4 shows a sample listing. Double-click on the width table you want to use, and then click on OK to return to the Ventura screen.

To use a different driver, click on the Device Name option. For best results, make sure the width table corresponds to the printer driver. If the default printer is a LaserJet (either 150 or 300 dpi), OUTPUT.WID can be used for both. But if you change to a different type of printer, select the appropriate width table, such as POSTSCPT.WID for the PostScript driver.

Combining Fonts in Width Tables

Having a large number of width tables that only support one or a few fonts is not very efficient. The best method is to merge the tables together into one, so all the fonts are available at the same time. Merge them with OUTPUT.WID to add them to the default fonts.

If you want to merge a table with OUTPUT.WID, just start Ventura and follow the steps below. Otherwise, use the Set Printer dialog box to

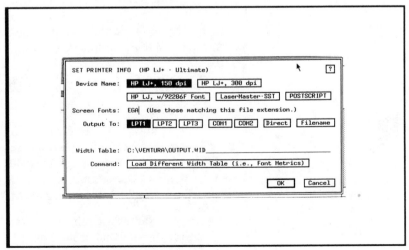

- Figure 10.3: *Ventura Set Printer Info dialog box*

select the first of the width tables to be merged, as described in the previous section, and then follow these steps to merge other tables with it.

1. Pull down the Options menu and click on Add/Remove Fonts to see the dialog box shown in Figure 10.5. The fonts available in the current width table will appear in the Face box on the left.

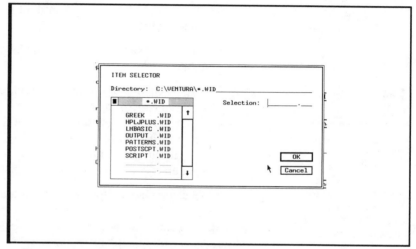

• Figure 10.4: *Sample Ventura width table listing*

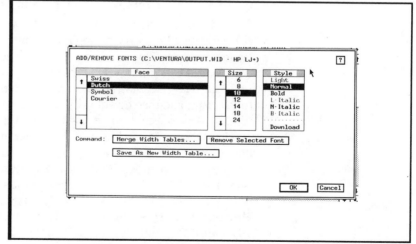

• Figure 10.5: *Ventura Add/Remove Fonts dialog box*

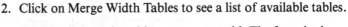
2. Click on Merge Width Tables to see a list of available tables.

3. Double-click on the table you want to add. The fonts in the merged table will now be listed in the Face box.

4. Delete any fonts you don't want in the resulting width table: Click on the Face, Size, and Style options, then on Remove Selected Font.

5. Repeat steps 2 through 4 until all the fonts you want in the new table are listed.

6. Click on Save As New Width Table to again display a list of width tables.

7. Type the name of a new width table then click on OK, or double-click on an existing table name. If you save a new table with the same name as an existing one, you'll be prompted to use another name or overwrite the existing file. Click on Overwrite to replace the current width table with that name, or click on New Name, type another file name, and then click on OK.

8. Click on OK to return to the Ventura window.

If you named the new table anything other than OUTPUT.WID, use the Set Printer Info dialog box to load it.

You can save the merged width table as OUT-PUT.WID. As long as the original table, such as HPLJPLUS, is not modified, you can always copy it to OUTPUT.WID to return to the default fonts.

Downloading Fonts for Ventura

The Style list box in the Add/Remove Fonts dialog box (select Add/Remove Fonts from the Options menu) includes the Download/Resident toggle. This means that you can select to have the listed font downloaded by Ventura when needed.

Since downloading takes time, you might want to change this setting to Resident, and then download your fonts manually before starting Ventura. This is especially time-saving if you use several applications that require the same softfonts. Load them once at the beginning of the day to have them available to all your programs.

To set a font as Resident, click on the font name, size, and style of the font. Then click on Download to change the setting to Resident.

When you use the font in a document, it won't be downloaded. However, Ventura has to know the ID number you used when you manually loaded the font. The font ID numbers are listed as Permfont entries in HPLJPLUS.CNF, a plain text file that contains information about resident fonts.

Use a word processing program to add a line to the beginning of the file in this format:

permfont(*Download-ID Fontname*)

For example, if you plan on manually downloading the 12-point Times Normal font as ID 1, add this line:

permfont(1 TMSN3012.SFP)

All the Ventura fonts are also listed as Fontspec entries in the CNF file. The Fontspec entry will be consulted by the driver if the font is flagged as Resident and included in a Permfont command. If you change the font back to Download status, just delete the Permfont entry—leave the Font-spec command there in case you ever need it again.

When you add your own softfont to the CNF file, such as SC100RPN.SFP, you must add a Fontspec entry as well as a Permfont entry:

permfont(2 SC100RPN.SFP)
fontspec(SC100RPN,99,10,0,0)

The file name in the Fontspec entry is followed by its Ventura ID number and point size. The third number indicates its weight: 0 for normal, 1 for bold, or 4 for italic. Make the last number 0.

Finally, be sure to save the edited file in ASCII, or plain text, format.

Using Fonts with Ventura

All the fonts available in the loaded width table can be used in your document. You select a font by either changing the font of the paragraph tag or by setting another font for the text:

- In the Paragraph Tag mode, select a paragraph, pull down the Paragraph menu, and then click on Font.

- In text-editing mode, highlight the text you want to format, and then click on Set Font.

You'll see a dialog box listing the fonts available. Figure 10.6 shows the fonts available in the table merging the SCRIPT and OUT-PUT files for the LaserJet.

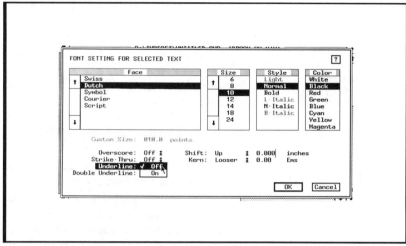

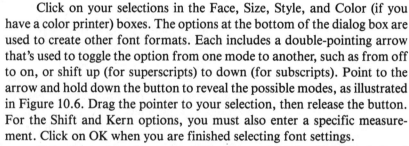

- Figure 10.6: *Ventura Font dialog box*

Certain options in the Size and Style boxes will turn gray, others black. Selections in gray are not available for that font.

Click on your selections in the Face, Size, Style, and Color (if you have a color printer) boxes. The options at the bottom of the dialog box are used to create other font formats. Each includes a double-pointing arrow that's used to toggle the option from one mode to another, such as from off to on, or shift up (for superscripts) to down (for subscripts). Point to the arrow and hold down the button to reveal the possible modes, as illustrated in Figure 10.6. Drag the pointer to your selection, then release the button. For the Shift and Kern options, you must also enter a specific measurement. Click on OK when you are finished selecting font settings.

If the font selected has a matching screen font, it will be loaded and used to display the characters on the screen. Other fonts will be displayed in the default screen font.

You set line spacing and leading through the Spacing option on the Paragraph pull-down menu. This displays the dialog box shown in Figure 10.7. Enter a point size for the Inter-Line option to control leading between lines in a paragraph.

Controlling Paper Size and Orientation through Ventura

Ventura provides a number of dialog boxes that allow you to precisely control the layout and spacing of pages. Four of the most common settings are in the dialog box displayed by the Page Size and Layout option on the Chapter pull-down menu, shown in Figure 10.8.

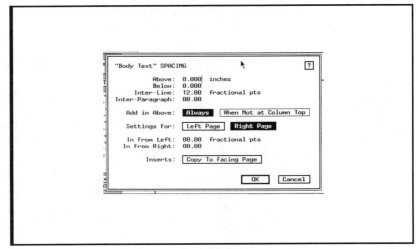

• Figure 10.7: *Ventura Spacing dialog box*

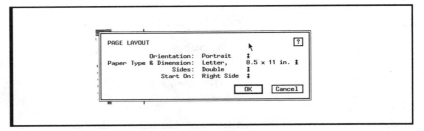

• Figure 10.8: *Ventura Page Layout dialog box*

Point to the double-pointing arrow following the option you want to change, and then hold down the mouse button to display alternatives. For example, the Paper Type & Dimensions option lists the following selections:

- **Half**: 5.5 by 8.5 inches

- **Letter**: 8.5 by 11 inches

- **Legal**: 8.5 by 14 inches

- **Double**: 11 by 17 inches

- **B5**: 17.6 by 25 centimeters

- **A4**: 21 by 29.7 centimeters

- **Broad Sheet**: 18 by 24 inches

Drag the pointer to your choice and release the mouse button. Click on OK after you've set the options.

Setting Ventura Printing Options

When you're ready to print the document, pull down the File menu and click on To Print to see the Print Information dialog box, shown in Figure 10.9. Enter your settings or select options using the selection arrows, as described in Table 10.2. Click on OK to start printing, or click on Cancel to remove the dialog box.

PostScript Printing with Ventura

If your LaserJet is equipped for PostScript printing, use the Post-Script driver in the PD_POSTS.SYS file. The POSTSCPT.WID width table supports the standard resident fonts found in Apple Laserwriter and compatible printers, as well as a number of softfonts.

If you purchase additional softfonts, store them in a directory called PSFONTS because the first line of the PostScript CNF file is

PSFONTS(C:\PSFONTS)

If you want to store PostScript fonts in some other directory, use a word processor to change the path on the PSFONTS command line.

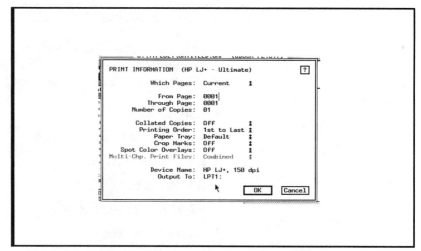

• Figure 10.9: *Ventura Print Information dialog box*

- Table 10.2: *Ventura Print Information Menu Options*

OPTION	SETTING
Which Pages	Choose All, Selection, Left, Right, or Current.
From Page Through Page	If you are printing selected pages, enter the starting and ending page numbers at the appropriate prompt.
Number of Copies	Enter the number of copies you want of each page.
Collated Copies	If you are printing multiple copies, set Collate On to print each entire copy separately. When set at Off, all the first pages will be printed, then all second pages, etc.
Printing Order	If your printer outputs pages in reverse order, set this option to Last to 1st for correct output order.
Paper Tray	Select from Default (continuous), Alt #1, Alt #2, or Manual. With the LaserJet 500 +, IID, and 2000, use default for tray 1 and Alt #1 for tray 2. Use Alt #2 for the LaserJet 2000's third tray.
Crop Marks	Set On to print short lines indicating the edges of the paper. These can be used to cut the final page down to size or for aligning various colors for commercial printing.
Spot Color Overlays	Set Yes to print a separate page for each color. If you have text in black and red, for example, one sheet will print with just the text marked black, a second page for red. Your commercial printer can use them to produce the final two-color job.
Multi-Chp Print Files	This is only active if you select to print to a file. It determines if multichapter documents are to be combined to one file or a separate file should be used for each chapter.

You can create Ventura VFM files from Adobe AFM fonts using the AFMTOVFM program in the PostScript directory of Utilities Disk #5. The syntax is

```
AFMTOVFM filename.AFM/F = Typeface-name/N = Ventura
ID#/W = weight
```

Refer to the section about adding softfonts for details.

You must also convert Adobe screen fonts to Ventura format before using them. Do this with the ABFTOFNT program, which is also on Utilities Disk #5. Make sure the screen fonts have the ABF extension, then use this command:

ABFTOFNT *filename*.ABF/F = *Typeface-name*/N = *Ventura*
ID#/W = *weight*

Screen font files ending with a PSF extension will be created. So be sure to enter PSF in the Screen Fonts option of the Set Printer Info dialog box.

Finally, you can speed up PostScript printing by about 10 seconds by preloading the Prologue file before starting Ventura. Normally, each time you print to a PostScript printer, the file PS2.PS—over 12,000 bytes long—is transmitted to the printer. Delete PS2.PRE from the Ventura directory, then copy PERMVP.PS from Utilities Disk #5. Before starting Ventura, enter this line from the DOS prompt (or add it to your AUTOEXEC file), replacing LPT1 with your own port indicator:

COPY \VENTURA\PERMVP.PS LPT1:

• *Printing with Aldus Pagemaker*

Bitstream fonts are discussed in Chapter 4.

Aldus Pagemaker earned its solid reputation in the Macintosh world. Now, as a Windows application, Pagemaker uses the printer driver and screen fonts in that environment. The package includes a run-time version of Windows. Version 3 of Pagemaker also comes with the Bitstream Fontware package for installing printer and screen fonts.

Pagemaker does not include a separate DeskJet driver. Contact the software manufacturer for recent developments.

Pagemaker comes with its own installation program and printer drivers, but you set up the program just as you would Microsoft Windows, discussed in Chapter 7. Use the Install program to select the driver; then use the Printer Setup procedure to select the communications port, install fonts, and select printer options. Use the Pagemaker printer drivers even if you've already set up the ones supplied with Windows. Once in Pagemaker, you can change the driver and install fonts by selecting Printer Setup from the File pull-down menu or Setup from the Print dialog box.

Controlling Page Size and Orientation through Pagemaker

When you start a new Pagemaker document (or select the Page Setup option from the File pull-down menu), you can set the size and shape of the

You can change the default driver, listed as the target printer in the Page Setup dialog box, by using the Printer Setup option on the File pull-down menu.

page through the Page Setup dialog box, shown in Figure 10.10.

Select from the page setup options as follows:

- **Page size**: Select one of the standard sizes shown or enter custom dimensions for the width and length. Even if your printer can handle only a maximum size of 8½ by 11 inches, you can lay out larger documents and print them in sections by tiling, as explained later in the chapter.

- **Orientation**: Choose Tall (portrait) or Wide (landscape).

- **Start page#**: Set the number of the current page. When printing facing pages of a double-sided document, make this an even number to place the page on the left side.

- **# of pages**: This keeps track of the size of your publication.

- **Options**: If you choose Double-sided, the inside and outside margins will automatically adjust for left and right pages. Select Facing Pages to display left and right pages at the same time.

- **Margins**: Enter a new value for the inside, outside, top, and bottom margins.

Using Pagemaker Screen Fonts

As explained in Chapter 7, Windows is supplied with a number of screen fonts that can be scaled to a variety of sizes. If you're using a printer

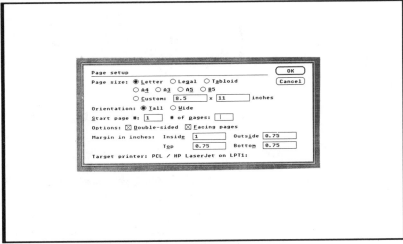

• Figure 10.10: *Pagemaker Page Setup dialog box*

Installing screen fonts is discussed in Chapter 4.

Greeked is a Pagemaker term for using shaded blocks to represent text.

font that's not matched by a specifically installed screen font, Windows applications will display the built-in font that most resembles it in its place: bit-mapped fonts for Times and Helvetica and vector fonts Roman, Modern, and Script for all others.

In Pagemaker, the display of screen fonts also depends on the page view selected, the point size of the screen font, and the settings in the Preferences dialog box.

The Pagemaker page view can be set to actual size; 75, 50, or 200 percent of the actual page; or reduced to fit in the window, the default setting. In the actual-size page view, Pagemaker will use the screen font that is the same size as the printer file. A 24-point screen font will be displayed for 24-point Times, for example. Figure 10.11 shows three type styles shown in their matching screen fonts—30, 24, and 18 points—in the actual-size page view.

When you change the display to 75 percent, Pagemaker will look for screen fonts 75 percent the printer font size, such as an 18-point screen font in the same family as the 24-point printer font. If it doesn't find a font in this size, the text will appear as shown in Figure 10.12. The greeked areas are in place of the text in 30-point Cooper Black and 18-point Universal Roman, fonts without matching screen fonts at 75 percent size. The characters in Times are displayed because an 18-point screen font existed.

You can use two different approaches to see your text at different display sizes:

- Create a range of screen fonts in various sizes. This is relatively common when you have a full set of printer fonts (such as Times in

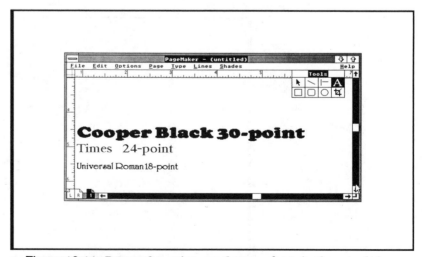

- Figure 10.11: *Pagemaker printer and screen fonts in the actual-size page view*

6, 8, 10, 12, 14, 18, and 24 points) and use a utility program to generate matching screen fonts for each one.

- Use the bit-map and vector fonts supplied with Windows. You won't get a true WYSIWYG display, but the built-in fonts will be used for all page views.

The screen font display is also controlled by the settings in the Preferences dialog box, which is accessed from the Edit pull-down menu. Figure 10.13 shows a sample Preferences dialog box with the following settings for screen fonts:

- All text below 6 points will be greeked.

- Characters between 30 and 72 points will be displayed by "stretching" the largest available matching screen font, if one the specific size is not provided. If no matching font is available, the built-in fonts will be substituted.

- Characters above 72 points will be replaced with vector fonts, even if suitable screen fonts have been created.

With these settings, if you have screen fonts up to 24 points for a particular type style, here's how a 24-point font would be displayed in the various

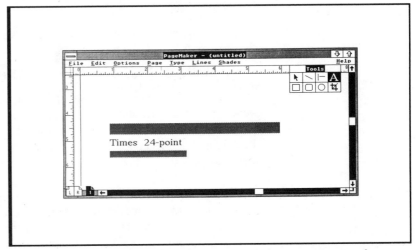

- Figure 10.12: *In Pagemaker's 75 percent view, some screen fonts are greeked*

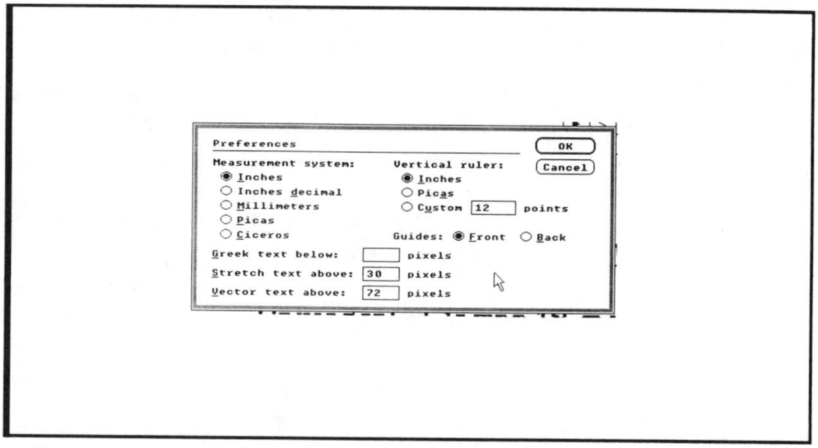

• Figure 10.13: *Pagemaker Preferences dialog box*

page views:

Actual size	24 points
75 percent	18 points
50 percent	12 points
Fit to page	6 points
200 percent	24-point font stretched to 48 points

Using Fonts with Pagemaker

By default, Pagemaker uses the internal Courier font. When you want to enter text in another font or reformat existing characters, press Ctrl-T or select Type Specs from the Type pull-down menu to display the Type Specifications dialog box, shown in Figure 10.14. Unlike Ami, Pagemaker doesn't show a preview sample of the font, but it does list each available font and size.

Click on the desired font and size—you may have to scroll through the selection boxes to display additional choices—then select the appropriate Type Style, Position, or Case options. Set leading by entering a specific point size at the Leading prompt or use Auto leading, which is by default a line height 120 percent the size of the largest font on the line. Using Auto leading and 10-point type, for example, the total line height will be 12 points. You can modify the

Reverse type will not print on a PCL printer. Small caps will be capital letters 70 percent of the selected font size.

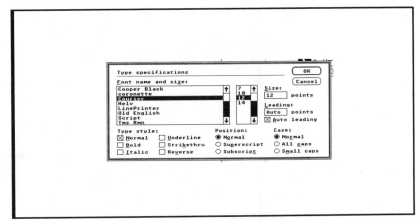

• Figure 10.14: *Pagemaker Type Specifications dialog box*

default Auto leading value in the Spacing dialog box, accessed from the Type pull-down menu. Click on OK when you're finished making selections.

The text you enter (or characters highlighted when you made your changes) will be displayed according to the screen fonts available and the other factors discussed in the previous section. The fonts will be downloaded when needed.

Printing Pagemaker Documents

Your own Print dialog box may contain different printers, depending on how you set up Windows and Pagemaker. If your printer isn't listed, click on Setup to install or modify the correct driver.

When you're ready to print your document, select Print from the File pull-down menu to see the dialog box shown in Figure 10.15. The page size and orientation set in the Page Setup dialog box are shown at the lower-right corner of the window.

In the example shown in Figure 10.15, the shaded options are not available for the selected printer, the HP LaserJet family, but would be if the Post-Script printer was selected. Since the possible selections depend on the printer, click on your printer first if it is not already selected.

Make your selections, as described in the following sections, and then click on OK to start printing (or choose Cancel to return to the document screen). Once printing starts, you'll see a dialog box with the Cancel option, which you can select to stop printing.

Standard Printing Options

The Print dialog box contains the following standard options:

• **Copies**: Enter the number of copies you want of each page.

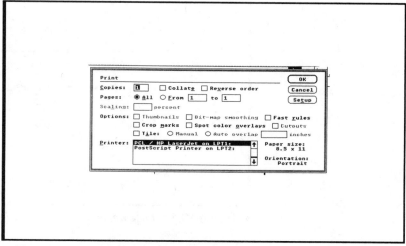

• Figure 10.15: *Pagemaker Print dialog box*

- **Collate**: If you are printing multiple copies, select this option to print each entire copy separately. Without collating, all the first pages will be printed, then all the second, etc.

- **Reverse**: If you have a printer that outputs the paper in reverse order, select this option to start printing at the last page, so the document will be output in the correct order.

- **Pages**: Enter the range of pages to be printed.

- **Scaling**: For PostScript printers only, enter a value to reduce or enlarge the printed page from 25 to 1000 percent of the original size.

Customized Printing Options

The choices listed next to Options in the Print dialog box allow you to customize the way the document appears. They include the following selections:

- **Thumbnail**: For PostScript printers only, prints a miniature copy of each page, numbered and shown in facing pages. Use this option to see a "dummy" of multipage documents.

- **Bit-map smoothing**: Adds extra dots to graphic images created with painting programs.

- **Fast rules**: For PCL printers only, speeds up the printing process if you have nonoverlapping objects and no cutouts.

If you're familiar with pasteup and color printing, you can also manually add registration marks and use the color palette to assign them the Registration color. The marks will be printed on all overlays, regardless of color.

- **Crop marks**: Prints short lines indicating the edges of the paper. These can be used to cut the final page down to size or for aligning various colors for commercial printing.

- **Spot color overlays**: Prints a separate page for each color. If you have text in black and red, for example, one sheet will print with just the text marked black, a second page for red. Your commercial printer can use them to produce a final two-color job.

- **Cutouts**: For PostScript printers only, prints spot color overlays so overlapping objects are cut out of the underlying color.

- **Tile**: Prints oversized pages in sections, each section on one sheet of paper, as illustrated in Figure 10.16. Manual tiling uses your zero-point to determine where each tile begins and ends. Use this method to make sure a graphic prints entirely in one tile. Auto Overlap divides the document into sections by itself, but overlaps the sections as set in the Inches option. The printed tiles can then be joined together for display or reproduction.

Printing Pagemaker Graphics

Pagemaker, like most desktop publishers, lets you combine graphics with text to produce professional-looking documents. The graphics can be

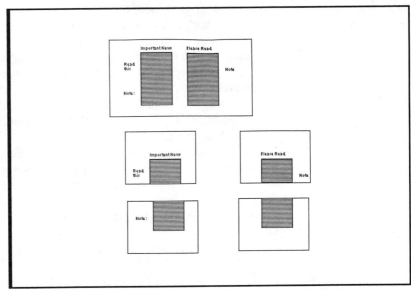

Figure 10.16: *Oversized documents can be printed in tiles*

the following types:

- Line graphics created with Pagemaker drawing tools

- Bit-map drawings produced with programs such as Windows Paint, PC Paint, and PC Paintbrush

- Object-oriented graphics, such as Lotus PIC and AutoCAD files, or drawings from programs like Windows Draw and Gem Draw

- Encapsulated PostScript (EPS) graphics—images created using a PostScript language program

- Scanned graphics, either bit mapped or halftone saved in TIFF format

Bit-map drawings may be distorted if scaled.

You import graphics by using the Place option on the File pull-down menu. All graphic images can be moved or copied, overlapped over text and other graphics, cropped, and resized. Remember that you'll need extra memory to print a full page of graphics at 300 dpi.

Using Scanned Images

In this discussion, the term *screen* refers to a pattern of dots or lines used to represent shades of gray, not the resolution of the video monitor.

Pagemaker provides a special feature for improving the appearance of scanned bit-map, gray scale, and halftone graphics. By selecting Image Control from the Options pull-down menu, you can adjust the lightness, contrast, and screen pattern (including both screen angle and lines-per-inch resolution) of the image.

A halftone, or screened image, is one in which the levels of gray are reproduced by various patterns of dots or lines. While this is similar to bit mapping, the screen resolution is a different setting than the dpi at which the LaserJet will print. Higher screen frequency settings in the Image Control dialog box result in less "grainy" images but fewer levels of gray.

Pagemaker automatically screens scanned images at 53 lines per inch. If you have special high-resolution equipment on your LaserJet, such as a LaserMaster card, increase the screen frequency to 90 or more.

In some cases, you might be scanning an already screened image, such as a photograph from a newspaper or magazine. These are harder to print because the Pagemaker screen pattern might cause unsightly patterns when superimposed over the original screen. Adjust the frequency and screen angle and test print the graphic until it appears satisfactory.

• *Printing with PFS: First Publisher*

For about one-quarter the cost of Pagemaker, First Publisher offers some sophisticated desktop publishing features. Although it is not as powerful and complete as Pagemaker or Ventura Publisher, the program is very useful for flyers, brochures, short newsletters, and similar publications.

Version 2 of First Publisher can import text files directly from popular word processing programs. But of more importance here, it can install Hewlett-Packard and third-party softfonts, and even creates its own screen fonts. Version 2.1 and later comes with Bitstream Fontware.

Accessing First Publisher Printer Drivers

When you install the program and designate your printer with the Printer program, a file called FPPRINT.DEF is created. This file contains driver information about your printer, such as the model number, port, and which cartridge you are using.

In addition to the printer file, you need one called MASTER.FNT that contains font definitions. The MASTER.FNT file supplied with First Publisher contains the dot-matrix font drivers. The other font drivers included with the program are HPLASER.FNT for PCL printers (on Program Disk 2) and APLASER.FNT for PostScript printers (on the Laser Support disk).

First Publisher always uses the file called MASTER.FNT for font information. To use the LaserJet fonts, you must rename the original MASTER.FNT file (DOTMATRX.FNT, for example), saving it for future use, and then rename the HPLASER.FNT file MASTER.FNT.

Installing Additional First Publisher Fonts

The program's LaserJet driver initially supports only internal fonts and the Hewlett-Packard B and F cartridges. If you don't have softfonts, you can add the lower resolution dot-matrix fonts to the driver. Even though First Publisher will smooth the rough edges somewhat, the fonts will not print as well as bit-mapped laser fonts. But, it's a viable alternative if you don't have softfonts.

If you do have softfonts, you can install them and even combine them with dot-matrix fonts. To install additional fonts, you use the Fontmove program supplied with the First Publisher software.

Adding Dot-Matrix Fonts

Follow these steps to add First Publisher's dot-matrix fonts to your MASTER.FNT file:

1. Type **FONTMOVE**, and then press ←┘. You'll see the Fontmove Main menu, as shown in Figure 10.17.

The DeskJet driver is DESKJET.FNT (on Program Disk 2).

If you have a floppy-disk system, copy the appropriate driver file to your working disk, then rename it MASTER.FNT.

With floppy-disk systems, place your working copy of Program Disk 1 in drive A and the Fonts Disk in drive B. When entering file names during this procedure, always include the drive letter. You might have to swap disks at certain points.

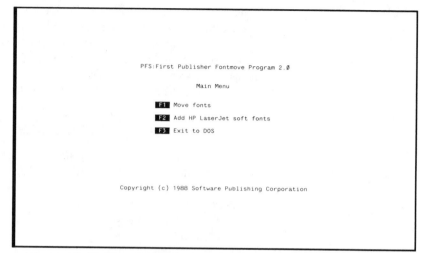

• Figure 10.17: *First Publisher Fontmove Main menu*

2. Press F1 to select Move Fonts.

3. Press F2, type **B:** (or the drive where your Fonts disk is located), and then press ←┘.

4. Press F3, type **MASTER.FNT**, and then press ←┘ to display a list of available dot-matrix fonts.

5. Press F4 to select Destination, type **A:MASTER.FNT**, and then press ←┘.

6. Use the arrow keys to highlight the font you want to install, and then press F6 to select Copy.

7. Repeat step 6 for all the fonts you want to add.

Adding Softfont Support

To add softfont support, note the drive and directory where the soft-fonts are stored. Then follow these steps:

1. From the First Publisher directory, type **FONTMOVE**, and then press ←┘. You'll see the Fontmove Main menu (Figure 10.17).

2. Press F2 to select Add HP LaserJet Softfonts. You'll see the menu shown in Figure 10.18.

3. Type the path and name of the softfont you want to install, such as C:\PCLFONTS\SC120RPN.USP, and then press ↓.

4. Type **MASTER.FNT**, and then press ↓.

5. Type a name you want to use to select the font from within First Publisher, such as Script, and then press ↓.

6. Type the path of the First Publisher program, and then press ⏎.

7. Repeat steps 3 through 6 until all your fonts are installed, and then press Esc.

The program will insert the necessary font information and width table into MASTER.FNT and create a screen font. Figure 10.19 shows an example of the screen font created for the 30-point Cooper Black Outline font.

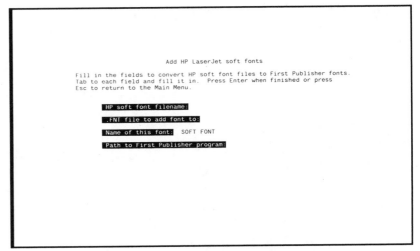

• Figure 10.18: *Menu used to add First Publisher softfonts*

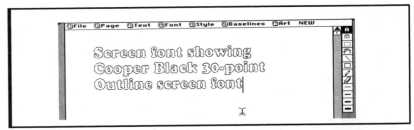

• Figure 10.19: *Screen fonts for First Publisher are automatically created when printer fonts are added*

First Publisher Layout Features

First Publisher is an easy-to-use program that only supports portrait orientation. Text is manipulated by moving, expanding, or reducing the baselines on which characters rest. It's a page-oriented program, so text doesn't flow smoothly from one page to the next. You must start a new page (press Shift-+) when the current page is full (you'll hear a beep).

Line and box drawing tools are provided, as well as the ability to import graphics files from PC Paintbrush, PC Paint, Microsoft Windows Paint, Publisher's Paintbrush, and LogiPaint. Scanned images (with a density of 72 dpi) can be stored in one of these file formats and read into First Publisher. Macintosh MacPaint files can also be imported if first transferred to an IBM-formatted disk. In fact, a sampling of MacPaint art files is provided (in .MAC files), along with a series of converted Macintosh fonts (in the EXTRA.FNT file).

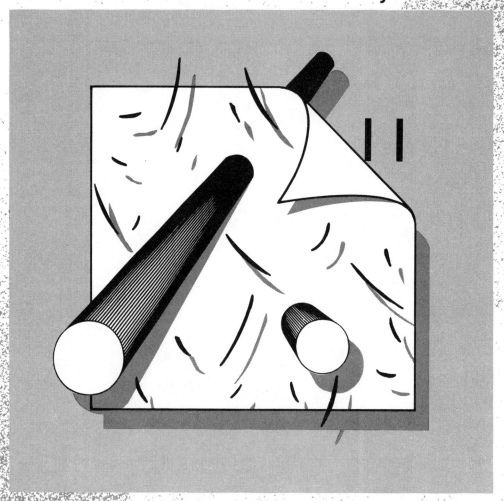

Database Publishing with dBASE

• The goal of database publishing is to produce professional-looking reports and other types of output from your data. With the LaserJet, this means printing in different fonts, orientations, and character styles.

Fortunately, dBASE IV comes with installable printer drivers that can print in portrait or landscape orientation, as well as in boldface, underline, subscript, superscript, and italics. You can also define five fonts by entering PCL commands in the program's configuration file.

Earlier versions of dBASE don't include printer drivers. However, there are a number of ways to access printing features.

• *Accessing Printing Features with Earlier dBASE Versions*

With the LaserJet II, LaserJet IID, and LaserJet 2000, you can select the font, symbol set, page size, and orientation from the control panel. However, you still have to adjust the dBASE report or label forms.

With all releases of dBASE, you can write small programs that set up the LaserJet, then format standard reports and labels to print properly. You can use this technique to print in landscape, select fonts and paper sizes, and even to print envelopes and labels. If you're an experienced dBASE programmer (or learning to be one), you can create complex command files that produce very professional-looking reports.

Another option is export your data to other programs that have more sophisticated printer drivers. For example, dBASE reports can be saved as text files on disk then transferred into Ventura Publisher or Pagemaker. The database itself can even be imported into merge files for creating form documents with programs such as WordPerfect. Still another alternative is to import the database into Lotus 1-2-3, then format and print it using add-on packages such as Always, described in Chapter 12, or database publishing programs such as DB Publisher from Digital Composition Systems.

If you have a version earlier than dBASE IV, skip to the section about programming with PCL commands later in the chapter. Don't worry if you've never written a dBASE program before. Most of the examples in this chapter are just a few lines long.

• *Accessing dBASE IV Printer Drivers*

The dBASE IV package includes four LaserJet printer drivers:

dBASE III Plus does not include printer drivers.

Driver File Name	Default Setup
HPLAS100.PR2	Portrait orientation, 100-dpi graphics
HPLASL.PR2	Landscape orientation, no graphics

Driver File Name	Default Setup
HPLAS2I.PR2	Portrait orientation, 300-dpi graphics (designed for the LaserJet II)
HPLAS2ID.PR2	Portrait orientation, 300-dpi graphics, duplex mode (designed for the LaserJet IID)

The DeskJet driver, HPDSK150, supports portrait orientation in 16, 10, and 12 pitch. Features include boldface, italic, underlining, superscripts and subscripts, and graphics at 150 dpi. Perforation skip is enabled for 60 lines per page.

The major differences between the drivers are orientation, the character formats available, and the default setup commands transmitted to the printer. Table 11.1 lists the features supported by the drivers.

All the printer drivers can be used with any LaserJet model, although you may not be able to access all the features. For example, if you have a LaserJet + with the A cartridge installed, you can print italics using the HPLAS2I.PR2 driver, even though that driver is designed for the LaserJet II. The HPLAS100.PR2 driver doesn't print italics (the text is underlined instead). If you use the HPLAS2ID.PR2 driver with the LaserJet +, the printer will ignore the duplex commands.

No facilities are provided for modifying the driver itself. However, if you have a utility program such as Debug or PCTools that lets you display

• Table 11.1: *Features Supported by dBASE IV Drivers*

FEATURE	HPLAS100	HPLASL	HPLAS2I	HPLAS2ID
Orientation	P	L	P	P
10 pitch	Yes	Yes	Yes	Yes
12 pitch	Yes	Yes	Yes	Yes
16 pitch	No	Yes	Yes	Yes
Bold	Yes	Yes	Yes	Yes
Italic	No	No	Yes	Yes
Underline	Yes	Yes	Yes	Yes
Superscript	Yes	Yes	Yes	Yes
Subscript	Yes	Yes	Yes	Yes
Graphics dpi	100	None	300	300
Character set	Roman-8	Roman-8	PC-8	PC-8

and change data directly on the disk, you could edit the driver; for example, you could add italic support in landscape orientation.

• *Installing dBASE IV*

When you install dBASE IV, you can designate up to four printer drivers. Two additional ones, for generic and ASCII printers, will also be copied onto the hard disk. Follow these steps to install your printer:

1. Insert the Installation disk in drive A, type **INSTALL**, and then press ←.

2. Follow the instructions on the screen until you see the Hardware Setup menu, shown in Figure 11.1.

3. Press ↓ to highlight Printers, and then press ← to see the printer selection screen.

4. Press Shift-F1 to display a list of available printers.

5. Press ↓ to scroll through the list until Hewlett-Packard is highlighted, and then press ← to see a list of alternative models and drivers, as shown in Figure 11.2.

6. Highlight one of the LaserJet selections, and check the name of the driver listed in the box to the right. When the driver you want to use appears, press ←. You'll return to the printer selection screen.

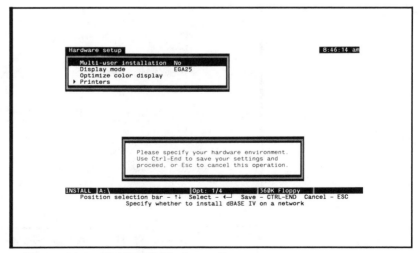

• Figure 11.1: *dBASE IV Hardware Setup menu*

Your HP LaserJet Handbook

7. Type the port (for example, LPT1 or COM1), and then press Shift-F1 to select another driver.

8. Repeat steps 4 through 6 for each driver you want to include. Figure 11.3 shows the printer selection screen after all four LaserJet drivers were added.

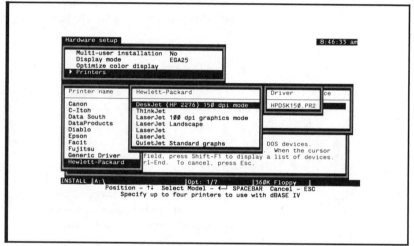

• Figure 11.2: *dBASE IV printer model and driver lists*

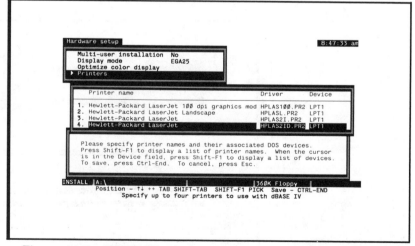

• Figure 11.3: *dBASE IV printer selection screen with LaserJet drivers installed*

9. Press Ctrl-End to save the configuration and display the default printer screen, as shown in Figure 11.4.

10. Highlight the driver you want to use as the default, and then press ◄─┘.

11. In a series of screens, you will be prompted to insert various disks in drive A. Follow the instructions given to complete the installation.

You can change printer drivers within dBASE.

When you're done, dBASE IV and the selected drivers will be on your hard disk. So will the file CONFIG.DB, which contains, among other default settings, a list of your installed printers. You can modify this file to change drivers or add fonts by using the DBSETUP program on the Installation disk or by editing the file with a word processor, as discussed later in the chapter.

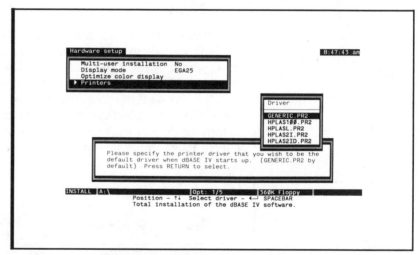

• Figure 11.4: *dBASE IV default printer screen*

Instead of specifying menu options, the instructions here are entered from the dot prompt (a single dot at the left edge of the screen). Display the dot prompt by pressing Esc Y (with dBASE III Plus, just press Esc), type the command shown, and then press ◄─┘. Redisplay the menus by entering Assist.

• *Changing dBASE IV Printer Drivers*

Any of the drivers you installed when you set up the program can be selected from the dot prompt. dBASE provides a special variable, _pdriver, which contains the name of the printer driver. If you enter

? _pdriver

at the dot prompt, you'll see the name of the current driver.

To change drivers, just assign the variable a new driver name. For example, to change to the driver that supports landscape orientation, enter this at the dot prompt

_pdriver = "HPLASL.PR2"

and dBASE will respond with:

Printer driver installed
HPLASL.PR2

• *Changing the Text Pitch with dBASE IV*

You can select from the available text pitches for a report when you create its form through the report form generator. The other printing features supported by the driver, such as boldface and underlining, must be included in a dBASE program or a print command from the dot prompt.

When you want to change the pitch for an entire report—perhaps to print a wide report in Line Printer font so it fits on an 8½- by 11-inch page—pull down the Print menu from the report form generator screen. Select the Control of Printer option to display the menu shown in Figure 11.5.

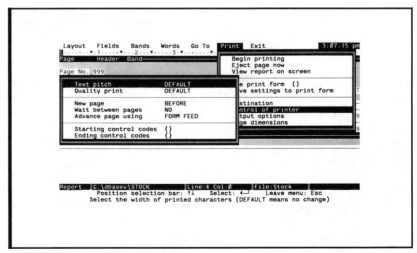

• Figure 11.5: *dBASE IV Control of Printer menu*

Similar techniques can be used to create and format label forms.

Use the arrow keys to highlight the Text Pitch option, and then press ← to cycle between Default, Pica, Elite, and Condensed. Press Esc to leave the menu. Figure 11.6 shows a sample report printed in the default Courier font, which is too wide to fit on the page. Figure 11.7 shows the same report printed in Line Printer font.

```
Page No.    1
06/01/89

ORDER_ID  PART_ID      PART_NAME                   DESCRIPT                          IT

87-105    C-111-6010   SOFA, 6-FOOT                LEATHER, BROWN, HIGHBACK
87-105    C-111-6015   SOFA, 6-FOOT                VELVET, GREY, FRENCH
87-106    C-111-8050   SOFA, 8-FOOT                VELVET, BLUE, FRENCH
87-107    C-222-1000   CHAIR, DESK                 LEATHER, BROWN, HIGHBACK
87-108    C-222-1000   CHAIR, DESK                 LEATHER, BROWN, HIGHBACK
87-109    C-400-2060   TABLE, END                  WOOD, OAK, 2-FOOT, SQUARE
87-109    C-500-6050   LAMP, FLOOR                 BRASS, 6-FOOT, ENGLISH
87-110    C-700-2020   FILE CABINET,2 DRAWER       METAL, BROWN
87-110    C-700-4020   FILE CABINET,4 DRAWER       METAL, BROWN
87-111    C-222-1001   CHAIR, DESK                 LEATHER, BROWN
87-112    C-222-3020   CHAIR, SIDE                 PLASTIC, GREY
87-113    C-300-2020   BOOKCASE                    WOOD, TEAK, 2-SHELF
87-114    C-500-6000   LAMP, FLOOR                 BRASS, 6-FOOT, ART DECO
87-115    C-500-6050   LAMP, FLOOR                 BRASS, 6-FOOT, ENGLISH
87-116    C-600-5000   DESK,EXECUTIVE 5-FOOT       WOOD, OAK, FANCY
87-116    C-700-2030   FILE CABINET,2 DRAWER       METAL, BLACK
87-116    C-222-1001   CHAIR, DESK                 LEATHER, BROWN

                                                                                      1
```

• Figure 11.6: *Sample dBASE IV wide report in Courier font*

```
Page No.   1
06/01/89

ORDER_ID  PART_ID    PART_NAME               DESCRIPT                   ITEM_COST   QTY

87-105    C-111-6010 SOFA, 6-FOOT            LEATHER, BROWN, HIGHBACK    1200.00     1
87-105    C-111-6015 SOFA, 6-FOOT            VELVET, GREY, FRENCH         650.00     1
87-106    C-111-8050 SOFA, 8-FOOT            VELVET, BLUE, FRENCH        1200.00     1
87-107    C-222-1000 CHAIR, DESK             LEATHER, BROWN, HIGHBACK    1250.00     1
87-108    C-222-1000 CHAIR, DESK             LEATHER, BROWN, HIGHBACK    1250.00     1
87-109    C-400-2060 TABLE, END              WOOD, OAK, 2-FOOT, SQUARE    250.00     1
87-109    C-500-6050 LAMP, FLOOR             BRASS, 6-FOOT, ENGLISH       165.00     1
87-110    C-700-2020 FILE CABINET,2 DRAWER   METAL, BROWN                  75.00     1
87-110    C-700-4020 FILE CABINET,4 DRAWER   METAL, BROWN                 100.00     1
87-111    C-222-1001 CHAIR, DESK             LEATHER, BROWN              1000.00     1
87-112    C-222-3020 CHAIR, SIDE             PLASTIC, GREY                350.00     2
87-113    C-300-2020 BOOKCASE                WOOD, TEAK, 2-SHELF          125.00     1
87-114    C-500-6000 LAMP, FLOOR             BRASS, 6-FOOT, ART DECO      150.00     3
87-115    C-500-6050 LAMP, FLOOR             BRASS, 6-FOOT, ENGLISH       165.00     1
87-116    C-600-5000 DESK,EXECUTIVE 5-FOOT   WOOD, OAK, FANCY            1500.00     1
87-116    C-700-2030 FILE CABINET,2 DRAWER   METAL, BLACK                  75.00     1
87-116    C-222-1001 CHAIR, DESK             LEATHER, BROWN              1000.00     1
                                                                        10505.00    20
```

• Figure 11.7: *Sample dBASE IV report in Line Printer font*

To change just one section of the report, such as the column headings or detail line, place the cursor on the section (band) in the report form generator screen, and press F10. Then pull down the Bands menu, which is shown in Figure 11.8. Set the Text Pitch for Band option, and then save and exit the report.

To print report forms from the dot prompt, enter the command:

report form *report name* to print

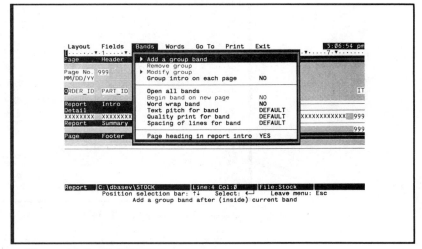

• Figure 11.8: *dBASE IV Bands menu*

• *Formatting in dBASE IV Programs*

The other printer driver features must be activated through dBASE programs. With dBASE IV, you can program with Style commands and memory variables, and even edit the configuration file. We'll discuss these techniques in the following sections and cover dBASE programming with PCL commands later in the chapter.

Writing dBASE Programs

You can use dBASE's built-in text editor to write a dBASE program. Table 11.2 lists the editor's most frequently used commands.

To enter the dBASE editor from the dot prompt, enter the command:

modify command *program-name*

The program name must be eight characters or less.

• Table 11.2: *dBASE Text Editor Commands*

COMMAND	dBASE III PLUS	dBASE IV
Copy selected text		F8
Delete line	Ctrl-Y	Ctrl-Y
Delete character	Del	Del
Find text	Ctrl-KF	Ctrl-KF
Insert line	Ctrl-N	Ctrl-N
Move selected text		F7
Quit and save	Ctrl-W	Ctrl-W
Quit without saving	Ctrl-Q	Ctrl-Q
Read file to screen	Ctrl-KR	Ctrl-KR
Replace text		Shift-F6
Select text		F6
Write selected text	Ctrl-KW	Ctrl-KW

Then press ◄─┘. For example, if you want to write a dBASE program to switch the LaserJet into landscape orientation, you might enter this command at the dot prompt:

    modify command landscp

Write your program, then press Ctrl-W to save it and return to the dot prompt (press Ctrl-Q to quit without saving the file).

Figure 11.9 shows an example of a dBASE program that prints one record from a database. The first line

    use stock

indicates the information should be taken from the Stock database. The next line

    set print on

directs output to the printer as well as the screen. The lines with just a single question mark will print a blank line. The lines with a single question mark

```
use stock
set print on
?
?"Inventory Report"
?
?
?
? "Order Number        :"
?? ORDER_ID
? "Part Number         :"
?? PART_ID
? "Item                :"
?? PART_NAME
? "Cost                :"
?? ITEM_COST
set print off
```

• Figure 11.9: *Sample dBASE IV program*

followed by text in quotation marks will print that text. A question mark command advances to the next line and prints.

Double question marks followed by a field name will print the contents of the field. A double question mark command prints on the current line.

Finally, the line

set print off

stops the output to the printer. Figure 11.10 shows the report generated by the sample program.

Adding dBASE IV Character Styles

In addition to a wide range of Picture and Functions commands for formatting output, dBASE IV provides five standard character formats, each associated with a style code:

To print italics, you must have a LaserJet with an internal italic font or a cartridge with an italic font. Using the HPLAS100 and HPLASL drivers, text formatted as italic will be underlined instead.

Code	Format
B	Bold
I	Italic
U	Underlined
R	Raised (for superscripts)
L	Lowered (for subscripts)

Figure 11.11 shows the commands for character styles added to the sample program. The program prints the title in italics, the headings in boldface, and the cost with an underline, as shown in Figure 11.12 (printed using the HPLAS2I.PR2 driver with a LaserJet +). Depending on your system, the boldfaced text might even appear brighter on the screen.

To format superscripts or subscripts, use the R or L command. Precede the elements you want on the same line with double question marks to

```
Inventory Report

Order Number        :87-105
Part Number         :C-111-6010
Item                :SOFA, 6-FOOT
Cost                : 1200.00
```

• Figure 11.10: *Printed report generated by the sample dBASE IV program*

```
use stock
set print on
?
?
? "Inventory Report" STYLE "I"
?
?
? "Order Number      :" STYLE "B"
?? ORDER_ID
? "Part Number       :" STYLE "B"
?? PART_ID
? "Item              :" STYLE "B"
?? PART_NAME
? "Cost              :" STYLE "B"
?? ITEM_COST STYLE "U"
set print off
```

• Figure 11.11: *Sample program with Style commands*

```
Inventory Report

Order Number        :87-105
Part Number         :C-111-6010
Item                :SOFA, 6-FOOT
Cost                : 1200.00
```

• Figure 11.12: *Printed report generated by the revised program*

print the text without performing a line feed/carriage return. For example, these lines

```
? "The sign for water is H"
?? "2" STYLE "L"
?? "O"
```

will print the character 2 subscripted between the H and O.

Formatting with dBASE IV Memory Variables

You can use the memory variables _pscode and _pecode to format your entire report rather than individual lines or characters.

Add the line

```
PRINTJOB
```

at the start of your program and the line

```
ENDPRINTJOB
```

at the end. The PCL commands following _pscode will be sent to the printer when the job begins; the commands following _pecode will be sent when it's done.

You can also use these variables from the dot prompt when printing a report or label. As an example, suppose that you want to print a report using the second tray in a LaserJet IID. Enter these commands at the dot prompt:

```
_pscode = "{27}{38}{108}{52}{72}"
_pecode = "{27}{38}{108}{49}{72}"
```

The PCL commands are the decimal equivalents for the Escape codes &l4H, which activates the lower tray, and &l1H, which returns feeding to the upper tray.

You can use these memory variables to transmit any type of codes to the printer, even to select fonts or paper size.

Editing the dBASE IV Configuration File

When you installed dBASE IV, the file CONFIG.DB was placed on your hard disk. This file, which is checked every time you start the program, contains the names of your default and available printers, as well as other specifics about the dBASE environment.

Figure 11.13 shows the CONFIG.DB file for an EGA system with all the LaserJet drivers installed. The PDRIVER command shows the default driver to be used, and all the selected drivers are listed in Printer commands, which include the driver file name, printer name, and port.

If you didn't install all the drivers when you set up dBASE, you can edit this file with a word processor or by using the DBSETUP program on the Installation disk. You could also edit it from within dBASE using the built-in editor. From the dot prompt, type

MODIFY COMMAND CONFIG.DB

Details on modifying the CONFIG.DB file are presented in Chapter 6 of the *dBASE Language Reference*.

One way to edit this file is to add Printer # Font commands to switch between fonts. For example, the Font commands in this section of a file switch between the Roman-8 and PC symbol sets:

PRINTER 3 = HPLAS2I.PR2 NAME "Hewlett-Packard LaserJet" DEVICE LPT1
PRINTER 3 FONT 1 = {Esc}(8U, {Esc}(#@ NAME "Roman 8"
PRINTER 3 FONT 2 = {Esc}(10U, {Esc}(#@ NAME "PC Set"

```
*
*          dBASE IV Configuration File
*          Thursday June 1, 1990
*

COMMAND            = ASSIST
DISPLAY            = EGA25
PDRIVER            = HPLAS100.PR2
PRINTER 1          = HPLAS100.PR2 NAME "Hewlett-Packard LaserJet 100 dpi graphics mod" DEVICE LPT1
PRINTER 2          = HPLASL.PR2 NAME "Hewlett-Packard LaserJet Landscape" DEVICE LPT1
PRINTER 3          = HPLAS2I.PR2 NAME "Hewlett-Packard LaserJet" DEVICE LPT1
PRINTER 4          = HPLAS2ID.PR2 NAME "Hewlett-Packard LaserJet" DEVICE LPT1
SQLHOME            = C:\dBASE\SQLHOME
STATUS             = ON
```

• Figure 11.13: *dBASE IV configuration file with all the LaserJet drivers installed*

On the screen, characters formatted in font styles may blink on and off.

You can type these lines directly into the CONFIG.DB file using a text editor, or you can use the DBSETUP program to make your changes. Follow these steps to edit the file using DBSETUP:

1. Insert the Installation disk in drive A, type **DBSETUP**, and press ◄─┘.

2. Select Config.db from the command line, then Modify Existing CONFIG.DB from the pull-down menu.

3. Type the drive and path where you installed dBASE IV, then press ◄─┘.

4. Pull down the Output menu, then select Printer. The options displayed let you set the default status of the printer, change or add drivers, set the default driver, and add fonts.

5. Select Fonts to display the menu for adding fonts.

6. Press PgDn or PgUp until the name of the driver you want to add fonts to is shown at the top of the box.

7. Type the name for the font and the beginning and ending codes in the appropriate columns. Figure 11.14 shows the two symbol sets installed as Font 1 and Font 2.

8. Press Ctrl-End to save the file; then Exit the program.

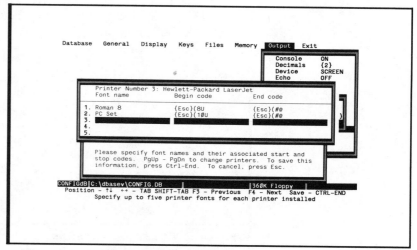

• Figure 11.14: *Two fonts installed in the dBASE IV configuration file*

• *dBASE Programming with PCL Commands*

If you want to do more than dBASE IV allows or have an earlier version of dBASE, you need to enter PCL commands directly in your programs in order to use printing features. Since you'll have to look up all the PCL commands, this might be a little more time-consuming than using drivers and Style and Print Font commands; however, you'll have greater flexibility and control over your printer.

The techniques discussed here can be used with all versions of dBASE. If you have dBASE IV, you can even combine these techniques with those already discussed. Because your programs are sending the codes, it really doesn't matter which driver is being used. You'll be able to print in landscape orientation with any driver—even GENERIC.PR2.

If you've never entered a dBASE program before, refer to the earlier section about writing dBASE programs.

Entering PCL Commands in dBASE Programs

With dBASE IV, you can also enter the Escape code as {Esc} or {27}.

All the PCL commands in your dBASE programs must begin with the Escape command, ASCII code 27. This tells the LaserJet that the characters that follow are commands, not text to be printed. The dBASE code for the Escape command is chr(27). Following the Escape command are one or more characters in quotation marks, such as

```
chr(27) + "&l10"
```

the PCL command for landscape printing.

If you leave out the Escape code, the remaining control characters will just print out. If you see &l10 printed on the first line of a report, it means that you forgot to start the command with chr(27). Don't worry if you enter an incorrect code—the most that you'll lose is a sheet of paper or two. An improper code cannot damage the printer.

Be sure to carefully read the commands in this chapter, distinguishing between a lowercase letter l and the number 1, and the uppercase letter O and the number 0 (zero). Copy the commands exactly as you see them, taking the time to understand what feature each code activates. Table 11.3 summarizes the PCL commands we'll be using.

• Table 11.3: *Common PCL Commands for dBASE Programs*

COMMAND	PCL CODES	COMMENTS
Reset printer	chr(27) + "E"	
Top margin	chr(27) + "&l#E"	# = top margin in lines
Vertical cursor positioning	chr(27) + "&aOR"	Activates top margin
Text lines per page	chr(27) + "&l#F"	# = text lines per page
Page length	chr(27) + "&l#P"	# = lines per page
Paper source	chr(27) + "&l#H"	# = source:
		0 eject page
		1 input cassette (or upper tray)
		2 manual sheet
		3 manual envelope
		4 lower tray
		6 envelope feeder
Vertical spacing	chr(27) + "&l#C"	# = $1/48$ inch units for line spacing
Lines per inch	chr(27) + "&l#D"	# = lines per inch (use this instead of vertical spacing when the measurement # is 1, 2, 3, 4, 6, 8, 12, 16, 24, or 48)
Left margin	chr(27) + "&a#L"	# = column position from left
Right margin	chr(27) + "&a#M"	# = column position from right
Pitch	chr(27) + "(s#H"	# = pitch
Landscape	chr(27) + "&l1O"	
Portrait	chr(27) + "&l0O"	

You direct output to the printer with the command

> set print on

Place all your PCL instructions after this command. Otherwise, the codes will go only to the monitor and not effect the printer. Your printer must be turned on and ready to print when the first line is transmitted to it. You stop output to the printer with the command

> set print off

Programs for Printing Database Reports

In order to use the examples that follow, you must first create a report form with the settings shown. Then enter the dBASE program—inserting your own database and report form name—to set the printer orientation, font, or spacing.

Each of these programs selects the correct database, resets the printer, and places it in the appropriate mode. Next it prints the report form, then resets the printer to the default font and orientation.

Some PCL commands will cause a blank page to first be ejected.

Using Letter-Size Paper

The following three programs print reports on 8½- by 11-inch paper, using continuous feed. Notice each program uses some combination of the commands listed in Table 11.3.

The following program prints a report in portrait orientation with the Line Printer font. Your report form must set the page width at 129, the lines per page at 55, the left margin at 8, and the right margin at 0.

```
use database name
set print on
?  chr(27) + "E" + chr(27) + "(s16.66H"
report form name
?  chr(27) + "E"
set print off
```

The next program prints in landscape orientation, with the default font. Your report form must set the page width at 100, the lines per page at 44, the left margin at 5, and the right margin at 0.

```
use database
set print on
? chr(27) + "E" + chr(27) + "&l1O"
report form name
? chr(27) + "E"
set print off
```

The third program prints in landscape orientation with the Line Printer font. Your report form must set the page width at 170, the lines per page at 44, the left margin at 5, and the right margin at 0.

```
use database
set print on
?  chr(27) + "E" + chr(27) + "&l1O" + chr(27) +
"(s16.66H"
report form name
? chr(27) + "E"
set print off
```

Using Legal-Size Paper

The following three programs print reports on 8½- by 14-inch legal paper using manual feed. If you have a legal-size paper tray, delete the command

```
chr(27) + "&l84p2H"
```

from each of the programs.

The following program prints a report in portrait orientation with the Line Printer font. Your report form must set the page width at 129, the lines per page at 77, the left margin at 8, and the right margin at 0.

The instruction chr(27) + "&l84p2H" is an abbreviated command combining chr(27) + "&l84P" and chr(27) + "&l2H". When the first two letters following chr(27) are the same, several instructions can be combined.

```
use database
set print on
?
chr(27) + "E" + chr(27) + "&l84p2H" + chr(27) + "(s16.66H"
report form name
? chr(27) + "E"
set print off
```

The next program prints in landscape orientation with the default font. Your report form must set the page width at 133, the lines per page at 44, the left margin at 5, and the right margin at 0.

```
use database
set print on
? chr(27) + "E" + chr(27) + "&l1O" + chr(27) + "&l84p2H"
report form name
? chr(27) + "E"
set print off
```

The third program prints in landscape orientation with the Line Printer font. Your report form must set the page width at 233, the lines per page at 44, the left margin at 5, and the right margin at 0.

```
use database
set print on
? chr(27) + "E" + chr(27) + "&l1O" + chr(27)
 + "&l84p2H" + chr(27) + "(s16.66H"
report form name
? chr(27) + "E"
set print off
```

Increasing Lines Per Page

The programs shown in the preceding sections print reports in the default six lines per inch. To fit even more on a single sheet of paper, add commands to increase the lines per page.

For letter-size paper, include one of the following lines in your program:

- Portrait, 66 lines per page:

    chr(27) + "&l7.27C" + chr(27) + "&l66F"

- Portrait, 89 lines per page:

    chr(27) + "&l5.39C" + chr(27) + "&l89F"

- Landscape, 66 lines per page:

    chr(27) + "&l5.45C" + chr(27) + "&l66F"

For legal-size paper, add one of these lines:

- Portrait, 104 lines per page:

    chr(27) + "18D" + chr(27) + "&l104F"

- Portrait, 150 lines per page:

    chr(27) + "&l4.16C" + chr(27) + "&l150F"

- Landscape, 66 lines per page:

  chr(27) + "&l5.45C" + chr(27) + "&l66F"

Duplex Printing

With the LaserJet IID, add one of these lines to your program to print in duplex:

- Long-edge binding:

  chr(27) + "&l1S"

- Short-edge binding:

  chr(27) + "&l2S"

Printing Envelopes

You can format and print envelopes by using either the dBASE label generator or your own program. The following sample program prints business envelopes using manual input. It first sets the orientation and margins for the printer, then loops through the database printing the addresses.

```
use clients
set talk off
set print on
? chr(27) + "E" + chr(27) + "&l1o3h27E" +
chr(27) + "&a52L" + chr(27) + "&a0R"
do while .not. EOF( )
? Trim(First) + " " + Last
? Address
? Trim(City) + " " + State + " " + Zip
eject
skip
enddo
? chr(27) + "E"
set print off
```

With the LaserJet +, substitute 38E for 27E in the PCL command line. If you have the optional envelope feeder on the LaserJet IID, substitute 6h for 3h in the PCL command line.

Formatting Characters with PCL Commands

The @ print command is used to control the cursor position on the page. See your dBASE manual for details.

You can select fonts and format characters in your programs by using the commands listed in Table 11.4. These commands can be added to either ?, ??, or @ output lines to produce a variety of results. For example, the program listed in Figure 11.15 produces the same report as the program listed in Figure 11.11, which used the dBASE IV Style commands.

To use softfonts in your program, download them manually, noting the font ID number assigned to each. Download them as permanent fonts if your program resets the printer with chr(27) + "E"; otherwise, the fonts will be erased. Then to use the font, insert the command

chr(27) + "(#X"

substituting the ID number for the # character.

• Table 11.4: *PCL Commands for Formatting Characters*

FORMAT	PCL CODES
Underline on	chr(27) + "&dD"
Underline off	chr(27) + "&d@"
Fixed-position underline on (LaserJet II, IID, and 2000)	chr(27) + "&d0D"
Floating-position underline (based on largest font on line) on (LaserJet II, IID, and 2000)	chr(27) + "&d3@"
Bold on	chr(27) + "(s3B"
Bold off	chr(27) + "(s0B"
Italic on	chr(27) + "(s1S"
Italic off	chr(27) + "(s0S"
Superscript on	chr(27) + "*p-20Y"
Superscript off	chr(27) + "*p + 20Y"
Subscript on	chr(27) + "*p + 20Y"
Subscript off	chr(27) + "*p-20Y"
Reset	chr(27) + "E"

```
use stock
set print on
?
?
? chr(27)+"(s1S"+"Inventory Report"+chr(27)+"(s0S"
?
?
? chr(27)+"(s3B"+"Order Number          :"+chr(27)+"(s0B"
?? ORDER_ID
? chr(27)+"(s3B"+"Part Number           :"+chr(27)+"(s0B"
?? PART_ID
? chr(27)+"(s3B"+"Item                  :"+chr(27)+"(s0B"
?? PART_NAME
? chr(27)+"(s3B"+"Cost                  :"+chr(27)+"(s0B"
?? chr(27)+"&dD"
?? ITEM_COST
?? chr(27)+"&d@"
set print off
```

• Figure 11.15: *dBASE program for formatting characters with PCL commands*

If you're mathematically inclined, the formula is Spacing = 48 × (1/lines per inch)

If you're using a font larger than 12 points, you'll also have to change the line spacing. Compute the number of lines that can fit in an inch, then divide that number into 48. Substitute that number for the # in this command:

chr(27) + "&l#C"

For example, suppose that you downloaded an 18-point font with ID 1. You can fit four 18-point lines per inch (72 points divided by 18), so the spacing command would be

chr(27) + "&l12C"

The dBASE language, especially dBASE IV, provides a full programming environment that can be used for a wide range of applications. In Part 4, you'll learn more about PCL commands to control every aspect of your printed output. Any of the commands can be included in a dBASE program by adding the characters after the Escape command.

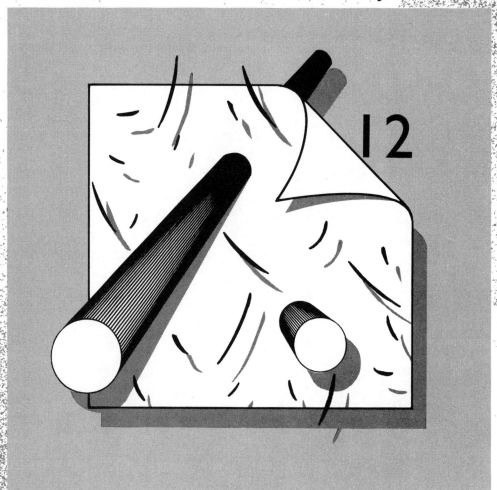

H·P L·A·S·E·R·J·E·T

12

*Spreadsheet Publishing
with Lotus 1-2-3*

• Because of the range of versions and products on the market, we'll look at printing with Lotus 1-2-3 from several viewpoints. First, we'll discuss features specific to Release 3, the most powerful 1-2-3 on the market. Many of the features available from add-on products have been integrated right into this release. Then you'll see how PCL commands can be used from within all versions of 1-2-3. Finally, we'll cover some powerful add-on products that can be used for spreadsheet publishing.

If you have a version of Lotus 1-2-3 other than Release 3, refer to the section about selecting a new default printer in the following section, then go on to the section about formatting with PCL commands.

• *Printing with 1-2-3 Release 3*

Release 3 has extensive features, such as three-dimensional worksheets, enhanced database commands, and a multitude of functions. Graphing is now totally integrated with the spreadsheet, so you don't have to save the file and load the Printgraph program separately. You can even use windows to display both the graph and spreadsheet at the same time and immediately see how a change in data affects the chart.

Release 3 also includes more powerful printer drivers that let you select fonts, orientation, pitch, and other features from the menus. These allow you to add printing features without manually embedding codes or setup strings in your spreadsheets.

Installing Release 3 Printers

When you install 1-2-3 for the first time, or change the configuration later on, you'll be prompted to select a printer, as shown in Figure 12.1. Selecting HP will display a second menu listing Hewlett-Packard printers for which drivers are provided, as shown in Figure 12.2. The added memory options for the LaserJet +, LaserJet 500 +, and LaserJet II allow you to print full-page graphics at 300 dpi.

After selecting your model, you'll see a list of cartridges to select from:

> No cartridge
> Z Microsoft 1A
> J Math Elite
> F TmsRmn2

DeskJet options are No Cartridge and Landscape cartridge.

Not many cartridges are supported, but it's possible to use the B and Pro cartridge in place of the F and Z options. This can be accomplished by modifying the driver, as explained in the next section.

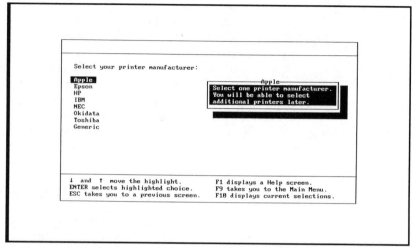

• Figure 12.1: *Printers supported by Lotus 1-2-3 Release 3*

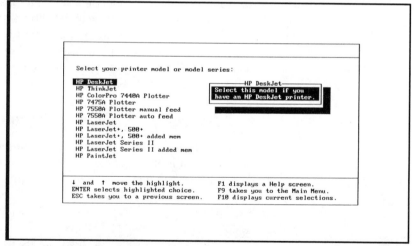

• Figure 12.2: *HP models supported by Lotus 1-2-3 Release 3*

The DeskJet drivers are
HPDJNO, no cartridge;
and HPDJLS, landscape
cartridge.

You can select up to 16 printers, or combinations of models and cartridges, then switch back and forth from within 1-2-3, as explained later in the chapter. The general driver information will be placed in a file called 123.DCF. Data for your selected cartridge is stored in files with a PBD extension, as listed in Table 12.1. Bit-map fonts for use with graphs are stored in files with an LRF extension.

• Table 12.1: *Lotus 1-2-3 Release 3 Printer Driver Files*

STANDARD MEMORY FILE	EXTRA MEMORY FILE	MODEL AND CARTRIDGES
HPJJ1NOL		Original LaserJet, no cartridge
HPLJ1JLO		Original LaserJet, J cartridge
HPLJ1FLO		Original LaserJet, F cartridge
HPLJ1ZLO		Original LaserJet, Z cartridge
HPLJPNOL	HPLJONOH	LaserJet +, no cartridge
HPLJPJLO	HPLJPJHI	LaserJet +, J cartridge
HPLJPFLO	HPLJPFHI	LaserJet +, F cartridge
HPLJZLO	HPLJZHI	LaserJet +, Z cartridge
HPLJNOLO	HPLJ2NOH	LaserJet II, no cartridge
HPLJ2JLO	HPLJ2JHI	LaserJet II, J cartridge
HPLJ2FLO	HPLJ2FHI	LaserJet II, F cartridge
HPLJZLO	HPLZZHI	LaserJet II, Z cartridge

Using Nonsupported Cartridges

Chapter 20 discusses disk-editing programs in more detail.

If you don't need to print any of the special characters in the Roman-8 symbol set, you can substitute the B cartridge for the F, or the Pro cartridge for the Z. However, you'll need a disk-sector editing program to modify the driver file.

First, when installing Lotus, select F TmsRmn2 if you have the B cartridge, Z Microsoft 1A if you have the Pro. Then make a backup copy of the driver using the same name but some other extension. Load your disk editor and look at the driver file. In several places, you'll see the PCL codes for selecting the 8U symbol set. Most editors show the disk information as both ASCII characters and hexadecimal numbers, something like this:

```
←       (       8       U
1B      28      38      55
```

Use your editor to change each 8U to 0U and the hexadecimal number 38 to 30. Then save the edited file and load 1-2-3.

Selecting Drivers from within 1-2-3 Release 3

The first printer or cartridge you installed becomes the default selection whenever you start 1-2-3. You can either select a new default printer or change the settings for the current worksheet.

Selecting a New Default Printer

If you set up more than one printer or cartridge, make sure the 1-2-3 setting agrees with the cartridge you have physically installed in the printer.

To select a new default printer and interface, use the /WGDP (Worksheet Global Default Printer) command. You'll see these options:

> Interface AutoLf Left Right Top Bottom Pg-Length Wait
> Setup Name Quit

Throughout this chapter, you'll be given instructions for selecting menu options by the series of keystrokes that navigate the hierarchy of menus. For example, the command /WGDP means to press the / key, then the characters WGDP. This enters the command structure, then selects the Worksheet Global Default Printer command through a series of menus.

Press N (Name) to see a menu listing the printers and cartridges you installed for your system and the numbers for their selection. As you highlight the numbers, the printer name and cartridge will appear on the second menu line. Type the number you want, or highlight it to see the description, and then press ◄──┘.

Press I for the Interface option to see the prompt:

> 1 2 3 4 5 6 7 8 9
> Parallel 1

As you highlight each option, the interface name will appear in the second menu line:

> 1   Parallel 1
> 2   Serial 1
> 3   Parallel 2
> 4   Serial 2
> 5   Output Device LPT1
> 6   Output Device LPT2
> 7   Output Device LPT3
> 8   Output Device COM1
> 9   Output Device COM2

Press the number corresponding to your interface. If you choose number 2 or 4 (your LaserJet is interfaced as a serial printer), you'll be prompted to select a baud rate between 1 and 9, corresponding to these settings:

1	110
2	150
3	300
4	600
5	1200
6	2400
7	4800
8	9600
9	19200

While some of the options may appear redundant, such as 1 and 5, and 2 and 8, there are subtle technical differences between them. When you select options 1 through 4, Lotus handles all communications between the computer and printer. That's why you have to tell Lotus the serial baud rate, for example, for options 2 and 4. The other selections channel printing through DOS. So, if you select either 8 or 9, you *must* have used the Mode command to set the baud rate and redirect output to the serial port. See Chapter 2 for details.

After you've selected the new default printer, press Q (Quit) until you return to a menu you want to use or to your spreadsheet.

Changing Printers for the Current Worksheet

In this and following sections, we'll refer to the menus in the Print Printer command chain, shown in Figure 12.3. Refer to the figure to see the flow of commands.

To select a different printer for a specific worksheet, press /PPOAD (Print Printer Options Advanced Device) to see the options Name and Interface.

Set the name and interface as explained above, then press Q until you return to the Printer menu. These settings will be used just for that worksheet and saved with the file.

You can always see a report of your printer settings by pressing /WGDS (Worksheet Global Default Status). The program will display a screen similar to the one shown in Figure 12.4.

1-2-3 Release 3 Default Settings

By default, 1-2-3 uses portrait orientation and font number 1. It uses the following default page settings:

- A two-line top margin

Print Printer
Range Line Page Options Clear Align Go Image Sample Hold Quit

Options
Header Footer Margins Borders Setup Pg-Length Other Name Advance Quit

Margins
Left Right Top Bottom None
Advanced
Device Layout Fonts Color Image Priority AutoLF Wait Quit

Device
Name Interface
Layout
Pitch Line-Spacing Orientation Quit

Pitch
Standard Compressed Expanded
Line-Spacing
Standard Compressed
Orientation
Portrait Landscape

Fonts
Range Header/Footer Border Frame Quit

1 2 3 4 5 6 7 8
Color
1 2 3 4 5 6 7 8
Image
Rotate Image-Sz Density Quit

Rotate
No Yes
Margin-Fill Length-Fill Reshape

Priority
Default High Low
AutoLF
Yes No
Wait
No Yes

• Figure 12.3: *Lotus 1-2-3 Release 3 Print menu hierarchy*

```
                                                                    STAT

            Printer:                        International:
              Interface..... Parallel 1       Punctuation..... A
              Auto linefeed. No                        Decimal Period
                                                      Argument Comma
            Margins                                   Thousands Comma
              Left 4          Top 2           Currency........ $ (Prefix)
              Right 76    Bottom 2            Date format D4.. A (MM/DD/YY)
                                              Date format D5.. A (MM/DD)
            Page length... 66                 Time format D8.. A (HH:MM:SS)
            Wait.......... No                 Time format D9.. A (HH:MM)
            Setup string..
            Name.......... HP LaserJet+, 500+ F TmsRmn2
                                              Negative........ Parentheses
            Automatic graph: Columnwise       Release 2....... LICS
                                              File translate.. Country
            File list extension: WK*
            File save extension: WK3          Clock on screen: File name
            Graph save extension: CGM         Undo: No      Beep: Yes
                                              Autoexec: Yes
            Default directory: C:\123R3
            Temporary directory: C:\123R3

            BUDGET.WK3
```

• Figure 12.4: *Lotus 1-2-3 Release 3 status report*

- A header line (which is blank until you enter a header)
- Two more blank lines before the worksheet
- Text prints up to line 61
- Two blank lines after the text
- A footer line (blank until you enter a footer)
- A two-line bottom margin
- Left and right margins at 4 and 76, for a line length of 72 characters

Before printing each page, you might want to use the Align command. This "homes" the cursor and sets the automatic page counter to 1.

To print using the default settings, press /PPR, select a range, then press ◄─┘ G. To print the same range again, just press /PPG.

The program, however, does not eject the page after printing. So if your worksheet (or graph) is less than a page, you have to eject it yourself. Instead of using the printer's control panel, you can select the Page command on the Print Printer menu.

After your spreadsheet is printed, the Print Printer menu will still be active. Press Q to return to the Main menu, then press Q again to work on your spreadsheet.

Changing 1-2-3 Release 3 Page Settings

To change any of the default page settings, use the Print Printer commands as follows:

- **Margins** (/PPOM): Set the top and bottom margins in lines, the left and right margins in columns.

- **Page Length** (/PPOP): Set the page length in lines. Page width is determined by the left and right margin settings.

- **Orientation** (/PPOALO): Select either portrait or landscape.

- **Pitch** (/PPOALP): Select standard, compressed (Line Printer), or expanded.

- **Spacing** (/PPOALL): Select standard or compressed line spacing.

- **Headers** (/PPOH): Enter a line of text to print below the top margin of every page.

- **Footers** (/PPOF): Enter a line of text to print above the bottom margin of every page.

- **Borders** (/PPOB): Choose Columns to specify worksheet columns to print down the left side of each page. Choose Rows to specify worksheet rows to print on the top of every page. Choose Frame to print row numbers and column letters along with the print range. Choose No-Frame to turn off frame printing.

Changing fonts, pitch, or orientation does not affect the margins; they keep their default settings until you change them. This means that simply setting the orientation to landscape will not let you print more than 72 characters on each line. You have to extend the right margin beyond position 76.

For example, to print a worksheet in landscape using the Line Printer font, use the command /PPR to set the range, press ↵, then press OMR (Options Margins Right), set the right margin to 176, and press ↵. Next press ALPC (Advanced Layout Pitch Compressed), then OL (Orientation Landscape). Press Q three times to return to the Printer menu. Press G to print, then PQ to eject the page and return to the Main menu.

The new settings you select will remain active until you change them, use the Clear command, or exit 1-2-3.

Printing 1-2-3 Release 3 Font Samples

Press /PPSG (Print Printer Sample Go) to generate a four-part sample printout of the fonts and features available with your driver:

- The first section lists the current printer settings.

- The second section lists the margin settings.

- The third section shows samples of the fonts, pitches, and line spacing options that you can use to print worksheet text. Figure 12.5 shows the fonts available using the Z cartridge.

- The final section includes a small sample graph and a list of font sizes and styles that you can use for chart text. Figure 12.6 shows an example.

```
PRINTER SETTINGS

Header =
Footer =
Margins:
   Left = 4 , Right = 76 , Top = 2 , Bottom = 2
Borders:
   Columns =  , Rows =  , No-Frame
Setup =
Pg-Length = 66
Other:
   As-Displayed , Formatted , Print Blank-Header
Device:
   Name = HP LaserJet+ , 500+ Z Microsoft 1A
   Interface = Parallel 1
Layout:
   Standard Pitch , Standard Line-Spacing, Portrait
Fonts:
   Range = 0 , Header/Footer = 0 , Border = 0 , Frame = 0
Image:
   No Rotate, Margin-Fill , Final Density

Color = 0, Default Priority, No AutoLf, No Wait

SAMPLE WORKSHEET

Left-aligned label                 54        69        $84.00
            Right-aligned label   599       614       $629.00
            Centered label      -1144     -1159    ($1,174.00)

PRINTER CAPABILITIES

FONT 1 and COLOR 1 were used to print this text.
FONT 2 and COLOR 2 were used to print this text.
FONT 3 and COLOR 3 were used to print this text.
FONT 4 and COLOR 4 were used to print this text.
FONT 5 and COLOR 5 were used to print this text.
FONT 6 and COLOR 6 were used to print this text.
FONT 7 and COLOR 7 were used to print this text.
FONT 8 and COLOR 8 were used to print this text.

This text is in STANDARD PITCH.
This text is in COMPRESSED PITCH.
This text is in EXPANDED PITCH.

STANDARD LINE SPACING was used for these three lines of text.
STANDARD LINE SPACING was used for these three lines of text.
STANDARD LINE SPACING was used for these three lines of text.
COMPRESSED LINE SPACING was used for these three lines of text.
COMPRESSED LINE SPACING was used for these three lines of text.
COMPRESSED LINE SPACING was used for these three lines of text.

SAMPLE GRAPH AND GRAPH TEXT OPTIONS
```

- Figure 12.5: *Lotus 1-2-3 Release 3 font samples for the Z cartridge*

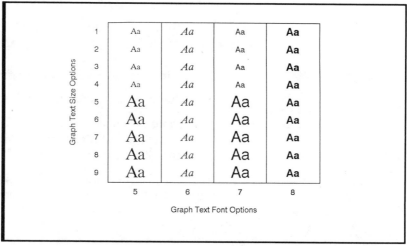

• Figure 12.6: *Fonts and sizes for Lotus 1-2-3 Release 3 chart text*

You should print a sample for each of the printers and cartridges you've installed. Keep the samples handy to help you select options when printing text or graphs.

Using 1-2-3 Release 3 Fonts

To use any of the fonts illustrated on your sample printout, issue the /PPOAF (Print Printer Options Advanced Fonts) command. This lets you set the font for a range of cells, the header and footer, the frame, and the border.

Select from the menu to see a list of the options:

```
1 2 3 4 5 6 7 8
Regular Serif, if available
```

"If available" means that not all the options listed on the screen may be available in your printer driver. As you move from one number to the next, the default font assignment will appear on the second menu line:

```
1    Regular Serif
2    Bold Serif
3    Italic Serif
4    Bold Italic Serif
5    Regular Sans Serif
6    Bold Sans Serif
```

7   Italic Sans Serif
8   Bold Italic Sans Serif

Printing the entire spreadsheet in one font is a simple process. Press /PPR and set the range to the entire spreadsheet, press OAFR (Options Advanced Fonts Range), select the font, return to the Printer menu, and then press G.

For example, these keystrokes print an entire spreadsheet in font 3:

/PPR *range* ↵ **OAFR3QQQG**

Formatting sections of your worksheet in different fonts is more complicated. You actually have to print it section by section, from top to bottom.

As an example, Figure 12.7 shows a worksheet printed in several fonts. Starting at the top, each section was selected as a range, the font was set, then the section was printed. Because the page was ejected only after all the sections were printed, the separate print jobs appear after each other, combined to form the entire worksheet. Be sure to include the blank rows in one of the ranges so they appear on the printout.

Here are the steps used to print the sample worksheet:

1. Use the Align command to home the printer's cursor.

2. Set the range to the top three rows, set the font to 6, then print with the Go command.

3. Set the range to the next four rows (4 to 7), set the font to 3, then print.

				Aardvark Corporation 1991 Budget	
	Quarter				*Annual*
	1	*2*	*3*	*4*	
Income	554	536	654	345	2089
Rent	12	12	12	12	48
Salaries	23	24	23	25	95
Supplies	10	9	9	9	37
Utilities	1	1	2	1	5
Taxes	124	124	124	122	494
Total	170	170	170	169	679
Net	384	366	484	176	1410
All figures in thousands					

• Figure 12.7: *Lotus 1-2-3 Release 3 worksheet rows can be printed in different fonts without embedding PCL commands*

4. Set the range to rows 8 to 17, set the font to 1, then print.

5. Set the range to rows 18 to 20, set the font to 2, then print.

6. Set the range to row 21, set the pitch to compressed, then print.

7. Eject the sheet with the Page command.

If you make a mistake anywhere in the process and print rows in the wrong font, eject the page and start all over.

Using Encoded Text Files

Unformatted ASCII files can be created using the /PF command.

To avoid having to print a worksheet in sections every time you want a copy of it, you can save the formatted worksheet to an encoded text file. This is a disk file that contains the worksheet along with the PCL commands for the font, pitch, and other formats you specify.

Press /PE (Print Encoded) to see the prompt

Enter name of encoded file: c:\123R3\

Type a file name with the .ENC extension, and then press ←┘. If that file already exists, you'll be prompted to replace it or rename the new file.

Now format and "print" the ranges as you would normally. When you exit the Print menu, all your formatting commands and worksheet ranges will be recorded on the disk.

After the information is on disk, you can print the formatted worksheet from the DOS prompt using the Copy command. For example, the command

COPY BUDGET.ENC/B LPT1

would print the Budget file to the first parallel port.

If you display the file on your screen with the Type command, you'll see the text and PCL codes that create the printed worksheet.

Printing 1-2-3 Release 3 Graphs

To set printing options for charts and graphs, press /PPOAI (Print Printer Options Advanced Image). Select from the options as follows:

- **Rotate** (/PPOAIR): Select No, the default, to print the chart in portrait orientation, or Yes for landscape orientation.

- **Image-Sz** (/PPOAII): Choose Margin-Fill (the default) to fill the area between the left and right margins and adjust the length to maintain the default 4 to 3 length-to-width ratio. Choose Length-Fill to enter the length of the graph and adjust the height to maintain the 4 to 3 ratio. Choose Reshape to enter a width and length. For the maximum size chart, enter the length and width of your page.

- **Density** (/PPOAID): Select Final or Draft. With standard printer memory, these are 150 and 75 dpi; with extended memory, 300 or 150 dpi.

To print the graph, return to the Print Printer menu, press I, then C, then G. The program will beep to warn you if a chart hasn't been defined.

The cursor remains at the last print position until you eject the page—either through the printer's control panel or the 1-2-3 Page command. So to combine a worksheet and graph on the same page, first print the spreadsheet, then the graph. Figure 12.8 shows an example of a worksheet and graph printed on the same page.

Just make sure there is enough room following the worksheet to hold the entire graph. Test print the worksheet, then select Length-Fill for the Image-Sz option. Enter the space remaining as the length in lines. The chart will fit in that space, adjusting the width to maintain the proper ratio.

If your chart is set up in color, 1-2-3 will automatically print black and white crosshatch patterns.

• *Formatting Worksheets with PCL Commands*

An add-on program is a separate program that gets "attached" to the Lotus 1-2-3 menu structure, making it a part of 1-2-3. These are explained in detail later in the chapter.

No matter what version of 1-2-3 you have—Release 3 with built-in drivers, or 2.1 and 2.2 with add-on formatting programs—there might be printing features that you would like to use that are not supported by the software. With all versions, you can format manually using PCL commands. These commands can be entered in two ways: using the Setup command or as printer codes inserted in worksheet cells.

Using Setup Strings for Formatting

The Setup command lets you insert PCL codes that are transmitted just before the worksheet is printed. This is useful for orientation settings or when you want the entire worksheet printed in one format.

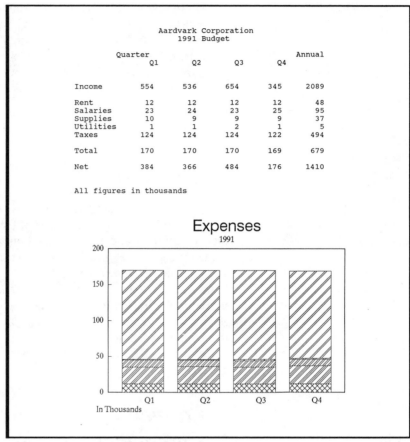

```
                    Aardvark Corporation
                       1991 Budget

          Quarter                                Annual
                  Q1        Q2        Q3      Q4

   Income        554       536       654     345     2089

   Rent           12        12        12      12       48
   Salaries       23        24        23      25       95
   Supplies       10         9         9       9       37
   Utilities       1         1         2       1        5
   Taxes         124       124       124     122      494

   Total         170       170       170     169      679

   Net           384       366       484     176     1410

   All figures in thousands
```

• Figure 12.8: *Lotus 1-2-3 Release 3 worksheet and graph printed on the same page*

To enter a setup string for just the current worksheet, press /PPOS (Print Printer Options Setup) to see the prompt:

Enter setup string:

To create a default setup string for use with every worksheet (until changed or overridden with /PPOS), press /WGDPS (Worksheet Global Default Printer Setup) to see the same prompt.

Now enter the PCL commands, using /027 as the Escape character, followed by the PCL characters. For example, type /027&l1O, then press ← to insert the landscape code. When you issue the Go command, that

Except where noted, use these same commands for the DeskJet +.

PCL code will be transmitted first, so the worksheet will be printed in landscape orientation.

When you change fonts, line spacing, or orientation with setup strings, you have to manually adjust 1-2-3's margin and page-length settings to get the desired results.

To delete a setup string, press /PPOS or /WGDPS, Esc, then ↵.

The most common use of setup strings is to increase the number of rows and columns that fit on one page. This is done by changing to the Line Printer font, landscape orientation, or legal-size paper.

Using Letter-Size Paper

The setup strings and right margin and page length settings can be used with any version of 1-2-3 and LaserJet model.

The following setup strings and settings are designed for 8½- by 11-inch paper. PCL commands that use the Line Printer font require a compatible internal font or cartridge.

The setup string to print in portrait orientation with the Line Printer font, the right margin at 132, and the lines per page at 60 is

    \027E\027(s16.66H

The setup string to print in landscape orientation with the default font, the right margin at 106, and the lines per page at 45 is

    \027E\027&l1O

The setup string to print in landscape orientation with the Line Printer font, the right margin at 176, and the lines per page at 45 is

    \027E\027&l1O\027(s16.66H

Using Legal-Size Paper

Load legal-size paper in the tray, and replace 84p2H with 84P in all the PCL commands. There is no manual feed command.

The following setup strings and settings are designed for 8½- by 14-inch paper and manual feed. If you have a legal-size paper tray, delete the command \027&l84p2H from each of the codes.

The setup string to print in portrait orientation with the Line Printer font, the right margin at 132, and the lines per page at 78 is

    \027E\027&l84p2H\027(s16.66H

The setup string to print in landscape orientation, with the default font, the right margin at 136, and the lines per page at 45 is

    \027E\027&l1O\027&l84p2H

The setup string to print in landscape orientation, with the Line Printer font, the right margin at 226, and the lines per page at 45 is

\027E\027&l1O\027&l84p2H\027(s16.66H

Increasing Lines per Page

To fit even more text on a sheet of paper, you can increase the page length setting and add the PCL commands to your setup string. Release 3 will accept page length settings up to 1000 lines, but other versions are limited to 100.

To print more than 100 lines per page with earlier versions, add the PCL commands to the setup string, but don't bother changing the page-length setting. Instead, use the /PPOOU (Print Printer Options Other Unformatted) command. This forces 1-2-3 to ignore its own page breaks, allowing the LaserJet to use the settings from the PCL commands.

For letter-size paper, add the following commands to your setup string:

When you're finished printing, remember to turn formatting back on using /PPOOF.

Orientation	Lines per Page	PCL Commands
Portrait	66	\027&l7.27C\027&l66F
Portrait	89	\027&l5.39C\027&l89F
Landscape	66	\027&l5.45C\027&l66F

For legal-size paper, add these commands to the setup string:

Orientation	Lines per Page	PCL Commands
Portrait	104	\027l8D\027&l104F
Portrait	150	\027&l4.16C\027&l150F
Landscape	66	\027&l5.45C\027&l66F

Duplex Printing

With the LaserJet IID, you can add PCL commands to the setup string for duplex printing. For long-edge binding, add

\027&l1S

For short-edge binding, add

\027&l2S

Embedding PCL Commands in Worksheet Cells

The vertical bar is over the backslash (\) key.

The same PCL commands can be embedded directly into a worksheet cell. Begin the cell entry by typing two vertical bars (| |), then type the setup string as explained in the previous sections, using \027 for the Escape code.

Format the entire spreadsheet by entering the command in cell A1, before any other text is printed.

Since you can place the code in any cell of the worksheet, you can format individual rows to print in different fonts or pitch settings. In an empty row before the one you want to format (insert one with /WIR if you have to), enter the commands that turn on the feature. Enter the commands that turn the feature off in an empty row after, or the effect will continue for the entire worksheet. Figure 12.9 shows an example of a worksheet with PCL commands embedded in cells.

Table 12.2 lists common formatting commands. PCL codes for selecting fonts are covered in Chapter 18.

Make sure the code is in the first column of the print range. If you're printing the entire spreadsheet, insert the code in column A. When you want to specify some other range, just copy or enter the code in the first column.

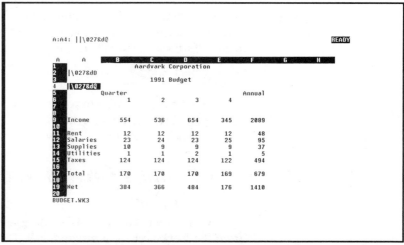

• Figure 12.9: *PCL commands embedded in Lotus 1-2-3 worksheet cells*

• Table 12.2: *PCL Commands for Formatting 1-2-3 Worksheets*

FEATURE	PCL CODE
Underline on	\027&dD
Underline off	\027&d@
Fixed-position underline on (LaserJet II, IID, and 2000)	\027&d0D
Floating-position underline based on largest font on line (LaserJet II, IID, and 2000)	\027&d3@
Bold on	\027(s3B
Bold off	\027(s0B
Italic on	\027(s1S
Italic off	\027(s0S
Superscript on	\027*p-20Y
Superscript off	\027*p + 20Y
Subscript on	\027*p + 20Y
Subscript off	\027*p-20Y
Reset	\027E

If you are planning to use this technique to create an underline that extends across the worksheet, as shown in Figure 12.10, you might have to include an extra column in the print range. For example, if the underlining codes were entered in the sample worksheet without printing an additional column, the underline would print like this, stopping at the last text character:

1991 Budget

To force the underline to go across the entire worksheet, enter several blank spaces in the column just beyond the end of the worksheet, cell G3 in this case. Then include that otherwise blank column in the print range.

• *Printing Graphs with Earlier 1-2-3 Versions*

With earlier versions of 1-2-3, the graph printing function is separate from the worksheet, in a program called Printgraph (accessed from the main 1-2-3 screen).

```
                        Aardvark Corporation
                             1991 Budget
              Quarter                              Annual
                 1         2         3        4

     Income     554       536       654      345      2089

     Rent        12        12        12       12        48
     Salaries    23        24        23       25        95
     Supplies    10         9         9        9        37
     Utilities    1         1         2        1         5
     Taxes      124       124       124      122       494

     Total      170       170       170      169       679

     Net        384       366       484      176      1410


     All figures in thousands
```

• Figure 12.10: *Lotus 1-2-3 worksheet underlining printed with PCL Commands*

Graph and paper size, orientation, text fonts, and colors are set from within this program, using the PIC file created and saved from the worksheet. Figure 12.11 summarizes the menu paths and functions in the Printgraph program.

Before printing with Printgraph, use the Settings option to configure the program for your hardware. Figure 12.12 shows an example of a completed Settings screen. With the LaserJet driver, use the Settings Hardware Printer option to select either low or high resolution, as shown in Figure 12.13.

• *Using Utilities for Spreadsheet Publishing*

A number of third-party software has been developed to create professional-looking printed worksheets. Some of this software is supplied free with new releases of Lotus 1-2-3. But if you'll still using an older version, you can purchase these utilities separately.

In this section, we'll look at three utility programs: Always, Datatype, and Sideways.

Always (supplied with Lotus 1-2-3 version 2.2) and Datatype are two general-purpose spreadsheet publishing programs that attach to 1-2-3 through the Add-On Manager, which is a Lotus program that lets you access utility programs from within the worksheet. Programs designed to work this way will include the Add-On Manager and instructions on how to use it. Once installed, the utility's own menus can be on the top of the worksheet, and the program can be used with 1-2-3 spreadsheets and graphs.

```
Image-Select Settings Go Align Page Exit
Image-Select
     (Load PIC files. Press F10 to display selected graph.)
Settings
     Image Hardware Action Save Reset Quit
          Image
               Size Font Range-Colors Quit
                    Size
                         Full Half Manual Quit
                    Font
                         1 2
                    Range-Colors
                         X A B C D E F Quit
          Hardware
               Graphs-Directory Fonts-Directory Interface
               Printer Paper-Size Quit
                    Graphs-Directory
                    (Specify path for PIC files)
                    Fonts-Directory
                    (Specify path for font files)
                    Interface
                         1 2 3 4 5 6 7 8
                    Printer
                    (Select printer and resolution)
                    Paper-Size
                         Length Width Quit
          Action
               Pause Eject Quit
          Save
          (Save current settings)
          Reset
          (Return to stored settings)
Go
(Print graph)
Align
(Home cursor)
Page
(Eject Page)
```

• Figure 12.11: *Lotus 1-2-3 Printgraph menu structure*

Sideways (supplied with Lotus 1-2-3 version 2.0), on the other hand, runs outside 1-2-3 and is designed to print your worksheets in landscape orientation. Because it is not an add-on program, you must first save your worksheets to an ASCII file (/PF), exit 1-2-3, then run the utility.

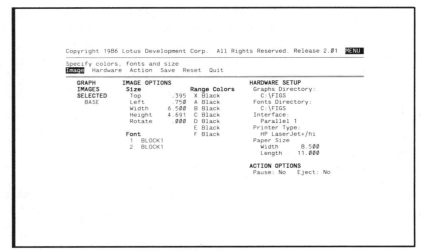

```
Copyright 1986 Lotus Development Corp.  All Rights Reserved. Release 2.01  MENU

Specify colors, fonts and size
Image  Hardware  Action  Save  Reset  Quit
─────────────────────────────────────────────────────────────────────────────
     GRAPH       IMAGE OPTIONS                          HARDWARE SETUP
    IMAGES       Size                Range Colors       Graphs Directory:
   SELECTED      Top        .395     X Black               C:\FIGS
     BASE        Left       .750     A Black             Fonts Directory:
                 Width     6.500     B Black               C:\FIGS
                 Height    4.691     C Black             Interface:
                 Rotate     .000     D Black               Parallel 1
                                     E Black             Printer Type:
                 Font                F Black               HP LaserJet+/hi
                  1  BLOCK1                               Paper Size
                  2  BLOCK1                                 Width    8.500
                                                           Length  11.000

                                                        ACTION OPTIONS
                                                         Pause: No   Eject: No
```

• Figure 12.12: *Lotus 1-2-3 Printgraph settings options*

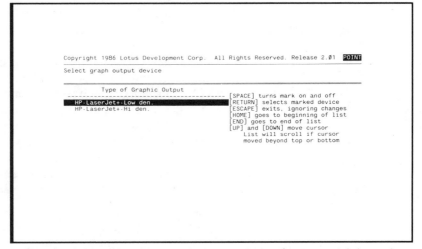

```
Copyright 1986 Lotus Development Corp.  All Rights Reserved. Release 2.01  POINT

Select graph output device
─────────────────────────────────────────────────────────────────────────────
        Type of Graphic Output
──────────────────────────────────────────   [SPACE] turns mark on and off
   HP·LaserJet+·Low den.                      [RETURN] selects marked device
   HP·LaserJet+·Hi den.                       [ESCAPE] exits, ignoring changes
                                              [HOME] goes to beginning of list
                                              [END] goes to end of list
                                              [UP] and [DOWN] move cursor
                                                 List will scroll if cursor
                                                 moved beyond top or bottom
```

• Figure 12.13: *Selecting the printing resolution for Lotus 1-2-3 graphs*

Printing Lotus Character Sets

Not all Lotus characters are supported by the LaserJet.

All three utilities include their own fonts that support the Lotus International Character Set (LICS). This set contains the standard characters in the ASCII range from 32 to 127, as well as international characters and symbols in the ASCII range 128 through 255. You can access them by using the Compose key, Alt-F1, followed by a specific sequence of keystrokes for each character, called the *compose sequence*. A complete list of compose sequences is in your Lotus manual.

For example, to create the Japanese yen sign, press Alt-F1, then Y=. The compose sequence for the British pound symbol is L=.

Using the Extended Character Set

Release 3 has an extended Lotus Multibyte Character Set (LMBCS), which includes all characters in the PC-8 symbol set, as well as many other graphic characters and symbols.

The LMBCS is divided into two groups:

- Group 0 is similar, but not identical to the PC-8 symbol set. Each of the characters are identified with an LMBCS code number from 32 to 255.

- Group 1 contains mainly graphic characters and symbols, associated with LMBCS code numbers 256 to 383. Each of these are also assigned a three-digit key code number from 000 to 127. This group includes characters with LMBCS code numbers 384 through 511, which duplicate group 0 characters 128 through 255.

Most of these characters can be created by pressing the Compose key and entering the compose sequence. All of them can be accessed through the @CHAR function or the Extended Compose key.

To use the @CHAR function, type

@CHAR(*LMBCS code number*)

Press ◄┘, and the character will be displayed on the screen (if it is part of the PC character set). To print the ← character, for example, type

@CHAR(283)

To use the Extended Compose key, press Alt-F1 twice, then enter the appropriate code. For group 1 characters, use the format

1-*LMBCS code number*

For example, to print ←, press Alt-F1 twice and enter

1-283

The versions of the add-on utilities discussed here support the LICS but, as of publication, not the LMBCS set.

The format for group 2 characters is

2-LMBCS key code number

Using Always

The Always utility offers extensive formatting capabilities. It includes three softfonts: Courier, Times, and Triumvirate (like Helvetica). These come in sizes from 6 to 20 points, and they can be set up to use internal and cartridge fonts. Text can be printed in bold, italic, or underlined, using up to eight fonts per worksheet.

When you want to format a worksheet, you create a font set of any eight available fonts, as shown in Figure 12.14. These are now available for formatting individual cells or cell ranges. To print in italics, you must select an italic font. But all other attributes, such as bold and underlining, are handled through the program's own /F (Format) menu.

In addition to formatting text with fonts, you can draw horizontal and vertical lines, enclose cells and cell ranges in boxes, and shade areas in three levels of gray.

Always is accessed using a hot key, by default Alt-F7. You can switch between text mode and graphics mode, which shows all the fonts and other formats. In the graphics mode, you can reduce the displayed screen to see more of your worksheet, or enlarge it to improve its appearance on low-resolution screens. Figure 12.15 shows an enlarged Always display.

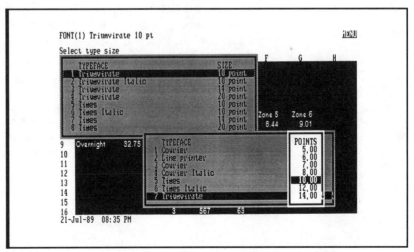

• Figure 12.14: *Creating an Always font set for Lotus 1-2-3*

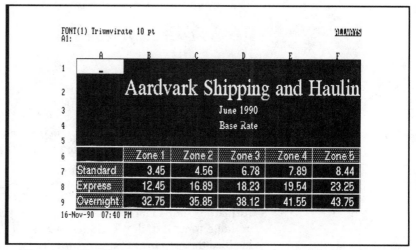

• Figure 12.15: *Always can enlarge the display*

Always also lets you format and print graphs from within the worksheet, a feature just included in Lotus 1-2-3 Release 3. This way, you can combine graphs and text on the same page. To access a graph, it must already be saved in the .PIC format. You can then load it into the worksheet, in the Always mode, and adjust its position and appearance. Figure 12.16 illustrates a worksheet and graph printed on the same page.

Like Printgraph, Always allows you to select colors and fonts. But you can also scale graph text by factors from .5 (half size) to 3 (triple the size). Because you can print the graph anywhere in relation to the worksheet, you can eliminate the graph's title, and then create your own using Always softfonts.

Using Datatype

The Datatype add-on program, manufactured by Swfte, includes Letter Gothic softfonts in sizes from 4 to 14 points and provides menu options for changing orientation and line spacing, from 4 to 12 lines per inch. You can also change margins, select paper size, and switch from the LICS to ASCII symbol set. The softfont has modified hyphen and equal sign characters that can be used for drawing solid single and double lines.

Using Sideways

Sideways was one of the first printing utilities designed for Lotus 1-2-3 worksheets. Its menu is shown in Figure 12.17. Its sole purpose is to print

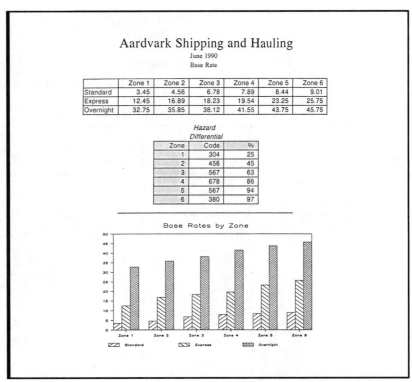

- Figure 12.16: *Lotus 1-2-3 worksheet and graph printed on the same page with Always*

```
                    S I D E W A Y S  version 3.21            S/N-61200-06
                                                             HP LaserJet Plus

        Printer port:                LPT1:

        Vertical form size (inches):    11.00
        Horizontal form size (inches):  8.00

        Character font:              Normal        5 x 18 dot matrix
        Density:                     Single
        Character spacing (dots):         1        12.50 characters per inch
        Line spacing (dots):              3         7.14 lines per inch

        Left margin (inches):          0.00
        Top margin (inches):           0.00
        Bottom margin (inches):        0.00            57 lines per page

        Starting page:                    1
        Glue lines:                       0
        Directory:   B:\
        Enter name of print .file:


        F1:help    F3:save options   F4:load options   F9:save defaults   F10:exit
```

- Figure 12.17: *Sideways menu*

ASCII text files in landscape orientation. While it was primarily meant for use with Lotus text files, it can be used with any file that is made up of unformatted ASCII characters.

You can print in one of nine different softfonts and set page size and spacing options. Table 12.3 lists the Sideways font options.

Table 12.3: *Sideways Font Options*

FONT	MATRIX	CPI	LINES PER INCH
Minuscule	4 × 11	15.00	11.53
Very Tiny	4 × 12	15.00	10.00
Tiny	4 × 15	15.00	8.33
Small	5 × 15	12.50	8.33
Normal	5 × 18	12.50	7.14
Large	7 × 15	8.33	8.33
Extra Large	7 × 10	8.33	7.14
Huge	9 × 15	6.81	8.33
Mammoth	9 × 18	6.81	7.14

Public Domain Support for Spreadsheet Printing

A number of useful utilities for Lotus 1-2-3 are available in the public domain or as shareware. Most bulletin boards and public domain libraries include small fonts, 6 points or less, designed to print wide worksheets on 8½-inch by 11-inch paper.

There is also a Lotus 1-2-3 macro program, HPLASER.WKS, in the public domain that lets you select fonts and page sizes from a two-line Lotus-like menu. The options available are shown in listed in Table 12.4.

The macro program runs automatically when you load it. If you're new to Lotus 1-2-3 macros, load the file, press Esc, then examine how the macros are structured.

- Table 12.4: *HPLASER.WKS Macro Options*

FONT	ORIEN-TATION	WEIGHT	PAPER	CHARACTERS	LINES
Courier	Landscape	Medium	Letter	98	45
Courier	Landscape	Medium	Legal	128	45
Courier	Portrait	Medium	Letter	72	76
Courier	Portrait	Medium	Legal	72	78
Courier	Portrait	Bold	Letter	72	78
Courier	Portrait	Bold	Legal	72	78
Courier	Landscape	Bold	Letter	98	45
Courier	Landscape	Bold	Legal	128	45
Line Printer	Portrait	Medium	Letter	124	104
Line Printer	Portrait	Medium	Legal	124	128
Line Printer	Portrait	Medium	Letter	124	80
Line Printer	Portrait	Medium	Legal	124	98
Line Printer	Landscape	Medium	Letter	165	60
Line Printer	Landscape	Medium	Legal	214	60
Line Printer	Landscape	Medium	Letter	165	45
Line Printer	Landscape	Medium	Legal	214	45

Note: Line Printer, bold, and landscape fonts require a compatible internal or cartridge font.

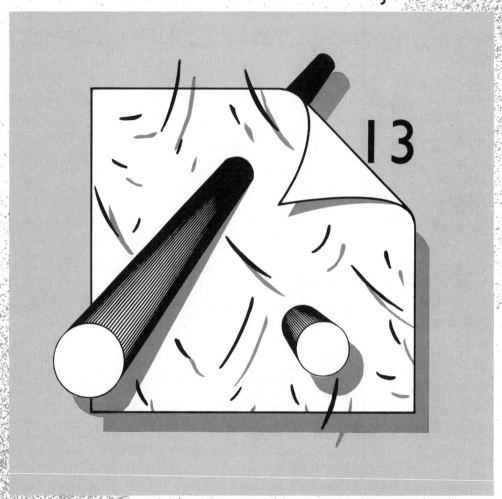

H · P L · A · S · E · R · J · E · T

13

Printing with Presentation Software

- Presentation programs produce visual images with high impact by blending elements of desktop publishing, graphic, drawing, and spreadsheet software. But in addition, they are specifically designed for professional-quality output on a wide range of devices. Instead of only generating printed output, these programs can present "slide shows" directly on the monitor, drive single and multicolor plotters, and produce color slides on film recorders such as the Polaroid Palette. Some programs even include communications software for automatically downloading files to vendors who can produce slides overnight.

In this chapter, we'll explore how two popular presentation packages, Harvard Graphics and Gem Presentation Team, work with LaserJet printers. These programs provide two different approaches to presentation development. Unfortunately, the black and white LaserJet cannot take full advantage of their powers.

• *Printing with Harvard Graphics*

In addition to text charts and signs, Harvard Graphics can produce statistical graphs and custom drawings. A number of graphic images suitable for presentations, called symbols, are provided with the package. It has the following LaserJet resources:

- Six built-in fonts

- Portrait and landscape orientation

- Graphics resolutions of 75, 150, and 300 dpi

You cannot modify the Harvard Graphics printer driver.

Harvard Graphics takes a totally graphic approach to laser printing. All characters are graphic fonts that can be scaled and rotated, not separate bit-mapped fonts for each type and size. Everything printed—even text—is actually in graphic form.

Setting Up for Printing with Harvard Graphics

The Install program on the Harvard Utilities disk copies the program files onto a directory that you name. All the font (with the FNT extension), symbol (SYM extension), and program files are copied. Printer selection and setup is performed within Harvard Graphics itself.

After you install Harvard Graphics, start it and follow these steps to set up your printer:

1. Select the Setup option from the Main menu. You'll see the Setup menu, as shown in Figure 13.1. This menu lets you designate default settings and the types of output devices attached to your system.

2. Select Printer 1 to display the Printer 1 Setup menu, as shown in Figure 13.2.

Select DeskJet from the Harvard Graphics Setup menu.

3. Using the mouse or keyboard, highlight the HP LaserJet, + ,500 + ,II option, or choose Apple LaserWriter if you have a PostScript-equipped LaserJet. If you're using a serial printer, you'll see the port and communications settings menu, as shown in Figure 13.3. Make your selections, and then press F10.

4. Repeat the process for Printer 2 if you are using two printers.

Using Fonts with Harvard Graphics

Harvard Graphics includes the six built-in fonts listed in Table 13.1. You cannot use internal fonts, cartridge fonts, or your own softfonts.

You can only print one font per page, but you can use all the font attributes. The default font is Executive. To change it to another font, select the Setup option from the Main menu, choose Default, and then select one of the six fonts.

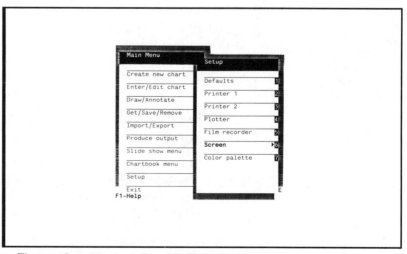

• Figure 13.1: *Harvard Graphics Setup menu*

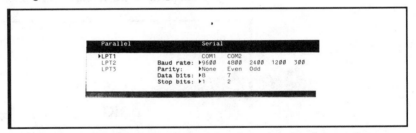

• Figure 13.2: *Printer 1 Setup menu*

• Figure 13.3: *Harvard Graphics port and communications settings*

While you're entering text, you can select font attributes, as well as size and color. Figure 13.4 shows the Text Options menu in Draw/Annotate mode. Figure 13.5 illustrates the available attributes.

Unfortunately, Harvard Graphics doesn't list the available sizes for each font. If you enter a size too large (usually anything above 100), nothing will appear when you preview the drawing. So, preview your work often (press F2) to make sure it appears balanced and well designed. You can always delete, move, or resize the text and graphic elements.

Changing the Orientation of Harvard Graphics Charts

The default setting is for landscape orientation. To change to portrait orientation, select the Setup option from the Main menu, and then choose

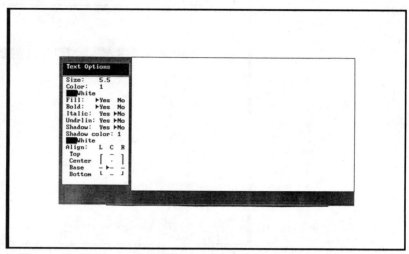

- Figure 13.4: *Harvard Graphics Text Options menu*

- Figure 13.5: *Harvard Graphics font attributes*

Defaults. Note that a half-page chart at the default landscape setting will actually print in portrait orientation.

Printing Harvard Graphics Charts

When you are ready to print your chart, press Esc to return to the Main menu and select Produce Output. Then choose Printer to see the Print

Chart Options menu, shown in Figure 13.6. Set the quality (see the following section for details) and size of the chart, paper size (Letter is 8½ by 11; Wide is 11 by 14), printer, and number of copies. Finally, press F10 to start printing.

• Table 13.1: *Harvard Graphics Fonts*

ATTRIBUTE				
Font	**Bold**	**Italic**	**No Fill**	**Underline**
Executive	Yes	Yes	Yes	Yes
Square Serif	Yes	Yes	Yes	Yes
Roman	Yes	Yes	No	Yes
Sans Serif	Yes	Yes	No	Yes
Script	Yes	No	No	Yes
Gothic	No	No	No	Yes

Note: Script and Gothic characters formatted as italic will print in Roman.

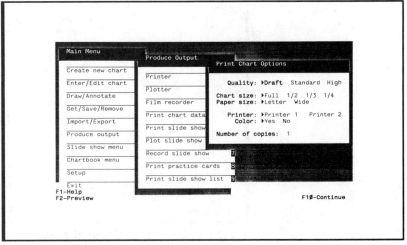

• Figure 13.6: *Harvard Graphics Print Chart Options menu*

PostScript printers will use internal fonts when you select Draft or Standard quality.

When selecting symbols for charts you are going to print, opt for ones that are black and white, or where the only color is in text.

Selecting Printing Quality

You can select from three printing qualities, or resolutions: Draft (75 dpi), Standard (150 dpi), and High (300 dpi). Draft is the default setting.

Since all printing is in graphic mode, you can't produce a full page at high resolution unless you have extra printer memory. The alternatives are to select a lower quality output or to reduce the size of the chart to one-half, one-third, or one-quarter page. Figure 13.7 shows an example of a three-dimensional line chart produced from data imported from Lotus 1-2-3, printed at high quality, ½ page.

At full size, lower quality text shows some jagged edges. So if quality is critical to your presentation, reduce the chart size, then enlarge the printout on a copy machine or at a local print shop.

Printing Color Symbols in Black and White

Harvard Graphics is designed to take full advantage of color output on the screen, plotters, or on film. When printing in black and white, fill patterns are substituted for chart colors, as shown in Figure 13.8. However, the results of printing some of the color symbols supplied may not be acceptable.

Figure 13.9, for example, shows six symbols. The three black and white graphics on the top line print nicely on the LaserJet + at high quality. The three bottom symbols, supplied in color, reproduce poorly. On a color screen, the map of the United States shows the states in various colors. The

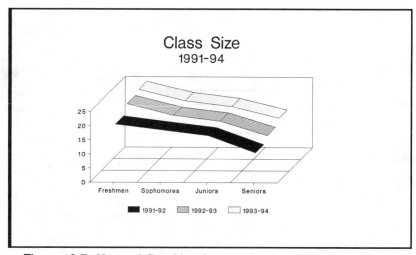

• Figure 13.7: *Harvard Graphics chart*

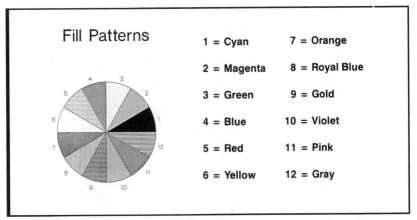

- Figure 13.8: *Harvard Graphics fill patterns substituted for colors*

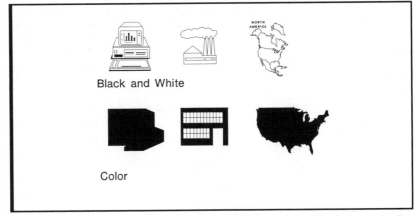

- Figure 13.9: *Harvard Graphics symbols: black and white (top) and color (bottom)*

other two color symbols also include details that appear in color but not on a black and white printout.

• *Printing with Gem Presentation Team*

The Gem Presentation Team package operates under the Gem Desktop, the same Windows-like environment that Ventura Publisher uses. It is actually a collection of the Desktop operating environment and four separate Gem applications. Because the system runs under the Gem interface, your work can be shared with other Gem applications. The presentation package provides the following LaserJet resources:

- Bitstream Fontware with Dutch, Swiss, and Charter fonts
- Portrait and landscape orientation
- Resolutions of 150 and 300 dpi

In addition, the package includes the Gem Business Library, a collection of borders and flow chart and electronic symbols.

Gem Applications

Gem Presentation Team includes the following programs:

- **Gem Draw Plus**: Use for free-hand drawing and text, or editing graphs, maps, and word charts from the other applications.
- **Gem Graph**: Use to create charts and graphics from data entered into its own spreadsheet. Graph can also make map charts in which data is plotted either statistically or by region.
- **Gem Map Edit**: Use to divide a map into regions and change displayed colors or patterns.
- **Gem Wordchart**: Use to create text-only charts, such as signs and cover pages.

Each of the applications can use all Gem resources and drivers for printers, plotters, and film recorders. The Bitstream Fontware, in fact, installs in Gem, not in any single application, so all the fonts you create are available no matter what program you're using.

The Bitstream fonts created for Gem can also be used in Ventura Publisher. See Chapter 4 for details on Bitstream Fontware.

Installing Printers for Gem

The Install batch file sets up the Gem environment and each of the applications. Bitstream Fontware must be installed separately, as discussed in Chapter 4.

During installation, you'll be asked to designate the type of system and mouse, then select one or more printer drivers, as shown in Figure 13.10. Select both of the HP LaserJet drivers so you have the choice of 150- or 300-dpi resolution. Select PostScript/LaserWriter Printer if your LaserJet is equipped for PostScript printing.

Contact Digital Research to order Driver Pack 14, which is a 300-dpi DeskJet printer driver.

Next, you'll have to designate the port for each printer, as shown in Figure 13.11. A warning box appears if you enter the same port for two printers. However, as long as you only output to one device at a time, you can connect them to the same port.

Using Fonts with Gem

When you use a LaserJet printer with Gem Presentation Team, you *must* install Bitstream fonts. You should make a full range of sizes, even though the process can take hours.

Originally, the Gem environment was shipped with two default graphic fonts, Swiss and Dutch. In all Gem applications, these two fonts, in a variety of sizes, will be listed as alternatives in the pull-down menus, as shown in Figure 13.12. Without Bitstream fonts installed, you'll still see Swiss and Dutch listed, but nothing will print.

```
▲▼ Digital Research Inc.                              GEM Setup R3.11

   Select the printer that you intend to use from the list below.

   ▯ Epson LQ Series Printers (180 x 180 Dots/Inch)
   ◀ HP Laserjet Series II Printer (300 x 300 Dots/Inch)
   ◀ HP LaserJet+ Printer (150 x 150 Dots/Inch)
   ◀ IBM/Epson High Resolution Printers (120 x 144 Dots/Inch)
   ◀ IBM Proprinter (120 x 144 Dots/Inch)
   ◀ HP Paintjet Printer (180 x 180 Dots/Inch) 8 colors
   ◀ Postscript / Laserwriter Printers
   ◀ Toshiba P321, P341, or P351 Printer (180 x 180 Dots/Inch)
   ◀ OTHER (Driver Pack)


   Press <F1> for device info, ↑ or ↓ to move cursor, <ENTER> to choose.
```

- Figure 13.10: *Gem printer selection menu*

```
▲▼ Digital Research Inc.                              GEM Setup R3.11

   Select a communications port for your printer:

   ▯ Parallel port #1 (LPT1)
   ◀ Parallel port #2 (LPT2)
   ◀ Parallel port #3 (LPT3)
   ◀ Communications port #1 (COM1)
   ◀ Communications port #2 (COM2)
```

- Figure 13.11: *Gem port options*

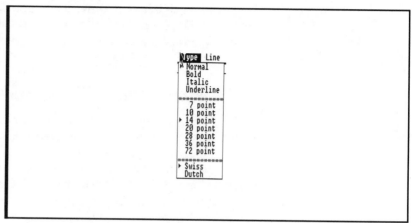

- Figure 13.12: *Gem font options*

If you select a font size that is not available, Gem will use the closest actual font but in the designated spacing. So if you select a 24-point font and only have a 12-point available, the characters will be spaced at twice the normal cpi, s o m e t h i n g   l i k e   t h i s.

Also, Gem doesn't offer a 12-point font in its menus. To use a 12-point font, you must select the listed font closest to it that is not matched by an existing printer font. For example, if you select the 10-point size, and there are no 10-point printer fonts, Gem will use the 12-point font instead.

As an example, I installed just three Bitstream fonts with my Gem system: 12- and 24-point Dutch and 18-point Swiss. When working with Word-chart, a program that makes signs and other all-text documents, I was able to create the report cover shown in Figure 13.13. Notice that the menu lists Swiss Bold sizes up to 72 points, the size used to format the words Annual Report. But look at the printed output shown in Figure 13.14. All the text printed in the one available Bitstream Swiss font.

To widen your selection, generate Bitstream fonts in all of the sizes you intend to use. If you don't make any Bitstream fonts, you'll still be able to create wonderful presentations, but you won't be able to print them on your LaserJet.

Selecting Orientation and Page Size for Gem Presentations

All Gem applications have similar dialog boxes to select orientation and page sizes. Pages larger than 8½ by 11 inches will be printed in four

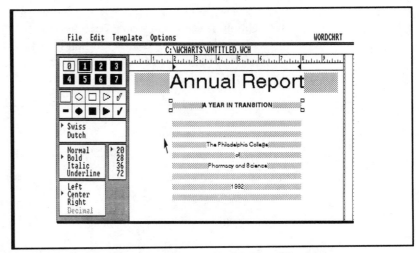

• Figure 13.13: *Report cover created with Gem Wordchart*

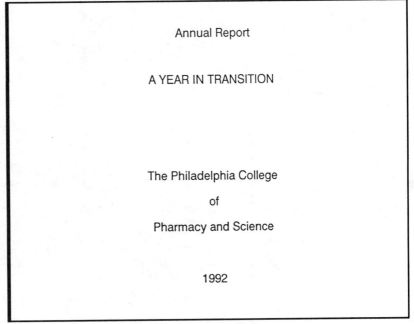

• Figure 13.14: *Printed report cover created with Gem Workchart*

tiles (separate sheets of paper) that can be pasted together.

A presentation can be made using just one application, or you could use several of them to merge text, graphs, and your own drawings. For instance, Figure 13.15 shows an illustration created using Gem Draw and Graph. It was printed on a LaserJet + at 150-dpi resolution. To create it, I started by running Gem Graph and used the Page Format dialog box to select portrait orientation and half-page size. I modified the chart shown in Figure 13.16 to display only the first series of data, saved that graph, then

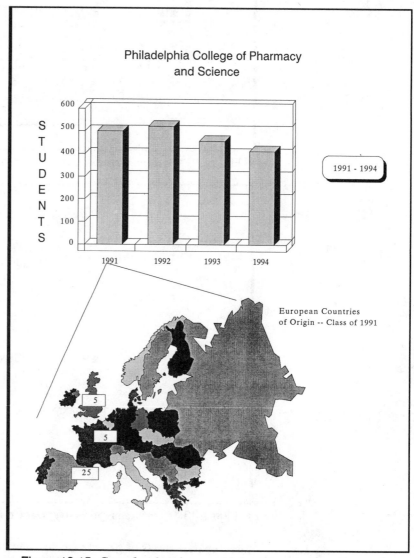

• Figure 13.15: *Complex drawing combining Gem graph and map charts*

Once loaded into Gem Draw, any part of the presentation can be edited.

loaded a map of Europe. I set up the map's region names as x-axis names, deleted the ones I didn't need, and then added the numbers for the y-axis.

With that done, I saved the map, loaded Gem Draw, and set the page at portrait orientation. Figure 13.17 shows the Draw Page Size dialog box. I then loaded each chart into its own Gem Draw application and copied the map under the bar chart. Using Gem Draw facilities, I changed some text and added a title and the lines extending from the first bar. With only three fonts available in my current setup, I had to carefully select sizes that I knew would print correctly.

You can also change the paper size using the Preferences pull-down menu. Select Paper Size to see the dialog box shown in Figure 13.18.

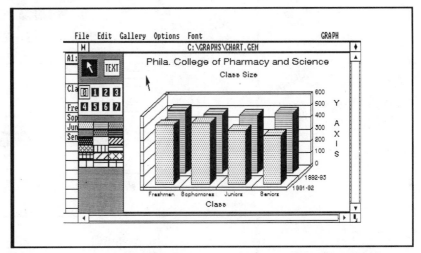

• Figure 13.16: *Three-dimensional bar chart created in Gem Graph*

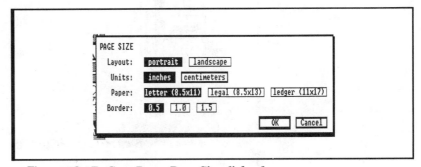

• Figure 13.17: *Gem Draw Page Size dialog box*

Printing Gem Presentations

When you're ready to print a publication, select To Output from the File pull-down menu. Figure 13.19 shows the output selection for my system, which includes a CGA display and both LaserJet drivers. By selecting the display as the device and clicking on the Start button, you can display a facsimile of the completed presentation.

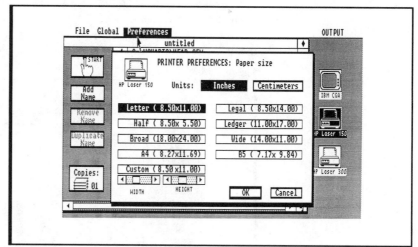

• Figure 13.18: *Gem Printer Preferences Paper Size dialog box*

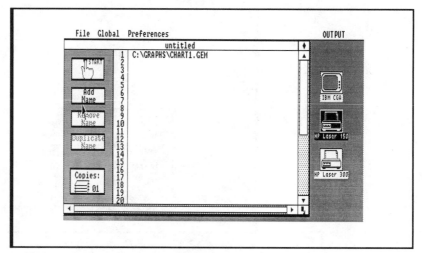

• Figure 13.19: *Gem output selection*

When printing color graphics, such as chart bars or pie slices, Gem substitutes different density dot patterns; the darker the color, the more dense the dots.

You can also select to print to a file. Pull down the Preferences menu, select Printer, and then choose File Redirect.

P · A · R · T   III

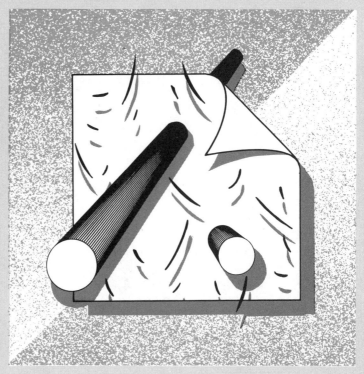

· *Enhancing Your System*

These three chapters will show you how to transport your LaserJet into another realm of productivity. If your printer is an important part of your office automation system, this part will help you get the largest return from your investment.

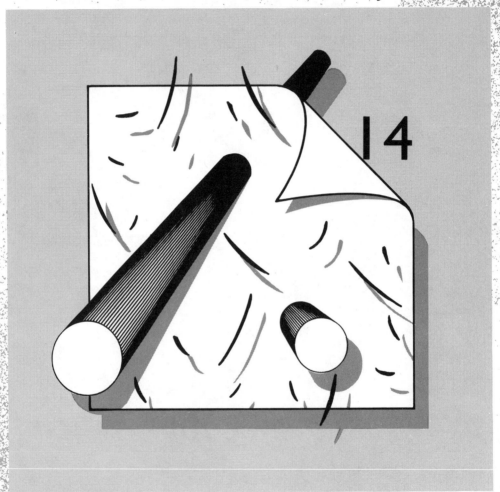

14

Printing Graphics: Scanners, Clip Art, and Colors

- Scanners and clip-art packages give you access to a wide variety of graphics. You can use special software and hardware to produce the highest possible quality printout. You may even be considering printing your publications in color. This chapter covers several different approaches to printing high-quality graphic images.

• *Printing Scanned Images*

A scanner directs light onto a printed surface, then uses a sensor to record the amount of reflected light at regular intervals—the scanning resolution. The data recorded by the sensor is converted into a graphic file that you can import into your application. The most popular formats are TIFF and PCX.

Scanners work by converting samples of the image into binary data. The number of samples taken per inch becomes the effective resolution of the scanned image. A 300-dpi scanner, for example, records samples at the rate of 300 per inch. Each sample, the same size as the LaserJet's dot, is read by the scanner, converted into binary, and transferred to your computer.

Full-Page Versus Hand Scanners

Scanners can either capture full pages or small sections of text. With full-page scanners, the sheet to be copied either sits flat under the scanning head or face down on glass, as on a photocopier. This makes it easy to scan pages from a book or magazine.

Recently, a number of lower cost hand scanners have become popular. You can scan images from 3 to 5 inches wide by slowly moving a hand-held device across or down the page.

Most hand scanners should be moved at about ¹/₂ inch per second.

Hand scanners are ideal for quickly capturing signatures and small drawings, but they have several drawbacks. Even though some scanner software lets you merge two scanned strips into one figure, their width will limit your scanning capabilities. Just the fact that they are hand operated can create problems. You must move the device straight down or across the page. If you shake or slide the device diagonally as you scan, the final image may be distorted.

In addition, hand scanners do not have the sophisticated technology to capture photographs. While some use the dithering technique that we'll discuss shortly, they can't capture true gray-scale images.

A typical full-page scanner can capture an 8¹/₂ by 11 inch page, at 300 dpi, in 24 seconds. With a hand scanner, you can quickly capture small areas in just a few seconds.

You can use more expensive scanners and printers to create images in high resolutions, such as the 1000-dpi LaserMaster 1000, 1270-dpi Linotronic L100, and 2540-dpi Linotronic L300.

Most full-page scanners use 300-dpi resolution to match that of your LaserJet. A few can capture at 400 dpi. Most hand scanners capture images at lower resolution, often about 200 dpi. To print images at more than 300 dpi, however, you need a special printer or enhancement hardware installed in your LaserJet.

Capturing the Gray Scale

Laser printers can only print one shade of black, and without special hardware, each dot printed is the same size. This is fine as long as the scanned image is just solid black and white, such as a signature. The scanner would convert each sample into either a black dot or white dot (a sample where no toner will be transferred to the paper), which would print nicely on the LaserJet.

But to reproduce photographs or other images that have shades of gray, the scanner must be able to simulate the gray scale. The results depend on the capturing mode used by your scanner: bit-map, dithered, or gray scale.

Bit-Map Scanners

The least expensive scanners only capture two shades: solid black and solid white. These are called bit-map, line-art, one-bit, or bilevel scanners. Every sample, even shades of gray, is converted into either a black or white dot. The scanner decides which shades are interpreted as black and which are white.

Most scanners have some sort of contrast dial that allows you to adjust the black-white cutoff point. But no matter where you set the dial, the image you see on the screen after scanning will be only black and white.

Obviously, this type of scanner is not suitable for capturing photographs and similar graphics.

Scanners that Use Dithering

Other scanners simulate the gray scale by a process called *dithering*. In dithering, each shade of gray is represented by a different number of dots in a square grid; the darker the shade, the more dots. The scanner reads a sample, then converts it into a dither pattern instead of a single black or white dot. When printed, the dither patterns give the illusion of gray.

The number of dots in the grid determine how many shades of gray can be simulated. A 4-by-4 grid, for example, can represent up to 16 different shades, as illustrated in Figure 14.1.

The more shades of gray, the more detail in the photograph. But as the number of shades increase, so does the size of the grid required to represent

• Figure 14.1: *Dither patterns in a 4-by-4 grid represent 16 shades*

Desktop publishers often refer to dithering as halftoning. But this is not the same as photographic halftoning used by commercial printers to reproduce continuous tone photographs.

each one, reducing the final printed resolution. Using a 4-by-4 grid, for instance, the effective resolution of the image is only 75 dpi—300 divided by 4. Using an 8-by-8 grid to represent 64 shades would result in an image with only 37.5-dpi resolution.

Gray-Scale Scanners

The more expensive scanners on the market capture gray scales digitally, instead of as collections of dots. Gray-scale scanners, also called multibit scanners, sample small sections of the photograph and record the sample as a series of bits representing the actual shade of gray.

Scanners like this come in 16-, 64-, or 256-level models, referring to the number of gray-scale levels that can be distinguished.

A 16-level scanner, for example, might sample the photograph at 300 dpi. Each sample is assigned a value from 0 (solid white) to 15 (solid black), and stored as 4 bits. Scanners that capture 64 or 265 levels work the same way, except more bits are required for each dot sample—6 bits for 64 levels, 8 bits for 256 levels.

Figure 14.2 shows how the number of bits used to represent one shade increases the number of shades that can be captured. A bit-map scanner can only store a 0 or 1, representing just white and black. But using 4 bits, 16 different binary combinations are possible, each used to store a specific shade between white and black. A 64-level scanner uses 6 bits for each gray tone, and a 256-level scanner uses 8 bits.

Gray-scale scanners come with special software that converts the scanned image into files, usually in TIFF format. But because 4, 6, or 8 bits are used to store each bit of the image, the files can be quite large—as much as 5 to 8 megabytes for an 8-inch by 10-inch photograph scanned at 256 levels.

Software for Manipulating Scanned Images

Some applications include options that allow you to manipulate scanned images. In addition, you can use programs designed specifically for this purpose.

Controlling Gray-Scale Images

Scanned images of photographs are screened to simulate the halftone effect of commercially printed photographs. The quality of the final output is affected by this screening. Screens can have various patterns, with different shapes, angles, and densities.

Unlike dithered scans that are screened when captured, gray-scale images are screened when printed. Applications that support gray-scale scans, such as Pagemaker, have options for controlling the line resolution and angle of the screens. Figure 14.3 shows the Pagemaker Image Control dialog box, which contains the options for screening images.

These programs can also use the binary information to resize the image without distortion and to control its brightness and contrast. (Pagemaker's Lightness and Contrast options are in the Image Control dialog box.) For example, if the original photograph was dark, all the samples would be in the higher binary range. To lighten the image, each of the captured levels would be reduced by the same amount, resulting in a printed image with the same range of grays but brighter.

	bitmap	16-level	64-level	256-level
White	0	0000	000000	00000000
		0001		
		0010		
		0011	64	256
		0100	levels	levels
		0101		
		0110		
		0111		
		1000		
		1001		
		1010		
		1011		
		1100		
		1101		
		1110		
Black	1	1111	111111	11111111

• Figure 14.2: *Binary patterns for gray-scale images*

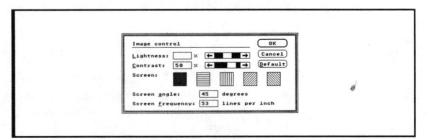

• Figure 14.3: *Pagemaker Image Control dialog box*

Other software, such as Publisher's Paintbrush and Picture Publisher, let you edit and manipulate the gray-scale patterns, controlling how the gray-scale data—up to 256 levels—will be converted into a halftone when printed. You can even use drawing tools to edit, size, crop, or mirror sections of the image, then save it in a format that can be imported into Pagemaker or Ventura Publisher.

Using PB/Scan with PC Paintbrush

For maximum control over scanned images, use scanning software such as PB/Scan, part of Publisher's Type Foundry. This program works directly from within PC Paintbrush for Windows, and it scans images into the Paintbrush environment. Driver files for the most popular scanners are included, so the program can be set up specifically for your hardware.

When you run PC Paintbrush, the Scan Image option will be listed on the File pull-down menu. This option gives you access to a range of selections, including the ability to set the brightness and contrast of the image. Figure 14.4 shows the PC Paintbrush Brightness and Contrast dialog box.

The Scanner Halftoning dialog box, shown in Figure 14.5, allows you to select the screen type. Some of the halftone patterns look better on the screen; others print better images on paper. The Bayer pattern, for example, produces a high-quality screen image, but prints in just fair quality on the LaserJet. Coarse Fatting, on the other hand, appears grainy on the screen but looks nice when printed. You can obtain a crisper printed image, but fewer shades of gray, with Fine Fatting.

Through PB/Scan, you can also select horizontal and vertical resolution and set a scaling factor to reduce or enlarge the image as it is scanned.

After you've set the scanning configuration, you can either scan or prescan the image. (Prescanning produces a quick low-resolution image of the entire page for testing settings and image size.) You designate which part of the page you want to capture and start the scan. The final image appears

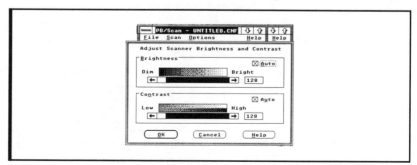

• Figure 14.4: *PC Paintbrush Brightness and Contrast dialog box*

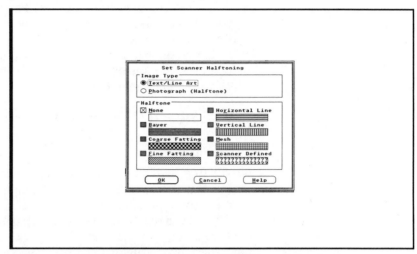

• Figure 14.5: *PC Paintbrush Scanner Halftone dialog box*

in the PC Paintbrush window, ready to be saved, edited, or printed though Windows.

Using Scanned Images as Fonts

Using Publisher's Type Foundry (or similar software), scanned images such as decorative characters can even be converted to downloadable fonts. Figure 14.6 shows a logo scanned into PC Paintbrush Plus, then transferred to the bit-map editor via the clipboard. This logo replaced the left bracket character ({).

Scanning Tips and Tricks

Printing faithful reproductions requires coordinated use of all your hardware—scanner, computer, and printer—and software—scanning, editing, and publishing. So it's important to consider the interactions of each component before beginning. Here are some points to remember:

- Check your desktop publishing or word processing software to see its graphic file requirements. Look for specifications regarding resolutions, file formats, and sizes. What functions can it perform on bit-map, dithered, and gray-scale scans?

- Does your scanner come with file-conversion utilities? You might be able to store large gray-scale files in a compressed format, then convert to TIFF format before use.

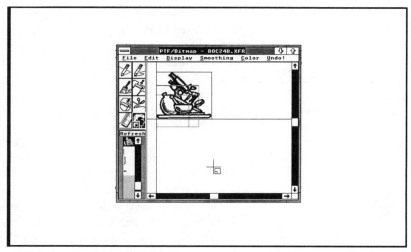

- Figure 14.6: *Scanned logo copied into bit-map font*

- Consider the type of document you are producing. If you're scanning an image for position only, select a bit-map or dithered format for its smaller file size.

- Don't screen photographs that are already halftones. Overlaying screen patterns creates a noticeable moire effect.

- Scan at the same size or larger than the final desired output. Enlarging a scanned image may reduce the resolution.

- For camera-ready copy, use the gray-scale setting, if available, and let your application screen the image.

- Create a one-page document containing just the scanned image. Make several test prints at various settings before merging the graphic into your document.

- Use a straight edge to guide your movement with a hand scanner. Attach the image you're copying firmly and squarely to a hard surface. If the image is small, tape a transparency over it to hold it in place.

Hardware for Enhancing Scanned Output

The problem with dithered and gray-scale halftoning is that LaserJet printers are still limited to 300 dpi and one size dot. Even after screening, the printed photograph might still be far from the quality of the original.

The JLaser card is discussed in detail in Chapter 15.

One solution to this problem is a hardware device that modulates the printer's laser beam to create dots of different sizes. This results in output more like the photographic halftones produced by a commercial printer.

The LazaGram Modulator Card is an example. This add-on requires a JLaser interface card. It installs between the printer's video interface and the JLaser switching assembly. A software driver installs embedded codes to turn the LazaGram off for text and line drawings, but on for pictures.

Some scanned images can be used directly by the system. Dithered images and several formats of gray-scale files must first be converted with software provided. These files can then be read directly by desktop publishing software. Even though the system can convert dithered files, gray-scale scans produce better output.

The LazaGram card is for laser printers only.

When the file is transmitted, the device uses the binary data to modulate the laser beam and define the size of the printed dot—from $1/300$ to $1/1500$ of an inch. When the image is printed using dots of different sizes, a greater number of gray shades can be represented by a smaller grid. The result is 64 possible shades of gray at 100 dpi, compared to the 37.5 dpi that would normally be printed. Figure 14.7 compares a dithered image with one printed using LazaGram.

Another beam-modulator device is Visual Edge, from Intel. Technically, photographs printed with these devices are at the same quality as a commercial printer can achieve using a 100-line halftone screen at a 45-degree angle. If you are producing camera-ready images to be reproduced commercially, tell your printing contractor not to rescreen the photograph.

Scanning Services

If you only have an occasional need for scanned image, such as a signature to add to form letters or a company logo, you might not want to invest in hardware. An alternative is to send the image to a scanning service, a company that will scan the image for you and return a graphic file that you can import into an application.

Macros are not available for DeskJet printers.

Some companies, such as Orbit Enterprises, can also provide a graphic macro to download to your printer. A macro is a series of PCL commands downloaded and stored in the printer's memory, much like keyboard macros in WordPerfect and Word. You later run the macro, which directs the printer to execute the PCL commands.

If you plan to use a scanned image often, such as the same signature at the bottom of 100 form letters, it is more efficient to download a macro one time instead of merging a graphic file with each letter.

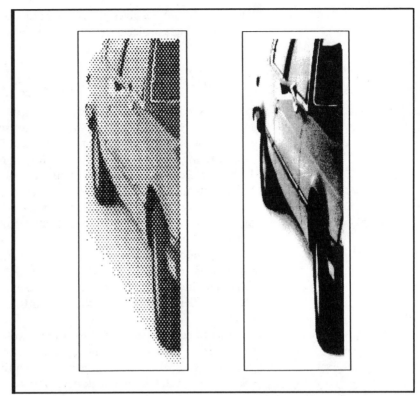

• Figure 14.7: *Dithered (left) and LazaGram output*

Orbit Enterprises also offers a program called Imagener that creates macros from your own scanner files. Macros are discussed in Chapter 19.

• *Printing with Clip Art*

Clip-art packages contain high-quality, ready-made images, either printed or on disk.

One of the most well known clip-art suppliers is Dover Publications. This company markets volumes of clip-art books, most specializing in one period or style of design, such as art deco, Victorian, and decorative initials. Better yet, the volumes range in price from $3.50 to $7.00 each.

Before you use clip art, check with the vendor to see if you can use it "copyright-free." In some cases, purchasing the clip art gives you the right to use it in any sort of publication. Other suppliers limit your right to in-house publications, or to a specific number of images from the collection.

Dover, for example, gives you the right to use up to ten images from a volume for a single project. Use of more images requires specific permission.

Disk Versus Printed Clip Art

Disk versions of clip art are convenient because they are ready to be merged into your application, but they have some drawbacks. Not only is there a limit to the number of images that can fit on one disk, but you must be able to use the format they are supplied in. Most come as either TIFF or PCX files. Be sure to check that your application accepts the disk format before you purchase the art (although there are file-conversion utilities you might be able to use, as discussed shortly). Also, make sure the disk supplied is for your type of computer. A great deal of clip art is sold on Apple Macintosh formatted disks.

A number of commercial, shareware, and public domain sources are available for clip art on disk. Public Brand Software offers at least 18 disks full of graphics, most archived to store two or three times the usual number. Other excellent sources are bulletin boards and services like Compuserve and Genie.

Hard-copy clip art offers its own advantages, but you need a scanner to use them. You can capture images in any format your software allows. Your own scanner might even be better than that used by some disk-based services, especially the public domain variety.

Converting Graphics Files to Your Application's Format

Have a favorite Printshop figure that you want to print with WordPerfect? Convert it to PCX format, then load it as a figure. If the figure is in dot-matrix resolution, first use a painting program to add pixels that smooth arcs and diagonal lines.

Although some application programs can handle more than one file format, many are limited to one specific type. But graphics files come in a variety of formats. Some programs use only their own proprietary format or just a limited number of others. If you purchase clip art on disk, or wish to use a design you created in one program with another application, you may have to convert the format of the file.

Fortunately, there are many ways to convert files. Several popular applications come with their own utilities that capture the displayed screen directly to their own format. Other utility programs can convert graphics to a variety of formats.

For example, Pizazz Plus not only captures and prints almost every type of screen image, but it can save the displayed screen in eight popular formats. So you could capture a graphics screen from one program, then use PC Paint to edit the image before printing it.

Other types of programs convert directly from file to file. This way you don't have to display the image before converting it. Harvard System's Graphic Link Plus, for example, converts between 20 different file formats. It can rotate an image as well as adjust up to 11 dithering patterns.

Iconvert is a commercial file-conversion program distributed in demonstration form through public domain libraries. It is a menu-driven program that requires a CGA monitor. The demonstration version performs the same conversions as the full release, but doesn't allow automatic conversion of multiple files. Figure 14.8 shows the formats that Iconvert can handle. The program can also mirror, expand, flip, and invert the image before conversion.

Some graphics programs have been designed to let IBM computer users display and print Macintosh computer drawings without conversion. Once Macintosh files have been transferred onto PC-formatted media, shareware programs such as ReadMac can display them on the screen, and PrintMac can output them to the LaserJet. Figure 14.9 shows an example of Macintosh art printed on a LaserJet + . Using ReadMac, Pizazz Plus, and a painting program, you could display a Macintosh file, capture it to PCX format, and then edit it.

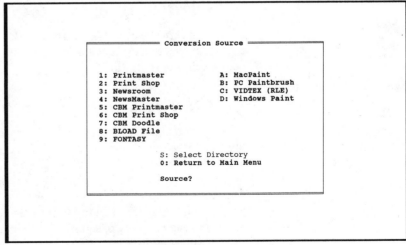

• Figure 14.8: *Conversion options in Iconvert*

• Figure 14.9: *Macintosh drawing printed on the LaserJet +*

• *Working with Color*

Scanners convert colors into gray-scale information for reproduction in black and white.

There are two ways that you can work with color using your LaserJet: to print images that are in color on the screen or to prepare publications for commercial color printing.

Printing Color Images in Black and White

What happens when you print a color image on the LaserJet depends on your software. In some cases, as with Lotus 1-2-3 Release 3, charts displayed in color will automatically be converted to black and white crosshatch patterns. Harvard Graphics converts chart colors to patterns, but it does not convert the colors in its symbol library. Gem Presentation Team prints colors as shades of gray using the LaserJet's dot patterns. So the results depend on the application and the image you're printing.

If you want to print a chart, drawing, or other graphic, try to set the application to black and white. When using a program with graphics libraries, such as Harvard Graphics, select only art that is black and white. Most spreadsheet and graphing programs let you select color or black and white.

Before you capture a color screen, refer to your application's manual for how to set the screen colors. For example, with Microsoft Windows, use the Control Panel to set the color preferences for each area of the screen. When you can't set the application to black and white, but still want to print screen dumps, consider using an image-capture program, such as one of those discussed in Chapter 3. Pizazz Plus, for example, will automatically convert colors to gray-scale patterns before printing. If you have an EGA or VGA monitor, it will even let you change screen colors, setting the gray-scale translation however you want.

Preparing for Commercial Color Printing

If you want your final output in color, you'll have to go to a commercial printer.

Some applications, such as Pagemaker 3.0 and Ventura Publisher 2.0, can be used for spot color. Separate sheets are printed (in black) for each color, and then the commercial printer overlays them on the press.

But from the commercial printer's viewpoint, there are two types of color printing: flat color and process color.

Flat Color

Flat color is the same as spot-color overlays. You supply the commercial printer with a separate sheet, printed in black, containing just the text and graphics for each color.

The printer prepares a "plate" from each sheet, then makes successive passes through the press until all the colors have been printed.

Premixed or custom-mixed inks are obtained for each color, using a matching system such as PMS (Pantone Matching System) to ensure the final colors are just what the client ordered. This allows the client to specify a unique color by its PMS number, which the commercial printer can mix exactly.

You can create color overlays even if you don't have a desktop publishing program. Two-color headlines, for example, can be created using outline and filler fonts, as shown in Figure 14.10. These two fonts were produced by Softcraft's Font Effects then installed in WordPerfect. To reproduce the headline, the commercial printer would make two plates, one for each font, then print them in different colors so the filler aligns inside the outline.

Flat color is fine if you don't have many colors to print, since a separate plate and press run is required for each. But at a certain point, the cost of multiple plates and press runs is not economically feasible.

Two-color Text
Two-color Text

• Figure 14.10: *Using fonts to create two-color text*

Process Color

The full range of colors in a color photograph can't be reproduced using flat colors. To reproduce color photographs or multicolored artwork, process color, also called four-color process, is used.

The picture or art to be printed is photographed as four special halftones, called separations. These separate the image into the four basic colors: yellow, magenta, cyan, and black. Each halftone consists of dots that represent varying degrees of the colors to be mixed. On the printed page, for example, a section that is light red will contain small, widely spaced red dots. A dark red area will contain large, close red dots.

When printed on the same page, the overlapping dots of these colors can combine to form literally thousands of different colors. No matter how many colors are in the original, only four plates and press runs are required.

If you have fewer colors to print, you may still save money by using two- or three-color process printing. This is possible when not all four process colors are needed to create the range of colors in the original.

Unfortunately, even though desktop publishing programs can output separate sheets for each of the four process colors, they cannot be used for separations. The printed sheets would be solid black, representing solid shades of yellow, cyan, magenta, and black. The commercially prepared separations, on the other hand, are halftones indicating degrees of each color, from light to dark. So you'll have to prepare your camera-ready copy and let the commercial printer produce the separations for process color from your original photographs or art.

Duotones are black and white photographs printed in two flat colors, using halftones created at different screen angles. In some applications, these offer a less expensive option to adding color to publications.

H·P L·A·S·E·R·J·E·T

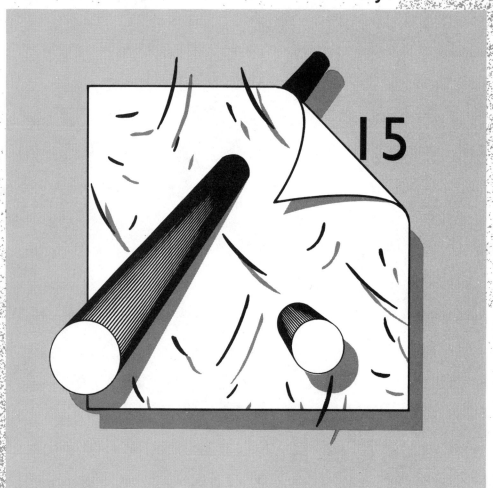

15

PostScript Solutions

• PostScript printing offers many advantages, such as the capability to produce a variety of special effects using fonts of any size. But PostScript printers are usually more expensive that LaserJet models. And if you do purchase a PostScript printer, you can't use any PCL or LaserJet drivers, still the most common in the PC world.

As an alternative, you can purchase hardware to implement PostScript on your LaserJet. The final cost may be about the same, but you'll get the best of both worlds—PostScript and PCL capabilities. You'll be able to use Laser-Jet, Apple LaserWriter, or generic PostScript drivers. If you don't have a rich uncle, there are software solutions; the cost of PostScript interpreters on disk starts at about $200.

Perhaps you don't need PostScript at all but just the ability to create special effects. There are ways to achieve these on the LaserJet without PostScript.

In this chapter, we'll explore ways to add PostScript to your LaserJet, as well as techniques for printing special effects. We'll review some examples of hardware and software solutions here, and a complete list of the alternatives is included in Appendix C. However, before you begin to apply these solutions, you should have a basic understanding of how PostScript works. We'll begin with a brief review.

• *Creating PostScript Programs*

Like PCL, the PostScript language is a carefully defined set of commands that control the printer. But while PCL is basically a series of Escape codes, PostScript has all the elements we've come to expect in a computer programming language: loops, conditionals, arrays, procedures, and even the ability to create library files of subroutines.

In fact, a PostScript program is really just a text file composed of English-language commands. For example, Figure 15.1 shows a PCL program followed by a PostScript program. Both programs print a 1-inch

PostScript is similar to Forth in that it is a stack-oriented language using postfix notation.

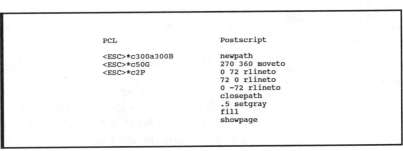

```
PCL                    Postscript

<ESC>*c300a300B        newpath
<ESC>*c50G             270 360 moveto
<ESC>*c2P              0 72 rlineto
                       72 0 rlineto
                       0 -72 rlineto
                       closepath
                       .5 setgray
                       fill
                       showpage
```

• Figure 15.1: *Comparing PCL and PostScript programs*

square filled with a 50 percent shade of gray. The PCL program contains three sets of Escape codes. If you know nothing about PCL, these lines appear meaningless. However, if you know nothing about PostScript but something about computer programming, you should be able to decipher how the PostScript program works.

You can create PostScript programs in three ways:

- Using an application with a PostScript driver
- Writing and downloading your own program
- Writing the program interactively

These methods are discussed in the following sections.

Using an Application's Driver

The easiest way to use a PostScript printer is with an application program that has a PostScript driver. You select and size fonts, set page formats, draw lines, and merge graphics through the application. The driver will convert your document or drawing into a PostScript program and transfer it to the printer. A PostScript interpreter built into the printer converts the commands into a graphic bit map that's placed on the laser's drum and then on paper.

The only drawback is that most applications cannot take full advantage of PostScript's power.

Writing Your Own Programs

You can print listings of your own programs, but not execute them, through your application. When your word processor prints the file, the driver assumes you simply want to print the text you entered.

Because PostScript programs are really just text files, you can also write your own programs using a word processor or text editor. Save the program as an ASCII (plain text) file; then download it through the printer's port. The PostScript interpreter will treat the program as if it was created by an application's driver. This method gives you access to all the PostScript features.

Writing Programs Interactively

Another way to create a program also involves writing it yourself, but in an interactive mode. Some PostScript printers, such as the Apple LaserWriter, can be placed in the interactive mode directly connected to your keyboard. This is normally done using a telecommunications program through the printer's serial port instead of a modem. Enter the command

> executive

to see the prompt

> PS>

on the screen. Now every line you type will be transmitted directly to the printer and interpreted immediately.

Entering commands one at a time is helpful when you're first learning PostScript. You can type small programs without having to switch in and out of a text editor.

Program Components

The preamble is similar to constant, variable, function, and procedure definitions that precede a Pascal program. It can also be compared to a library file of functions merged into a C language program.

PostScript programs may contain two parts: the preamble (sometimes called the prologue) and the script. The preamble, transmitted to the printer first, contains definitions used in the script. For example, the preamble used by WordPerfect 5.0 contains these definitions to turn on (_SH) and off (_sh) shadow characters:

```
/_SH  {bon {/bon false def} if
  /_S /sshow load def /sflg true def
  } bdef
/_sh  {/_S /show load def /sflg false def bflg {_B} if} bdef
```

When you format text in a shadow font (by pressing Ctrl-F8 A A), something like this will appear in the script:

```
/Times-Roman 1210 _ff
_SH (This)_S 167 _rm (is)_S 167 _rm (a)_S 167 _rm (test)_S _sh
```

The interpreter knows what _SH and _sh are because their definitions are in the preamble.

Every application program has its own unique preamble—WordPerfect's preamble will not work with Microsoft Word files, for instance. But the application's preamble is the same for every script (document or file) that it prints.

In some cases, such as with Microsoft Word and Ventura Publisher, the preamble is a separate file on your disk that is transmitted to the printer before every script. When you print a PostScript document, only the script is created by the driver. But before the script is sent to the printer, the preamble file is transmitted. With these type of programs, the preamble file must be present on the disk for any document to print on a PostScript device.

Other programs, such as WordPerfect, combine the preamble with every script. That's why the print file to produce a single line of text might be 7000 bytes, while the same Word file is less than 200.

If you write your own PostScript programs, you don't need a preamble unless you want to define functions and procedures ahead of time. However, if your programs are complicated, a preamble can serve as a basic library of commands. For example, you could include this definition for a 1-inch square in your preamble:

You'll cause an error if you transmit a script that uses definitions not found in a preamble.

```
/square
{0 72 rlineto
72 0 rlineto
0 -72 rlineto
closepath} def
```

Then to print a square, you would specify the position on the page and the fill pattern in your program, such as

```
newpath
270 360 moveto square
.5 setgray
fill
showpage
```

PostScript will use the commands in the preamble's /square definition when these lines are executed.

• *Using PostScript Fonts*

PostScript uses outline rather than presized fonts like PCL. When you want to print in a particular font and size, the driver (or your own program) will include the commands that create the characters "on the fly." This means that specifically sized and formatted characters are made at the time of printing. You only need the outline available, not separate fonts in every size.

Two standard sets of fonts are usually supplied with PostScript. Printers compatible with the original Apple LaserWriter have 13 fonts: a symbol set of Greek characters, and Courier, Times, and Helvetica in Normal, Bold, Italic, and Bold Italic. LaserWriter NTX compatible printers have those 13 fonts, plus Zapf Chancery Medium Italic; Zapf Dingbats; and four fonts each of Palatine, ITC Avant Garde, ITC Bookman, Helvetica Narrow, and New Century Schoolbook.

There are several advantages to using PostScript fonts:

- You don't have to waste storage space with different sized fonts in each typeface you want to use. You only need the basic outlines.

- You aren't limited to predefined sizes. With PostScript, you can usually enter any point size up to 120 points, depending on your application.

- You aren't restricted to a maximum font size. The largest PCL font that you can print on the LaserJet + might be 32 points; you can print any size—limited only by total printer memory—using PostScript.

- PostScript can create special graphic and text effects. Although most applications are very limited in using this capability, you can take advantage of it in your own programs.

- Portrait and landscape orientations can be included on the same page.

Figure 15.2 shows some examples of effects created with PostScript fonts. The top shows a basic Times font scaled in five different sizes, rotated, and converted to outline. The same font was used to create the word *PostScript* in the lower-left corner, where the characters are "masked" with a series of radiated lines. The three-dimensional effect for the word *Sybex* was created by printing it a number of times in varying levels of gray, each word offset slightly from the one before. All these examples were created with short PostScript programs entered in the interactive mode.

The only real disadvantage of using PostScript fonts is that printing them can be a slow process. Rasterizing text (creating bit maps on the fly from outlines) can take a long time. Slow speed, in fact, is the most common complaint about PostScript.

Fortunately, many of the hardware solutions to implementing PostScript on the LaserJet overcome the speed problem. We'll discuss hardware alternatives after we explore the software possibilities.

• *Implementing PostScript with Software*

If you want to use PostScript occasionally, consider a low-cost software solution. Instead of having the PostScript interpreter built into the printer,

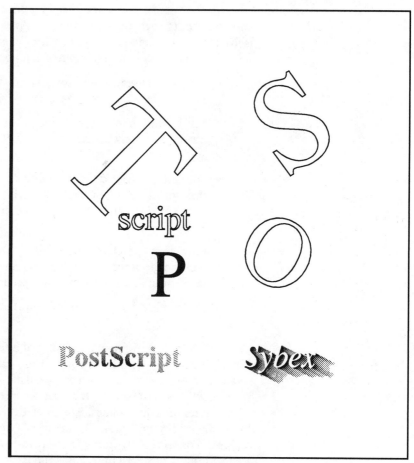

● Figure 15.2: *Effects with PostScript fonts*

software interpreters translate PostScript scripts into PCL commands. Like PostScript, these interpreters use outline fonts to scale type on the fly. The names and widths of the fonts are compatible with their PostScript counterparts, so you can use your application's standard PostScript driver.

Printing with these programs involves several steps. First, you set up your application for PostScript, create the document, then save the printer output to a file. (Most applications have a means of sending printer output to a disk file.) Exit the application, and then run the interpreter. It reads the PostScript file, scales the fonts, and sends the bit-map data for both text and graphics. You can't print a PostScript file directly from within an application.

In some cases, software interpreters are faster than PostScript printers. In one test, GoScript printed a PostScript graphics benchmark in 75 percent of the time it took the Apple LaserWriter IINT (*PC Magazine*, "Post-Purchase PostScript," 4/11/89).

A DeskJet driver, DeskJet.DRV, supports full-page graphics at 300 dpi without additional memory.

However, this is not an ideal way to implement PostScript if it is your primary method of printing. Rasterizing the fonts usually takes much longer than with hardware solutions and not all PostScript commands may be supported. But software interpreters are an excellent way to see if Post-Script is really for you; they can serve as an inexpensive introduction to PostScript.

Using GoScript

An example of a PostScript software interpreter is GoScript. It comes in two versions: a $195 package with 13 outline fonts, and GoScript Plus, a $395 package with 35 fonts.

GoScript installs on your hard disk, along with its own outline fonts, which are compatible with PostScript fonts. The files supplied with the base package are listed in Table 15.1. The LaserJet driver, LJII.DRV, supports all models but the original and can print a full page of graphics at 300 dpi on the LaserJet II and IID without any additional memory. A 150-dpi setting supports full-page graphics on the LaserJet +, although smaller 300-dpi pages can still be printed.

• Table 15.1: *Fonts Supplied with GoScript*

FONT FILE NAME	TYPEFACE
F_3000.GSF	Roman (similar to Times Roman)
F_3001.GSF	Roman Italic
F_3002.GSF	Roman Bold
F_3003.GSF	Roman Bold Italic
F_3004.GSF	Sans (similar to Helvetica)
F_3005.GSF	Sans Italic
F_3006.GSF	Sans Bold
F_3007.GSF	Sans Bold Italic
F_3008.GSF	Courier
F_3009.GSF	Courier Oblique
F_3010.GSF	Courier Bold
F_3011.GSF	Courier Bold Oblique
F_3012.GSF	Symbol

Use the /L option to print at 150 dpi. Output is faster than the default 300 dpi, but the quality is significantly reduced.

The installation program creates a configuration file, named GSCONFIG.CFG, on the hard disk, using the default settings for your printer. The LaserJet configuration file for 300 dpi is shown in Figure 15.3.

If you plan on printing full pages on a LaserJet + , modify the Driver command in the configuration file to read

DRIVER = LJII.DRV /L

This sets GoScript to 150 dpi. The best setup for the LaserJet + , however, is to create two configuration files: one for 150 dpi and the other for 300 dpi. Use the /L option to create a file called LJ150.CFG that includes the modified Driver command and a file called LJ300.CFG, which is just a copy of the default file. Before printing a full page, copy the LJ150.CFG file to GSCONFIG.CFG. To return to the default 300 dpi, copy LJ300.CFG to GSCONFIG.CFG.

The other settings in the GoScript configuration file usually don't have to be changed. Table 15.2 defines these settings, as well as some other configuration options that may not be included in the default configuration file.

Printing with GoScript

When you're ready to print with GoScript, save your PostScript document to a file, and then exit the application. Before you use GoScript, you need to know how your application handles the PostScript preamble. If it is included with the script as one file (such as with WordPerfect), log onto the GoScript directory, then enter

GS *filename.extension*

```
;Size of virtual memory in Kbytes
VMSIZE = 130
;font cache file name
FONTCACHE = C:\GS.CHE
;directory for temporary page image file
TEMP = C:\
;if YES, expanded memory is enabled, if available
EMS = YES
;paper size for laser and ink jet printers
PAPERSIZE = LETTER
;if YES, printer has single sheet feed operation
MANUALFEED = NO
;printer driver file name, for example DRIVER = EPSONFX.DRV
DRIVER = LJII.DRV
; preamble
;printer parallel port number
LPTDEVICE = 1
```

Figure 15.3: *GoScript configuration file for LaserJet II at 300-dpi resolution*

• Table 15.2: *GoScript Configuration File Settings*

SETTING	FUNCTION
VMSIZE	Specifies the amount of memory, in kilobytes, that GoScript uses to store PostScript variables, dictionaries, and functions. Increase this value if you receive an out of virtual memory error.
DEFAULTFONT	The name of the font substituted when unsupported fonts are requested in a program.
FONTFILE	File names of additional resident fonts from the GoScript library.
FONTCACHE	The path and file name of the font cache file. If you start GoScript with the /S option, processed fonts will be saved to this file. To speed up processing, use the /R option the next time a program requires the same fonts.
TEMP	The path where all temporary processing files are stored.
EMS	Set to Yes to allow use of expanded memory, if available.
PAPERSIZE	Specify Letter, Legal, A4, or Custom. Custom is supported by drivers for the Canon BubbleJet BJ-130 printer.
MANUALFEED	Set to Yes to feed paper manually.
DRIVER	Path and name of driver file (DRV extension), followed by applicable parameters. Use /L for 150 dpi.
PSPREAMBLE	Path and file name of your application's preamble file.
LPTDEVICE	Communications port: LPT1, LPT2, LPT3, COM1, COM2, or COM3.

Include the full path and file name.

GoScript processes the program, reporting on the screen the percentage of the file interpreted, as shown in Figure 15.4. It builds the bit map for the entire page in your computer's memory, or in temporary disk files, and then prints the document.

```
C>gs logo.ps
GoScript Printing Utility Version 2.07
Copyright (C) LaserGo Inc., 1988.  All rights reserved.

LaserJet II Printer Driver Version 2.0
300-dpi Mode
GoScript Initializing Bitmap ... Size = 1008 Kbytes of Disk File
Ready

Available memory=383384 bytes  VM=133120 bytes  Heap memory=89960 bytes
Reading "logo.ps"   File Size = 891 bytes
Processing... 35%
```

• Figure 15.4: *GoScript displays messages while processing a PostScript program*

You can print several files at one time by listing them on the command line in this format

GS *filename.extension filename.extension filename.extension*

However, if you're using a program with a separate preamble file, you must specify its name before the name of the PostScript file. For example, to print a Microsoft Word PostScript file called WORD.PS, you would enter a command similar to this from the DOS prompt (using your own drive and path):

GS C:\WORD5\POSTSCRP.INI C:\WORD5\WORD.PS

If you always plan to print files from that application, add a line similar to this to the GoScript configuration file:

PSPREAMBLE = C:\WORD5\POSTSCRP.INI

In this example, whenever a document is printed with GoScript, the Word preamble file will first be interpreted. Using this technique, you don't have to include the preamble name in the command from the DOS prompt.

If the interpreter encounters any problems, you'll see an error message on the screen. A full list of error messages and possible solutions is given in Appendix A of the GoScript manual.

Printing Multiple Copies

Along with the preamble (if needed) and file name, you can specify the number of copies of the document to be printed with GoScript. The command

GS /N10 FILE1.PS

for example, will print ten copies of FILE1.PS. The script is interpreted once, and then all ten copies are produced at your printer's full speed.

Using Interactive Mode

Like the Apple LaserWriter, GoScript provides an interactive mode for entering commands directly to the interpreter. If you enter GS from the DOS prompt without a file name, you'll see the prompt

GS>

Each command you type will be interpreted. Enter

Quit

to exit GoScript and return to the DOS prompt.

Using a new approach, Pacific Page, from Pacific Data Products, provides PostScript compatibility in a font-type cartridge.

• *Hardware PostScript Solutions*

If you're looking for a faster and more complete way to implement PostScript, you can install special hardware. The PostScript interpreter and fonts can be actually installed in your LaserJet, or they can be on a circuit card in your computer. With these configurations, you use your application just as if you have a PostScript printer instead of a LaserJet. You print documents from within your application using its own PostScript driver, without first saving documents to a file.

While hardware solutions can cost several thousand dollars, they offer some real advantages:

- In some cases, the cost of the LaserJet and the additional hardware is still less than a PostScript printer.

- Most of the add-on boards are faster than PostScript printers.

- In most cases, you can still use your LaserJet as a PCL printer.

Here we'll review two hardware solutions: the PS-388 Accelerator for the LaserJet II, and PS Jet for the LaserJet and LaserJet +. Additional hardware alternatives are listed in Appendix C.

Adding PostScript to the LaserJet II with the PS-388 Accelerator

Hewlett-Packard now markets a PostScript cartridge for the LaserJet IID.

The PS-388 Accelerator, from Princeton Publishing Labs, is one example of how PostScript can be added to a LaserJet II. The system contains a clone of the PostScript interpreter, 35 resident Bitstream outline fonts, and 3 megabytes of memory for processing fonts and graphics.

Like most add-on PostScript systems, it consists of two circuit boards. One installs in a slot in your computer and is configured for parallel port LPT2. You could change the port assignment, but it is assumed you want to keep the LaserJet connected to LPT1 for use as a standard PCL printer. The other card fits into the optional interface slot in the back of the printer. A special cable connects the two cards. Installing the system takes only a few minutes and screwdriver.

This system, and those like it, works by bypassing the LaserJet's internal controller card—the hardware that converts text and graphics into bit maps. The rasterizing of text and graphics is performed on the add-on card, then the rasters are transmitted directly to the LaserJet's video circuits that place the bit map on the drum. In benchmark tests, the PS-388 Accelerator printed Post-Script graphics in 1/38th the time it took the Apple LaserWriter IINT (*PC Magazine*, "Post-Purchase PostScript," 4/11/89).

To use the card, you install several programs and a batch file on your hard disk. When you start your computer, you'll see the message

> Princeton Publishing Labs, Inc.
> Downloading Interpreter
> with 35 different typefaces

Princeton Publishing Labs also offers a video board and monitor that displays a full page in WYSIWYG mode. Using this hardware and software provided with the PS-388 Accelerator, you can preview your own PostScript programs to see how the results will appear when printed.

Just configure your application for PostScript using LPT2, and then print documents as you would normally.

The system doesn't provide an interactive mode, but you can download your own PostScript programs from the DOS prompt, using the form

> COPY *filename.extension* LPT2

If you are working with an application that doesn't support Post-Script, you can bypass the PS-388 Accelerator and use your LaserJet as a standard PCL printer.

Adding PostScript to Earlier LaserJet Models with PS Jet

Since the earlier LaserJet models do not have an optional interface, some other means of installing PostScript hardware is necessary. PS Jet from Laser Connection is one system that will work with the original LaserJet and the LaserJet +. PS Jet comes with 13 PostScript fonts; PS Jet + has 35.

To install PS Jet, you have to actually remove the LaserJet controller and interface connectors. This requires taking off the top section of the printer that contains the PCL circuitry and control panel. Since PS Jet has its own special ports, you also must remove the LaserJet's serial and parallel connectors.

PS Jet comes with software for both DOS and Macintosh systems.

After you've taken these components off, you first install a new interface containing both 25-pin (for use with PCs) and 9-pin (for Macintosh systems) serial ports. Then you install a new top section containing the PostScript controller, fonts, and control panel. The panel includes indicator lights for ready (on line), active (receiving data or idle), paper out, and paper jam conditions. Laser Connection estimates the procedure should take about one hour.

The printer is connected to your computer's serial port, which must be set at 9600 baud.

Every time you turn on your printer, a startup page is printed. This page lists the resident fonts, interface settings, and the number of pages printed up to that time.

For all practical purposes, you now have a PostScript printer, 100 percent compatible with Adobe PostScript, complete with an interactive mode. Some applications include a separate PS Jet driver. If yours doesn't, you can use those for the Apple LaserWriter or generic PostScript. Select one of the PostScript drivers, and then create and print your documents.

The default PS Jet settings should work with most systems. However, you can test the hardware and make adjustments using the setup program supplied with PS Jet. The setup options are listed in Table 15.3.

Emulation Modes

If you're using an application that doesn't support PostScript, you can use PS Jet to have your printer emulate another output device. The printer can be set to act like the LaserJet +, HP 7475A plotter, or Diablo 630 daisy-wheel printer. Emulation modes are set using a switch on the interface panel.

The LaserJet emulation even improves upon original PCL performance. Up to 64 fonts can be resident and printed per page at an estimated 20 percent increase in speed. In addition, your PCL driver can access the built-in Courier,

• Table 15.3: *PS Jet Setup Options*

OPTION	FUNCTION
Align PS Jet	Prints a test pattern of two intersecting lines, 1 inch from the bottom-left corner of the page. If the position is incorrect, menu options let you change the horizontal or vertical alignment.
Print PostScript Samples	Lets you select from a menu of options, including printing PS Jet specifications, typeface samples, and pie and bar charts. The print samples are a good test of newly installed systems.
Change Printer Name	This is useful if you're using the printer in a network.
Set Printer Protocol	Changes between DTR and XON/XOFF protocols.
Manual Feed Control	By default, PS Jet uses continuous feed from the paper cassette. Use this option to select manual feed.

Times, and Helvetica fonts in Roman, Bold, Italic, and Bold Italic and scale the fonts to any size in portrait or landscape orientation.

By emulating the 7475A plotter, your printer can produce spreadsheet, CAD (computer-aided drafting), and presentation program documents containing HP Graphic Language commands. Not all plotter functions are available, however. The only text font is Courier in the ASCII symbol set, and a 0.3-mm pen is assumed as the default.

The Diablo emulation can be used for printing text files, particularly with older applications that provide limited driver support. You can use any one of the built-in fonts for printing, but Courier will produce the best results because character spacing will be controlled by the application, not the printer.

• *Printing PostScript Effects without PostScript*

Hardware and software solutions are also available for those of you who would like to get some of the benefits of PostScript without actually adding it. In this section, we'll review several alternatives for producing PostScript-like effects.

Installing Hardware PostScript Alternatives

Several add-on hardware systems are available that can scale fonts on the fly and create PostScript-like special effects from within application programs. Because these aren't PostScript systems, to use them you need special drivers supplied by either the hardware or application manufacturer.

LaserMaster Corporation produces one such system for use with all LaserJet models except the 2000. The boards come in a wide range of configurations, differing in memory, available fonts (13 or 35), and emulation modes.

The LX6 series can be used with the LaserMaster 1000 printer for 1000 × 400 dpi resolution.

An example is the LX6 Professional series, which comes with 2 to 6 Mb of memory and creates all fonts from outlines. The older LC2 series includes 2 Mb of memory. Fonts smaller than 18 points are stored as individually sized bit maps, but they can be downloaded in about one second by special software. Larger fonts are scaled on the fly when needed.

Why install hardware that isn't PostScript? Two good reasons are higher resolution and speed. LaserMaster can print high-quality final output at *600-dpi* horizontal resolution at remarkable speeds. A Ventura Publisher test page that takes several minutes to print in PostScript can be produced by the LaserMaster system in seconds. The speed is achieved by caching fonts in the card's memory, then transferring bit maps at high speed (over a million pixels per second) to image memory when needed.

If your final output will be produced on a Linotronic, you can quickly print proof pages using LaserMaster because all its fonts are the same width as PostScript fonts. Then use a PostScript driver to prepare a print file for the typesetter. (You can't download a PostScript program to LaserMaster or enter commands interactively.)

In addition, some of the drivers supplied by LaserMaster can access special effects such as rotation and character fill from within the application. Figure 15.5 shows the patterns that can be selected when using the Ventura Publisher driver. Text can also be stretched, squeezed, rotated, or slanted in any amount.

The main problem with this system is obtaining drivers. You can't use an application's PostScript driver—you need one specially made for Laser-Master. Drivers are currently available for WordPerfect, Ventura Publisher and other Gem applications, Windows and Aldus Pagemaker, and Auto-CAD. No doubt other drivers will be available by the time this book is published. Just keep in mind that while LaserMaster has a full PCL mode, you need a special driver to get PostScript-like effects.

Using Software PostScript Alternatives

If you just want special effects, plus the security of using only Laser-Jet drivers and applications, consider a software alternative.

Your HP LaserJet Handbook

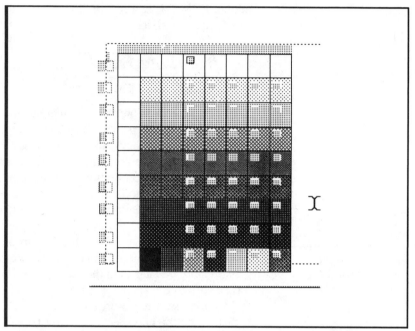

• Figure 15.5: *Fill patterns selectable from within Ventura Publisher using LaserMaster*

Using special-effects software, you can produce custom fonts that can be downloaded by your application or create graphic files that can be imported and printed. However, the procedure usually isn't automatic—it's not like selecting an effect from within Ventura Publisher.

Glyphix 3.0 is one exception. It allows WordPerfect 5.0 and Microsoft Word to scale fonts on the fly from outlines while printing. Text can be printed in sizes from 3 to 120 points in bold, italic, bold italic, outline, and shadow styles.

But with most software, after creating a new font, you have to install it in an application before printing. For graphics, you'll need an application that can import files in TIFF or PCX format. But if you don't mind working this way, special-effects software can offer tremendous flexibility and power.

Softcraft manufactures two such programs: Font Effects and Spinfont. They can be purchased separately or as part of the Font Solu-

Building New Fonts with Font Effects

Font Effects creates new fonts from your current ones. Figure 15.6 shows examples of a standard Helvetica font and two custom ones. The pattern font example uses one of 15 available designs, shown in Figure 15.7, that can be used for character fill and background. The shadow font example uses one of 14 predefined styles that can be selected from the menu shown in Figure 15.8.

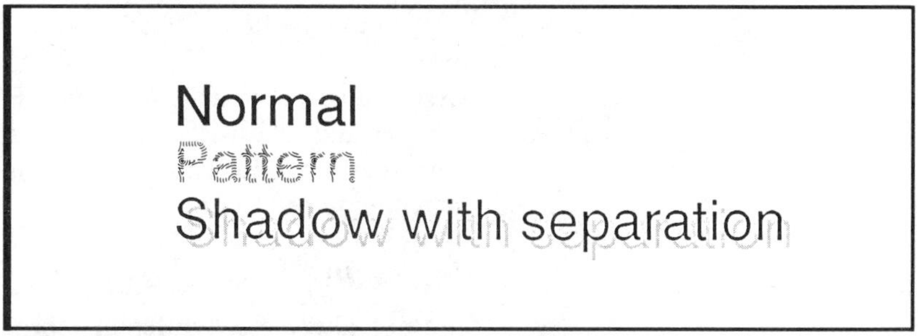

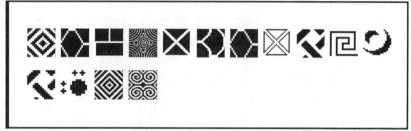

• Figure 15.6: *Fonts created with Font Effects*

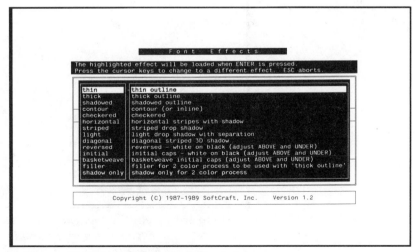

• Figure 15.7: *Font Effects patterns for character fill and outlines*

• Figure 15.8: *Font Effects predefined styles*

To create a new font, you designate the one to use as the base, then select from styles, patterns, and custom options that are available. For example, Figure 15.9 shows a 24-point Helvetica font that was converted into a shadowed outline, a pattern added, and then scaled horizontally and vertically. You can use Font Effect's preview mode to see how the new font will appear.

After you accept your design, Font Effects adjusts the bit map for each character and then writes the new font on your disk. If you have a font-installation program, you can then add the font to an application or create matching screen fonts.

Producing Special Effects with Spinfont

Spinfont takes a much different approach. It uses Bitstream font outlines to create graphic files that can be printed, edited with drawing programs, or imported into your documents. Because it scales fonts on the fly,

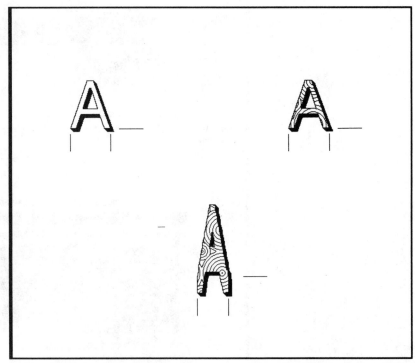

• Figure 15.9: *Helvetica character converted to shadowed outline, filled with a pattern, and scaled in the x and y dimensions using Font Effects*

characters of all sizes and orientations can be generated to produce a wide range of results. Figure 15.10 shows a ring design created with Spinfont and printed with WordPerfect.

Characters generated by Spinfont on the fly can also be processed by Font Effects. The programs are integrated, so just those characters needed by Spinfont will be modified in Font Effects. The design shown in Figure 15.11 was created with Spinfont's Spoke option, using outline letters formed by Font Effects.

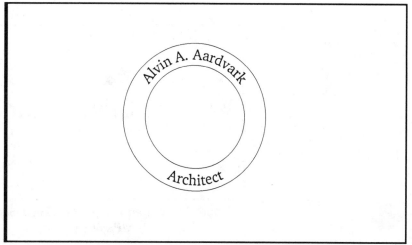

• Figure 15.10: *Spinfont ring design*

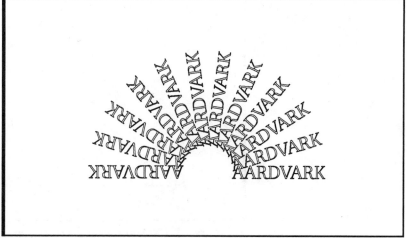

• Figure 15.11: *Spinfont spoke design with outline letters*

Spinfont also has a graphic option that lets you combine lines, circles, and rectangles with your text, or create files with graphics alone. For the letterhead shown in Figure 15.12, the radiating lines in the logo were created by Spinfont and saved in a TIFF formatted file. That file was imported into WordPerfect (using Alt-F9), the text was added, and then the document was printed at 300 dpi on a LaserJet + using softfonts.

Spinfont even lets you preview approximately how the final graphic file will appear when printed, including its size. A preview of a design made with the curve option is shown in Figure 15.13. By looking at the scales, you

• Figure 15.12: *Spinfont graphic design merged and printed with WordPerfect*

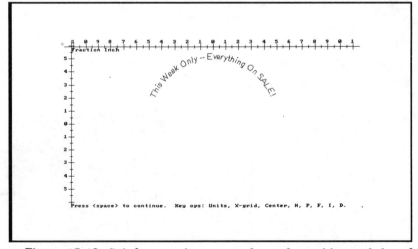

• Figure 15.13: *Spinfont preview screen shows the position and size of characters*

can tell the figure is 5 inches wide and about 1½ inches high. Both x and y axis scales use a center zero reference, but they can be moved on the screen by pressing the arrow keys.

If your application has the capability, the graphic files can be reduced or enlarged after being imported. But for best results, print the file the same size created by Spinfont. The exact size will be displayed on the screen after the file is generated.

Font Effects, Spinfont, and similar programs provide a way to create a wide range of special effects—even some that would be quite difficult using PostScript. You just have to be willing to work with several different programs, rather than access all your printer's capabilities through one application.

H·P L·A·S·E·R·J·E·T

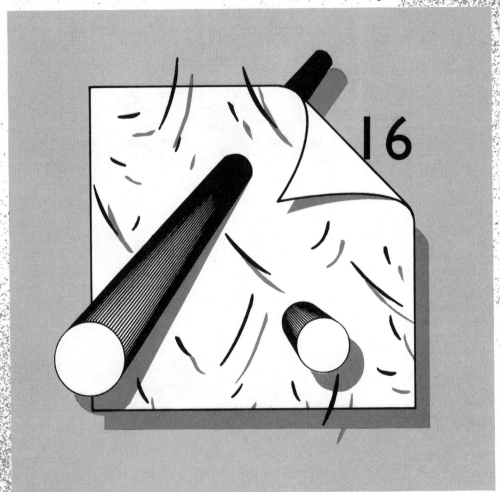

16

Improving Office Productivity

- The speed and quality of the LaserJet make it an excellent business tool. But when you combine the cost of the printer, fonts, and applications, you'll find that your printing system has been quite an investment. To compete successfully in the business world, you have to get the best return from your money. Your LaserJet is no exception.

In this chapter, you'll learn how to increase your printer's productivity. We'll discuss printer sharing networks, text-scanning systems, and facsimile output. Implementing any of these features will cost you yet more money. But in the long term, your net return can improve substantially.

• *Sharing Printers*

If you have just one computer connected to your LaserJet, you might not be using it to its full capacity. How many minutes or hours does it sit idle? What percentage of the time is it used for routine tasks that don't take advantage of its fonts and graphic capabilities?

You could improve your productivity through a computer network system, but when all you really want to do is get the most out of your printer, there are some simpler and less expensive alternatives.

A printer sharing network is a system in which two or more computers can share one or more printers. These types of networks don't provide electronic mail or the ability to share applications; from a processing standpoint, each computer is still an isolated machine. But from a productivity viewpoint, printer sharing is a powerful alternative.

In Chapter 1, I mentioned that a simple A-B switch, which can be purchased for as little as $40, can connect one computer to two printers. The same type of switch can give two computers access to one printer, as illustrated in Figure 16.1. Devices like this also come in three-to-one, four-to-one, and greater combinations.

But a simple switching mechanism has a number of disadvantages. Even though multiple computers are connected, only one can use the printer at a time. If station B wants to use the LaserJet while station A is printing a document, it has to wait patiently until the printer is free. And when the printer is available, someone has to physically move the switch from one position to the next, completing the connection between station B and the printer. These problems can be solved by using an intelligent device that provides a buffer and automatic switching.

Storing Data in a Buffer

Even though your LaserJet is fast, it still can't print pages as quickly as information is transmitted by the computer. So as one page is being

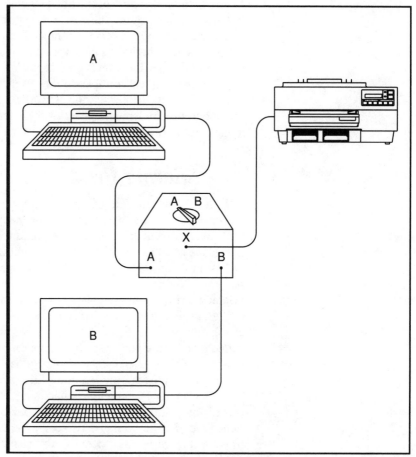

• Figure 16.1: *A-B switch connecting two computers to a LaserJet*

converted to a bit map, your system just has to wait. The situation is worse when you're connected through a simple switching device. If you give a print command while someone else is using the printer, your system might "hang up" or give a DOS error message to abort.

Some applications have the ability to print in the background, letting you continue working while they print or wait for access to the printer. But this usually slows system response, making the application's reaction to the keyboard sluggish.

A buffer is random access memory (RAM) where a document can be stored while the printer is busy. When you give a command to print, your application transmits a document at its full speed, not knowing or caring if the data is going to the printer or buffer. The buffer stores text until the printer is free, then transmits the next page to be printed.

It's possible to use your computer's memory as a printing buffer by running special software. The program intercepts characters going to the printer and stores them in RAM if the printer is occupied. However, the buffer might take up memory needed for the application. If you set aside too much memory for the printing buffer, your application may not be able to run.

The solution is to have a hardware buffer, which is a separate device connected between the computer and printer. It accepts your full document (as much as its own memory allows) so your application thinks the job was completely printed.

The Quick-Link Inline Buffer is one example of a hardware buffer. It is a small box (about 3 inches square) that connects to the parallel cable between the computer and printer. With 64K to 128K of memory, it accepts data at the computer's full speed and holds it until the printer is free.

A related process is spooling. Like a buffer, a print spooler can accept and store output to be printed. Spoolers are more active devices, however, that can keep track of multiple print jobs on a first-come, first-printed basis. Many spoolers allow you to cancel or repeat specific printing jobs and even change the order they will be printed to accommodate priority requests.

Using Automatic Switching

The other disadvantage of a simple switch is that someone has to physically turn the dial or push a button to change from one computer to the other. The user with this dubious honor is always responding to calls from others connected to the unit—who no doubt get annoyed if the switching isn't completed fast enough.

An automatic unit has the ability to switch by itself. It "polls" the computers connected to it, scanning back and forth between input ports looking for incoming data. If the printer is free when a request to print is received, the unit accepts the data and switches the printer to that computer.

If the switching device also contains a buffer, it then continues scanning, looking for additional printing jobs. If another is located, it buffers the data until the printer is free, and then prints the next job in sequence.

As long as its memory is not full, the operation is completely transparent to the user.

Using Printer Sharing Devices

Some printer sharing devices can be installed in the optional interface of your printer (a LaserJet II or IID). Others are separate, stand-alone units.

Most of the devices discussed in the following sections are manufactured by either ASP Computer Products or Intellicom, Inc., but there are many suppliers of similar equipment. These resources are listed in Appendix C.

Printing with ServerJet

The ServerJet, one model of which is shown in Figure 16.2, is an example of a printer sharer specifically made for the LaserJet II and IID. This device installs in the optional interface slot of the LaserJet II or IID and can accept input from up to ten computers. It comes standard with 256K of buffer memory, expandable to 1.25 Mb. All the models contain multiple serial ports; several also include a parallel port.

To access the device, use the printer's control panel to select I/O = Optional on the Configuration menu and reset the printer. ServerJet will perform a self test, and then print a status report. Figure 16.3 shows a sample ServerJet report. The details on the status report will vary depending on the amount of memory installed and the port configuration.

All users can access the printer as if they had their own LaserJet. One computer can be connected to the unit's parallel port, and up to ten to its serial ports.

Since the serial ports use RJ-11 modular telephone-type connectors, special cables are needed to connect with 25- or 9-pin serial ports on your computer. The cable configurations are shown in Figure 16.4. Although this seems like an added expense, this type of cable offers some real advantages. Cheaper, thinner and more flexible than standard serial cable, it can be run

Although the printer's built-in serial and parallel ports can still be used, they are not controlled by the ServerJet. If you want to access the printer from its own interface, you have to reset the I/O menu option.

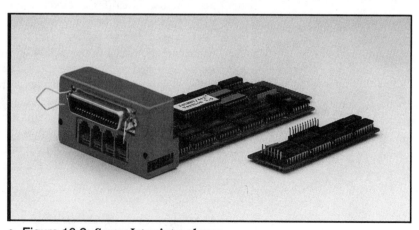

• Figure 16.2: *ServerJet printer sharer*

```
OPTION I/O SELF-TEST DIAGNOSTICS REPORT
Version 1.3
ROM TESTED OK
Installed Memory=256KBytes
BASE MEMORY OK
Serial Port A = 9600 Baud
Serial Port B = 9600 Baud
Serial Port C = 9600 Baud
Serial Port D = 9600 Baud
ALL SERIAL PORTS FIXED AT: 8 bits, no parity, 1 start and 1 stop
bit
```

• Figure 16.3: *ServerJet status report*

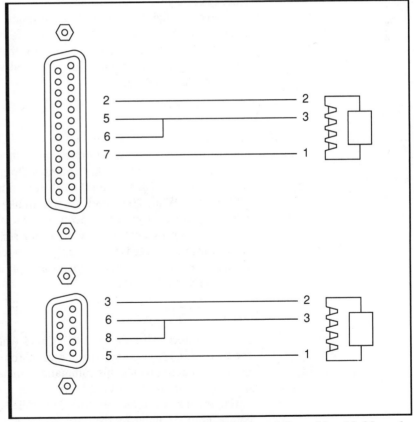

• Figure 16.4: *Connections for using RJ-11 modular cable with 25- and 9-pin serial ports*

over longer distances and concealed along floors and walls. Depending on the baud rate and electrical noise in the environment, the printer can be up to 200 or more feet from the computer.

The serial ports can be configured individually, so the ten computers connected don't have to use the same baud rate. A small dip switch on the side of the unit contains two switches for each port. Settings are available from 1200 to 115,200 baud.

With its own buffer memory and automatic switching, the ServerJet accepts data from all users practically simultaneously. In addition, the device resets the printer after each job, so you don't have to worry, for example, if the previous user set it for landscape orientation. After printing a partial page, such as a directory listing or screen dump, it issues a form feed, ejecting your page automatically.

Even though the ServerJet is automatic, it has its own set of control codes for performing special functions. Each of the codes start with two tildes (˜ ˜) and can be typed as text on the first line of a document or embedded in setup commands like PCL codes.

The ServerJet code

    ˜ ˜T#

determines the end-of-file timeout. After receiving a file, the unit waits this amount of time before assuming the printing job is completed. The default is 20 seconds, and # represents a number from 0 to 9. Numbers from 1 to 9 are multiplied by 10; a 1 would set the timeout to 10 seconds. A 0 sets it to 100 seconds. While 20 seconds may seem like a long time to wait until the page is ejected, setting the timeout too short could cause problems. For example, your application may pause for some time to process a graphic file. If the pause exceeds the timeout, the ServerJet assumes the document is complete, ejects the page, and then starts printing the next file.

The ServerJet code

    ˜ ˜C#

sets the number (#) of copies to be printed. Valid numbers are 1 to 9, and 0 for ten copies. If you want to print multiple copies of a document, it may be more efficient to include this command than use your application's number of copies function. For example, if you set some word processors to print ten copies of a document, ten complete copies will be transmitted, taking up computer time and buffer memory. You would also have to wait until all the copies were printed before exiting the program. Using the command

    ˜ ˜C0

your application is free after transmitting the job once, and only one copy is buffered.

The other valid ServerJet code is

~ ~ S"*xxxx*"

This is a convenient way to send PCL commands to the printer with applications that don't allow embedded codes. Include up to 255 ASCII codes for the command, using ^ for the Escape character. For example, to print a document in landscape, enter

~ ~ S"^&l1O"

as the first line. You can also send a text string to print at the start of every document. Enter

~ ~ S"MIS Department"

for example, to print the words MIS Department at the top of every page. Send a blank string

~ ~ S""""

to cancel the setup.

Printing with the SimpLan Intelligent Buffer

If you have a printer other than the LaserJet II or IID or are already using your optional I/O slot, you need a switching device that's a separate unit. Many of these stand-alone devices provide the same functions as the ServerJet, if not more.

The SimpLan Intelligent Buffer is an example of a switching unit that comes in both parallel and serial versions. The parallel unit connects up to three computers to one printer using standard parallel cables and connections. With 265K of standard memory (expandable to 512K), it buffers printing jobs and switches automatically, polling the input ports for incoming data.

Switches in the back of the unit control the length of timeout (the amount of time the unit waits before assuming the job is completed) and automatic form feed. To issue a page eject at the end of every printing job, set the form feed switch to on.

Four indicator lights on the front panel show the amount of buffer memory that's being used. When all four lights are on, the buffer is full and no additional data can be accepted.

The buttons on the buffer's front panel allow you to override the automatic operations, as follows:

- **Channel**: Allows you to manually select which computer to connect to the printer.

- **Copy**: Press this button once for each copy desired.

- **Bypass**: Press this button to suspend the current job to print a priority document. The original job will resume printing after the priority document is generated.

- **Pause**: Press this button to suspend printing until the button is pressed again.

- **Form Feed**: When the rear form feed switch is set to off, press this button to send a form feed command at the end of the current job.

- **Erase**: Press this button to delete the printing jobs for the current channel.

The serial buffer model is identical except that all input and output must be by serial interface. The communications protocol for each port can be set independently.

Printing with the SimpLan Printer Server

Some printer sharing devices allow a greater number of computers and printers to be connected. The SimpLan Printer Server, for example, can connect six computers to four different printers, all using parallel interfaces. You can connect laser, daisy-wheel, and dot-matrix printers on the same printer server network.

Like the other devices, the printer server polls the input ports looking for data to be printed. By default, all computers are connected to printer 1 on the network. Other printers can be selected manually from the front panel or by transmitting a code from the computer. To output to printer 2, for example, type these lines from the DOS prompt:

```
COPY CON PRN
(ST PTR2)
```

Next press the F6 key, and then press ◄─┘.

Indicator lights on the printer server's front panel show which input and output ports are being used, as well as the status of the Pause button. The Reset button clears all buffers and directs all output back to printer 1.

Using the Simplan Printer Server (or a similar device) to mix different types of printers in the same network can be quite efficient in a busy office. You can choose the LaserJet for final copies and use a dot-matrix or daisy-wheel printer for draft copies, continuous labels, envelopes, and checks.

Laying Out and Connecting Printer Networks

The efficiency of a printer network depends a great deal on the physical layout and procedures established for its use. It's always wise to physically locate printers near the people who will use them the most, unless one person has the task of collecting and distributing output. Before laying out the network, estimate the percentage of printer time that each user requires, the type of output desired, and the availablilty of space for cables and sharing devices.

Connecting Remote Devices

Layout is critical when you're using standard parallel or serial cables. Serial cables can extend 80 feet or more; the parallel interface usually isn't effective further than 15 feet or so.

To connect a computer and printer over greater distances, you need hardware that uses telephone-type modular cords and connectors, such as the ServerJet. If you don't need to connect multiple computers or don't have a LaserJet II or IID, you can use an interface extender. For example, Long-Link is a system that converts standard parallel interfaces into RJ-11 modular telephone-type, allowing a maximum distance of 7000 feet. A transmitter unit, about 3 inches square, plugs into the computer's parallel port. It is connected by telephone cable to a receiving unit attached to the printer.

Interface extenders are commonly used to connect two computers to one printer through an A-B switch when one computer is further away, as illustrated in Figure 16.5.

Using Protocol Converters

If you want to connect the original LaserJet or some other serial-only printer to a parallel interface and your printer sharing device doesn't accept a mix of serial and parallel input and output, you can use a protocol converter.

Protocol converters convert parallel signals to serial, and serial to parallel, so you can use a combination of devices. One converter even includes a 16K or 64K buffer.

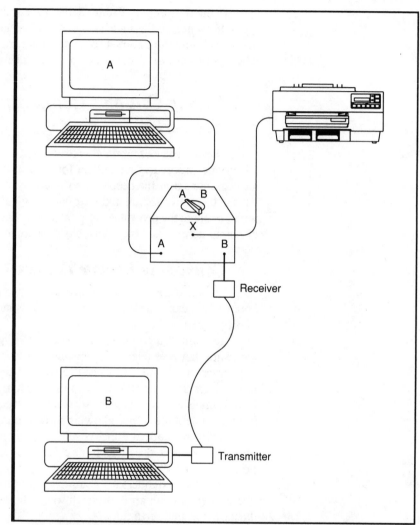

• Figure 16.5: *Using interface extenders to connect a distant computer*

Since serial cable can extend further than parallel, protocol converters can also be used to increase the distance between two parallel devices, as illustrated in Figure 16.6.

• *Supercharging the LaserJet*

To increase your LaserJet's speed and resolution, you can expand its memory or install an accelerator system. This section describes the memory-expansion options and the JLaser system for enhancing printer performance.

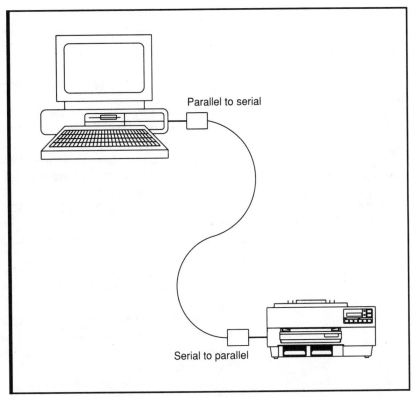

- Figure 16.6: *Using protocol converters to extend the distance between parallel devices*

Expanding Printer Memory

One way to boost printer performance is to install additional memory so a full page can be printed at 300-dpi resolution. With extra memory, there is room for downloaded fonts as well the page bit map.

Hewlett-Packard markets a line of memory-expansion boards. If you have the LaserJet II or IID, you can purchase and install 1 Mb, 2 Mb, or 4 Mb upgrades. Adding a 1 Mb board gives you a total of 1.5 Mb of memory—enough for a full page with some softfonts at 300 dpi.

If you have the original LaserJet, LaserJet + , or LaserJet 500 + , your only option from Hewlett-Packard is to purchase the 2 Mb board and have it installed by a service technician. It's not recommended that you try to install the board yourself.

You can't add more memory to the cards, so plan ahead of time how much memory you really need. If you purchase a 1 Mb board then decide you need more, you'll have to purchase a full 2 Mb or 4 Mb upgrade.

Using the JLaser Accelerator

The LaserMaster card, discussed in Chapter 15, not only provides scalable fonts and special effects, but also increases printing speed and resolution. Spinfont is also described in Chapter 15.

The JLaser series from Tall Tree Systems offers increased speed and full-page 300-dpi resolution. (A few graphic programs even support 600-dpi horizontal resolution with JLaser cards.) Like PostScript add-on cards, JLaser systems increase speed by communicating directly with the printer's video interface. The system combines some of the benefits of LaserMaster and Spinfont at a lower price.

Since the system requires at least 1 Mb of expanded memory, most models include a JRAM memory-expansion card. Without that card, you'll need to supply your own memory compatible with the LIM extended memory specification.

Systems for the LaserJet II and LaserJet IID include circuit cards for your computer and the printer's optional interface. Installing the cards in earlier LaserJet models requires some internal tinkering. You must remove the back panel of the printer to install a separate video switching mechanism, then connect it to the computer with cables. It's not a complicated task, but should only be attempted by those who feel relatively comfortable with a screwdriver and pliers.

The series includes several models, as listed in Table 16.1. All the models come with the Bitstream Fontware package.

JLaser Drivers

To take advantage of the JLaser's increased performance, you need special drivers. JLaser drivers are currently available for Ventura Publisher and Microsoft Windows.

With Ventura Publisher, just copy the driver to the Ventura directory. Versions are provided for Ventura 1.X (PD_JLASS.B30) and Ventura 2.0 (VENTURA2.0).

Using Microsoft Windows, copy the driver JLASER.DRV to the Windows directory. Then load it using the Add New Printer command from the Control Panel. A separate program (JBSTOJWF) is provided to convert Bitstream fonts to JLaser Windows format.

PCL Emulation

The emulator can't access the printer's internal or cartridge fonts.

If your application doesn't have a JLaser driver, you can use a LaserJet driver by running JLaser LP, a PCL emulator that supports full-page graphics at 300 dpi.

- Table 16.1: *JLaser Systems*

MODEL	FEATURES
Plus PC	Includes the scanner interface and an 8-bit memory board with a 2 Mb capacity.
Plus AT	For machines running up to 8 MHz. Supplied with a 16-bit memory board with 2 Mb capacity and the scanner interface.
Plus AT-2	For AT and 386 systems running up to 16 MHz. Includes the scanner interface and a 16-bit memory board with 2 Mb capacity.
Plus AT-4	For AT and 386 systems running up to 16 MHz. Includes the scanner interface and a 16-bit memory board with 2 Mb capacity.
Plus SA	For IBM PC, XT, AT, and compatible computers with their own EMS memory. The 8-bit board includes the scanner interface.
SA	Same as the Plus SA but without the scanner interface.
CR1	For PC, AT, and 386 systems. Laser interface with 4 Mb EMS memory capacity on one 8-bit board.

The emulator uses the softfonts listed in Table 16.2. The fonts are in a special JLaser format and are similar to the internal fonts and those in the F cartridge. You access the fonts from your applications by choosing their HP equivalents. The JLaser softfonts can also be downloaded manually to the printer with no conversion.

When you start JLaser LP, fonts supported by the emulator are loaded into EMS memory for faster downloading to the printer. You can add your own HP or Bitstream fonts to the driver, but they must first be converted to JLaser format. You can use the conversion programs provided with the emulator.

JLaser Special Effects

The JBanner program, provided with the JLaser card, allows you to create special font effects. Like Spinfont, JBanner scales Bitstream outlines

Your HP LaserJet Handbook

• Table 16.2: *JLaser Softfonts and Their HP Equivalents*

JLASER NAME	HP EQUIVALENT	POINT SIZE	WEIGHT
Redwood	Times	10	Medium
Redwood	Times	10	Bold
Redwood	Times	10	Medium Italic
Redwood	Times	8	Light
Cedar	Courier	12	Medium
Cedar	Courier	12	Medium Landscape
Linden	Line Printer	8.5	Medium
Magnolia	Helvetica	14	Bold

on the fly to produce graphic files that can be imported into your applications. Files can be output in TIFF, PCX, or IMG format.

The range of effects are more limited than those produced by Spinfont, but characters from 2 to 720 points can be generated, then rotated, slanted, condensed, expanded, kerned, and reversed. All effects are created using a PostScript-like command language that can be entered interactively or as a complete program.

Figure 16.7 shows a JBanner program that creates the TIFF formatted image file illustrated in Figure 16.8. It uses the Bitstream Charter font and creates a file called SAMPLE.TIF on the WordPerfect directory.

```
preview
fontfile \fontware\bco\cq0648.bco
output \wp50\sample.tif
start_h .25 inches
move_v 72 points
pointsize 72
angle 45
text SAMPLE
end
```

• Figure 16.7: *A JBanner program*

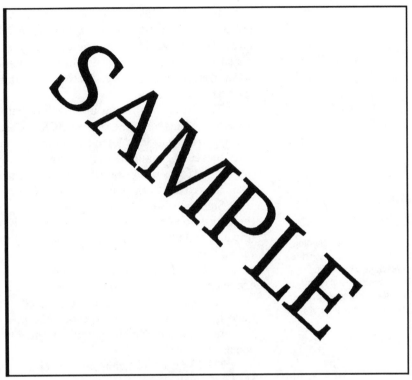

• Figure 16.8: *Output from JBanner program*

Graphic scanners are discussed in Chapter 14.

You can import existing image files into JBanner and add text. Files can also be scanned into JBanner using Canon IX-12-based devices. Most JLaser models can be purchased with built-in support for Canon scanners. A dedicated 9-pin port on the interface that installs in the computer is designed to connect directly to the scanner.

• *Scanning Text*

One time-consuming task when an office becomes computerized is reentering old documents into the new word processor. OCR (optical character recognition) scanning could simplify the conversion. In this process, each character in the text is read and transferred to the computer by ASCII code.

Unfortunately, OCR scanning technology is still in its infancy compared to graphic scanning. OCR devices cost more than graphic scanners, and sometimes they cannot accurately transfer all text.

Because OCR systems not only have to sense the image on the paper but convert each character to the correct ASCII code, they usually recognize only a few typefaces and sizes, typically 10- and 12-point Courier. Some systems contain a number of other font matrices in memory, which you select from before scanning. These are generally classed as matrix-matched systems.

The problem with this approach is that the scanner is limited to the fonts it stores as matrices. Newer OCR systems are called ICR (intelligent character recognition). When the system doesn't recognize a font, its characteristics can be "taught" to the software. After learning more characteristics of the font, the program may even go back to previously scanned characters to assign the correct ASCII codes.

Since no system is 100 percent accurate, however, you must still check the entire document for errors, particularly when scanning low-quality originals and photocopies. Light, thin, and broken lines in poor copies are very difficult to reproduce. Even some copies with good contrast may be unreadable if the copy machine slightly enlarged or reduced the image so characters do not match the original point size in the matrix.

Another problem is that the scanned text does not always maintain the original formatting. Tabs, indentations, centering, and other formats are often lost. So, after scanning, you may have to reformat most of the document.

The Kurzweil System from Xerox is one well-known scanning system. Model K-5000, for example, can handle both text and graphics in high volume and costs more than $15,000.

If you already have a less expensive scanner, you can add a third-party ICR solution, such as the Caere Corporation's OmniPage. This system includes an expansion board for the computer and Windows-compatible software that interprets scanned images directly in WordPerfect, Word, WordStar, MultiMate, and DisplayWrite formats. Because this is an "intelligent" scanner, its speed increases as it advances in the document.

As OCR and ICR technology improves and costs come down, text scanning will become more practical for word processing and office automation.

As text-scanning technology improves, the accuracy rate is reaching 95 percent. However, that still means that there will be a dozen errors or so per page of text.

• *Fax on the LaserJet*

As the telephone did many years ago, the facsimile (or just fax) machine is becoming a standard communications tool. But both regular fax machines and fax boards that install in your computer have the same problem: the printed quality of received messages. Text and graphics reproduce poorly, and the thermal paper used will not withstand the test of time.

You can use the JetFax even if you don't have a computer. Connect it directly to the printer for a dedicated high-quality fax.

Hijaak PS, from Inset Systems, and GammaScript, from Grammalink Inc., translate PostScript output to a fax-formatted file.

It was only a matter of time until someone combined the convenience of the fax with the quality of the LaserJet. The JetFax is a receive-only machine that installs between your computer and printer by parallel cable. It automatically receives incoming fax messages and prints them on the LaserJet, on plain paper, at full 300-dpi resolution. Plain paper output reduces your overall costs.

If the printer is busy, JetFax can store up to 60 fax pages in its own memory, then output them when the printer becomes available. Switches on the unit control the paper size (letter or legal, corresponding to the printer's setting), and the number of copies of each message to be printed (up to five). With a LaserJet IID, JetFax can detect the size of incoming pages and select the appropriate tray. An optional accelerator card, which can double printing speed, is also available.

A recent enhancement to the JetFax is delayed polling, which lets the unit dial out to receive messages at user-specified times. The JetFax can store up to 64 fax telephone numbers and be programmed to request transfer at a given time. JetFax can also reduce incoming fax pages up to 12 percent, shrinking an originating message on A4 paper to fit on letter-size paper.

The JetFax can share the telephone line with a standard fax machine. When the JetFax's memory is full, it passes messages to the other fax.

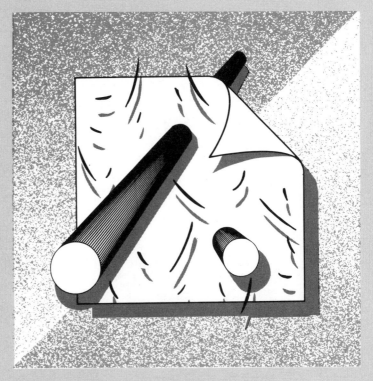

· *Programming Your LaserJet*

If you write your own programs, or want to learn in detail how to control your LaserJet, these four chapters will prove invaluable. Here you'll learn all the commands that make up the PCL language and see practical programming examples. You'll also learn the fundamentals of writing printer drivers and programming the LaserJet for fonts and graphics.

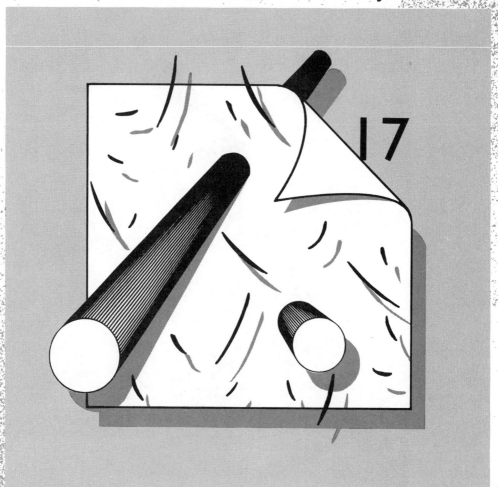

17

An Introduction to PCL

- The preceding chapters have touched on what PCL is all about, covering the subject from an application user's point of view. This and the following chapters cover PCL in detail, describing how to access all the LaserJet's features from within your own programs.

In this chapter, we'll review the basic structure of PCL commands. You'll learn how to control the LaserJet from within C, Pascal, and Basic programs and how to construct simple printer drivers for your own applications.

Chapter 10 discusses using PCL commands in dBASE programs.

• *The PCL Hierarchy*

PCL was developed by Hewlett-Packard as a standard interface between users and HP printers. The goal was to provide a common control structure for different printers and a platform for further development.

But one problem in reaching this goal is the wide range of user needs, budgets, and sophistication. So Hewlett-Packard developed PCL in four distinct levels, each building on the other to satisfy the diversity of printer needs. Each level consists of a collection of printer commands and functions, as follows:

- **Level 1**: The Print and Space level. This contains the most fundamental printer functions and commands—the ones necessary for printing basic text and raster graphics.

- **Level 2**: The EDP/Transaction level. Implements all level 1 features but can also change symbol sets and font pitch and adjust right and left margins, text lines per page, and page length.

- **Level 3**: The Office Word Processing level. Performs all level 1 and 2 functions but with higher quality output and formatting capabilities. Font styles and spacing can be selected, including various typefaces and stroke weights, and horizontal and vertical motion can be controlled. Level 3 printers cannot accept downloaded fonts.

- **Level 4**: The Page Formatting level. The highest level of HP printer at this time. It performs all office word processing functions, accepts softfonts and macros; and prints lines, rectangles, patterns, and gray scales. It offers horizontal and vertical movement in 1/300 inch (dots). Note that not every level 4 printer can follow all level 4 commands. For example, special instructions for duplex printing on the LaserJet IID and LaserJet 2000 will be ignored on other level 4 devices.

All LaserJet models are level 4 machines except for the original LaserJet, which is classified as level 3.

An application written at the most basic level 1 will run properly on any HP printer. A level 4 printer, the most sophisticated device, can run any HP application.

You can run a program designed for a high-level printer on any lower level machine because the more sophisticated commands will be ignored. For example, if you run a program that selects a softfont on the original LaserJet, the command will be ignored and the default internal font will be used. Similarly, a command to select duplex printing on the LaserJet II will be ignored.

If you're writing a program specifically for LaserJet printers, you can include all level 3 commands. You can be sure the program will output properly on all models. But if your program is designed for all HP printers, not just the LaserJet, consider which features you want to access. You can always include a basic level 1 set of functions that every HP printer can use.

• *The PCL Command Structure*

PCL isn't a natural language program, such as Cobol, Basic, Pascal, or even PostScript. It does not contain arithmetic operators or conditional or repetition structures. About the only "traditional" programming it includes are push and pop instructions that move the cursor position on and off the stack.

PCL has only one function: to change and control the printer's environment. But because of that, PCL is a concise language that's remarkably easy to learn and use after you've mastered its basic concepts.

All commands to the LaserJet can be divided into three general classes: ASCII control codes, two-character Escape sequences, and parameterized Escape sequences.

ASCII Control Codes

Every printer made to work with PC-compatible computers recognizes a basic set of eight control codes in the range from 0 to 31, as listed in Table 17.1. There are other control codes in this range, but not every printer responds to them in the same way.

No matter what printer you have, these codes perform the same functions. For instance, ASCII 12 always performs a form feed, ejecting the current page in the printer; ASCII 10 is always a line feed.

The control code you will be using the most in your programs is ASCII 27. This is the Escape character, used to signify that additional printer codes follow.

- Table 17.1: *ASCII Control Codes*

CODE	HEXADECIMAL	DECIMAL	PURPOSE
Backspace	08	8	Moves the cursor one character position to the left, but not past the left margin. To move the cursor one character to the right, use the spacebar or ASCII 32.
Line feed	0A	10	Moves the cursor to the next line, at the same column position.
Carriage return	0D	13	Moves the cursor to the left margin of the current line.
Shift out	0E	14	Selects the following characters from the secondary font.
Shift in	0F	15	Selects the following characters from the primary font.
Escape	1B	27	Begins the control sequence.

• Table 17.1: *ASCII Control Codes (Continued)*

CODE	HEXADECIMAL	DECIMAL	PURPOSE
Horizontal tab	09	9	Moves the cursor to the next tab position.
Form feed	0C	12	Ejects the current sheet of paper.

Every PCL command except the ASCII control codes must start with the Escape character, which is why PCL is often referred to as Escape sequences or Escape codes. In this and the next chapters, you'll see the Escape character shown in several forms. In text (not program listings), it will be represented by <Esc>. The command <Esc>E is an Escape code followed by the capital letter E. In program listings, the Escape code is usually shown in its decimal (27) or hexadecimal (1B) equivalent.

Two-Character Escape Codes

There are five PCL commands that contain just the Escape character and one other character:

- **<Esc>E**: Resets the printer to its default environment, deleting any temporary softfonts and macros. Its function is similar to the control panel Reset button, except it prints whatever is currently in memory and ejects the page. The Reset button erases memory without printing.

- **<Esc>9**: Clears (resets) the right and left margins to the default values.

- **<Esc>=**: Performs a half-line feed from the current cursor position. The distance is ½ of the current line-spacing setting.

- **<Esc>Y**: Turns on the display function. In this mode, all PCL commands except carriage returns and <Esc>Z are printed and not executed. Use this to obtain a hard copy of the exact data being sent to the printer and as an aid in debugging your PCL programs. For instance, with the display function on, a text line to be printed in boldface would appear like this:

(s3BThis line is bold (s0B

The <Esc> code itself will not appear in the printout.

- **<Esc>Z**: Cancels the display function. PCL commands will now be executed as normal.

These commands perform fixed functions and cannot be modified in any way.

Parameterized Commands

All other PCL sequences are parameterized commands. These require a series of characters, including a user-specified value followed by a parameter that signifies the function you want the printer to perform.

Parameterized commands can be simple or complex. Simple commands contain just one instruction for each <Esc> code. Complex commands combine any number of simple ones following a single <Esc> code.

Simple Commands

Throughout the remainder of this book, make sure you carefully distinguish between the character 0 (zero) and the uppercase letter O, and the number 1 and the lowercase letter l.

Commands such as <Esc>&l1O, which sets the landscape mode, and <Esc>(1X, which selects the softfont with ID 1, are examples of simple commands.

Each simple command is in the format:

<Esc> *X y # Z [data]*

where

<Esc> = The Escape code.

X = The parameterized character, which informs the printer that the command includes a parameter. Valid characters are in the ASCII range from 37 (the ! character) to 47 (/).

Some commands do not contain a group character but use the parameterized character as the group indicator. For instance, many font selection commands have no group letter but are identified by the (parameterized character.

y = The group character, which signifies the general class of the instruction. Valid characters are in the range from 95 (') to 126 (˜). For example, font selection commands are usually in group s and format controls in group l.

= A user-specified field value for the specific parameter that follows. Valid characters are from 0 to 9, +, −, and .(period). Some commands do not require a value. If they do, and you do not include one, a 0 is assumed.

Z = The parameter character that indicates to which parameter the previous value applies. The group letter only identifies the general class of command; the parameter signifies the exact function. For example, a group letter l indicates a formatting command, but the parameter indicates which format is being set. In a simple PCL command, this also serves as the terminator character and, if a letter, *must* be capitalized. This lets the printer know it has reached the end of the command. Terminating characters are in the range 64 to 94.

[data] = The binary data following commands to download softfonts and raster graphics. Usually, the field value indicates the number of data bytes included in the command.

Unfortunately, not every command fits neatly into a category. Although all d group commands control underlining, for instance, others cannot be so uniquely classified. Some *c commands relate to graphics, others to font management. Most formatting commands are &l, but several begin with &a.

To help you understand what the parts of a simple command mean, we'll examine some simple commands in detail. We'll begin with

<Esc>&l#D

This command means that all sequences starting with &l are parameterized (&) formatting commands (group l). The D parameter signifies that the value preceding is the amount of line spacing. Values can be 1, 2, 3, 4, 6, 8, 12, 16, 24, or 48. The command

<Esc>&l2D

for example, assigns the D format parameter the value 2, for double spacing.

This is similar to another command in the group:

<Esc>&l#E

In this case, the E indicates the value is the top margin in lines. To set the top margin to 2 inches, use the command

<Esc>&l12E

Here, the E format parameter is assigned 12.

Keep in mind that not all commands have a group letter, such as

<Esc>(8U

This is a symbol set selection command that sets the primary font at HP Roman-8. The (parameterized character indicates it is a font command. (Commands with the) parameterized letter always refer to the secondary font.) All commands in the general format <Esc>(#Z are symbol set commands except

>   <Esc>(3@

which selects the default primary font.

Some commands have no value field, such as

>   <Esc>&d@

This is in group d, which controls underlining. In this case, the @ parameter character turns off automatic underlining, and no value is required.

In all these cases, when the terminating character is a letter, it must be capitalized.

Some commands include binary data, such as

>   <Esc>*b4W 255 255 255 255

This command transfers a group of four bytes of raster graphics, in this case a line of 32 black dots. The * parameterized character means that the command is either for font management or graphics. The group and parameter characters, however, indicate it is a raster transfer of four—the value field—characters. Following the command are four bytes of graphics.

In your own programs, you can include more than one command on the same program line. For example, to set the printer at landscape and select the softfont with ID 2, use this code:

>   <Esc>&l1O<Esc>(2X

In this case, each command is preceded by <Esc>, and each has its own parameterized and group characters. The terminating parameter character in each command is uppercase.

Complex Commands

In certain circumstances, you can save typing by creating a complex command containing a series of Escape sequences that share the same

<Esc> and parameterized and group characters. In order to combine commands, however, they must follow two rules:

- The parameterized and group characters must be the same for all commands.

- All alphabetic characters in the command must be lowercase except for the final parameter character, which serves as the command terminator. Parameter characters not terminating the code must be in the range 96 to 126; terminating parameter characters must be in the range 64 to 94.

All commands will be performed in the order given, from left to right. As an example, here's a command for the LaserJet IID:

<Esc>&l1s4h12E

This is a combination of three Escape sequences.
The first sequence

<Esc>&l1S

sets duplex printing with long-edge binding. In the complex command, the parameter character no longer terminates the sequence, so it is lowercase.
The next sequence

<Esc>&l4H

says paper is obtained from the lower tray. In the complex command, the <Esc>&l commands are dropped and the parameter letter is lowercase.
The final sequence

<Esc>&l12E

sets a top margin of 12 lines. The <Esc>&l characters are dropped in the complex command but the parameter character, which terminates the entire sequence, remains uppercase.

If you want to enter a complex command and one from a different group on one line, be sure to include all necessary characters. For example:

<Esc>(2X<Esc>&l1s4h12E

selects the softfont with ID 2, then issues the complex command just discussed. Since the font command has different parameterized and group characters, it terminates with an uppercase letter, and the next command has its own <Esc> and parameterized and group characters.

• *Programming with PCL Commands*

You can include PCL commands in any language that has a way of transmitting the <Esc> character to the printer. You can't use the Esc key since it will not enter a character or code into your program line. Instead, you must send the character using its decimal (27), hexadecimal (1B), octal (033), or binary (00011011) equivalent.

Fortunately, most languages have a standard function for sending the <Esc> character. The following sections explain how C, Pascal, and Basic handle the <Esc> character.

As an aid in debugging problems, remember you can use the <Esc>Y command to print rather than execute PCL commands.

Programming in C

To print anything in C, you have to open a file accessing the DOS printer device. The way you open this file varies between implementations of the language, so check your C manual.

Once the file is open, transmit the PCL commands as a text string starting with \x1B. The characters \x indicate that a hexadecimal number follows.

For example, this is a C program designed for Turbo C from Borland International:

```
#include <stdio.h>
main( )
{
FILE *fptr;
char string[81];
if( (fptr = fopen("prn", "w")) = = NULL)
{ printf("Sorry, can't access printer"); exit ( ); }
fputs("\x1B&dDThis is underlined\x1B&d@", fptr);
fclose(fptr);
}
```

The program includes the stdio.h header file, then creates and opens a file (fptr) accessing the printer. It uses the built-in "prn" file handle to link the file with the DOS printing device.

The sample output line

```
fputs("\x1B&dDThis is underlined\x1B&d@", fptr);
```

transmits the PCL command for underlining, the text to be underlined, and then the code to turn underlining off. If you didn't turn underlining off, all other printing would be underlined until you reset the printer.

Notice that the codes and text are included in the same quotation marks. The printer knows when the PCL command ends and the text begins because of the terminating character. The command ends when it encounters the first terminating character—a parameter character in the range 64 to 94—following an <Esc>. The LaserJet then prints all the text between the terminating character and the next <Esc> code. The file is closed before ending the program.

Use the same techniques to transmit ASCII control codes and two-character PCL commands. This C program line, for instance, resets the printer, then issues a line feed:

```
fputs("\x1BE\x0A", fptr);
```

Both the <Esc> and line feed codes are output in their hexadecimal format.

Programming in Pascal

Here is an example of a Turbo Pascal 5.0 program that uses PCL codes:

```
program sample;
uses printer;
begin
write (lst, chr(27) + '(s1SThis is italic' + chr(27) + '(s0S');
end.
```

This program prints a line of text in italics. It uses the built-in printer unit which contains the predefined lst printer file.

The <Esc> code is transmitted by its decimal number 27. Chr is a built-in function that returns the character equivalent of the number in parentheses. So, the code chr(27) sends to the printer the ASCII character represented by decimal 27, the <Esc> code.

Notice that chr(27) is not surrounded by quotation marks, but the remaining sequence characters are included along with the text to be printed.

Other control codes would be issued like this:

write (lst, chr(13) + chr(27) + ' = ');

These codes first perform a carriage return with the ASCII code 13, then a half-line feed using the two-character PCL command <Esc> = .

Programming in Basic

All printer output in Basic is transmitted by the LPRINT command. As in Pascal, <Esc> is transmitted by the decimal 27 using a number-to-character conversion function. With Basic, the code must be identified by the string character function $: chr$(27). For example, this command:

10 LPRINT chr$(27);"(s3BThis is Bold";chr$(27);"(s0B"

changes the stroke weight to bold.

Also as in Pascal, ASCII control codes are entered as the chr$ parameter, such as

10 LPRINT chr$(12)

which issues a form feed.

Using Decimal and Hexadecimal Numbers

With the exception of the <Esc> code, all the PCL commands illustrated so far were transmitted as characters. This is the easiest technique because the Hewlett-Packard manuals show the codes in that format.

But just as <Esc> can be sent as either the decimal 27 or hexademical 1B, all PCL characters can be transmitted in their numeric equivalent. Using a high-level language like C, Pascal, or Basic, there's really no need to do so. But if you're programming in Assembler, you might find it easier to use the hexadecimal or decimal numbers.

Refer to an ASCII chart to convert the characters to numbers. For example, the code for landscape orientation (<Esc>&l1O) would be transmitted with these numbers:

Decimal: 27 38 108 49 79

Hexadecimal: 1B 26 6C 31 4F

• *Creating a Printer Driver*

If you are writing a program designed just for the LaserJet, you only have to know the PCL codes and how to access them in your language.

However, this method is rather limiting if you hope to sell your application to the mass market. Wouldn't you like to sell your software to owners of dot-matrix and daisy-wheel printers as well?

Throughout this book, we've talked about using PCL *drivers* to operate your printer. Most applications that supply drivers include them for a variety of printers. By using this approach, the application can create reports and other printed output using boldface, underlining, and other formatting effects, as long as the user has a printer supported by a driver. How difficult it is to create drivers depends on the range of features you want to include and the number of printers you want to support.

As an example, in the following sections we'll use Basic to create a driver that supports all LaserJet models, as well as IBM Graphics (dot-matrix) and compatible printers. It will include these features:

- Boldface

- Underlining

- Italic

- Reset

- Page eject

Writing the Driver

The first task is to identify the codes for the supported features. In some cases, such as for boldface, underlining, and italic, separate codes are needed to turn on and off the feature. Other features, such as reset and eject, require only one command. The codes for our sample driver are listed in Table 17.2.

In this case, all the codes except form feed (to eject the page) begin with the <Esc> character. This will make it easy to use the drivers in the application.

Once you have the codes, you must create driver files containing them. For this application, we'll create two files. The LASER.DRV file contains the codes for LaserJet printers:

```
(s3B
(s0B
```

• Table 17.2: *PCL Codes for the Sample Driver*

FUNCTION	LASERJET	DOT-MATRIX
Bold on	\<Esc\>(s3B	\<Esc\>G
Bold off	\<Esc\>(s0B	\<Esc\>H
Underline on	\<Esc\>&dD	\<Esc\>-1
Underline off	\<Esc\>&d@	\<Esc\>-0
Italic on	\<Esc\>(s1S	\<Esc\>I1
Italic off	\<Esc\>(s0S	\<Esc\>I0
Reset	\<Esc\>E	\<Esc\>@
Eject	ASCII 12	ASCII 12

```
&dD
&d@
(s1S
(s0S
E
```

The IBMGRAPH.DRV file is for dot-matrix printers:

```
G
H
-1
-0
I1
I0
@
```

To save space and typing, certain common elements have been left out. We can enter the form feed character (12) and \<Esc\> codes directly in the application instead. The drivers are actually plain ASCII text files that can be created with any word processing program.

Our instructions to users will explain that they have to rename their specific driver DRIVER.DRV. A small batch file can be included with the application to select and rename the file.

Writing the Application

We now need a mechanism for accessing the driver (DRIVER.DRV) in the application. Here's a short Basic program that reads the commands from the driver and embeds them in the appropriate locations to format output:

```
10 E$ = chr$(27)
20 EJECT$ = chr$(12)
30 OPEN "I",1,"DRIVER.DRV"
40 INPUT #1, BON$, BOFF$, UON$, UOFF$, ION$,
    IOFF$, RST$
50 CLOSE
60 LPRINT E$ + RST$
70 LPRINT E$ + UON$;"This is underlined";
    E$ + UOFF$
80 LPRINT E$ + BON$;"This is bold";E$ + BOFF$
90 LPRINT E$ + ION$;"This is italic";E$ + IOFF$
100 LPRINT EJECT$
```

Let's review each of the lines to see exactly how the driver is being used. The first line

```
10 E$ = chr$(27)
```

assigns the <Esc> code to the string E$. Making this initial assignment saves typing the full chr$(27) every time the code is required.

The next line

```
20 EJECT$ = chr$(12)
```

assigns the ASCII form feed code (12), which both printers use to eject pages, to a variable.

The line

```
30 OPEN "I",1,"DRIVER.DRV"
```

opens the specific driver, which has been renamed DRIVER.DRV.

The following line

```
40 INPUT #1, BON$, BOFF$, UON$, UOFF$, ION$,
IOFF$, RST$
```

reads the seven commands in the driver file into variables. Easy to remember mnemonic names have been assigned. They stand for Bold ON, Bold OFF, etc.

The line

    50 CLOSE

closes the driver file after the codes are read into memory, so the file will not be corrupted by any hardware or software error.

The next line

    60 LPRINT E$ + RST$

resets the printer by combining <Esc> with the printer's reset command. This line is equivalent to chr$(27)"E" on the LaserJet and chr$(27)"@" on a dot-matrix printer.

The three lines that follow

    70 LPRINT E$ + UON$;"This is underlined"; E$ + UOFF$
    80 LPRINT E$ + BON$;"This is bold";E$ + BOFF$
    90 LPRINT E$ + ION$;"This is italic";E$ + IOFF$

add the <Esc> characters and formatting codes to sample output lines. The text will be formatted properly on either LaserJet or IBM Graphics-compatible printers.

The last line

    100 LPRINT EJECT$

ejects the current page from the printer.

The same process can be used in more sophisticated Basic programs or converted to equivalent code in any other language. The basic features described here can be quite effective in your own applications, giving them the edge on those written by competitors who don't understand printer technology.

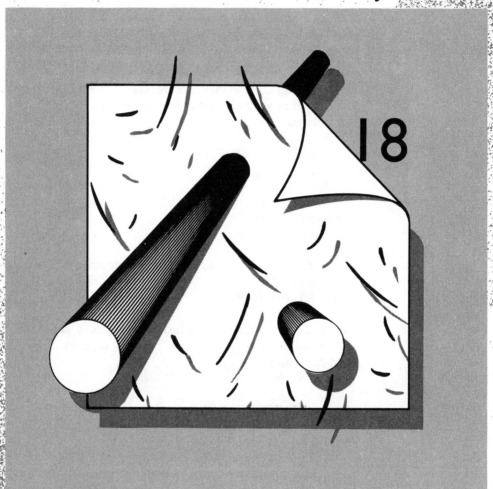

Programming Special Functions

- When you use a daisy-wheel printer, you can view the printed page as a series of individually formed letters. You can see the print head move across and down the page, imprinting each character against the ribbon.

  With the LaserJet, the page can be viewed as a canvas on which the printer will paint its image with dots. All text and graphics that you transmit to it are formed into a single bit map. It's the individual dots that form the page, much like the artist's individual brushstrokes form the finished picture. This view of the laser-printed page requires a whole set of functions for controlling the placement of each dot and the arrangement of the final image.

  In this chapter, we'll describe the PCL commands for these functions. We'll examine cursor movement and page layout, as well as selecting the type and source of paper.

• *PCL Measurement Systems*

The LaserJet has many ways to measure a page and positions within it, which you will be using to work with PCL.

It uses the following three fixed measurement systems:

- **Decipoint**: Equals $1/720$ inch, or one tenth of a point. This small measurement can be used for precisely placing text on the page. An $8^1/2$- by 11-inch page is 6120 decipoints wide and 7920 decipoints long.

- **Dots**: Equals $1/300$ inch. Working with measurements in dots is convenient because it relates directly to the actual dots that will print on the page. Letter-size pages are 2550 dots by 3300 dots.

- **Inches**: PCL commands that deal with inches—the vertical and horizontal motion indexes—use increments of either $1/120$ or $1/48$ inch.

Some PCL commands use the measurements of lines (also called rows) and columns, which are dependent upon the current font or other PCL settings. If you use the PCL command to move the cursor one line, for example, the actual distance moved depends on the size of the font. Using a 12-point font with no leading, each line is $1/6$ inch; a 24-point font makes each line $1/3$ inch.

The column, or character, measurement is even more difficult to deal with. For fixed-width fonts, each position is an even increment of the pitch; 12 pitch means that each character is $1/12$ inch. With proportionally-spaced fonts, each character is a different width, so the width of the font's space character (ASCII 32) is used as the column width.

Before using either lines or columns for page layout, you have to know exactly how much space each occupies.

• *The Printer's View of the Page*

Before looking at how we can layout the page, it's important to understand a page from the LaserJet's point of view. In fact, there are three "pages" in every sheet of paper:

- **Physical page**: The actual sheet of paper you load into the printer, measured from side to side, top to bottom. When you select a page size, such as letter or legal, it is the physical page. This measurement establishes the size of the logical and printable pages.

- **Logical page**: The area of the physical page in which dots can be placed. Commonly referred to as the *addressable* area, it is the same length as the physical page but narrower by about 50 dots ($\frac{1}{6}$ inch) on the left and right. You can place the cursor anywhere in the logical page, but you can't print outside the printable page.

- **Printable page**: The region where text and graphics can actually be printed. It is the same width as the logical page but 50 dots shorter on the top and bottom, leaving a printable length of 10.66 inches on letter-size paper. However, the default LaserJet setting includes $\frac{1}{2}$-inch top and bottom margins, 150 dots each. Unless you manually change the margins with PCL commands, the printable area is just 10 inches long by the logical page width of 8.17 inches.

Figure 18.1 shows the relationship between these three pages.

• *The Printer's Coordinate System*

When you lay out a page, you have to tell the LaserJet where to place characters or dots. This is done through cursor-movement commands that point to locations on the page using an x-y coordinate system. The x-axis runs along the width of the page, the y-axis down the side, as illustrated in Figure 18.2.

Like the coordinate system of your monitor, there is a "home" position at the upper-left corner of the page. But in this case, the x-axis zero position is at the left edge of the logical page, and the y-axis zero position is

The LaserJet doesn't have a cursor in the same sense as your monitor. Here, *cursor* refers to the current x-y coordinate position where the next character or dot will be placed.

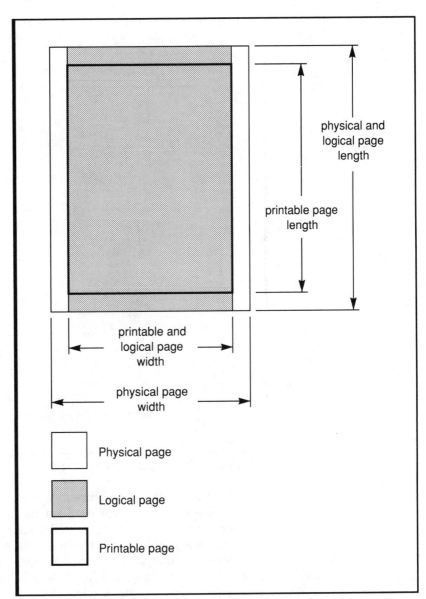

• Figure 18.1: *LaserJet pages*

at the *current* top margin. Using default settings, the top margin is ¹/₂ inch. So, the home position is 50 dots from the left and 150 dots from the top of the page.

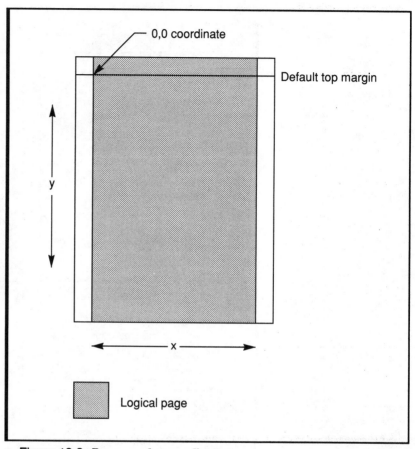

• Figure 18.2: *Page x and y coordinates*

If you change the top margin setting using PCL commands, the y-axis home position moves also. Setting the top margin to 2 inches, for example, places the home position 50 dots from the left and 600 dots from the top of the page, as shown in Figure 18.3. If you manually set the top margin to 0, the home coordinate (0,0) moves to the very top of the page at the left border of the logical page, as shown in Figure 18.4. While this position is within the addressable area, it is outside the printable page. So, even though you can use PCL commands to place the cursor in that region, nothing will print.

Knowing the position of the nonprinting region is particularly critical when you're using large fonts. With all models except the LaserJet IID and 2000, if any portion of a character extends into a nonprinting area, the entire character will not print. The LaserJet IID and 2000, however, have

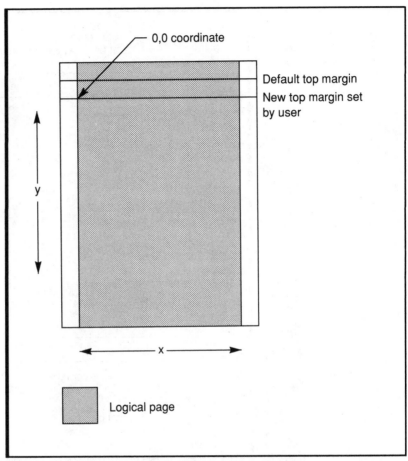

0,0 coordinate

Default top margin

New top margin set by user

y

x

Logical page

• Figure 18.3: *The top margin affects the 0,0 coordinate*

pixel level clipping. This means that only the portion of the characters extending into the nonprinting area will be clipped, or lost. Figure 18.5 shows how characters in the nonprinting area are handled.

The cursor position becomes the lower-left corner of the character, approximately aligned with the font's baseline. So even though the cursor position is in the printable area, a portion of the character may extend outside and be clipped.

For example, if you position the cursor 75 dots (1/4 inch) from the top margin, it will be 175 dots within the printable region. If you then print a 48-point headline, which is about 200 dots high, 25 dots of the text will extend into the nonprinting area.

Make sure the entire character can fit within the printable region. If not, it will be clipped.

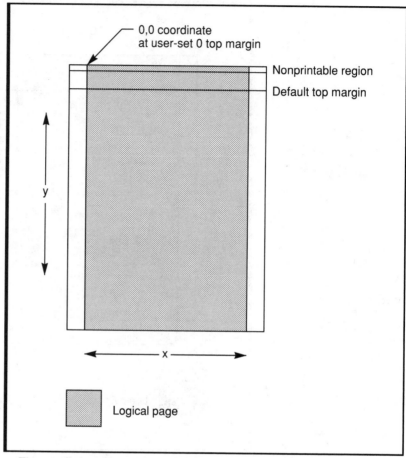

- Figure 18.4: *You can address but not print in all positions of the logical page*

• *Cursor Movement*

The original LaserJet cannot set cursor position
by dots.

Cursor movement is performed using PCL commands, in either decipoints, dots, lines, or columns. Movement can be absolute—measured
from the 0,0 coordinate—or relative to the current coordinate. The same
commands are used for both absolute and relative movement.

The PCL commands in this book show a # to refer to the value field.
If you enter a number without a sign in this field for a cursor-movement
command, the cursor is positioned absolutely from the coordinate 0,0. A
plus (+) or minus (−) sign indicates relative movement to the right or left
of the current position.

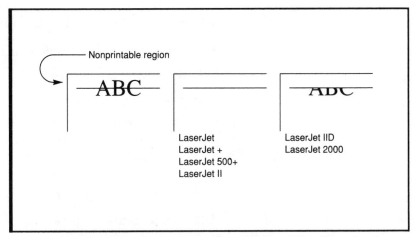

- Figure 18.5: *All models but the LaserJet IID and 2000 clip entire charac-*
ters if any portion enters the nonprinting area

Horizontal Positioning

The PCL command to set the horizontal cursor position by column
number is

<Esc>&a#C

The width of each column is based on the horizontal motion index, which
will be described later.

To set the horizontal cursor position by decipoints, use the command

<Esc>&a#H

The value (#) can include up to two decimal places. The original LaserJet
accepts only integer numbers.

To set the position by dots along the horizontal axis, use

<Esc>*p#X

Remember that several ASCII control codes and the space character
discussed in Chapter 17 also affect the cursor position. These are the carriage return, backspace, and horizontal tab.

Valid cursor positions depend on the size of the page and the measurement system. To compute the maximum position, figure the width of the

logical page in inches. Then multiply that width as follows:

- **Columns**: Logical page width × font pitch.
- **Decipoints**: Logical page width × 720.
- **Dots**: Logical page width × 300.

For letter-size paper with 10-pitch spacing, the valid horizontal cursor positions would be 0 to 79 for columns, 0 to 5875 for decipoints, and 0 to 2448 for dots.

Vertical Positioning

The PCL comand to set the vertical position by row (line) number is

<Esc>&a#R

The size of each row is set by the vertical motion index, normally the point size of the font. The first row, defined by the top margin, is row 0.

To set the position by decipoints along the vertical axis, use

<Esc>&a#V

The value can include up to two decimal places. The original LaserJet accepts only integer numbers.

The command to set the vertical position by dots is

<Esc>*p#Y

For half lines, use the command

<Esc>=

The size of the half line is based on the current vertical motion index.

Vertical cursor movement is also performed by the line feed and form feed ASCII control codes.

To determine valid cursor positions, figure the length of the printable page in inches, and then multiply that value as follows:

- **Rows**: Printable page length × number of lines per inch.
- **Decipoints**: Printable page length × 720.
- **Dots**: Printable page length × 300.

For letter-size paper with six lines per inch and the default margins, the valid vertical positions would be 0 to 60 for rows, 0 to 7199 for decipoints, and 0 to 2999 for dots.

Line Termination Control

The exact effect of the carriage return, line feed, and form feed ASCII codes can be adjusted using the line termination command

<Esc>&k#G

The field value, 0 through 3, sets how the cursor reacts when one of these commands is received. A 0 simply performs the action of the code. The other values work as follows:

Value	Code Sent	Action
1	Carriage return	Carriage return and line feed
	Line feed	Line feed
	Form feed	Form feed
2	Carriage return	Carriage return
	Line feed	Carriage return and line feed
	Form feed	Carriage return and form feed
3	Carriage return	Carriage return and line feed
	Line feed	Carriage return and line feed
	Form feed	Carriage return and form feed

Saving the Cursor Position

When you issue a command that changes the cursor position, the cursor moves and the previous position is forgotten. There may be times, however, when you want to return to the original position.

The push/pop command

<Esc>&f#S

saves the current coordinate in an area called the *stack*. A stack is series of memory addresses that are used to store up to 20 coordinate positions in a

You can't save the cursor position with the original LaserJet.

last-in, first-out basis. The first item in the stack will be the last one removed; the last one in the stack will be the first removed.

Performing a push instruction with the command

    <Esc>&f0S

places the current coordinates on the top of the stack.

Performing a pop instruction using

    <Esc>&f1S

removes the last inserted coordinates from the stack and positions the cursor at their setting.

These instructions are most commonly used with graphics and macros, which will be discussed in Chapter 19. Some other useful examples are presented later in this chapter.

• *Page and Sheet Controls*

The next series of PCL commands controls the overall layout and size of the page. These can be generally classified into three categories: job controls, text area, and spacing settings.

Job Controls

The job control commands set the overall nature of the printing job, including the type, source, and size of the paper.

To set the number of copies of each page printed, use the command

    <Esc>&l#X

Copies are produced uncollated: all of page 1, then page 2, etc. The maximum field value is 99.

The command to reset the printer is

    <Esc>E

This resets the printer to its default environment, deleting any temporary fonts and macros, but printing the current page.

To select the paper source, use the command

    <Esc>&l#H

The field value depends on the LaserJet model, as listed in Table 18.1. Using a field value of 0 will issue a form feed.

The command to specify paper size is

<Esc>&l#A

The field values are listed in Table 18.2. This command is not available on the original LaserJet, LaserJet +, and LaserJet 500 +. With these models, use the following page length command instead.

To set the page length in lines of the logical page, use the command

<Esc>&l#P

To calculate the maximum setting, multiply the logical page length in inches by the lines per inch of the current font. Since the page size command is not

• Table 18.1: *Values for Paper Source (<Esc>&l#H)*

Field Value	Source	LaserJet 2000	LaserJet IID	LaserJet II	LaserJet +	LaserJet 500 +
0	No change	•	•	•	•	•
1	Upper tray	•	•	•	•	•
2	Manual paper		•	•	•	•
3	Manual enve-lope		•		•	•
4	Lower tray	•	•			•
5	Paper deck	•				
6	Enve-lope feeder		•			

• Table 18.2: *Values for Paper Size (<Esc>&l#A)*

Field	Size	LaserJet 2000	LaserJet IID	LaserJet II
1	Executive (7.25" × 10.5")	•	•	•
2	Letter (8.5" × 11")	•	•	•
3	Legal (8.5" × 14")	•	•	•
6	Ledger (11" × 17")	•		
26	A4 (210 mm × 297 mm)	•	•	•
27	A3 (297 mm × 420 mm)	•		
Envelopes				
80	Monarch 7 3/4 (letter)		•	•
81	Commercial 10 (business)		•	•
90	International DL		•	•
91	International C5		•	•

available for earlier LaserJet models, use this setting instead to make your programs compatible with all LaserJet printers.

The command to set the orientation is

    <Esc>&l#O

A field value of 0 is portrait; 1 is landscape.

Display Modes

In Chapter 17, you learned that <Esc>Y turns on the display function, causing the LaserJet to print Escape codes instead of executing them. The command <Esc>Z turns the function off. A related command is

<Esc>&p#X

This is called the transparent print data function. It provides access to symbol set characters in the ASCII range below 31. Normally, these characters are interpreted as ASCII control codes. If you transmit ASCII 27, for example, the LaserJet recognizes it as the <Esc> character and waits for additional PCL commands. On the other hand, the ASCII 7, used to sound a bell on most devices, is ignored.

Some symbol sets have graphic characters mapped to these codes. The PC-8 set assigns a left-pointing arrow (←) to ASCII 27 and a bullet (•) to ASCII 7.

The transparent print data command tells the LaserJet to treat these ASCII numbers as print data instead of control codes. The field value (#) specifies the number of characters to treat this way.

For example, to print the ←, use this code

<Esc>&p1X<Esc>

To print the four card suits, use this command

<Esc>&p4X

followed by the ASCII numbers 3, 4, 5, and 6.

A space will print if no character exists for the ASCII code given.

Duplex Printing

Duplex printing commands are available only for the LaserJet IID and LaserJet 2000.

The command for simplex/duplex printing is

<Esc>&l#S

This selects either single- or double-sided printing and the binding edge, as explained in Chapter 2. The field values are 0 for simplex; 1 for duplex, vertical binding; or 2 for duplex, horizontal binding.

For left-offset registration, use the command

<Esc>&l#U

This sets the vertical position of the logical pages in relation to the physical page. The field value, which can contain up to four decimal positions, represents the number of decipoints of extra binding space on the side of each page. A positive value shifts the logical page toward the right, away from the left margin. When printing on the back side of vertical-binding duplex pages, text is shifted to the left, away from the right margin. A negative field value shifts the logical page toward the left, away from the right margin. When printing on the back side of vertical-binding duplex pages, text is shifted to the right, away from the left margin.

Set the top-offset registration with the command

<Esc>&l#Z

This determines the horizontal position of the logical page in relation to the physical page. The field value, which can contain up to four decimal positions, represents the number of decipoints of extra binding space on the top of each page. A positive value shifts the logical page down, away from the top margin. When printing on the back side of horizontal-binding duplex pages, text is shifted up, toward the top margin. A negative field value shifts the logical page toward the top margin. When printing on the back side of horizontal-binding duplex pages, text is shifted down.

To specify the duplex page side, use the command

<Esc>&a#G

This controls the side of the sheet a page will print on, overriding normal duplex printing. Field values are 0 for next side, 1 for front side, or 2 for back side. For example, perhaps you've typed a multichapter document as one file. During printing in duplex, you want the first page of each chapter to start on the front side of a page. Use the command

<Esc>&a1G

at the start of each chapter. If the page before was printed on the front side, the printer will eject the page with a blank back side, then start printing on the front of the next sheet.

Controlling Multiple Print Jobs

When you're printing several jobs at one time, dividing the output stack into separate documents can be time consuming. The LaserJet 2000 and LaserJet 500+ will do this for you when you use the job separation command

<Esc>&l1T

With the LaserJet 2000, a sheet of paper with a heavy black bar along one edge will be inserted between jobs. The black bar makes it easy to identify separate documents.

The LaserJet 500+ will output alternate jobs slightly offset in the tray.

Setting the Text Area

After the page size is set, you can use PCL commands to determine the number of lines and characters that will print on each page. You can specify the top margin, but no PCL command directly establishes the bottom margin. Instead, the bottom margin is calculated by subtracting the top margin and text length from the physical page size.

There is, however, a command to enable or disable the perforation area. This command might appear odd for a printer that uses individual sheets of paper, but remember that PCL was designed for all HP printers.

The left margin is specified with

<Esc>&a#L

which sets the left margin in columns, based on the current horizontal motion index.

For the right margin, use

<Esc>&a#M

to set the right margin in columns.

The command to reset margins is

<Esc>9

This returns margins to the left and right boundaries of the logical page.

The command for the top margin is

<Esc>&l#E

This determines the top margin in lines, based on the current vertical motion index or line spacing. The top margin becomes the y-axis 0 coordinate.

You can set the text length with

<Esc>&l#F

This specifies the number of lines that will print starting at the top margin.

The perforation command is

<Esc>&l#L

The perforation area is defined as the distance from the bottom of text on one page to the start of text on the next. When enabled (the default setting with a field value of 1), a line feed or half-line feed placing the cursor beyond the text area will cause a page eject and place the cursor at the first text line of the next page. When disabled, with a field value of 0, print lines could be lost.

The end-of-line command

<Esc>&s#C

determines the action when the cursor reaches the right margin. When disabled (the default setting with a field value of 1), characters extending into the right margin are clipped. The default setting doesn't affect programs with LaserJet drivers and printing jobs that fit within the printable page. However, screen dumps and ASCII text files may extend into the nonprintable region and be clipped. To enable the setting, use a field value of 0. Any character or space that would move the cursor into the nonprintable region will cause a carriage return and line feed.

Spacing Commands

The spacing commands control the distance the cursor moves with each line or character printed.

For line spacing, use the command

<Esc>&l#D

This sets the number of lines per inch, with a default value of 6. Valid field values are 1, 2, 3, 4, 6, 8, 12, 16, 24, and 48. Using the default font, setting a field value larger than 6 will cause lines to overlap. Compute the maximum setting by dividing the point size into 72.

The vertical motion index command is

    <Esc>&l#C

It sets the number of 1/48-inch increments between rows, which is 8 by default for six lines per inch. Use this command as an alternative method of changing line spacing, particularly for settings not available with the line spacing command. Field values range from 0 to 336 and may contain up to four decimal positions.

    The vertical motion index affects all commands using lines (or rows) as a measure. For example, this command changes line spacing to four lines per inch:

    <Esc>&l12C

If you then used the command

    <Esc>&a6R

to move the cursor down six lines, the cursor moves $1\frac{1}{2}$ inches. The same command at the default vertical motion index would move the cursor just 1 inch.

    The horizontal motion index command is

    <Esc>&k#H

It sets the number of $\frac{1}{120}$-inch increments between columns. The default value of 12 accommodates 10-pitch characters ($\frac{12}{120}$ inch equals $\frac{1}{10}$, or 10 characters per inch). Field values range from 0 to 840 and may contain up to four decimal positions.

    The horizontal motion index affects all commands using columns as a measure. Use this command to add extra space between characters or compress text.

• *Avoiding Programming Pitfalls*

After you understand the structure of PCL and the various methods of measurement, using the commands can be as easy as working with any programming language. Still, keep in mind that the LaserJet is a sophisticated device and that the interaction of settings can present some subtle traps.

This section reviews some of the potential problems and their solutions. The examples are written in Basic, but the same algorithms can be applied to any language.

Working with the Top Margin

If you set the top margin to 0 and increase the lines per page setting, you'll be able to fit the maximum number of lines on each page. Unfortunately, your very first line will be in the nonprintable region and will not appear. So if you use this command:

<Esc>&l0E

to set the top margin to zero, start each page with a blank print statement. The carriage return/line feed after the blank line will push the first actual line of text into the printable region. As an alternative, use the command <Esc>&l1E to set the top margin at one line.

Creating Overstriking Characters

The cursor-movement commands can be used to create special characters and symbols that might not be available in your symbol set. Accented characters, for example, can be formed by printing the first character, backing up, then printing the next.

In some instances, the effects are not exactly as planned. Figure 18.6, for example, shows slashed zeros created from two different fonts with the commands

```
10 LPRINT "0";
20 LPRINT chr$(27);"&a-1C/"
```

The PCL command in line 20 backs up the cursor one character position then prints the slash.

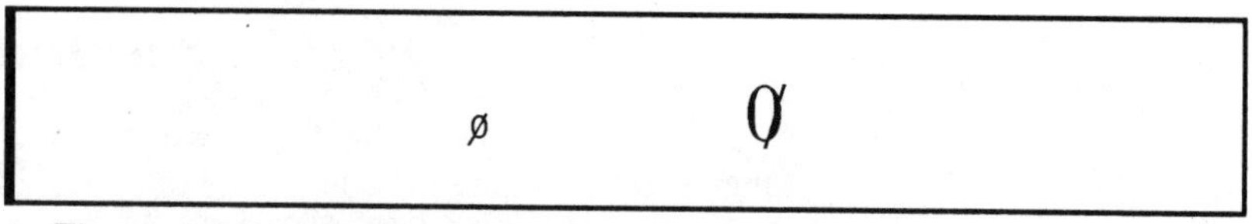

• Figure 18.6: *Moving by column widths often results in improperly aligned characters*

With the fixed-width font on the left (10-pitch Courier), the slash is correctly centered horizontally over the zero, but extends too far down. The results are worse with the proportionally-spaced font (24-point Times). Column widths in proportional fonts are determined by the size of the space character, ASCII 32. In this case, that width is not sufficient to center the slash over the zero.

In the case of the fixed-width font, the starting position of the slash should be raised slightly to center it vertically. But this would move it off-center horizontally. So, the cursor must be repositioned along both axes using either decipoints or dots.

The slash on the proportionally-spaced font is not far enough to the left and must be moved further back, again by decipoints or dots.

Horizontal or vertical cursor movements by decipoints would properly position the slash in both cases. But what if you wanted to print a second character immediately afterward? This program for the fixed-width font:

```
10 LPRINT "0";
20 LPRINT chr$(27);"&a-65h-10V/1";
```

or this one for the proportionally-spaced font:

```
10 LPRINT "0";
20 LPRINT chr$(27);"&a-100H/1";
```

would properly position the slash, but leave the cursor in the wrong position for the number 1, as shown in Figure 18.7. On the left, the 1 is still 10 decipoints higher than the zero; on the right, it's too close.

The solution is to save the cursor position immediately after the zero, back up to print the slash, and then return the cursor to the saved position for the next character. For the fixed-width font, the commands are

```
10 LPRINT "0";
20 LPRINT chr$(27);"&f0S";
30 LPRINT chr$(27);"&a-65h-10V/";
40 LPRINT chr$(27);"&f1S1";
```

• Figure 18.7: *Moving the cursor corrects the slash, but results in improperly aligned characters that follow*

For the proportionally-spaced font, use

```
10 LPRINT "0";
20 LPRINT chr$(27);"&f0S";
30 LPRINT chr$(27);"&a-100H/";
40 LPRINT chr$(27);"&f1S1";
```

The push and pop instructions on lines 20 and 40 save the cursor position immediately after the 0 in the stack, then restore it before printing the number 1. Figure 18.8 shows the printed results.

• *Programming Special Effects*

Logos, graphics, and other effects can be formed with creative use of cursor-movement commands. For example, the logo shown in Figure 18.9 was formed by carefully positioning two letter C's in 30-point Cooper Black. The cursor was placed using absolute positioning in dots:

```
10 LPRINT chr$(27);"*p300x300Y";
20 LPRINT "C";
30 LPRINT chr$(27);"*p350x350Y";
40 LPRINT "C"
50 LPRINT chr$(12)
```

More complex designs can be created using repetition statements. Figure 18.10 shows a "staircase" effect formed by the letter Z in the word *Zip*,

---

01   01

• Figure 18.8: *Saving and restoring the cursor position properly aligns characters*

• Figure 18.9: *A double-C logo*

using 18-point Helvetica. The cursor was manipulated to link the letters together diagonally:

```
10 WIDTH "LPT1:",255
20 A = 300
30 B = 300
40 FOR X = 1 TO 10
50 LPRINT chr$(27);"*p";A;"x";B;"Y";
60 LPRINT "ZIP";
70 A = A + 40
80 B = B + 48
90 NEXT X
100 LPRINT"ZIPZIPZIPZIPZIPZIPZIPZIPZIPZIPZIPZIP"
```

This program is interesting because of the use of variables in PCL commands. In line 50, the program variables A and B are used to represent the horizontal and vertical positions. Notice that they are not included in the quotation marks because their value is to be transmitted to the printer.

The width command in line 10 is needed to prevent the Basic interpreter from issuing its own carriage return/line feed command when it thinks it has reached the end of a line. The syntax for this command in your own version of Basic might be different.

Each of these examples used one font size and face for all the characters. By combining cursor movement with the font and graphic commands you're about to learn, you can create some startling effects.

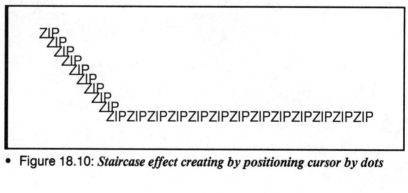

• Figure 18.10: *Staircase effect creating by positioning cursor by dots*

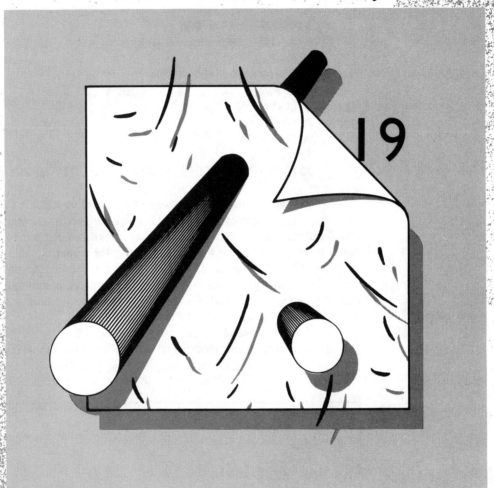

H·P L·A·S·E·R·J·E·T

19

Programming Fonts and Graphics

• In Chapter 18, you learned PCL commands that control where and how much text goes on the page. After you position the cursor and lay out the page, you must program what prints on that page.

In this chapter, you'll learn how to use PCL commands to select and control fonts, print graphics, and program macros.

• *Selecting Fonts in Your Programs*

By default, the LaserJet uses the internal 12-point Courier font for all text. Using an application with a LaserJet driver, you can select any supported font, and then format characters with attributes, such as size, boldface, and italic.

Using PCL commands to select fonts gives you even more capabilities. You select the font to use, called the *primary* font, by specifying its attributes or, for a softfont, its ID. You can also choose a *secondary* font, then quickly switch between the two. Use the shift-out code (ASCII 14) to select the secondary font; use the shift-in code (ASCII 15) to return to the primary font, like this:

```
10 LPRINT chr$(14);"This is the secondary font"
20 LPRINT chr$(15);"This is the primary font"
```

Font Selection Priority Rules

The LaserJet uses a priority system to respond to PCL font commands. For example, suppose that you have fonts available in all three resources: softfonts, cartridges, and internal, as well as a collection of font faces and styles. Now suppose you use PCL commands that designate Times 12-point Bold as the primary font. All LaserJet models, except the original, will first look in RAM for a matching softfont, starting with the lowest ID number. If one isn't found, it looks at loaded cartridges, then at the internal fonts.

If the printer can't find a font matching all the characteristics specified by PCL commands, it uses a priority system in this order:

In selecting cartridge fonts, the priority is left, center (LaserJet 2000), then right.

1. Orientation

2. Symbol set

3. Spacing

4. Pitch

5. Height

6. Style

7. Stroke weight

8. Typeface

For example, if you used the PCL command to select a font having the PC-8 symbol set, in fixed 10-pitch spacing, the printer will first look through each source for a font that matches all three characteristics. If it can't find one, it next looks for fonts meeting the first two of the characteristics, then one, until a font is selected. This means that if no font has both the first two characteristics, the first font (by source) with the PC-8 symbol set, no matter what typeface, will be selected.

In addition to this, priority is given to the current font. For instance, if you're already using 12-point Times Roman, a PCL command to use bold will first see if 12-point Times Roman Bold is available. If not, the first bold font will be selected based on the priority rules.

If matching fonts in both portrait and landscape are found, priority will be given to the current orientation. With the LaserJet IID and 2000, if the orientation of the matching font is incorrect, the printer automatically turns it in the proper direction.

Selecting Fonts by Attribute

In all the commands for selecting fonts by attribute, the parameterized character (represents selection of the primary font. To select the secondary font, use) as the parameterized character.

To specify a font by symbol set, use

<Esc>(*set-ID*

This designates the font with the specified symbol set ID the primary font. The *set-ID* is a unique two- or three-character code that is assigned to all HP compatible symbol sets, as listed in Table 19.1. If this symbol set is not found, the default set will be used. To select the PC-8 set, for example, use the command

<Esc>(10U

Set the font spacing with the command

<Esc>(s#P

Two additional priorities are used: after symbol set, fonts are selected by placement (subscript or superscript), and the final priority is print quality (draft or letter quality).

Remember that orientation is set by <Esc>&l0O for portrait and <Esc>&l1O for landscape.

Additional symbol set values are 0Q for Math-8a, 1Q for Math-8b, and 2Q for HP Pi font a.

• Table 19.1: *ID Field Values for Symbol Sets (<Esc>set-ID)*

SET ID	SYMBOL SET
0A	HP Math-7
0B	HP Line Draw
0D	ISO 60: Norwegian version 1
1D	ISO 61: Norwegian version 2
0E	HP Roman Extension
1E	ISO 4: United Kingdom
0F	ISO 25: French
1F	ISO 69: French
0G	HP German
1G	ISO 21: German
8G	HP Greek-8
0H	HP Hebrew
8H	HP Hebrew-8
0I	ISO 15: Italian
0K	ISO 14: JIS ASCII
1K	HP Katakana
2K	ISO 57: Chinese
8K	HP Kana-88
9K	HP Korean
0L	HP Line Draw (same as 0B)
1L	HP Block Characters
0M	HP Math-7 (same as 0A)
1M	Technical-7
8M	HP Math-8
0N	ISO 100: ECMA-94 (Latin 1)
0O	OCR A
1O	OCR B
2O	OCR M

Your HP LaserJet Handbook

• Table 19.1: *ID Field Values for Symbol Sets (<Esc>set-ID) (Continued)*

SET ID	SYMBOL SET
0P	APL (typewriter)
1P	APL (bit paired)
0R	HP Cyrillic ASCII
1R	HP Cyrillic
0S	ISO 11: Swedish
1S	HP Spanish
2S	ISO 17: Spanish
3S	ISO 10: Swedish
4S	ISO 16: Portuguese
5S	ISO 84: Portuguese
6S	ISO 85: Spanish
0T	HP Thai-8
8T	HP Turkish-8
0U	ISO 6: ASCII
1U	HP Legal
2U	ISO 2: International
5U	HP HPL Language Set
7U	OEM-1
8U	HP Roman-8
9U	Windows
10U	PC-8
11U	PC-8 (D/N)
12U	PC-850
15U	HP Pi font
0V	HP Arabic (McKay's version)
8V	HP Arabic
nX	Downloaded font n

Note: ISO is the International Standards Organization.

The spacing of the primary font is either fixed (0), or proportional (1). If a font with the selected spacing is not available, a fixed-pitch font will be used.

The command for setting font pitch is

<Esc>(s#H

The field value is the pitch in characters per inch of the primary font. When one with this value isn't found, the LaserJet first looks for the next greater value, then the closest lower value.

To set the font height, use

<Esc>(s#V

This selects the point size of the primary font. If the exact point size isn't found, the closest font will be selected.

You can specify the style of a font with

<Esc>(s#S

The style of the primary font will be either upright (0) or italic (1).

To set font weight, use

<Esc>(s#B

This determines the stroke weight of the primary font using these values:

−7	Ultra thin
−5	Thin
−3	Light
0	Medium
3	Bold
5	Black
7	Ultra black

If the designated weight isn't located, the next thickest is used, and if not found, the next thinnest.

The command to set a typeface is

<Esc>(s#T

This determines the font family of the primary font, using the field values listed in Table 19.2.

Selecting Entirely New Fonts

The command to set all new characteristics can be quite complex. As an example, suppose that you want to select an 18-point proportionally-spaced, Helvetica Bold Italic font in the ASCII symbol set, printed in landscape orientation. Because the font is not fixed-width, you don't have to specify the pitch.

Here are the individual commands:

Landscape orientation	<Esc>&l1O
Symbol set: ASCII	<Esc>(0U
Spacing: Proportional	<Esc>(s1P
Height: 18 points	<Esc>(s18V
Style: Italic	<Esc>(s1S
Weight: Bold	<Esc>(s3B
Typeface: Helvetica	<Esc>(s4T

Putting the commands on one line yields

> <Esc>&l1O<Esc>(0U<Esc>(s1P<Esc>(s18V<Esc>(s1S <Esc>(s3B<Esc>(s4T

Then combining the codes (using the rules outlined in Chapter 18), the final code is

> <Esc>&l1O<Esc>(0U<Esc>(s1p18v1s3b4T

In Basic, the command would look like this:

```
10 LPRINT
chr$(27);"&l1O";chr$(27);"(0U";chr$(27);"(s1p18v1s3b4T"
```

• Table 19.2: *Field Values for Typeface (<Esc>s#T)*

VALUE	TYPEFACE
0	Line Printer
1	Pica
2	Elite
3	Courier
4	Helv
5	TmsRmn
6	Letter Gothic
7	Script
8	Prestige
9	Caslon
10	Orator
11	Presentations
12	Helv Condensed
13	Serifa
14	Futura
15	Palatino
16	ITC Souvenir
17	Optima
18	ITC Garamond
19	Cooper Black
20	Ribbon (Coronet)
21	Broadway
22	Bauer Bodini Black Condensed
23	Century Schoolbook
24	University Roman
25	Helv Outline
26	Futura Condensed
27	ITC Korinna

Table 19.2: *Field Values for Typeface (<Esc>s#T) (Continued)*

VALUE	TYPEFACE
28	Naskh (Arabic)
29	Cloister Black
30	ITC Galliard
31	ITC Avant Garde Gothic
32	Brush
33	Blippo
34	Hobo
35	Windsor
36	Helv Compressed
37	Helv Extra Compressed
38	Peignot
39	Baskerville
40	ITC Garamond Condensed
41	Trade Gothic
42	Goudy Old Style
43	ITC Zapf Chancery
44	Clarendon
45	ITC Zapf Dingbats
46	Cooper
47	ITC Bookman
48	Stick
49	HP-GL Drafting
50	HP-GL Spline
51	Gill Sans
52	Univers
53	Bodoni
54	Rockwell
55	Melior

Table 19.2: *Field Values for Typeface (<Esc>s#T) (Continued)*

VALUE	TYPEFACE
56	ITC Tiffany
57	ITC Clearface
58	Amelia
59	Park Avenue
60	Handel Gothic
61	Dom Casual
62	ITC Benguiat
63	ITC Cheltenham
64	Century Expanded
65	Franklin Gothic
66	Franklin Gothic Expressed
67	Franklin Gothic Extra Condensed
68	Plantin
69	Trump Mediaeval
70	Futura Black

Changing Attributes

If you're using the default font or have already selected a new primary font, you can change specific attributes by just specifying their characteristics. For example, to print in bold using the current font, use the command

    <Esc>(s3B

To select italic print, use the command

    <Esc>(s1S

As with all PCL commands, codes that have the same parameterized and group characters can be combined. So the commands to change to the 14-point italic font:

    <Esc>(s14V<Esc>(s1S

would be entered like this

<Esc>(s14v1S

Selecting Automatic Underlining

The possible field values for underlining are 0 and 1 for single fixed position, 2 for double fixed, 3 for single floating, and 4 for double floating.

Underlined characters are not created with a font but with the printer's automatic underline feature. Turn on underlining with the command

<Esc>&d#D

The field value, either 0 or 3, determines the position of the underline. If the field value is 0 (or not included) the line is drawn starting on the fifth dot under the baseline, three dots thick. This is called *fixed-position underlining*.

With the original LaserJet, LaserJet +, and LaserJet 500 +, turn on underlining with the command

<Esc>&dD

If you have several typefaces and sizes on one line, fixed-position underlining might not fit well under certain characters. When this happens, try floating-position underlining.

These printers have only fixed-position underlining and do not recognize a field value.

With a field value of 3, the other models determine the line position by the fonts on the line. As you'll learn in Chapter 20, the data downloaded for a font contains a descriptor called underline distance, the recommended starting position under the baseline. Using *floating-position underlining*, as this mode is called, the line is placed at the lowest underline distance of all the fonts on the current line.

Turn underlining off with the command

<Esc>&d@

Selecting Softfonts by ID

Because so many codes are needed to select a unique font by attribute, it is more efficient to select downloaded softfonts by their ID number using the command

<Esc>(#X

Select the secondary font with

<Esc>)#X

The field value is the ID number assigned to the font when it was downloaded. To use the font with ID 5 as the primary font, for example, use this command

<Esc>(5X

You can use a short Basic program to select the primary font by ID:

```
10 PRINT "WHICH FONT DO YOU WANT TO USE"
20 INPUT A
30 LPRINT chr$(27);"(";A;"X";
```

If you have several consecutively numbered fonts downloaded, use this program to print a sample of each:

```
10 PRINT "ENTER THE STARTING ID NUMBER"
20 INPUT A
30 PRINT "ENTER THE ENDING ID NUMBER"
40 INPUT B
50 FOR X = A TO B
60 LPRINT chr$(27);"(";X;"X";
70 LPRINT "FONT "X;"  ABCDEFabcdef"
80 LPRINT
90 NEXT X
```

Unique visual effects can be created by combining font selection and cursor movement commands. For example, the three-dimensional effect shown in Figure 19.1 was created with this program:

```
10 WIDTH "lpt1:", 255
20 X = 300:Y = 300:X1 = 10:Y1 = 10
30 FOR A = 0 TO 5
40 LPRINT chr$(27);"(";A;"X";
50 FOR B = 1 TO 5
60 LPRINT chr$(27);"*p";X;"x";Y;"Y";
70 LPRINT "Sybex"
80 X = X + X1:Y = Y + Y1
90 NEXT B
100 X1 = X1 + 2:Y1 = Y1 + 2
110 NEXT A
120 X = X + 50:Y = Y + 50
```

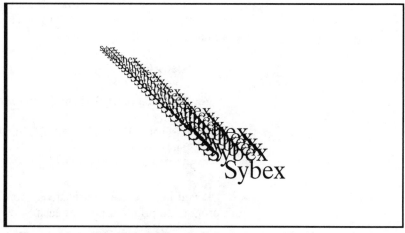

• Figure 19.1: *Three-dimensional effects created with PCL commands*

```
130 LPRINT chr$(27);" * p";X;"x";Y;"Y";
140 LPRINT "Sybex"
150 LPRINT chr$(12)
```

The program gradually increases the font size while moving the cursor diagonally. In this case, the program uses ID numbers of six fonts loaded in size order, starting with ID 0. The cursor was moved in two-dot increments, starting at ten dots down and to the right of the previous starting position. At the end, a final string was printed offset by 50 dots.

Selecting by Pitch

With the original LaserJet, LaserJet +, and LaserJet 500 +, you can quickly change from standard 10-pitch Courier to the 16.66-pitch Line Printer font.

The command

        \<Esc>&k2S

selects Line Printer as the current primary and secondary font. Reselect the 10-pitch font with the command

        \<Esc>&k0S

The reselect command is not available on the original LaserJet.

Returning to the Default Font

To return to the default font after selecting fonts, use the command

      <Esc>(3@

This sets all the attributes to those of the default font. Reselect the secondary font with

      <Esc>)3@

You can also use the default reset command to set symbol sets by entering the appropriate field value:

Field Value	Primary (<Esc(#@)	Secondary (<Esc)#@)
0	The default font's symbol set is selected as the symbol set for the primary font.	The default font's symbol set is selected as the symbol set for the secondary font.
1	Same as field value 0.	The primary font's symbol is selected as the symbol set for the secondary font.
2	Sets the currently used symbol set of the primary font as the default symbol set of the primary font. This forces the printer to check available fonts for one matching the new attributes.	Sets the currently used symbol set of the secondary font as the symbol set of the secondary font.

• *Managing Softfonts*

This section is not applicable to the original LaserJet.

When you download softfonts through a font downloading program, the assignment of ID numbers and permanent or temporary status is handled for you. This is also the case when you download certain fonts using the DOS Copy command. The ID and status information is contained in the binary data, along with the font bit map itself.

Most softfont files, however, do not contain this information. They can only be downloaded with the DOS Copy command by manually specifying the ID number and status using PCL commands.

These commands, and the PCL code to delete fonts, are classified as font management instructions. There are other PCL commands used to create the softfont itself, which will be discussed in Chapter 20.

Specify the font ID number with the command

    <Esc>*c#D

The field value is the ID number of the next font downloaded to the printer. If you are about to download a font as ID 3, for example, use the command

    <Esc>*c3D

To designate font status, use

    <Esc>*c#F

Use this command immediately after the softfont has been downloaded. A field value of 4 designates the font as temporary. A value of 5 sets it as permanent. Until you designate a font as permanent, it is considered temporary. For example, if you just downloaded font 1, make it permanent with the command

    <Esc>*c5F

Use a field value of 4 to change a permanent font to temporary.

This command changes the status of the last softfont referenced. To make sure you're setting the correct font, combine the font ID command with the status command. For example, to set font number 0 as permanent (at any time) use the command

    <Esc>*c0d5F

The command to delete fonts is

    <Esc>*c#F

To delete all softfonts from memory, use a field value of 0. Use a value of 1 to delete only temporary softfonts. If you want to delete a specific font, use the field value 2, but first designate the font's ID. For example, delete font 3 with the command

<Esc>*c3d2F

The LaserJet + and 500+ accept two additional field values for the delete fonts command: 3 deletes the last character code downloaded and 6 assigns the current font the last ID number specified in a font ID command. Character codes will be discussed in Chapter 20.

As an example, here is how you would download a font called TM2400RPN.USP, with ID 2 and permanent status:

1. If this is the only font you want loaded, delete all current softfonts with the command **<Esc>*c0F**.

2. Send the PCL code to designate the font ID: **<Esc>*c2D**.

3. Use the DOS Copy command with the /B option to download the bit map: enter **c:> COPY /B TM240RPN.USP LPT1**.

4. Make the font permanent with the command **<Esc>*c5F**.

5. If you want to use the font immediately, select it as the primary font with the command **<Esc>(5X**.

To program this in Basic, you need these two short programs:

```
10 PRINT "WHAT FONT ID DO YOU WANT TO ASSIGN"
20 INPUT A
30 LPRINT chr$(27);"*c";A;"D";
```

```
10 PRINT "WHAT FONT ID DID YOU JUST DOWNLOAD"
20 INPUT ID
30 PRINT "DO YOU WANT TO MAKE THE FONT
      PERMANENT -- Y OR N?"
40 INPUT PERM$
50 IF PERM$ = "Y" OR PERM$ ="y" THEN LPRINT
      chr$(27);"*C5F";
60 PRINT "DO YOU WANT TO USE THE FONT
      IMMEDIATELY -- Y OR N?"
70 INPUT NOW$
80 IF NOW$ = "Y" OR NOW$ = "y" THEN LPRINT
      chr$(27);"(";ID;"X";
```

```
90 PRINT "DO YOU WANT A SAMPLE OF THE FONT –
    Y OR N";
100 INPUT SAM$
110 IF SAM$ = "N" OR SAM$ = "n" GOTO 160
120 LPRINT "ABCDEFGHIJKLMN"
130 LPRINT "OPQRSTUVWXYZ"
140 LPRINT "abcdefghijklmn"
150 LPRINT "opqrstuvwxyz"
160 LPRINT "01234567890!@#$%^&*()?><.,':;}{][" 
170 LPRINT chr$(12)
180 END
```

Run the first program to designate the ID, and then return to the DOS prompt to download the font with the Copy command. Next run the second program to select permanent status and, if you want, make the font current and print a sample. If you have a Basic compiler, create executable versions of both programs and use a batch file to run the programs and copy the font.

• *Programming Graphics Printing*

Throughout this book, we've described ways to select graphic resolution and print graphic files from application programs. In the following sections, we'll examine graphics from a programming viewpoint.

There are two categories of PCL commands for printing graphics: raster graphics and rectangular area fill. We'll discuss the more complex raster approach first.

Creating Raster Graphics

The size of bit-map graphics is limited by your printer's memory.

Raster graphics commands are used to print images that are transferred to the LaserJet bit by bit. This provides complete control over the design, but it is really only practical if you are reproducing very small images (or have a great deal of time).

At 300-dpi resolution, a 1-square inch graphic image is 90,000 dots. It's one thing to draw a small figure on paper. It's another to know where each of these dots should be placed to be reproduced accurately by the printer.

Graphics Resolution

Before you begin working with raster graphics, you should thoroughly understand the concept of resolution. Figure 19.2 illustrates how each dot is handled at resolutions of 300, 150, 100, and 75 dpi.

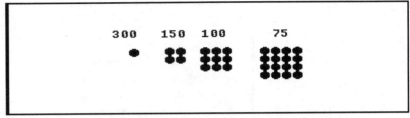

• Figure 19.2: *The physical image of a single dot at 300, 150, 100, and 75 dpi*

When the LaserJet is set at 300 dpi, each dot you transmit is printed as one 1/300th-inch dot. When you transmit a graphic that's 300 dots high and 300 dots wide, the printed image will be 1 inch square.

At 150 dpi, however, the LaserJet prints each transmitted dot as a two-by-two matrix, using four printed dots for each dot in the graphic. This doubles the size of the image. A graphic designed to be 300 dots square will print 600 dots high and 600 dots wide, 2 inches square.

The same dot prints as a three-by-three matrix at 100 dpi, for three times the size, and a four-by-four grid at 75 dpi for four times the size.

As the matrix used to represent each dot grows, the quality of the image declines. Each white space where a dot doesn't print ("white dot") is the same enlarged size. These wider white areas give the image a more grainy, less defined look. Additionally, the larger grid gives diagonal lines a stepped look. The dots appear to have a rectangular shape.

Figure 19.3 shows how the same graphic image appears at all four resolutions. The arrows were printed with a Basic program using raster graphics commands. Notice the differences in the diagonal lines that form the point. With each decrease in resolution, and a corresponding increase in size, the jagged edges become more pronounced. At 75 dpi, it appears that the point is made from rectangles, not round dots.

This same effect is also created by many application programs. Windows Paint images, for example, can be printed in either high or low resolution. Graphics printed at low resolution are twice the size as their high-resolution counterparts.

Word processing and desktop publishing programs, on the other hand, deal with resolution differently. Rather than use different sized grids for each dot, these programs print fewer dots as resolution decreases, so the size of the image doesn't change.

Figure 19.4 shows how WordPerfect printed the same graphic image, an Old English letter C, at 300, 150, and 75 dpi. Each letter is the same size, but at 75 dpi, the curved and diagonal lines are less smooth.

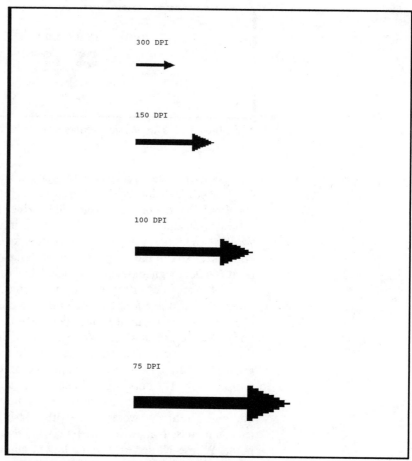

• Figure 19.3: *Raster graphic shown at four resolutions*

Designing a Raster Graphic

To start planning a raster graphic, draw the image on graph paper with the smallest grid possible, where each block can represent a single printed dot. Because you can't print parts of a dot, fill in each block completely.

This might seem like a lot of work, but it is only the beginning of the effort required to create raster graphics. Remember, a design 1 inch long will require rows of 300 dots.

When you're satisfied with the design, draw a rectangle around it. Make the rectangle as small as possible but completely enclose the image. Now reproduce everything within the rectangle on another piece of graph

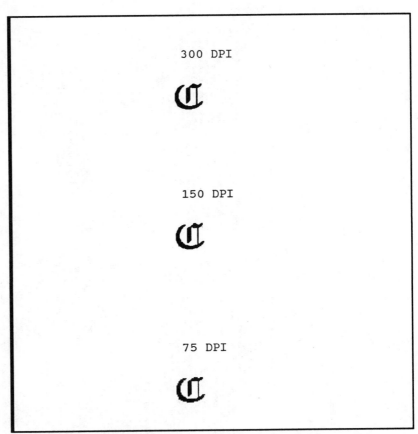

• Figure 19.4: *Graphic character printed at three resolutions with WordPerfect*

paper, this time placing a 0 on every empty block, a 1 on each filled one. Figure 19.5 shows the pattern used to create the arrows shown in Figure 19.3. Each row of blocks will become a printed row of dots, a black dot for every 1, a white space for each 0.

Converting the Drawing to Decimal

The next step is to divide the rectangle into groups of columns, each eight blocks wide. Start at the left and work toward the right. If the last column isn't a full eight blocks, extend the rectangle and fill in the extra blocks with zeros.

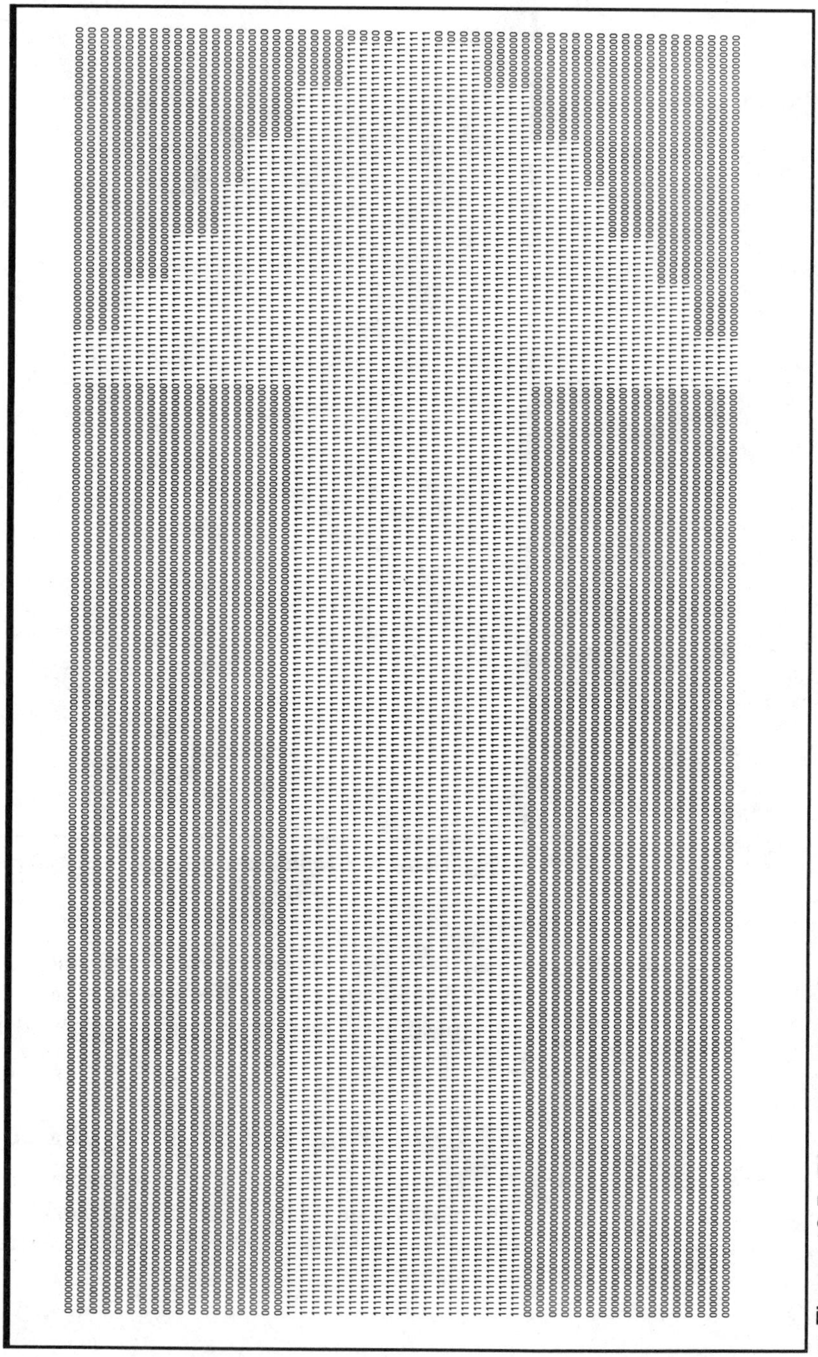

• Figure 19.5: *Bit-map pattern for arrow*

You now have to convert each set of eight blocks to a decimal number that will be transmitted to the printer. This is done using the binary numbering system, assigning each of the eight blocks a value, then adding them together. The place holders in the binary system have these values, from left to right: 128 64 32 16 8 4 2 1.

Assign the numbers to each of the blocks, like this:

128 64 32 16 8 4 2 1

0 1 1 1 1 0 0 0

Add up the numbers for each 1 in the group and record the total. In this case, the series of eight blocks will be transmitted to the printer as the number 120 (64 + 32 + 16 + 8).

Do this for each block in each row, recording the numbers like this:

01111000	00000000	00000000	00000000	120	0	0	0
00000111	00000000	00000000	00000000	7	128	0	0
00000000	01111000	00000000	00000000	0	120	0	0
00000000	00000111	11111111	11111111	0	7	255	255

Using PCL Raster Graphics Commands

See Appendix D for a description of PCL commands unique to DeskJet printers.

After your design is planned and converted to decimal bytes, you can use PCL commands to transmit and print the image. Begin with the cursor-movement commands to place the cursor at the top-left corner where you want to start the graphic.

Next, set the resolution of the image with the command

<Esc>*t#R

The field value is the resolution in dots per inch: 75, 100, 150, or 300. Then give the start raster graphics command

<Esc>*r#A

A field value of 0 starts each line at the left edge of the printable page; a value of 1 sets the current x coordinate as the graphic's left margin.

For each printed row, issue the transfer command

<Esc>*b#W

followed by the data for each line. The field value represents the number of bytes for the line, as explained shortly. When the entire image has been transferred, use the end raster graphics command

<Esc>*rB

Figure 19.6 shows a portion of the Basic program used to print the arrow illustrated in Figure 19.3. Only five of the data statements containing the raster data are included in the figure. The entire drawing requires 55 rows of 33 bytes, with 264 dot positions in each row.

Each data command contains the decimal numbers for one row of data. The program sets the resolution, issues the start raster graphics command, and then repeats the transfer command for each row. It certainly is a great deal of work for an arrow less than 1 inch long.

Raster Graphics Orientation

Most LaserJet models cannot rotate bit maps automatically. To print a graphic in landscape mode, you must issue the landscape PCL command and transmit the graphic in the proper sequence.

For example, if you wanted to print a graphic that's 320 dots wide and 2400 dots tall in portrait mode, you would have to transmit 2400 lines, each 40 bytes long. To print the same graphic in landscape orientation, you have to "turn the graphic around," transmitting it in 320 lines of 300 bytes each.

```
10 WIDTH "lpt1:"; 255
20 OPEN "lpt1:" as #1
30 PRINT #1, chr$(27);"*t300R";
40 PRINT #1, chr$(27);"*r0A";
50 FOR X=1 to 55
55 PRINT #1, chr$(27);"*b33W";
60 FOR Y = 1 to 33
65 READ A
70 PRINT #1, chr$(a);
80 NEXT Y
90 NEXT X
100 PRINT #1, chr$(27);"*rB";
120 CLOSE
1000 DATA    0,0,0,0,0,0,0,0,0,0,0,0,0,0,0,0,0,0,0,0,0,0,0,3,254,0,
0,0,0,0,0,0,0,0
1010   DATA   0,0,0,0,0,0,0,0,0,0,0,0,0,0,0,0,0,0,0,0,0,0,0,3,254,0,
0,0,0,0,0,0,0,0
1020   DATA   0,0,0,0,0,0,0,0,0,0,0,0,0,0,0,0,0,0,0,0,0,0,0,3,254,0,
0,0,0,0,0,0,0,0
1030   DATA   0,0,0,0,0,0,0,0,0,0,0,0,0,0,0,0,0,0,0,0,0,0,0,3,254,0,
0,0,0,0,0,0,0,0
1040 DATA 0,0,0,0,0,0,0,0,0,0,0,0,0,0,0,0,0,0,0,0,0,0,0,3,255,255,
0,0,0,0,0,0,0,0
```

• Figure 19.6: *Basic program to print arrow*

However, the command

<Esc>*r#F

takes advantage of the ability of the LaserJet IID and 2000 to rotate bit maps in either orientation. With a field value of 0, raster graphics are printed according to the current orientation setting. Using 8½- by 11-inch paper, graphics will print across the 8½-inch width in portrait orientation, across the 11-inch width in landscape.

If you change the field value to 3, however, the graphic will print across the 8½-inch width of the page (sometimes called the physical width) no matter what the orientation. This has no effect in portrait orientation but can create problems in landscape. The image will print down the 8½-inch "height" of the page, each line moving toward the left side, the physical top margin. Unless you start with a cursor position far enough along the x-axis, some of the image may get clipped in the nonprintable region.

Creating Rectangular Fill Graphics

Rectangular fill graphics commands are not available for DeskJet printers.

With any model but the original LaserJet, you can more easily print graphics using PCL rectangular fill graphics commands. These define the shape of the rectangle and density and pattern used to fill it. Rectangles can be empty or filled with various degrees of gray or one of six different patterns. Figure 19.7 shows the gray scale shades, and Figure 19.8 illustrates the patterns.

You can specify the length and height of a rectangle in dots or decipoints. Set its length (horizontal size) in dots with the command

<Esc>*c#A

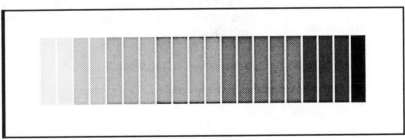

• Figure 19.7: *Gray scale rectangular fill*

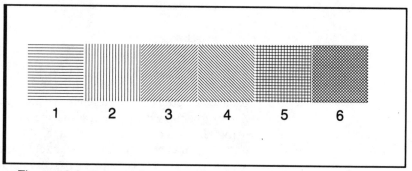

• Figure 19.8: *Patterns for rectangular fill*

To set the length in decipoints, use

<Esc>*c#H

The command to set the height of a rectangle (vertical size) in dots is

<Esc>*c#B

Specify the height in decipoints with

<Esc>*c#V

To fill a rectangle with a shade of gray or a pattern, use the command

<Esc>*c#G

The field values are 1 to 100 for a gray-scale value or 1 to 6 for a pattern. You specify pattern or gray-scale fill when you give the command to print the rectangle. You don't need to use this command if the rectangle will be solid black.

Although the field value for a gray scale can be between 1 and 100, only eight levels will print:

Field Value	Printed Level
1 or 2	2
3 to 10	10
11 to 20	15

21 to 40	30
41 to 60	45
61 to 80	70
81 to 99	90
100	100

Print the rectangle with the command

<Esc>*c#P

The field value determines the type of fill: 0 for solid black, 2 for gray scale, or 3 for pattern.

You can create solid lines, or rules, by using small horizontal or vertical values. For example, this Basic program prints a solid 1/4-inch line, 5 inches long:

```
10 LPRINT chr$(27);"&a720h3960V";
20 LPRINT chr$(27);"*c3600h180V";
30 LPRINT chr$(27);"*c0P";
```

As with all graphic programs, it begins by using the cursor-movement commands to designate the upper-left starting position. The line starts 1 inch from the left and 5½ inches down. All measurements are given in decipoints.

Figure 19.9 shows the program used to print the gray scale shown in Figure 19.7. Figure 19.10 lists the program for the patterns shown in Figure 19.8. Notice how the gray-scale values, patterns, and cursor positions were changed by using a FOR loop.

```
10 WIDTH "lpt1:", 255
20 X=720
30 Y=1440
40 FOR H = 1 TO 20
50 LPRINT chr$(27);"&a";X;"h";Y;"V";
60 LPRINT chr$(27);"*c160h720V";
70 F=H*5
80 LPRINT chr$(27);"*c";F;"G";
90 LPRINT chr$(27);"*c2P";
100 X=X+180
110 NEXT H
120 LPRINT chr$(12)
```

• Figure 19.9: *Program to print gray scale*

Rectangular fill graphics, however, are not boxed; they aren't surrounded by lines or borders. If you want to enclose the rectangle in a box, use the commands to draw four solid lines. For example, this program prints a 1-inch box made with 50-dot wide lines:

```
  5 WIDTH "lpt1:", 255
 10 LPRINT chr$(27);"*p600x600Y";
 20 LPRINT chr$(27);"*c300a50b0P";
 30 LPRINT chr$(27);"*c50a300b0P";
 40 LPRINT chr$(27);"*p+250X";
 50 LPRINT chr$(27);"*c50a300b0P";
 60 LPRINT chr$(27);"*p-250x+250Y";
 70 LPRINT chr$(27);"*c300a50b0P";
 80 LPRINT chr$(27);"*p650x650Y";
 90 LPRINT chr$(27);"*c200a100B";
100 LPRINT chr$(27);"*c3G";
110 LPRINT chr$(27);"*c3P";
120 LPRINT chr$(27);"*p650c750Y";
130 LPRINT chr$(27);"*c200a100B";
140 LPRINT chr$(27);"*c4G";
150 LPRINT chr$(27);"*c3P";
```

For an unusual effect, two different diagonal patterns were used (3 and 4), each filling half of the box. This program illustrates both absolute and relative cursor positioning, as well as graphic commands. The image created by the program is shown in Figure 19.11.

```
10 WIDTH "lpt1:", 255
20 X=200
30 Y=1440
40 FOR H= 1 TO 6
50 LPRINT chr$(27);"&a";X;"h";Y;"V";
60 LPRINT chr$(27);"*c720h720V";
70 LPRINT chr$(27);"*c";H;"G";
80 LPRINT chr$(27);"*c3P";
90 X=X+730
100 NEXT H
```

• Figure 19.10: *Program to print patterns*

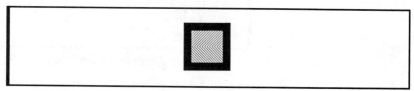

• Figure 19.11: *Boxed rectangle with two patterns*

• *Using Printing Macros*

Macros are not available for DeskJet printers.

A macro is a series of PCL commands stored in the printer's memory. Macros can include any combination of PCL commands, control codes, text, and bit-map data. (Macros are available for all LaserJet models except the original.)

In Chapter 14, you learned that scanned images can be supplied as macros. After they are downloaded, you can print the image without retransmitting the bit map, saving a great deal of time. Macros are excellent for printing the same graphic signature at the bottom of form letters, placing a logo on the top of every page, or repeating complex formatting or font selection commands quickly.

Creating a Macro

Since each macro must be assigned a unique ID number, start by issuing the command

<Esc>&f#Y

The field value must be an integer number between 1 and 32767. This assigns the ID number to the next macro downloaded, much like an ID is assigned to a softfont. All other macro commands are variations of the command

<Esc>&f#X

After you specify the macro ID, transmit the command

<Esc>&f0X

followed by the body of the macro: the commands, codes, or data that you want to be repeated. To stop the macro definition, use the command

<Esc>&f1X

This ends the recording of the macro.

Like softfonts, macros can be permanent or temporary. When you reset the printer (with <Esc>E), all temporary macros and softfonts will be erased. By default, all macros are temporary until assigned permanent status. To make the last macro identified permanent, use the command

<Esc>&f10X

If you can't remember which macro was last referenced by the ID command, specify the ID and change the status at the same time. For example, the command

<Esc>&f1y10X

makes macro 1 permanent. Use a field value of 9 to change the status to temporary.

As an example, here's a program that creates a macro for printing a small logo (a 1-inch, pattern-filled rectangle) and address at the top of the page:

```
 5 WIDTH "lpt1:", 255
10 LPRINT chr$(27);"&f1Y";
20 LPRINT chr$(27);"&f0X";
30 LPRINT chr$(27);"*p100x0Y";
40 LPRINT chr$(27);"*t300R";
50 LPRINT chr$(27);"*c300a300b6g3P";
60 LPRINT chr$(27);"*p410x75Y";
70 LPRINT chr$(27);"(2X";
80 LPRINT "Alvin A. Aardvark Apple Company"
90 LPRINT chr$(27);"(1X";
100 LPRINT chr$(27);"*p410x120Y";
110 LPRINT "346 Chestnut Street, Philadelphia, PA
       19116 (215) 555-1111"
120 LPRINT chr$(27);"&f1X";
130 LPRINT chr$(27);"&f3X";
```

The program downloads the ID number 1 (line 10) then starts recording the definition (line 20).

The cursor is positioned 1/2 inch down from the top and 1/2 inch in from the left edges of the paper (line 30). Using x and y coordinates of 150 would not accomplish this; those coordinates would place the cursor 1/2 inch in from the logical page left boundary and 1/2 down from the default top margin. The x coordinate of 100 and y coordinate of 0 position the cursor correctly.

Graphics resolution is set at 300 dpi (line 40), then line 50 sets the rectangle size to 1 square inch, by dots, selects pattern 6, and then prints the graphic.

The cursor is repositioned for the first line of the address (line 60), then the softfont with ID 2 (24-point Helvetica) is selected in line 70. After the first line of text prints (line 80), another font (10-point Helvetica with ID 1) is selected (line 90), the cursor is repositioned (line 100), and then the last line is printed (line 110). Finally, the macro definition ends (line 120).

The spacing of the text is specific to the size of the two fonts used. In this case, the second line is positioned close to the line above and the telephone number is moved over to avoid collision with the descenders. Figure 19.12 shows the letterhead created by the macro.

Executing Macros

There are three ways to run a macro, or recall its contents from memory:

- Execute the macro
- Call the macro
- Activate a macro overlay for every page

When you execute the macro with the command

       `<Esc>&f2X`

any changes made by the macro are retained when it ends. For example, if the macro prints text at eight lines per inch, text following the macro will use the same line spacing unless you explicitly change it.

Changes made by a called macro, using the command

       `<Esc>&f3X`

are not retained. The settings in effect before the macro's execution will again be in effect when it ends. For example, to call the sample letterhead created by the program in the previous section, use the command

       `<Esc>&f1y3X`

An overlay macro, run with the command

       `<Esc>&f4X`

- Figure 19.12: *Printout of letterhead macro*

will repeat automatically for every page until it is turned off with the command

        `<Esc>&f5X`

This type of macro is ideal for printing headers, footers, borders, or other graphics on every page. As with a called macro, the original settings are in effect when the macro ends.

The most important thing to remember is that the position of the cursor before the macro is executed is *never* retained. If you want to return to that position after execution, use the push (`<Esc>&f0S`) and pop (`<Esc>&f1S`) commands.

Deleting Macros

To delete all your macros from memory, use the command

        `<Esc>&f6X`

If you want to delete just temporary macros, use the command

        `<Esc>&f7X`

Resetting the printer (with `<Esc>E`) also deletes all temporary macros.

To clear the last macro identified, use

        `<Esc>&f8X`

Graphic macros can be very handy for images that you use often, but they can be quite complicated to plan and execute. It's a good idea to first test your graphic in a Basic program. Then, when you're sure it prints properly, add the macro commands.

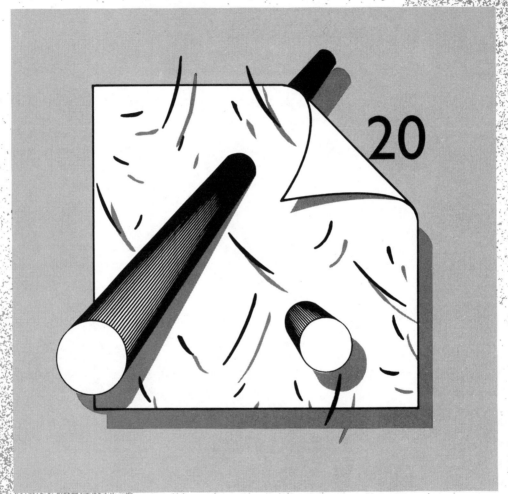

H·P L·A·S·E·R·J·E·T

20

An Inside Look at Softfonts

Font headers are 92 bytes.
See Appendix D for details.

• Your knowledge of PCL commands and raster graphics now equip you for a detailed look at softfonts. So far, we've treated softfonts simplistically, calling them a collection of bit maps for the characters.

But a softfont is actually a series of PCL commands and data. Some of the data, usually about 64 bytes, describes the general characteristics of the font itself. The bulk of the file details each character. In many ways, characters are just raster graphics. Each is stored in memory as a series of ones and zeros, every row representing a one-dot high slice of the character.

Just like raster graphics, with all LaserJet models except the IID and 2000, the bit-map pattern is specific to the orientation. Programs such as PORTOLAN rewrite all portrait bit maps to the proper proportions for landscape orientation.

In this chapter, we'll look inside a softfont to see exactly what gets transmitted to your printer.

Fonts designed to be downloaded with the DOS Copy command include information about ID and status.

• *Softfont Organization*

Each softfont starts with the font descriptor command

<Esc>)s#W

followed by data which describes its overall characteristics. This data is called the *descriptor*, or *font header*.

Following the font descriptor data, and for *each* character in the font, is a set of three components. The first is a character code command

<Esc>*c#E

This signifies the ASCII code of the character about to be downloaded. Next comes a character descriptor command

<Esc>(s#W

This details the overall layout of the character. Finally, there is the raster data for the character itself.

For example, the first character is typically the exclamation point, ASCII 33. So following the font descriptor data, will be the command

<Esc>*c33E

This tells the LaserJet that the next character downloaded will be associated with ASCII 33. Following that command will be

        `<Esc>(s#W`

then the bit map for the ! character. The next character is normally the quotation mark, ASCII 34. So following the bit map for the exclamation point will be the codes

        `<Esc>*c34E`

and

        `<Esc>(s#W`

then the raster graphics for ("). If the font has 127 characters, there will be 127 character code commands, character descriptor commands, and sets of bit maps.

Variations in LaserJet Models

The general patterns for font and character descriptors you're about to see can be used with all LaserJet models. However, certain models ignore some of the fields, and some don't even list them in their technical manuals. Other fields are reserved for use with the DeskJet printer or for future functions.

For example, all models ignore the underline height descriptor and use a three-dot thick underline instead. Since the LaserJet IID and 2000 can rotate fonts to either orientation, these models ignore settings that are orientation-dependent on other printers, such as baseline distance, cell width, and cell height. The technical manual for the LaserJet+ doesn't even list font descriptor fields past byte 25.

For reserved fields, always use a value of 0. Check your technical manual for suggested settings and the maximum values that can be used in the field.

Font Descriptor Data

The field value in the font descriptor command represents the number of bytes of data that follow. Most HP LaserJet font descriptors are 64 bytes long, so the most common format of the command is

        `<Esc>)s64W`

DJ

Descriptors for DeskJet softfonts are discussed in Appendix D.

Third-party fonts, however, may have longer descriptors; values up to 65535 are valid. The main variation in length comes in the last part of the descriptor, which contains the font's name. Some vendors extend HP's standard 16-bytes to include their own name and copyright information.

Figure 20.1 illustrates some of the concepts and terms used in the font descriptor information. Table 20.1 describes the data in byte order.

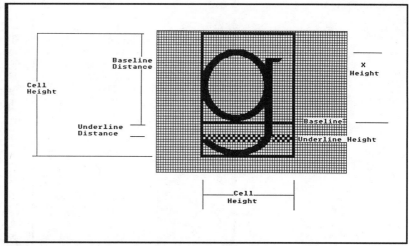

• Figure 20.1: *Font descriptor concepts*

• Table 20.1: *Font Descriptor Data*

BYTE	FUNCTION	SETTING
0 and 1	Font descriptor size	The number of bytes in the descriptor.
2	Descriptor format	Set to 0.
3	Font type	A 0 signifies a 7-bit font with characters from ASCII 32 to 127; 1 is an 8-bit font including ASCII characters 160-255; and 2 is a PC-8 font.
4 and 5	Reserved	
6 and 7	Baseline distance	Distance, in dots, from the top of the cell to the baseline.

Table 20.1: *Font Descriptor Data (Continued)*

BYTE	FUNCTION	SETTING
8 and 9	Cell width	Width of the cell in dots.
10 and 11	Cell height	Height of the cell in dots.
12	Orientation	0 represents portrait; 1 is landscape.
13	Spacing	0 represents fixed width; 1 is proportional spacing.
14 and 15	Symbol set	Designates the symbol set calculated from the *set ID* discussed in Chapter 19. Each ID consists of a number (called the PCL Escape sequence field value) followed by a letter (the termination character). The formula for obtaining the field value here is: *PCL Escape sequence field value* * 32 + ASCII *code of termination character* − 64.
16 and 17	Pitch	Pitch in $1/4$ dots. This defines the default horizontal motion index.
18 and 19	Height	Height of the font in $1/4$ dots. This field is converted to points and used when fonts are selected by point size.
20 and 21	X height	The height of the lowercase x in $1/4$ dots.
22	Width type	The value can be −2 for condensed, −1 for semicondensed, 0 for normal, 1 for semiexpanded, or 2 for expanded.
23	Style	0 is upright; 1 is italics.
24	Stroke weight	Use the same field values as for selecting fonts.

- Table 20.1: *Font Descriptor Data (Continued)*

BYTE	FUNCTION	SETTING
25	Typeface	Use the same field values as for selecting fonts. This field contains the font's least significant byte.
26	Typeface	Most significant byte of the typeface number.
27	Serif style	The value can be 0 for sans serif square, 1 for sans serif round, 2 for serif line, 3 for serif triangle, 4 for serif swath, 5 for serif block, 6 for serif bracket, 7 for rounded bracket, or 8 for flair stroke.
28 and 29	Reserved	
30	Underline distance	The distance, in dots, from the baseline to the top row of dots in the underline. A 0 designates that the underline starts at the baseline; a positive number for the underline above the baseline; a negative value for the underline below the baseline.
31	Underline height	The thickness of the underline in dots.
32 and 33	Text height	Optimal interline spacing in $1/4$ dots.
34 and 35	Text width	Optimal character spacing in $1/4$ dots.
36 to 39	Reserved	
40	Pitch extended	An extension of the pitch field (bytes 16 and 17), in 1024ths of a dot, used for more exact measurements that can be stored in 2 bytes. For example, when defining a 17-pitch font,

Table 20.1: *Font Descriptor Data (Continued)*

BYTE	FUNCTION	SETTING
		70 in the pitch field represents 17.5 dots or 17.1429 cpi. Placing 150 in the pitch extended field adds another 0.1465 dots, bringing the pitch to 17.0005.
41	Height extended	An extension of the height field (18 and 19), in 1024ths of a dot.
42	Cap height	Percentage of the font height from the top of unaccented uppercase letters to the baseline. A 0 in the field designates the default value of 70.87%. The calculation is done in decipoints. For instance, a 10-point font is 120 decipoints. The default cap height for this font is 120 times 0.7087, or 85.04 decipoints (8.504 points).
43 to 47	Reserved	
48 and up	Font name	The remainder of the descriptor contains the font name in ASCII characters. The standard HP field is 16 characters.

Character Descriptors

After the font descriptor, the codes, descriptors, and raster data for each character are downloaded. The character code command

<Esc>*c#E

The font descriptor and character descriptor commands have the same group and terminator character, but in this case, the) and (parameterized characters do not signify a primary or secondary font. Instead,) designates a font descriptor, and (designates a character descriptor. Primary and secondary status are assigned after the font has been downloaded.

designates the ASCII value. The character descriptor command

<Esc>(s#W

represents the number of bytes of descriptor and raster data for the character.

The descriptor is 16 bytes long. For example, when downloading a character requiring 128 bytes of raster data, use the command

<Esc>(s144W

Figure 20.2 illustrates some of the terms and concepts used in the character descriptor information. Table 20.2 describes the data in byte order.

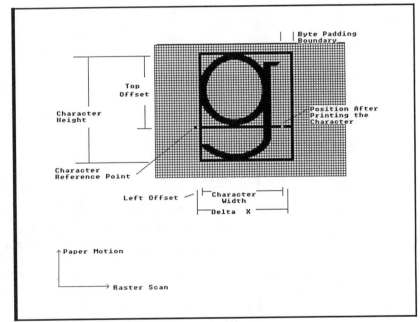

- Figure 20.2: *Character descriptor concepts*

- Table 20.2: *Character Descriptor Data*

BYTE	FUNCTION	SETTING
0	Format	The bytes should be set at 4 for all LaserJet models.

Table 20.2: *Character Descriptor Data (Continued)*

BYTE	FUNCTION	SETTING
1	Continuation	If total descriptor and character data requires more than 32,767 bytes, the character must be downloaded in two blocks. If this block is not a continuation of the previous (it is its own character), the field is 0. A 1 in this field signifies that the block is a continuation of the last character. In this case, all the following fields are replaced by the actual character data. (See byte 16.)
2	Descriptor size	The size of the character descriptor. Set this at 14 for all LaserJet models. Even though the descriptor contains 16 bytes, there are only 14 from here to the first data byte.
3	Class	Set at 1 for all LaserJet models.
4	Orientation	0 represents portrait; 1 is landscape. This must match the orientation of the font.
5	Reserved	Set at 0.
6 and 7	Left offset	The distance, in dots, from the character reference point to the left side of the character. The character reference point is the current cursor position when the character is printed.
8 and 9	Top offset	The distance, in dots, from the reference point to the top of the character.
10 and 11	Character width	The width of the character in dots.
12 and 13	Character height	The height of the character in dots.

• Table 20.2: *Character Descriptor Data (Continued)*

BYTE	FUNCTION	SETTING
14 and 15	Delta x	The number of ¼-dot units that the cursor moves after printing the character. Used only for proportionally-spaced characters.
16 and up	Raster data	The remainder of the block contains the actual raster data for the character. The printer knows the number of bytes by subtracting 14 from the field value in the <Esc>(s#W command.

• *Exploring Font Bit Maps*

If you want to see the exact dot pattern for characters, you need to look at the font file with some sort of disk-sector editor. Figure 20.3 shows a portion of a 14-point Helvetica font file displayed by PC Tools. The section on the left shows the hex values on the disk; those on the right show their ASCII equivalent. Each two-character hex value, such as 33 and 1B, represents 8 bits, or some combination of 8 ones and zeros.

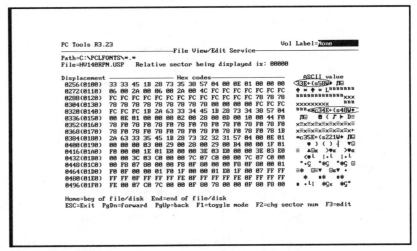

• Figure 20.3: *Font file data displayed with disk editor*

In the ASCII section, I've circled the first two character code and character descriptor commands. (Part of the first character code is not displayed because it's on the "previous" section for the file.) The ← represents the <Esc> code.

The first code signifies that ASCII 33, the exclamation point, will be downloaded next. The character descriptor code

<Esc>(s58W

indicates that the descriptor and raster data are 58 bytes long: 16 bytes for the descriptor followed by 42 of data.

To see how a character is formed, you have to convert the bytes between the character descriptor and the code for the next character from hex to binary. In order to do this, you need to know where the raster data starts and ends.

In Figure 20.3, the hex bytes for the PCL commands that appear on the first line are:

3	3	E	←	(	s	5	8	W
33	33	45	1B	28	73	35	38	57

The next 16 hex bytes represent the descriptor itself:

Byte	Hex	Decimal
0 (format)	04	4
1 (continuation)	00	0
2 (descriptor size)	0E	14
3 (class)	01	1
4 (orientation)	00	0
5 (reserved)	00	0
6 and 7 (left offset)	00 06	6
8 and 9 (top offset)	00 2A	42
10 and 11 (character width)	00 06	0
12 and 13 (character height)	00 2A	42
14 and 15 (delta x)	00 4C	76

The next 42 hex bytes represent the raster data for the character. These start with FC (following 4C) and end at the 45, just before the <Esc> code 1B starting the next character code command.

To determine how many hex bytes represent each row of data, look at the character height field. The value here is 2A, or 42 in decimal numbers. Since the height is 42, and there are only 42 hex bytes of raster data, each one is a single row.

For example, the second character in the font, the quotation mark, is 16 dots high, a hex byte of 10. Since there are 32 hex bytes (48 − 16), every two must be one row.

Now that you know that the next 42 hex bytes represent the raster data, you can convert them to their binary (1 and 0) counterparts. This is really very easy. Each character in a hex byte represents four bits:

0	0000
1	0001
2	0010
3	0011
4	0100
5	0101
6	0110
7	0111
8	1000
9	1001
A	1010
B	1011
C	1100
D	1101
E	1110
F	1111

Write down the binary equivalent for each of the characters, disregarding the decimal value.

Your HP LaserJet Handbook

The hex byte 1F represents this pattern:

1 F

0001 1111

The hex byte 3A would be:

3 A

0011 1010

The hex bytes for ASCII 33 shown in Figure 20.3 would be converted to the raster pattern shown in Figure 20.4. Because this is a Helvetica font, the character is straight, without serifs.

```
FC          11111100
FC          11111100
FC          11111100
FC          11111100
FC          11111100
FC          11111100
FC          11111100
FC          11111100
FC          11111100
FC          11111100
FC          11111100
FC          11111100
FC          11111100
FC          11111100
FC          11111100
FC          11111100
FC          11111100
FC          11111100
FC          11111100
FC          11111100
78          01111000
78          01111000
78          01111000
78          01111000
78          01111000
78          01111000
78          01111000
78          01111000
78          01111000
78          01111000
78          01111000
78          01111000
00          00000000
00          00000000
00          00000000
00          00000000
FC          11111100
FC          11111100
FC          11111100
FC          11111100
FC          11111100
FC          11111100
```

• Figure 20.4: *Hex bytes converted for ASCII 33*

If you used the same procedure for the next character, you would see it is a series of 16 rows of F0 78, or the pattern

F	0	7	8
1111	0000	0111	1000

The converted character would appear as shown in Figure 20.5.

This same technique can be used to reveal the bit-map pattern for any raster graphic image, even those created with painting or drawing programs. Load the graphic into a word processor such as WordPerfect or Word, and then print the document to a disk file. Look at the disk file using a program such as PC Tools. After the resolution and start raster graphics commands, you'll see a series of hex bytes representing the raster pattern. Convert the hex numbers to binary to see the ones and zeros. Just remember that a large graphic requires a great many dots.

Designing and downloading fonts and graphics are perhaps the most challenging uses of the LaserJet. Fortunately, you don't have to understand all the technical details of laser printing to produce high-quality documents. As new products become available, your laser printer will have even greater capabilities. You are now ready to use the best of current technology and are prepared for the future.

```
FO  78          1111000001111000
FO  78          1111000001111000
FO  78          1111000001111000
FO  78          1111000001111000
FO  78          1111000001111000
FO  78          1111000001111000
FO  78          1111000001111000
FO  78          1111000001111000
FO  78          1111000001111000
FO  78          1111000001111000
FO  78          1111000001111000
FO  78          1111000001111000
FO  78          1111000001111000
FO  78          1111000001111000
FO  78          1111000001111000
FO  78          1111000001111000
```

• Figure 20.5: *Hex bytes converted for ASCII 34*

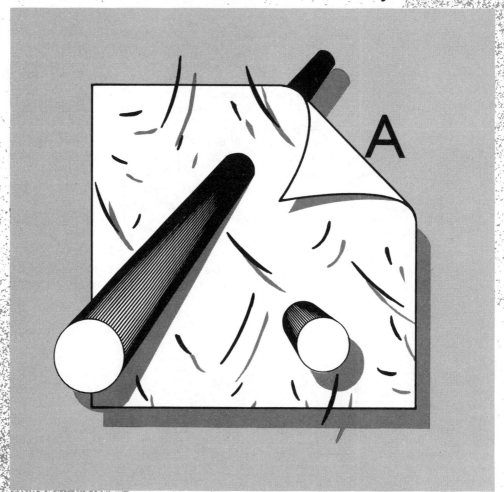

LaserJet
Equipment and Maintenance

• With luck, you might never have to perform any maintenance on your printer beyond replenishing toner cartridges and paper. The most common problems, however, only require minor cleaning that you can do yourself in a few seconds. When major problems occur, you'll need the services of a trained technician. But the LaserJet is a well-built printer that will provide service a long time without the need for serious repair.

This appendix covers equipping your LaserJet and performing minor maintenance tasks. The only consumable supplies you have to worry about are toner cartridges and paper. Both require careful selection to avoid potential maintenance and repair problems.

See your printer manual for detailed diagrams of the location and handling of the LaserJet components described in this appendix.

• *Selecting and Maintaining Toner Cartridges*

The electrophotographic cartridge contains much more than toner. Each houses the photosensitive drum and other components that transfer the image to be printed and clean the drum after each page. When you install a new cartridge, you are actually replacing a majority of the parts used in the imaging process. This should tell you how important cartridge selection is to proper maintenance of the printer.

The LaserJet II and IID use different cartridges than earlier models. They are not interchangeable. Adding toner to the LaserJet 2000 is discussed separately.

Cartridge Life

Toner cartridges are rated for the average number of full text pages they can print: 4000 for the LaserJet II and IID and 3000 for earlier models. But actual toner life depends more on the amount of ink coverage than the number of pages. If you print a great deal of short half-page memos, for example, your cartridge will last much longer. Pages that are full of text or 300-dpi graphics will use the toner more rapidly.

One way to extend cartridge life is by regulating the density dial. Place it on the highest setting possible that still produces suitable density. If you're printing a special graphic page where you want a solid dark black, turn the dial down to a lower setting for that page.

If you turn the density dial to a low setting for a special page, remember to return the dial to a higher setting afterward.

As the toner level decreases, your printed image will become light, and you might even notice patches of missing text. Turn the density dial down until the output improves.

When lowering the density dial has no effect, you can still extend cartridge life for another 100 pages or so. Remove the cartridge, then rock it back and forth several times to distribute the remaining toner evenly. But when the image starts getting light again, it's time to replace the cartridge.

Toner Indicators

Eventually, with the LaserJet II and IID, the message 16 TONER LOW will appear on the control panel display. This indicates enough toner remains for no more than 100 pages of double-spaced text.

The toner indicator on earlier models serves as an estimate of toner level, turning from green to yellow to red. In reality, it only measures the number of drum rotations, not the amount of toner remaining. When testing the PCL commands and programs in this book, for example, I printed hundreds of pages containing only a few lines. The indicator quickly moved to red even though very little toner was consumed. I was still able to print several thousand pages before changing the cartridge. However, if you do print dense pages of text and graphics, the toner indicator is relatively accurate.

Selecting Cartridges

The toner cartridge is not an inexpensive item. One cartridge can cost up to $125 compared to the $2 to $12 you might spend for the typical dot-matrix or daisy-wheel printer ribbon. However, the toner cartridge provides consistent performance over its entire life. If you compute the cost of replacing ribbons, particularly the expensive cartridge type, to maintain high density printing, you would find that toner cartridges compare favorably.

Even so, the cost of a cartridge does take a bite out of a tight budget. So, you should consider the best way to replace your cartridges when they are depleted.

You can purchase new cartridges, reconditioned ones, or refill your cartridges yourself. Without a doubt, buying new cartridges is the safest route, even if the most expensive. Many computer stores stock cartridges, or you can order them from Hewlett-Packard and a number of third-party suppliers. Each cartridge is supplied with a new fusing roller cleaning pad that keeps excess toner from smearing your output.

As an alternative, you can purchase reconditioned cartridges. Check the back pages of most computer journals for companies advertising this service. For less than half the cost of a new cartridge, you get a used cartridge that has been cleaned and refilled. Some vendors will ship you a reconditioned unit from stock; others require you to send in your empty cartridge for processing.

However, cartridges cannot be reused indefinitely. After a while, the photosensitive drum and other components can wear down, making replacing the toner a waste of money. But even more important, an improperly refilled cartridge could leak toner inside the printer, requiring an expensive service call.

This doesn't condemn the entire refilling industry. There are individuals and companies that use reconditioned cartridges almost exclusively. Just be careful in selecting your vendor. Use one who has been in operation a while or can supply names of satisfied clients. Before using a reconditioned cartridge, examine it carefully. Look for loose toner, broken pieces, or signs of excessive wear. The cartridge should be wrapped in opaque material and supplied with a clean fusing roller cleaning pad.

One final option is to refill the cartridge yourself. You can purchase a supply of toner and a special kit for drilling access holes in the cartridge. But unless you're down to bread and water, this isn't really a practical or safe alternative.

Replacing the Cartridge

The procedure for installing cartridges varies with LaserJet models.

If you plan on having your old cartridge refilled, wrap it in protective opaque material and store it in its original carton, along with the old fusing roller cleaning pad and the plastic separator strip that you'll be removing from the new cartridge. Most vendors will give you credit for these materials.

Replacing LaserJet, LaserJet +, and LaserJet 500 + Cartridges

Follow these steps to replace the cartridge in earlier LaserJet models:

1. Open the printer's main body by pulling up on the green lever on the right side.

2. Open the access door, to the right of the lever, by pulling it out, then down. You can't open the access door until the main body is open.

3. Pull the old cartridge straight out.

4. Remove the new cartridge from its aluminum foil wrapper, then rock it back and forth several times.

5. Insert the new cartridge by sliding it all the way into the printer.

6. You now have to remove the strip of plastic that separates the photosensitive drum from the toner supply. Hold the end of the cartridge and bend the plastic tab (protruding from the end of the cartridge) up and down several times until it breaks loose from the cartridge. It will still be attached to the plastic strip.

The opaque wrapper prevents light from exposing the photosensitive drum. Always store your cartridges in the wrapper and away from light.

For safety, turn the printer off before replacing the cartridge.

7. Pull the tab straight out, firmly and evenly, until it clears the cartridge. If the strip breaks as you're removing it, grab the exposed end with your fingers or pliers, then pull it straight out.

8. Close the access door.

9. Raise the fusing assembly cover, a green covered plate near the front of the printer.

10. Slide out the fusing roller cleaning pad by pulling the green tab straight out.

11. Unwrap the new cleaning pad and slide it into the assembly.

12. Close the assembly cover, and then close the printer's main body.

Be careful. The fusing assembly area may be hot!

Replacing LaserJet II and LaserJet IID Cartridges

Follow these steps to replace the cartridge in a LaserJet II or IID:

1. Open the printer's main body by pulling back the release lever, on top of the printer, then pressing it down.

2. Grasp the cartridge with both hands, then pull it straight back and out of the printer.

3. Remove the new cartridge from its aluminum foil wrapper, then rock it back and forth.

4. Insert the new cartridge by sliding it all the way into the printer.

5. You now have to remove the strip of plastic that separates the photosensitive drum from the toner supply. Hold the end of the cartridge, bend the plastic tab (protruding from the end of the cartridge) back and forth several times until it breaks loose from the cartridge. It will still be attached to the plastic strip.

6. Pull the tab straight out, firmly and evenly, until it clears the cartridge. If the strip breaks as you're removing it, grab the exposed end with your fingers or pliers, then pull it straight out.

8. Raise the green covered fusing assembly cover.

9. Pull out the old fusing roller cleaning pad.

Be careful. The fusing assembly area may be hot!

10. One end of the new cleaning pad contains a cloth cover. Use this end to wipe along the length of the roller to remove any excess toner.

11. Remove the cloth end and throw it away.

12. Insert the new cleaning pad, and then lower the assembly cover.

13. Close the top of the printer.

Replacing LaserJet 2000 Cartridges

The LaserJet 2000 uses a refillable toner supply hatch located on the top of the developing unit. Instead of installing a sealed cartridge, as with other LaserJet models, a new supply of toner is poured into the hatch. Although the toner is nontoxic, avoid letting it contact skin, clothing, or the inner workings of the printer.

When the toner level gets low, you'll see the message 14.1 ADD TONER on the control panel display. An empty toner hatch can hold two new packages of toner, about 1 kilogram.

Some excess used toner is also stored inside the printer, in a disposable box. You'll see the message 14.2 EMPTY WASTE TONER when the box is full.

Follow these steps to replenish the toner supply:

Dispose of empty toner boxes carefully. Wrap them securely in a plastic bag before placing them in a waste basket.

Hewlett-Packard warns never to recycle used toner, and that using non-Hewlett-Packard toner voids the warranty.

1. Make sure the printer is off line.

2. Pull open the printer's right door. If you have the duplex option installed, only open the top right door so you don't disturb the paper path.

3. Unlock the developing unit by swinging the green release lever to the right.

4. Slide the developing unit out of the printer until it stops.

5. On top of the developing unit is a small hatch door. Hold the door on the right side and swing it up to open it.

6. Open a fresh box of toner. Pull the perforated tab, then remove the top to expose a sealed inner envelope.

7. Shake the box several times, then tap the bottom on a desk or other flat surface.

8. Cut open the inner envelope, along the dotted line just below the top.

9. Being careful not to spill any toner, turn the box upside down into the hatch door. When all the toner has poured in, lightly tap the bottom.

10. Carefully remove and discard the toner box, and then close the hatch door.

11. Push the developing unit back into the printer, then swing the green release lever toward the left until it locks.

12. Close the printer door.

Follow these steps when it's time to dispose of the collected waste toner:

1. Have a new disposal box ready.

2. Open both top printer doors. You'll see a cardboard box on the left side.

3. Tap on the tube going into the box to dislodge any excess toner.

4. Pull the box straight out of the printer, seal the top with tape, and then throw it away.

5. Follow the instructions packaged with the new box to prepare and insert it.

6. Close both printer doors.

• *Cleaning and Maintaining the LaserJet*

While you're inserting a cartridge, it pays to take a moment to perform some simple maintenance tasks. These may save you from having to stop a printing job because of image problems.

You should clean the primary corona wire, which charges the photosensitive drum; the transfer corona wire, which charges the paper; and all the areas where particles of toner and dirt collect.

To clean the transfer corona wire, open the top of the printer to expose a thin wire sitting under the cartridge. Dip a cotton swab in alcohol, and rub it gently back and forth across the wire several times. Make sure the swab is not dripping. (With the LaserJet II, you can use the small green brush that is packed inside the printer, to the left of the paper guides.)

With the LaserJet II and IID, also clean the areas around the transfer corona wire, including the orange pads (along the back of the casing) and the length of the plastic lip.

The primary corona wire is located on the toner cartridge. The wire on cartridges for the LaserJet II and IID is very delicate and should only be cleaned when necessary. Black strips on the printed page may be a sign that the primary wire needs cleaning.

To clean the primary corona wire, remove the toner cartridge and the green handled wire cleaner (with a felt pad on the bottom), which is packed inside the printer. Insert the felt pad on the cleaner into the long slot on top of the cartridge, then slide it back and forth several times.

To clean the transfer guide, open the printer, then use a damp cloth to wipe the area behind and around the transfer corona wire.

Also clean the paper path. Use a damp cloth or cotton swab to wipe any excess toner from the rollers, guides, or other areas the paper contacts.

Preventing Ozone Emissions

Ozone is a natural byproduct of the laser process used in your printer. The gas levels emitted are quite safe but may cause a slight odor if you're working in a poorly ventilated area.

The LaserJet IID, however, has a disposable ozone filter designed to prevent the gas from escaping. The filter is located inside the printer, within a small housing on the right side. Replace the filter about every 50,000 pages or so by opening the printer, then pulling down a small cover on the filter housing. Pull the filter out by its plastic tab, insert a new filter, then close the housing cover and printer door.

Cleaning the LaserJet 2000

The LaserJet 2000 has three separate corona assemblies that require cleaning every 10,000 pages. If you open both of the upper doors, you'll see a label pointing to the three assemblies. Remove, clean, then reinsert each of the wires separately, as follows:

- **Primary corona wire (1)**: The first corona is located above the label. Remove the assembly by pulling it out by the green handle. The assembly has two sets of wires: inner and outer. Clean the inner wires by moving the built-in wire cleaner back and forth several times. Clean the outer wires with a cotton swab dipped on alcohol. Wipe the swab in only *one direction*, not back and forth.

- **Pretransfer corona wire (2)**: This wire is located at the bottom right of the label. Remove the assembly by the handle, then rub the wire in *one direction* with a cotton swab dipped in alcohol.

- **Transfer/separation corona (3)**: This is located at the bottom of the label. Remove the assembly by the handle, then rub the wire in *one direction* with a cotton swab dipped in alcohol.

Troubleshooting

Even with some preventive maintenance, problems may occur that indicate that cleaning is required or that the toner cartridge should be replaced. Here are some guidelines for solving output problems:

Problem	Solution or Cause
Faded areas running the length of the page	Lower density dial; replace toner cartridge; paper is too humid.
Dropouts—patches of faded areas	Paper is too humid; the transfer corona wire needs cleaning.
Vertical black streaks on the front of pages	Clean or replace the fusing roller cleaning pad; clean along the paper path; clean the primary corona wire; replace the cartridge.
Horizontal black lines	Clean the transport rollers and paper path; clean or replace the fusing roller cleaning pad; try another brand of paper; replace the toner cartridge.
Vertical white streaks	Clean the transfer corona wire; replace the toner cartridge; clean or replace the fusing roller cleaning pad.
Horizontal white lines	Paper is too humid.
Black stains on the back of pages	Clean the paper feed path and rollers; clean the transfer corona wire; remove and clean the bottom of the toner cartridge; clean the fusing roller cleaning pad. With the LaserJet 2000, clean the fusing roller, registration rollers, or feeder belts.
Strip along the right edge	Clean the primary corona wire; clean the separation belt (refer to your printer's manual).
Marks that repeat at regular intervals	Clean all rollers in the paper path; replace the toner cartridge.

• *Supplying the LaserJet with Paper*

Using the improper paper could result in poor quality output, paper jams, and more frequent cleaning of rollers and corona wires. Table A.1 lists the technical specifications for paper type. Here are some general guidelines to follow when you select paper:

- Never use paper that is wrinkled, folded, not rectangularly shaped, or with high humidity. Store paper flat, in an area with low relative humidity. Keep the paper sealed in original cartons or packaging until you are ready to use it. Then insert just what you'll need for the day in the LaserJet.

- Because the fusing rollers can reach over 200 degrees Celsius, never use paper susceptible to high temperatures. Some adhesive on labels or envelopes tend to melt at temperatures this high. The stock could curl up and jam the printer, or even stick inside, resulting in expensive repair.

- Some printing and duplication inks used on preprinted forms, printed letterheads, and envelopes soften at high temperatures. The inks will adhere to fusing and paper path rollers, then rub off on following pages. If you're purchasing a large supply of paper, get a few test sheets first and run them through the printer several times when the printer is hot.

- Never use paper smaller than the minimum recommended size.

- Don't use carbonless or multipart forms, cardboard, high-gloss, textured, or coated paper, or paper with cutouts or perforations.

Special consideration is needed if you have a LaserJet 2000. The path the paper follows is more complex than the other models, and there are more opportunities for paper jams and other problems. With this model especially, use only the recommended the types of paper.

Selecting Envelopes

Several manufacturers sell envelopes designed specifically for laser printers, but you can use regular envelopes (without windows) if you select them wisely. Standard commercial envelopes, with diagonal seams and gummed flaps, are recommended.

Avoid envelopes more than 24 pounds thick or those with pressure-sensitive adhesive, the type with a pull-off strip that exposes the adhesive.

Hewlett-Packard does not recommend printing envelopes on the LaserJet 2000.

• Table A.1: *Paper Specifications*

PAPER ELEMENT	SPECIFICATION
Weight	16 to 24 pounds. The LaserJet IID can accept paper up to 36 pounds in the top tray in simplex mode. The original LaserJet, LaserJet +, 500 +, and II can accept paper up to 35 pounds.
Fusing	Must not scorch, melt, or offset at 200 degrees Celsius.
Composition	100% chemical wood pulp and/or cotton fiber "bond" paper.
Curl	None on printing side, 15-inch radius of curvature minimum on the other.
Brightness	83% minimum.
Caliper	3.75 to 7.5 (up to 5.5 on the LaserJet 2000).
Cut edge	No visible fray.
Grain	Long.
Moisture	4% to 6% maximum.
Opacity	85% minimum.
Type	Cut sheet.
Minimum width	3.9 inches (8.5 inches on the LaserJet 2000).
Minimum length	7.5 inches (10.5 inches on the LaserJet 2000).
Maximum width	8.5 inches (297 mm on the LaserJet 2000).
Maximum length	14 inches (17 inches on the LaserJet 2000).
Acid content	5.5 pH to 8.0 pH (7.4 with the LaserJet 2000).
Ash content	Not more than 10% and no large amounts of clay.

Never use envelopes with edges that are more than two layers thick, or that have clasps or snaps.

Test a sample envelope to ensure the heat of the fusing roller doesn't seal it shut, especially if the moisture content is high.

Selecting Labels

Here are some guidelines for selecting labels:

- There must not be any exposed adhesive. Take a plain piece of paper the same size as the label sheet and press it as firmly as possible in contact with the printing side of the labels. The paper should not adhere.

- The adhesive must be able to withstand 200 degrees Celsius.

- There should be no spaces between labels. These spaces make it easy for individual labels to peel off and stick inside the printer. It's acceptable if there's a border around the entire page. But the border must be made of the same printable material as the labels, not exposed adhesive.

- Never use a sheet if you see labels starting to peel off.

Printing Transparencies

Overhead transparency film may be used as long as it meets the criteria for heat sensitivity and size. Feed the sheets so they have the straightest transport path. For example, with the LaserJet II and IID, use the rear output tray to avoid excessive bending inside the printer. On earlier models, feed the sheets manually through the rear tray.

Remove each sheet before printing the next. This prevents hot ink from rubbing onto the next sheet.

• Clearing Paper Jams

A warning message will appear on the display if your paper gets stuck somewhere in the printer:

Pressing Continue or Reset has no effect until you remove the jammed page.

Model	Message
LaserJet, LaserJet +, LaserJet 500+	13
LaserJet II and LaserJet IID	13 PAPER JAM
LaserJet 2000	13.1 PAPER JAM
	13.2 OUTPUT JAM
	13.3 DUPLEX JAM

Except for duplex operation, there are only three areas where paper can jam: the input area, in and around the imaging area, and the output area. With the LaserJet IID and 2000, the duplex path adds another possible trouble spot. After you clear the jam, clear the error message, and then you can continue printing.

Clearing the Input Area

If paper becomes jammed as it is feeding into the printer, remove the input cassette, then look into the printer for one end of the paper sticking out. Firmly but gently pull the page straight out. In some cases, pressing Continue will not clear the error message; you will have to open and close the printer's cover.

When paper jams after manual feeding, raise the paper tray, pull down the rear door, then remove the paper.

With the LaserJet II and IID, the paper might be jammed just before the transfer guide tray. Open the printer body and pull out the paper from above. You might have to remove the paper tray and open the transfer guide lock tray, but do not bend it past the upright position. Then, pull the page straight out.

If you have a LaserJet 2000, never attempt to pull out a sheet after it has been grasped by the pickup rollers. Instead, clear the paper as if it were an internal jam, as discussed next.

Clearing the Image Area

Once the sheet has left the input area, you have to open the printer to clear jams.

Open the upper body and look for the paper. The page is usually in the separation/transfer guide area, under the location of the cartridge. Grasp the paper and pull it firmly straight out. With the LaserJet II and IID, the paper might be caught around the transfer guide tray. Open the guide tray lock by the handle to remove the paper.

With the LaserJet 2000, open both front doors, then push the corona assembly lever down and to the left. Remove any paper in that area. Turn the registration knob counter-clockwise until any other paper is free. In some cases, the paper might be stuck in the pickup area, too far in the printer for removal from the input trays. If rotating the registration knob doesn't free the sheet, release the pressure on the rollers with the green lever, then remove the paper.

Clearing the Output Area

With most models, the paper will be stuck under the fusing roller assembly. Open the assembly, then pull the paper straight out.

If you have a LaserJet 2000, there are several areas where paper may jam. Check the fusing area, vertical guide, and output stacker.

Clearing Duplex Areas

When you are printing in duplex, the printer must rotate the paper so the second side comes in contact with the photosensitive drum. This lengthens the paper path and provides two spots where paper may jam: the switchback area where the sheet is fed back into the printer and rotated, and the duplex area, which feeds the page back into the main paper path.

With the LaserJet IID, open the printer and transfer guide tray and look for the jammed paper. If you don't see it, open the left side door or rear output tray cover.

Clearing the duplex areas in the LaserJet 2000 is more complex. First, try three spots near the output area: the duplex path diverter, the switchback transport door, and the inner paper guide door. If this doesn't clear the jam, open both lower front doors. Rotate the green knob labeled 5B clockwise to remove any paper from the feed belt area. Paper may also be stuck in the holding tray. Move the tray's release lever (marked 4A) to the left and inspect the tray for paper. Also check the guide plate and vertical guide areas.

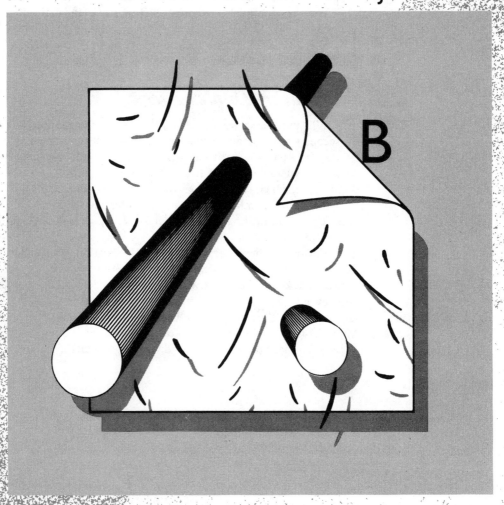

H · P L · A · S · E · R · J · E · T

B

Symbol Sets

- This appendix includes three common font symbol sets. Figure B.1 shows the PC-8 set, Figure B.2 shows the Roman-8 set, and Figure B.3 illustrates decimal to hexadecimal conversion.

- Figure B.1: *PC-8 symbol set*

- Figure B.2: *Roman-8 symbol set*

```
DECIMAL TO HEX

     0   1   2   3   4   5   6   7   8   9  10  11  12  13  14  15  16  17  18  19
0    0   1   2   3   4   5   6   7   8   9   A   B   C   D   E   F  10  11  12  13
20  14  15  16  17  18  19  1A  1B  1C  1D  1E  1F  20  21  22  23  24  25  26  27
40  28  29  2A  2B  2C  2D  2E  2F  30  31  32  33  34  35  36  37  38  39  3A  3B
60  3C  3D  3E  3F  40  41  42  43  44  45  46  47  48  49  4A  4B  4C  4D  4E  4F
80  50  51  52  53  54  55  56  57  58  59  5A  5B  5C  5D  5E  5F  60  61  62  63
100 64  65  66  67  68  69  6A  6B  6C  6D  6E  6F  70  71  72  73  74  75  76  77
120 78  79  7A  7B  7C  7D  7E  7F  80  81  82  83  84  85  86  87  88  89  8A  8B
140 8C  8D  8E  8F  90  91  92  93  94  95  96  97  98  99  9A  9B  9C  9D  9E  9F
160 A0  A1  A2  A3  A4  A5  A6  A7  A8  A9  AA  AB  AC  AD  AE  AF  B0  B1  B2  B3
180 B4  B5  B6  B7  B8  B9  BA  BB  BC  BD  BE  BF  C0  C1  C2  C3  C4  C5  C6  C7
200 C8  C9  CA  CB  CC  CD  CE  CF  D0  D1  D2  D3  D4  D5  D6  D7  D8  D9  DA  DB
220 DC  DD  DE  DF  E0  E1  E2  E3  E4  E5  E6  E7  E8  E9  EA  EB  EC  ED  EE  EF
240 F0  F1  F2  F3  F4  F5  F6  F7  F8  F9  FA  FB  FC  FD  FE  FF
```

- Figure B.3: *Decimal to hexadecimal conversion*

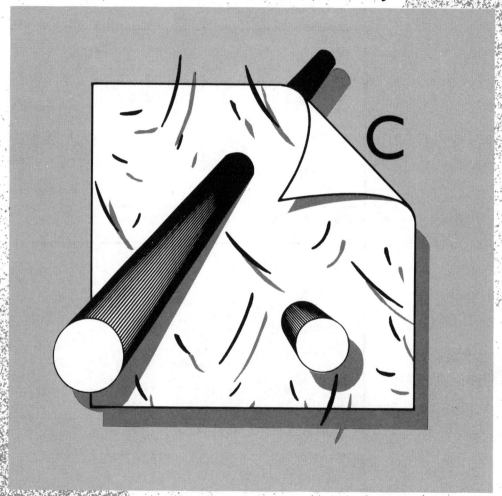

H·P L·A·S·E·R·J·E·T

C

Hardware and
Software Resources

• This appendix lists the sources of the hardware and software described in this book, as well as related products that were not discussed.

Clip Art, Screen, and Graphic Utilities

Arts and Letters
Computer Support Corporation
15926 Midway Road
Dallas, TX 75244
(214) 661-8960

Clickart
T/Maker Company
1390 Villa Street
Mountain View, CA 94041
(415) 962-0195

Collage Display Utilities
Stephens and Associates
10106 Halberns Boulevard
Santee, CA 92071
(619) 562-5161

Collage Plus
Inner Media, Inc.
60 Plain Road
Hollis, NH 03049
(603) 465-3216

Dover
Dover Publications, Inc.
31 East 2nd Street
Mineola, NY 11501
(516) 294-7000

EPSF Clip Art
Image Club Graphics
1902 11th Street
Calgary, Alberta, Canada T2G 3G2
(403) 262-8008

Grafplus
Jewell Technologies
4740 44th Avenue, S.W.
Suite 203
Seattle, WA 98116
(206) 937-1081

Graphic Link Plus
Harvard Systems Corporation
1661 Lincoln Boulevard East
No. 190, Suite 101
Santa Monica, CA 90404
(213) 392-8441

Hijaak, Hijaak PS
Inset
71 Commercial Drive
Brookfield, CT 06804
(203) 775-5866

Hotshot Graphics
Symsoft
444 First Street
Los Altos, CA 94022
(415) 941-1552

Iconvert
John Paul Michalski
Infinity Engineering Services
P.O. Box 812
Chandler, AZ 85224-0812

PC Graphics Deluxe
GoldMind Publishing
12155 Magnolia Avenue   Suite 3-B
Riverside, CA 92503
(714) 785-8685

Clip Art, Screen, and Graphic Utilities

PC Paintbrush, Publisher's Paintbrush
ZSoft
450 Franklin Road
No. 100
Marietta, GA 30067
(404) 428-0008

PC Tools
Central Point Software
9700 SW Capitol Highway
Portland, OR 97219
(503) 244-5782

Picture Paks
Marketing Graphics, Inc.
4401 Dominion Boulevard
Suite 201
Glen Allen, VA 23060
(804) 747-6991

Picture Publisher
Astral Development Corporation
Londonderry Square, Suite 112
Londonderry, NH 03053
(603) 432-6800

Pizazz Plus
Application Techniques
10 Lomar Park Drive
Pepperell, MA 01463
(508) 433-8464

Quick-Art
PC Quick-Art, Inc.
394 S. Milledge Avenue
Suite 200
Athens, GA 30606
(800) 523-1796

Scanart, Drawart
Migraph, Inc.
200 S. 33rd Street
Federal Way, WA 98003
(206) 838-4677

Theme, The Music Editor
Theme Software Company
P.O. Box 8204
Charlottesville, VA 22906
(804) 973-6919

World Geography Clip Art
Micrografx Inc.
1303 Arapaho Street
Richardson, TX 75081
(214) 234-1769

Color

Page Express
(PostScript to color separation)
Network Picture Systems, Inc.
2953 Bunker Hill Lane
Suite 202
Santa Clara, CA 95054
(408) 748-1677

Connectivity

3X-Link 16
3X USA Corporation
1 Executive Drive
Fort Lee, NJ 07024
(800) 327-9712

BayTech Print Master
Bay Technical Associates, Inc.
200 N. Second Street
P.O. Box 387
Bay St. Louis, MS 39520
(601) 467-8231
(800) 523-2702

Lasertorq
Lasertools Corporation
5900 Hollis Street
Suite G
Emeryville, CA 94608
(415) 420-8777

Long-Link, Quick-Link
Intellicom, Inc.
9259 Eton Avenue
Chatsworth, CA 91311
(818) 882-8877
(800) 992-2882
(800) 422-4428 (CA)

Master Link, Master Switch
Rose Electronics
P.O. Box 642571
Houston, TX 77274
(713) 933-7673

Master Share
Dual Group
P.O. Box 13944
Torrance, CA 90503
(213) 542-0788

Print Sharers
Fifth Generation Systems
11200 Industriplex Boulevard
Baton Rouge, LA 70809
(504) 291-7221
(800) 873-4384

ServerJet, SimpLan
ASP Computer Products, Inc.
1026 W. Maude Avenue, Suite 305
Sunnyvale, CA 94086
(408) 746-2965
(800) 445-6190

Database and Database Publishing

dBASE
Ashton-Tate, Inc.
20101 Hamilton Avenue
Torrance, CA 90502
(213) 329-8000

Data Tag
Dynamic Graphics, Inc.
205 E. 78th Street
Suite 17-T
New York, NY 10021
(212) 288-2470

Database and Database Publishing

Database Publisher
Original Software Concepts Ltd.
Kent Lodge
38 Castle Hill
Maidenhead, Berkshire, SL6 4JJ
England

DB Publisher
Digital Composition Systems
1715 W. Northern Avenue
Phoenix, AZ 85021
(602) 870-7667

Drivers

Publisher's Powerpak
Atech Software
5962 LaPlace Court
Suite 245
Carlsbad, CA 92008
(619) 438-6883

Desktop Publishing and Support

Aldus Corporation
411 First Avenue, South
Seattle, WA 98104-9926
(206) 622-5500

Ventura Publisher
Xerox Corporation
101 Continental Boulevard
El Segundo, CA 90245
(800) 822-8221

PSF:First Publisher
Software Publishing Corporation
1901 Landings Drive
Mountain View, CA 94039
(415) 962-8910

VP Toolbox
SNA, Inc.
P.O. Box 3662
Princeton, NJ 08543
(609) 799-9605

Environments

Windows
Microsoft Corporation
16011 N.E. 36th Way
Redmond, WA 98073-9717
(206) 882-8080

Fax and Support

AT&T Fax Connection
AT&T
1 Speedwell Avenue
Morristown, NJ 07920
(800) 257-1212

Brother IntelliFAX
Brother International Corporation
8 Corporate Place
Piscataway, NJ 08855
(201) 981-0300

Connections CoProcessor
Intel PCEO
Mailstop CO3-07
5200 N.E. Elam Young Parkway
Hillsboro, OR 97124-6497
(800) 538-3373

FaxMail 96
Brook Trout Technology, Inc.
110 Cedar Street
Wellesley Hills, MA 02181
(617) 235-3026

Fascimile Pack
DEST Corporation
11201 Cadillac Street
Milpitas, CA 95035
(408) 946-7100

FAX/PC Connection
(Ventura to fax)
Jon Kee Groep
Thorn Prikkerstraat 58
1062 BR
Amsterdam, The Netherlands
31-20-170806

JetFax
Hybrid FAC, Inc.
1733 Woodside Road
Suite 335
Redwood City, CA 94061
(415) 369-0600

Faxit
(Pagemaker to fax)
Alien Computing
37919 50th Street, East
Palmade, CA 93550
(805) 947-1310

GammaFAX, GammaScript
GammaLink
2452 Embarcadero Way
Palo Alto, CA 94303
(415) 856-7421

JT-Fax 9600
Quadram Limited Partnership
1 Quad Way
Norcross, GA 30093
(800) 548-3420

MicroFax
Xerox Imaging Systems
Datacopy Corporation
1215 Terra Bella Avenue
Mountain View, CA 94043
(415) 965-7900

MicroLink Fax LC96
Microlink International, Inc.
4064 McConnell Drive
Burnady, B.C.
Canada V5A 3A8
(604) 420-0366

Fax and Support

Omnium PC Fax System
Omnium Corporation
1911 Curve Crest Blvd.
Stillwater, MN 55082
(800) 328-0233

Pamirs FA10
Pamirs Business
   International Corporation
550 Lake Site Drive, #2
Sunnyvale, CA 94086
(408) 736-2583

Panasonic FX-BM89
Panasonic Corporation
Panasonic Industrial Co.
2 Panasonic Way
Secaucus, NJ 07094
(201) 348-7000

SMARTFAXplus
American Data Technology, Inc.
44 W. Bellevue Drive, #6
Pasadena, CA 91105
(818) 578-1339

The Complete Fax
The Complete PC
521 Cottonwood Drive
Milpitas, CA 95035
(408) 434-0145

Fonts and Font Utilities

Backloader
Roxxolid Corporation
3345 Vincent Road
Pleasant Hill, CA 94523-4318
(415) 256-0105

Bitstream
Bitstream, Inc.
215 First Street
Cambridge, MA 02142
(617) 497-7512

E-Z Set, E-Z Dump,
   Softfonts, Imagener
Orbit Enterprises
P.O. Box 2875
Glen Ellyn, IL 60138
(312) 469-3405

Font Solution Pack
Softcraft Inc.
16 N. Carroll Street
Suite 500
Madison, WI 53703
(800) 351-0500

Glyphix 3.0
Swfte International
P.O. Box 219
Rockland, DE 19732
(301) 429-8434

LJ Fonts, Laser Fonts
Keller Software
1825 Westcliff Drive
Newport Beach, CA 92660
(714) 854-8211

Fonts and Font Utilities

More Fonts
Micrologic Software
6400 Hollis Street
Suite 9
Emeryville, CA 94608
(408) 262-9400

Publisher's Type Foundry
ZSoft
450 Franklin Road
No. 100
Marietta, GA 30067
(404) 428-0008

TSR Download and Softfonts
Elfring Softfonts
P.O. Box 61
Wasco, IL 60183
(312) 377-3520

Type Director
Hewlett-Packard
Boise Division
11311 Chinden Boulevard
Boise, ID 83714

General

Upstart Services
12 Springdale Road
Cherry Hill Industrial Center, Building 11
Cherry Hill, NJ 08003
(609) 424-2266
(800) 288-8778

Hewlett-Packard

LaserJet:
Hewlett-Packard
Boise Division
11311 Chinden Boulevard
Boise, ID 83714

DeskJet:
Hewlett-Packard
Vancouver Division
Vancouver, WA 98668-8906

Supplies:
(800) 538-8787

Customer Support and Repairs:
(208) 323-2551
(800) 835-4747

Labels

Compusoft, Inc.
2191 Northlake Parkway
Suite R
Tucker, GA 30084
(404) 496-0814
(800) 826-1988

Hi-Tech Printing Company
653 N. Wayne Avenue
Cincinnati, OH 45215
(513) 563-4455

Label America
P.O. Box 1245
Stone Mountain, GA 30086
(404) 934-8040
(800) 232-7833

Spreadsheet and Spreadsheet Publishing

Always, Sideways
Funk Software
222 Third Street
Cambridge, MA 02142
(617) 497-6339

Datatype
Swfte International
P.O. Box 219
Rockland, DE 19732
(301) 429-8434

Impress
PC Publishing
1801 Avenue of the Stars
Los Angeles, CA 90067
(213) 556-3630

Lotus 1-2-3
Lotus Development Corporation
55 Cambridge Parkway
Cambridge, MA 02142
(617) 577-8500

Table Manners
(Lotus to Ventura)
The Desktop Publishing Group
978 Douglas Avenue
Altamonte Springs, FL 32714
(800) 257-8087

PostScript and PostScript Alternatives

ConoDesk 6000
Conographic Corporation
16802 Aston Street
Irvine, CA 92714
(717) 474-1188

EiconScript
Eicon Technology Corporation
2196 32nd Avenue
Montreal, Quebec
Canada H8T-3H7
(514) 631-2592

PostScript and PostScript Alternatives

Freedom of the Press
Custom Applications, Inc.
900 Technology Park Drive
Building 8
Billerica, MA 01821
(508) 667-8585

Font Solution Pack
Softcraft Inc.
16 N. Carroll Street
Suite 500
Madison, WI 53703
(800) 351-0500

GoScript
LaserGo, Inc.
9235 Trade Place
Suite A
San Diego, CA 92126
(619) 530-2400

JetScript, PS Jet
QMS, Inc.
1 Magnum Pass
Mobile, AL 36618
(205) 633-4300

LaserMaster
LaserMaster Corporation
7156 Shady Oak Road
Eden Prairie, MN 55344
(612) 944-6069

Pacific Page
Pacific Data Products
6404 Nancy Ridge Drive
San Diego, CA 92121
(619) 552-0880

Pagestyler
Destiny Technology
300 Montague Expressway
Suite 150
Milpitas, CA 95035
(408) 262-9400
(800) 874-5553

PS-388 Accelerator
Princeton Publishing Labs, Inc.
19 Wall Street
Princeton, NJ 08540
(609) 924-1153

Super Cartridge
IQ Engineering
586 Weddell Drive
Sunnyvale, CA 94089
(408) 734-1161

Presentation Software

Gem Presentation Team
Digital Research, Inc.
Box DRI
Monterey, CA 93942

Harvard Graphics
Software Publishing Corporation
1901 Landings Drive
Mountain View, CA 94039
(415) 962-8910

Presentation Software

HP Graphics Gallery
Hewlett-Packard Corporation
3000 Hanover Street
Palo Alto, CA 94304
(415) 857-1501
(800) 538-8787

Productivity

JLaser, JBanner
Tall Tree Systems
2585 E. Bayshore Road
Palo Alto, CA 94303
(415) 493-1988

RAM Upgrades
Micron Technology, Inc.
2805 E. Columbia Road
Boise, ID 83706
(206) 383-4000

LaserFeeder
(Envelope feeder)
BDT Products, Inc.
17152 Armstrong Avenue
Irvine, CA 92714
(800) 346-3238

Programs cited in the text but not listed here are not identified or supported by their authors, but are available from public domain libraries and bulletin boards. Several of the programs listed are not public domain or shareware, but are distributed in limited or demonstration form through public domain libraries. The features available in those versions, however, were used for discussions in this book.

Public Domain/Shareware

Libraries and General Sources:

ACC Software
1621 Fulton Avenue
Sacramento, CA 95825

AP-JP Enterprises
P.O. Box 1155
West Babylon, NY 11704

Compuserve
P.O. Box 20212
Columbus, OH 43220-0212

Genie
GE Information Services
401 N. Washington Street
Rockville, MD 20850
(800) 638-9636

PC Sig
103D East Duane Avenue
Sunnyvale, CA 94086
(408) 730-9291

Public Domain/Shareware

PSL Computer Products
P.O. Box 35705
Houston, TX 77235-5705
(800) 242-4775

Public Brand Software
P.O. Box 51315
Indianapolis, IN 46251
(800) 426-DISK
(800) 727-3476 (IN)

Products:

Claser LG
Keith P. Graham
Graham Systems
(914) 353-2176

ENVLJ
Steven D. Stern
JMB Realty Corporation
875 N. Michigan Avenue
Chicago, IL 60612

EP2HP
Thomas Giacchi
256 White Oak Ridge Road
Bridgewater, NJ 08807-1532

Fontview
S.H. Moody & Associates, Inc.
1810 Fair Oaks Avenue
South Pasadena, CA 91030

4UP
Hexagon Products
P.O. Box 1295
Park Ridge, IL 60068-1295

FT10.SFP
Orbit Enterprises
P.O. Box 2875
Glen Ellyn, IL 60138
(312) 469-3405

HPL2VEN
Vince Campbell
P.O. Box 8313
Atlanta, GA 30306
(404) 872-0334

HPPS
Darin May
Society of Critical Care Medicine
251 E. Imperial Highway
Suite 480
Fullerton, CA 92635

HPSTUFF, ANSFONT
Rip Toren
P.O. Box 674
Columbia, MD 21045

LaserJet 4.4
Guy Gallo
P.O. Box 344
Piermont, NY 10968

LJ2
Keller Software
1825 Westcliff Drive
Newport Beach, CA 92660

LJSP
Sterling Pacific International
1889 Green Street
San Fransisco, CA 94123

Public Domain/Shareware

LPTX
Mark DiVecchio
9067 Hillery Drive
San Diego, CA 92126
(619) 566-6810

MAKEHOLL, MAKESHAD
Jim Bumgardner
(818) 766-0594

Pamphlet
Martin C. Beattie
9190 Rolling Tree Lane
Fair Oaks, CA 95628
(916) 988-9117

Qfont
Kenn Flee
Jamestown Software
2508 Valley Forge Drive
Madison, WI 53719

Snapshot
ButtonWare
P.O. Box 5786
Bellevue, WA 98006

SU
Alex Sass
381 Evergreen Drive
Brick, NY 08723

Scanners and Scanning Hardware and Utilities

ART Turboscan
AST Research, Inc.
2121 Alton Avenue
Irvine, CA 92714
(714) 863-9991

Canon Image Scanner
Canon, Inc.
1 Canon Plaza
Lake Success, NY 11042
(516) 488-6700

CAT Image Scanner
Computer Aided Technology
7411 Hines Place
Dallas, TX 75235
(214) 631-6688

Data Sweep OCR Reader
Soricon Corporation
4725 Walnut Street
Boulder, CO 80301
(303) 440-2800
(800) 541-SCAN

Datacopy
Datacopy Corporation
1215 Terra Bella Avenue
Mountain View, CA 94043
(415) 965-7900

DS-2000/3000
Chinon America, Inc.
660 Maple Avenue
Torrance, CA 90503
(213) 533-0274

Scanners and Scanning Hardware and Utilities

Handy Scanner
Diamond Flower Electric, Inc.
5C Joanna Center
East Brunswick, NJ 08816
(201) 390-2815

IS-300
Laser Connection
7852 Schollinger Part West
Mobile, AL 36608
(205) 633-7223
(800) 523-2696

JX300 Color
Sharp Electronics Corporation
Sharp Plaza
Mahwah, NJ 07430
(201) 529-9500

Kurzweil
Kurzweil Computer Products
185 Albany Street
Cambridge, MA 02139
(617) 864-4700

Kyocera A-800 Scanner
Kyocera Unison, Inc.
1321 Harbor Bay Parkway
Alameda, CA 94501
(415) 748-6680
(800) 367-7437

LazaGram
FX Unlimited
4151 Middlefield Road
Suite 110
Palo Alto, CA 94303
(415) 494-0888

LS-300 Image Scanner
Princeton Graphics Systems
601 Ewing Street
Princeton, NJ 08540
(609) 683-1660

MegaScan
Advanced Vision Research, Inc.
2201 Qume Drive
San Jose, CA 95131
(408) 434-1115

Motif 3.0
Neotech Systems, Inc.
103 West 61st Street
Westmont, IL 60559
(312) 963-1202

MSF Gray-Scale Scanners
Microtek Lab, Inc.
680 Knox Street
Torrance, CA 90502
(213) 321-2121

OmniPage
Caere Corporation
100 Cooper Center
Los Gatos, CA 95030
(408) 395-7000

PB/Scan
ZSoft
450 Franklin Road
No. 100
Marietta, GA 30067
(404) 428-0008

Scanners and Scanning Hardware and Utilities

PCS Page Reader
Compuscan, Inc.
300 Broadacres Drive
Bloomfield, NJ 07003
(201) 338-5000

Pentax Image Scanner
Pentax Technologies
880 Interlocken Parkway
Broomfield, CO 80002
(303) 460-1600

Picture Publisher
Astral Development Corporation
Londonderry Square, Suite 112
Londonderry, NH 03053
(603) 432-6800

Pocket Scanner
Packard Bell
21800 Oxnard Street, #700
Woodland Hills, CA 91367
(818) 704-3905

QCS Scanner
Imapro Corporation
2081 Business Center Drive
Suite 371
Irvine, CA 92715
(714) 752-2043

Ricoh RS312
Richo Corporation
5 Dedrick Place
West Caldwell, NJ 07006
(201) 882-2000

ScanDo
Hammerlab Corporation
938 Chapel Street
New Haven, CT 06510
(203) 624-0000
(800) 351-4500

ScanJet Plus
Hewlett-Packard
700 71st Avenue
Greeley, CO 80634
(303) 350-4000

ScanMan
Logitech, Inc.
6505 Kaiser Drive
Fremont, CA 94555
(800) 231-7717

Scanmaster
Howtek, Inc.
21 Park Avenue
Hudson, NH 03051
(603) 882-5200

Scanning Service
Orbit Enterprises
P.O. Box 2875
Glen Ellyn, IL 60138
(312) 469-3405

SX-1000
Desktop Technology
986 Mangrove, Suite B
Sunnyvale, CA 94086
(408) 737-1992

Scanners and Scanning Hardware and Utilities

The Complete Page Scanner
The Complete PC
521 Cottonwood Drive
Milpitas, CA 95035
(408) 434-0145
(800) 544-3888

TrueScan
Calera Recognition Systems
2500 Augustine Drive
Santa Clara, CA 95054
(408) 986-8006

Visual Edge
Intel Corporation
5200 N.E. Elam Young Parkway
Hillsboro, OR 97124
(503) 681-8080

Wang PC Scan Plus
Wang Laboratories
1 Industrial Drive
Lowell, MA 01851
(508) 459-5000
(800) 835-9264

WorkLess Station
PC Scan
DEST Corporation
11201 Cadillac Street
Milpitas, CA 95035
(408) 946-7100

Word Processing

Ami
Samna Corporation
5600 Glenridge Drive
Atlanta, GA 30342
(404) 851-0007

Microsoft Word
Microsoft Corporation
16011 N.E. 36th Way
Redmond, WA 98073-9717
(206) 882-8080

MultiMate
Ashton-Tate, Inc.
20101 Hamilton Avenue
Torrance, CA 90502
(213) 329-8000

WordPerfect
WordPerfect Corporation
155 N. Technology Way
Orem, UT 84058
(801) 225-5000

WordStar
WordStar International
33 San Pablo Avenue
San Rafael, CA 94903
(800) 227-8320

XYQuest, Inc.
XYWrite III Plus
44 Manning Road
Billerica, MA 01821
(508) 671-0888

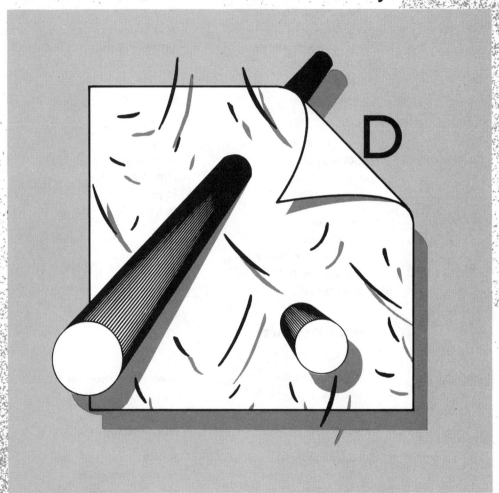

D

Using DeskJet Printers

Keep print cartridges away from children; the ink is toxic if swallowed.

• The HP DeskJet and DeskJet+ are ink-jet printers that produce the printed image by ejecting streams of ink through a small ink-spraying mechanism, called the print cartridge. The cartridge contains 50 dot-sized ink jets with a 600-dpi horizontal and 300-dpi vertical resolution. Because of the way the dots are placed, the effective resolution is a maximum of 300 dpi.

In many ways, DeskJet printers are similar to LaserJet models. They print graphics and softfonts using the same PCL commands, and can even use LaserJet printer drivers. DeskJet models are classified as PCL level 3 devices, although they do provide some powerful additional features.

• *Connecting and Using Your DeskJet*

See Chapter 2 for instructions for configuring your computer for serial or parallel transmission.

DeskJet printers have both serial and parallel connectors, located on the bottom of the machine. To use either connector, just install the correct cable. You don't have to configure the printer for serial or parallel transmission, but if you're using a serial protocol other than the default (9600 baud, no parity, 8 data bits), you'll have to change dip switches located on the front of the machine, under the paper tray.

There are 16 switches divided into two banks. Tables D.1 and D.2 show how each of the switches are used. The default factory setup has all switches in the down position.

• Table D.1: *DeskJet Switch Functions (Bank A)*

CHARACTER SET	A1	A2	A3	A4
PC-8	down	down	down	down
HP Roman-8	down	down	down	up
PC-8 Denmark/Norway	down	down	up	down
United Kingdom (ISO 04)	down	down	up	up
Germany (ISO 21)	down	up	down	down
France (ISO 69)	down	up	down	up
Italy (ISO 15)	down	up	up	down
Norway (ISO 60) V. 1	down	up	up	up

Table D.1: *DeskJet Switch Functions (Bank A) (Continued)*

CHARACTER SET	A1	A2	A3	A4
Sweden (ISO 11)	up	down	down	down
Spain (ISO 17)	up	down	down	up
ASCII	up	down	up	down
Portugal (ISO 16)	up	down	up	up
PC-850	up	up	down	down
ECMA-94 Latin 1	up	up	down	up
Lega	up	up	up	down
Default in font cartridge	up	up	up	up

PAPER SIZE	A5	A6
Letter (8½ by 11)	down	down
A4 (210 by 297 mm)	down	up
Legal (8½ by 14)	up	down
Envelope (#10)	down	down

CARRIAGE RETURN DEFINITION	A7
CR and LF	up
CR only	down

PERFORATION SKIP	
Disable	up
Enable	down

• Table D.2: *DeskJet Switch Functions (Bank B)*

TEXT SCALE MODE			
LINES PER PAGE		**B1**	
66		up	
63		down	
GRAPHICS DENSITY		**B2**	
300 dpi		up	
75 dpi		down	
TERMINAL MODE		**B3**	
Enable		up	
Disable		down	
BAUD RATE		**B4**	**B5**
1200		up	up
2400		up	down
9600		down	down
19200		down	up
PARITY	**DATA BITS**	**B6**	**B7**
None	8	down	down
Odd	7	down	up
Even	7	up	down
None	8	up	up

• Table D.2: *DeskJet Switch Functions (Bank B) (Continued)*

TEXT SCALE MODE			
HANDSHAKING		**B8**	
DTR DTR and XON/OFF		up down	

After you connect the cables and set the switches, install the print cartridge following the instructions packaged with it.

Available Fonts

LaserJet and DeskJet
cartridges and softfonts are
not interchangeable.

Like the LaserJet models, DeskJet printers use internal fonts, cartridges, and softfonts. The DeskJet + can handle fonts up to 30 points; the original DeskJet prints up to 14 points. Table D.3 lists the fonts available.

Two cartridge slots are located on the top right of the printer. They can be used for any combination of font and RAM cartridges. Since the printers have no internal memory, one or two 128K or 256K RAM cartridges are required to use softfonts. The original DeskJet can access a maximum of 256K memory, using 128K RAM cartridges only.

DeskJet Printer Drivers

Refer to earlier chapters and
the application notes later in
this appendix for specific
details on using DeskJet
drivers.

Use a DeskJet + or DeskJet printer driver if your application has one. Drivers for the original DeskJet will work with the DeskJet + but in a limited way. They don't support cartridges and softfonts designed just for the DeskJet +, and they will not automatically access internal italic or landscape fonts. However, you might be able to access these internal fonts if the driver supports the A and K cartridges. Select the A cartridge for italic and the K cartridge to use landscape. The driver's PCL commands to use the cartridge fonts will probably access the internal ones.

When DeskJet drivers aren't available, try using one for the LaserJet + or LaserJet II. While some DeskJet features will not be accessed, text and graphics should print.

Hewlett-Packard also markets a cartridge (HP22707F) that emulates the Epson FX-80 printer. With this cartridge installed, you can use a driver for the Epson FX-80 printer.

• Table D.3: *Available DeskJet Fonts*

INTERNAL COURIER FONTS	STYLE
6 points; 5, 10, and 16.67 pitch	Normal
6 points; 20 pitch	Normal, Bold, Italic*, Bold Italic*
12 points; 16.67 pitch	Normal
12 points; 5, 10, and 20 pitch	Normal, Bold, Italic*, Bold Italic*
CARTRIDGES	**FONTS AND POINT SIZES** (most supplied in a variety of styles and pitches)
A	Courier 6 and 12; Line Draw 12
B	Prestige Elite 5, 7, and 10; Line Draw 6 and 12; Math Prestige 5 and 10
C	Letter Gothic 4.75, 6, 9.5, and 12; Line Draw 6 and 12
D	TmsRmn 4, 5, 8, and 10
E	TmsRmn 6 and 12
F	TmsRmn 7 and 14
G	Helv 4, 5, 8, and 10
H	Helv 6 and 12
J	Helv 7 and 14
K	Landscape, Courier 6 and 12
L	Landscape, Courier 6 and 24; Letter Gothic 6, 9.5, 19, and 24
M	Presentations 7, 8, 9, 14, 16, 18; Letter Gothic 7 and 14; Line Draw 6 and 12
P	TmsRmn ASCII 4, 5, 6, 7, 8, 10, 12, and 14
Q	Helv ASCII 4, 5, 6, 7, 8, 10, 12, and 14
R*	TmsRmn 5, 6, 10, 12, and 14

• Table D.3: *Available DeskJet Fonts (Continued)*

CARTRIDGE	FONTS AND POINT SIZES (most supplied in a variety of styles and pitches)
T*	Helv 5, 6, 10, 12, and 14
U*	TmsRmn 15 and 30
V*	Helv Headlines 15 and 30
WP1	CG Times 6, 8, 10, 12, and 14
WP2*	CG Times 24; Univers 14, 18, and 24
SOFTFONTS (require RAM cartridge)	FONTS AND POINT SIZES
A	TmsRmn/Helv 8, 10, 12, and 14
C*	TmsRmn/Helv 8, 10, 12, 14, 15, and 30
D*	Univers Condensed 5, 6, 7, 8, 9, 10, 12, 14, 15, 18, 24, and 30

* *Note*: DeskJet + only

DeskJet Paper

Because of the ink-jet mechanism, you should take some time to make sure you're using the correct paper. Do not use paper specially made for ink-jet printers; choose quality copying or bond paper. If you're using copying paper, check the package to see which is the printing side, usually marked with an arrow. Load the paper in the tray with the printing side facing down. The paper tray holds about 100 sheets.

Printing Envelopes

Print envelopes on DeskJet printers in portrait orientation. Load envelopes, either #10 or DL size, in the OUT tray, lengthwise. Insert the top of the envelope in, printing side down, the right side against the side of the

DeskJet printers have 1/4-inch unprintable areas on the left and right, and 1/2-inch default top and bottom margins. The top margin can be eliminated using PCL commands to disable perforation skip.

tray. Press the Up and Down arrow keys on the control panel at the same time to feed the envelope into the printer.

Select a portrait font, either through your application or the printer control panel.

Set the following envelope margins:

- **Top**: 2 to 2$^1/_2$ inches

- **Bottom**: 0

- **Left**: 4$^1/_2$ inches

- **Right**: 0

- **Page length**: 4 inches

If your application lists specific envelope settings, use them.

• *The DeskJet Control Panel*

The DeskJet control panel has eight buttons and nine indicator lights. Changes made on the control panel are temporary; they are erased when you turn the printer off. Most of the control panel functions can also be performed by using PCL commands.

The On Line Indicator and Button

When the printer is "on line," the indicator light on the button is lit and the printer is ready to accept characters from the computer. When the On Line indicator is off, the printer is "off line," and the computer will not transmit any characters. To switch between on and off line mode, press and release the On Line button. For example, to pause printing, press the On Line button to switch to off line.

To use any other control on the panel, the printer must first be off line.

If the paper jams during a printing job, the DeskJet stops and the On Line and Busy lights will blink. Clear the paper, then press the On Line button.

Other Controls

The DeskJet control panel also includes the following buttons and indicators:

- **Busy light**: When this indicator light is on, the printer is receiving data from the computer.

The DeskJet + prints text twice as fast, and graphics up to five times as fast, as the original DeskJet.

Press Reset to quickly return to the default settings.

- **Reset**: Press this button to return the printer to its default settings. Any text or graphics in the printer will be lost.

- **Mode**: When you turn on the printer, it defaults to the 120 character per second letter quality mode. Press the Mode button to activate draft quality, about 240 characters per second. (Character cells are 30 by 50 in letter quality; 15 by 50 in draft.)

- **Draft light**: When this indicator light is on, the printer is in draft mode, which is faster, uses less ink, and produces poorer quality than letter quality.

- **Prime**: Press this button *before* starting a printing job to activate a new cartridge or when printing becomes light.

- **Font**: Press this button to select internal fonts, printer orientation, and cartridge fonts. As you press the Font button, the printer cycles between Courier 10 (the default), 16.67, and 20 pitch in portrait, then Courier 10, 16.67, and 20 pitch in landscape, then through the available cartridge fonts. To print a self test, turn the printer off, hold down the Font button, and then turn on the printer. A test pattern will print in both portrait and landscape orientations. (The original DeskJet will not print the landscape test pattern.)

- **Font lights**: As you press the Font button, lights on the control panel indicate the pitch and orientation. If you have a cartridge installed, lights on the end of the cartridge will indicate the selected font.

- **FF**: Press FF (form feed) to eject a sheet of paper or envelope already in the printer. You can also press the FF button to manually load a sheet of paper from the IN tray.

- **Up and Down**: These buttons are used to move the paper in and out of the printer in small increments. Press both keys at the same time to manually load an envelope from the OUT tray.

When you're using the control panel to select fonts, remember that bold and italic fonts are internal, but they must be selected with PCL commands. Also graphics and automatic underlining are not supported in landscape orientation. With the original DeskJet, italic and landscape fonts are not internal.

• *PCL Programming*

In addition to the differences noted earlier, certain PCL commands are unique to DeskJet printers.

By default, the printer switches into unidirectional printing when in landscape mode. Use a field value of 1 to print bidirectional.

You can specify the print direction with

<Esc>&k#W

The field value determines the direction of print: 0 for unidirectional left to right, 1 for bidirectional (default), or 2 for unidirectional right to left.

To enable text scaling, using the command

<Esc>&k#W

This compensates for the default 1/2-inch bottom margin by scaling the text. A field value of 6 enables text scaling, printing 66 lines when set at 6 lines per inch, and 88 lines at 8 lines per inch on 81/2- by 11-inch paper. The field value of 5 returns the printer to the default condition. This works in portrait orientation only.

To request the model, use

<Esc>*rK

The printer will transmit its model number back to the computer. This works with serial interfaces only.

You can issue an I/O status request with

<Esc>? *D1*

D1 represents the device control 1 code: 17 decimal or 11 hexadecimal. The printer responds with a status byte, as listed in Table D.4. This works with serial interfaces only.

To print subscripts or superscripts, use

<Esc>(s#U

This sets the line position. Field values are -1 for begin subscript, 0 for normal position, or 1 for begin superscript.

Set the print quality with

<Esc>(s#Q

Use a field value of 1 for draft quality or 2 for letter quality.

To specify the underline mode, use

<Esc>&k#E

- Table D.4: *I/O Status Request Reponses (<Esc>?D1)*

BITS		MEANING
7	0	
6	0	
5	1	
4	1	
3	1	An I/O error has occurred since the last request.
	0	No error has occurred.
2	1	The printer is off line.
	0	The print is on line.
1	1	The printer is busy.
	0	The print is not busy.
0	1	Paper is out.
	0	Paper is not out.

With a field value of 1, the default, when turned on, automatic underlining will remain on until the command

<Esc>&d@

is transmitted. Using a field value of 0, underlining is turned off at the end of the line.

You can control the shift in/shift out codes with

<Esc>&k#F

With a field value of 1, the default, shift in and shift out control codes stay in effect until changed. Using a field value of 0, the last received shift in or shift out will be cancelled at the end of the current line.

Graphics Commands

A number of commands have been added to the PCL language to increase the speed of printing graphics with DeskJet printers.

You can set the width of a raster graphic with the command

<Esc>*r#S

The field value is the width in dots of the graphic image about to be down-loaded. When printing graphics, the printer by default allocates enough internal memory for a graphic the full width of the page. If your graphic is smaller, use this command to limit the amount of memory allocated.

Set a temporary left margin offset with

<Esc>*b#X

The field value represents a temporary left margin (in dots) for the next row to be transmitted.

To set raster graphics quality, use

<Esc>*r#Q

A field value of 1 sets the print quality to draft; a 0 or 2 sets letter quality. Use the faster draft printing for test prints, then switch to quality for the final version.

The command to specify the graphics mode is

<Esc>*b#M

The field value determines the format in which repeated characters or blocks of characters are transmitted to the printer. A field value of 0 is the default standard mode.

Values of 1 and 2 change the format of the data transfer

<Esc>*b#W

command. The field value 1 sets compaction graphics mode 1. If you want to transmit several of the same characters in a row, use this mode to reduce the actual number of characters transmitted. The transfer command is modified to include a repeat count in this format:

<Esc>*b2W *(repeat-count minus 1) character*

For example, to print a row of 60 *X*s, use these commands after setting the resolution and starting raster graphics:

<Esc>*b1M
<Esc>*b2W 3B X

The first code turns on compaction mode 1, and the second signifies that two bytes will be transmitted. The first byte represents the number of times you want to print the character, less 1. Hex byte 3B is 59 decimal. The second byte is the character that you want to repeat.

The field value 2 sets compaction graphics mode 2. Use this mode to transmit repeated characters (same as mode 1) or repeated blocks of different characters. The command

<Esc>*b2M

turns on the mode. The data transfer command is now modified to these two formats:

<Esc>*b2W *(−1 to −127) byte*
<Esc>*b#W *(1 to 127) block*

The first code means that a repeat count of −1 to −127 represents the number of times (less one) to repeat the following character. The negative repeat count differentiates the command from a block repeat. The second code signifies that a repeat count of 1 to 127 represents the number of times (less one) to repeat the following block of characters. For example

<Esc>*b 6 W 63 SYBEX

repeats the word SYBEX 100 times. (The hex byte 63 is 99 decimal.)

• *DeskJet Resources*

Many of the sources listed in Appendix C also support DeskJet printers. Both Hewlett-Packard and Elfring Softfonts, for example, carry a line of DeskJet softfonts.

Public Brand Software, the public domain library, offers two DeskJet support disks. Disk UP13 contains several 10-, 12-, and 18-point fonts; a landscape Courier font in normal and italic; and a downloading program. Disk UP23 contains nine fonts, a download program, a utility that prints samples and character maps for softfonts, and a general information file.

Check with the vendors listed to see if their hardware and software is compatible with DeskJet printers.

• *Using DeskJet Softfonts*

Although LaserJet and DeskJet softfonts are not interchangeable, the first 64 bytes of font headers contain the same information. DeskJet fonts, however, are more complicated in many ways, as well as less documented. Font headers contain the 28 additional bytes listed in Table D.5.

• Table D.5: *Additional DeskJet Font Header Bytes*

BYTE	FUNCTION	SETTING
64 and 65	Horizontal resolution	Set at 600
66 and 67	Vertical resolution	Set at 300
68	Top of double underline	The distance, in dots, from the baseline to the top row of dots in the underline
69	Top underline height	The thickness of the top underline in dots
70	Bottom underline	The distance to the bottom underline
71	Bottom underline height	The thickness of the bottom underline in dots
72 and 73	Extra block size	Set at 20
74 and 75	Font data size	Ignored by printer
76	Unidirectional flag	Set at 0 for bidirectional
77	Compress flag	Set at 1 if compressed
78	Reserved	
79	Half-pitch flag	Set at 0 if half pitch
80	Double-pitch flag	Set at 0 if double pitch

• Table D.5: *Additional DeskJet Font Header Bytes (Continued)*

BYTE	FUNCTION	SETTING
81	Half-height flag	Set at 0 if half height
82	Bold flag	Set at 0 for automatic boldface
83	Draft flag	Set at 0 if draft quality is recommended
84	Bold method	Set at 0 for single dot; 1 for double-dot bolding
85	Reserved	
86 and 87	Tall baseline	
88 and 89	Hold delay	
90 and 91	Reserved	

• *Application Notes*

This section contains some additional information not included in margin notes in previous chapters. Since the DeskJet + is a relatively new printer, check your application's documentation for the latest support details. Contact the manufacturer if your version doesn't support the Desk-Jet or DeskJet + .

Printer drivers are also available through manufacturer support groups on Compuserve. If you are a Compuserve member, there are no fees beyond connection charges to join the support group and download the latest driver files. Support groups on the system include Aldus, Ashton-Tate, Digital Research, Enable, Lotus, Microsoft, Software Publishing Corporation (PFS), WordPerfect, and WordStar.

Printing with WordPerfect

WordPerfect 5.0 supports both the DeskJet and DeskJet + printers through drivers HPDESKJE.PRS and HPDESPLU.PRS.

When printing envelopes, the minimum margins are:

- **Left**: 0.25 inch

- **Right**: 1.50 inch

- **Top**: 0.10 inch

- **Bottom**: 0.25 inch

When printing in landscape, the minimum top and left margins are 0.3 and 0.7 inch.

The driver supports two special DeskJet WordPerfect cartridges. One contains CG Times in sizes from 6 to 18 points; the other includes CG Times in 24-point Bold and Univers in 14, 18, and 24 points.

Printing with Microsoft Word

DeskJet support is provided in several PRD files. Drivers for DeskJet + cartridges and softfonts are on Microsoft's supplemental printer disk #3. Each PRD file includes two models: HP DESKJET (no cartridge) for just internal fonts and HP DESKJET followed by supported cartridges, such as HP DESK-JET [A/B/C].

The following driver files are included:

HPDESK.PRD	Internal and cartridge A
HPDESK1.PRD	Internal and cartridges A, B, and C
HPDESK2.PRD	Internal and cartridges A, D, E, and F
HPDESK3.PRD	Internal and cartridges A, G, H, and J
HPDESK4.PRD	Internal and cartridges A, M, P, and Q
HPDESK5.PRD	Landscape cartridges K and L

There are four drivers designed for the DeskJet + :

HPDESKPC.PRD	Softfont set A (requires HPDESKPC.DAT)
DESKJET1.PRD	Cartridges R, T, U, V, and softfont set C and D, PC symbol set (requires DESKJET1.DAT)
DESKJET2.PRD	Same fonts as DESKJET1.PRD but the Legal character set (requires DESKJET2.DAT)
DESKJET3.PRD	Same as DESKJET1.PRD but the ASCII character set (requires DESKJET3.DAT)

PRD files can be combined using MergePRD, as discussed in Chapter 6. Graphics are supported in 75-, 150-, and 300-dpi resolution. Word assumes the following nonprintable areas:

- **Top**: 0.04 inches

- **Left**: 0.25 inches

- **Bottom**: 0.34 inches

- **Right**: 0.25 inches

To print envelopes, use a portrait font and set the page as follows:

- **Top margin**: 2 inches

- **Left margin**: 4.5 inches

- **Right margin**: 0

- **Page length**: 4 inches

Printing with WordStar

The version of the WordStar DTF printer database dated June 1989 supports softfonts on the DeskJet +. In addition to cartridges A, B, C, L, M, P, Q, R, T, U, and V, the file allows use of these softfonts:

Univers is supported in both ASCII and PC-8 symbol sets.

Font	Sizes
Helvetica	4, 5, 6, 7, 8, 10, 12, 14, 15, 30
TmsRmn	4, 5, 6, 7, 8, 10, 12, 14, 15, 30
Univers	6, 7, 8, 9, 10, 14, 15, 18, 24, 30

Because of the number of internal symbol sets, WordStar recommends using only one symbol set per driver. For example, if you want to use the PC-8 symbol set, delete any fonts that use the Legal character set from the driver.

Printing with MultiMate

Several sets of files (with PAT, SAT, and CWT extensions) are available for the DeskJet printer:

- **DESKJET.PAT**: Supports the DeskJet and DeskJet +. Bin 1 is portrait, and bin 2 is landscape. When printing in landscape with the DeskJet +, only cartridges A, B, E, F, L, M, N, and P are available.

- **DJRANDU.PAT**: Supports cartridges R and U, using the font assignments listed in Table D.6.

- **DJTANDV.PAT**: Supports cartridges T and V and softfonts using the font assignments shown in Table D.7.

- Table D.6: *MultiMate DJRANDU.PAT Font Assignments*

# FONT	SIZE AND STYLE	# FONT	SIZE AND STYLE
A TmsRmn	12 Regular	N TmsRmn	5 Regular
B TmsRmn	12 Bold	O TmsRmn	5 Italic
C TmsRmn	12 Italic	P TmsRmn	4 Regular
D TmsRmn	12 Bold-Ital	Q TmsRmn	14 Regular
E TmsRmn	10 Regular	R TmsRmn	14 Bold
F TmsRmn	10 Bold	S TmsRmn	15 Regular
G TmsRmn	10 Italic	T TmsRmn	30 Regular
H TmsRmn	10 Bold-Ital	U Courier	10 cpi
I TmsRmn	8 Regular	V Courier	10 cpi Bold
J TmsRmn	8 Bold	W Helv	14 Regular
K TmsRmn	7 Regular	X Helv	14 Bold
L TmsRmn	6 Regular	Y Helv	15 Regular
M TmsRmn	6 Italic	Z Helv	30 Regular

Table D.7: *MultiMate DJTAND V.PAT Font Assignments*

# FONT	SIZE AND STYLE	# FONT	SIZE AND STYLE
A Helv	12 Regular	N Helv	5 Regular
B Helv	12 Bold	O Helv	5 Italic
C Helv	12 Italic	P Helv	4 Regular
D Helv	12 Bold-Ital	Q Helv	14 Regular
E Helv	10 Regular	R Helv	14 Bold
F Helv	10 Bold	S Helv	15 Regular
G Helv	10 Italic	T Helv	30 Regular
H Helv	10 Bold-Ital	U Courier	10 cpi
I Helv	8 Regular	V Courier	10 cpi Bold
J Helv	8 Bold	W TmsRmn	14 Regular
K Helv	7 Regular	X TmsRmn	14 Bold
L Helv	6 Regular	Y TmsRmn	15 Bold
M Helv	6 Italic	Z TmsRmn	30 Bold

When using a proportionally spaced font, pitch settings are ignored. MultiMate recommends, however, that you select pitch numbers using these guidelines:

Pitch Setting	Fonts
1	S, T, U, V, Y, and Z
2	Q, R, W, and X
3	A, B, C, and D
4	E, F, G, and H
5	E, F, G, and H
6	I and J
7	K
8	L and M
9	N, O, and P

. *Index*

Selections from
The SYBEX Library

SPREADSHEETS AND INTEGRATED SOFTWARE

Visual Guide to Lotus 1-2-3
Jeff Woodward

250pp. Ref. 641-3

Readers match what they see on the screen with the book's screen-by-screen action sequences. For new Lotus users, topics include computer fundamentals, opening and editing a worksheet, using graphs, macros, and printing typeset-quality reports. For Release 2.2.

The ABC's of 1-2-3 Release 2.2
Chris Gilbert/Laurie Williams

340pp. Ref. 623-5

New Lotus 1-2-3 users delight in this book's step-by-step approach to building trouble-free spreadsheets, displaying graphs, and efficiently building data-bases. The authors cover the ins and outs of the latest version including easier calculations, file linking, and better graphic presentation.

The ABC's of 1-2-3 Release 3
Judd Robbins

290pp. Ref. 519-0

The ideal book for beginners who are new to Lotus or new to Release 3. This step-by-step approach to the 1-2-3 spreadsheet software gets the reader up and running with spreadsheet, database, graphics, and macro functions.

The ABC's of 1-2-3 (Second Edition)
Chris Gilbert/Laurie Williams

245pp. Ref. 355-4

Online Today recommends it as "an easy and comfortable way to get started with the program." An essential tutorial for novices, it will remain on your desk as a valuable source of ongoing reference and support. For Release 2.

Mastering 1-2-3 Release 3
Carolyn Jorgensen

682pp. Ref. 517-4

For new Release 3 and experienced Release 2 users, "Mastering" starts with a basic spreadsheet, then introduces spreadsheet and database commands, functions, and macros, and then tells how to analyze 3D spreadsheets and make high-impact reports and graphs. Lotus add-ons are discussed and Fast Tracks are included.

Mastering 1-2-3 (Second Edition)
Carolyn Jorgensen

702pp. Ref. 528-X

Get the most from 1-2-3 Release 2 with this step-by-step guide emphasizing advanced features and practical uses. Topics include data sharing, macros, spreadsheet security, expanded memory, and graphics enhancements.

The Complete Lotus 1-2-3 Release 2.2 Handbook
Greg Harvey
750pp. Ref. 625-1

This comprehensive handbook discusses every 1-2-3 operating with clear instructions and practical tips. This volume especially emphasizes the new improved graphics, high-speed recalculation techniques, and spreadsheet linking available with Release 2.2.

The Complete Lotus 1-2-3 Release 3 Handbook
Greg Harvey
700pp. Ref. 600-6

Everything you ever wanted to know about 1-2-3 is in this definitive handbook. As a Release 3 guide, it features the design and use of 3D worksheets, and improved graphics, along with using Lotus under DOS or OS/2. Problems, exercises, and helpful insights are included.

Lotus 1-2-3 Desktop Companion SYBEX Ready Reference Series
Greg Harvey
976pp. Ref. 501-8

A full-time consultant, right on your desk. Hundreds of self-contained entries cover every 1-2-3 feature, organized by topic, indexed and cross-referenced, and supplemented by tips, macros and working examples. For Release 2.

Advanced Techniques in Lotus 1-2-3
Peter Antoniak/E. Michael Lunsford
367pp. Ref. 556-5

This guide for experienced users focuses on advanced functions, and techniques for designing menu-driven applications using macros and the Release 2 command language. Interfacing techniques and add-on products are also considered.

Lotus 1-2-3 Tips and Tricks
Gene Weisskopf
396pp. Ref. 454-2

A rare collection of timesavers and tricks for longtime Lotus users. Topics include macros, range names, spreadsheet design, hardware considerations, DOS operations, efficient data analysis, printing, data interchange, applications development, and more.

Lotus 1-2-3 Instant Reference Release 2.2 SYBEX Prompter Series
Greg Harvey/Kay Yarborough Nelson
254pp. Ref. 635-9, 4 ¾" × 8"

The reader gets quick and easy access to any operation in 1-2-3 Version 2.2 in this handy pocket-sized encyclopedia. Organized by menu function, each command and function has a summary description, the exact key sequence, and a discussion of the options.

Lotus 1-2-3 Instant Reference SYBEX Prompter Series
Greg Harvey/Kay Yarborough Nelson
296pp. Ref. 475-5; 4 ¾" × 8"

Organized information at a glance. When you don't have time to hunt through hundreds of pages of manuals, turn here for a quick reminder: the right key sequence, a brief explanation of a command, or the correct syntax for a specialized function.

Mastering Symphony (Fourth Edition)
Douglas Cobb
857pp. Ref. 494-1

Thoroughly revised to cover all aspects of the major upgrade of Symphony Version 2, this Fourth Edition of Doug Cobb's classic is still "the Symphony bible" to this complex but even more powerful package. All the new features are discussed and placed in context with prior versions so that both new and previous users will benefit from Cobb's insights.

The ABC's of Quattro
Alan Simpson/Douglas J. Wolf

286pp. Ref. 560-3

Especially for users new to spreadsheets, this is an introduction to the basic concepts and a guide to instant productivity through editing and using spreadsheet formulas and functions. Includes how to print out graphs and data for presentation. For Quattro 1.1.

Mastering Quattro
Alan Simpson

576pp. Ref. 514-X

This tutorial covers not only all of Quattro's classic spreadsheet features, but also its added capabilities including extended graphing, modifiable menus, and the macro debugging environment. Simpson brings out how to use all of Quattro's new-generation-spreadsheet capabilities.

Mastering Framework III
Douglas Hergert/Jonathan Kamin

613pp. Ref. 513-1

Thorough, hands-on treatment of the latest Framework release. An outstanding introduction to integrated software applications, with examples for outlining, spreadsheets, word processing, databases, and more; plus an introduction to FRED programming.

The ABC's of Excel on the IBM PC
Douglas Hergert

326pp. Ref. 567-0

This book is a brisk and friendly introduction to the most important features of Microsoft Excel for PC's. This beginner's book discusses worksheets, charts, database operations, and macros, all with hands-on examples. Written for all versions through Version 2.

Mastering Excel on the IBM PC
Carl Townsend

628pp. Ref. 403-8

A complete Excel handbook with step-by-step tutorials, sample applications and an extensive reference section. Topics include worksheet fundamentals, formulas and windows, graphics, database techniques, special features, macros and more.

Excel Instant Reference SYBEX Prompter Series
William J. Orvis

368pp. Ref.577-8, 4 ¾" × 8"

This pocket-sized reference book contains all of Excel's menu commands, math operations, and macro functions. Quick and easy access to command syntax, usage, arguments, and examples make this Instant Reference a must. Through Version 1.5.

Understanding PFS: First Choice
Gerry Litton

489pp. Ref. 568-9

From basic commands to complex features, this complete guide to the popular integrated package is loaded with step-by-step instructions. Lessons cover creating attractive documents, setting up easy-to-use databases, working with spreadsheets and graphics, and smoothly integrating tasks from different First Choice modules. For Version 3.0.

Mastering Enable
Keith D. Bishop

517pp. Ref. 440-2

A comprehensive, practical, hands-on guide to Enable 2.0—integrated word processing, spreadsheet, database management, graphics, and communications—from basic concepts to custom menus, macros and the Enable Procedural Language.

Mastering Q & A
(Second Edition)
Greg Harvey
540pp. Ref. 452-6

This hands-on tutorial explores the Q & A Write, File, and Report modules, and the Intelligent Assistant. English-language command processor, macro creation, interfacing with other software, and more, using practical business examples.

Mastering SuperCalc5
Greg Harvey/Mary Beth Andrasak
500pp. Ref. 624-3

This book offers a complete and unintimidating guided tour through each feature. With step-by-step lessons, readers learn about the full capabilities of spreadsheet, graphics, and data management functions. Multiple spreadsheets, linked spreadsheets, 3D graphics, and macros are also discussed.

ACCOUNTING

Mastering DacEasy Accounting
Darleen Hartley Yourzek
476pp. Ref 442-9

Applied accounting principles are at your fingertips in this exciting new guide to using DacEasy Accounting versions 2.0 and 3.0. Installing, converting data, processing work, and printing reports are covered with a variety of practical business examples. Through Version 3.0

DATABASE MANAGEMENT

The ABC's of Paradox
Charles Siegel
300pp. Ref.573-5

Easy to understand and use, this introduction is written so that the computer novice can create, edit, and manage complex Paradox databases. This primer is filled with examples of the Paradox 3.0 menu structure.

Mastering Paradox
(Fourth Edition)
Alan Simpson
636pp. Ref. 612-X

Best selling author Alan Simpson simplifies all aspects of Paradox for the beginning to intermediate user. The book starts with database basics, covers multiple tables, graphics, custom applications with PAL, and the Personal Programmer. For Version 3.0.

Quick Guide to dBASE:
The Visual Approach
David Kolodney
382pp. Ref. 596-4

This illustrated tutorial provides the beginner with a working knowledge of all the basic functions of dBASE IV. Images of each successive dBASE screen tell how to create and modify a database, add, edit, sort and select records, and print custom labels and reports.

The ABC's of dBASE IV
Robert Cowart
338pp. Ref. 531-X

This superb tutorial introduces beginners to the concept of databases and practical dBASE IV applications featuring the new menu-driven interface, the new report writer, and Query by Example.

Understanding dBASE IV
(Special Edition)
Alan Simpson
880pp. Ref. 509-3

This Special Edition is the best introduction to dBASE IV, written by 1 million-reader-strong dBASE expert Alan Simpson. First it gives basic skills for creating and manipulating efficient databases. Then the author explains how to make reports, manage multiple databases, and build applications. Includes Fast Track speed notes.

SYBEX®

TO JOIN THE SYBEX MAILING LIST OR ORDER BOOKS
PLEASE COMPLETE THIS FORM

NAME _____ COMPANY _____

STREET _____ CITY _____

STATE _____ ZIP _____

☐ PLEASE MAIL ME MORE INFORMATION ABOUT **SYBEX** TITLES

ORDER FORM (There is no obligation to order)

PLEASE SEND ME THE FOLLOWING:

TITLE	QTY	PRICE
_____	____	____
_____	____	____
_____	____	____
_____	____	____

TOTAL BOOK ORDER ____ $____

CUSTOMER SIGNATURE _____

SHIPPING AND HANDLING PLEASE ADD $2.00 PER BOOK VIA UPS _____

FOR OVERSEAS SURFACE ADD $5.25 PER BOOK PLUS $4.40 REGISTRATION FEE _____

FOR OVERSEAS AIRMAIL ADD $18.25 PER BOOK PLUS $4.40 REGISTRATION FEE _____

CALIFORNIA RESIDENTS PLEASE ADD APPLICABLE SALES TAX _____

TOTAL AMOUNT PAYABLE _____

☐ CHECK ENCLOSED   ☐ VISA
☐ MASTERCARD   ☐ AMERICAN EXPRESS

ACCOUNT NUMBER _____

EXPIR. DATE _____ DAYTIME PHONE _____

CHECK AREA OF COMPUTER INTEREST:

☐ BUSINESS SOFTWARE

☐ TECHNICAL PROGRAMMING

☐ OTHER: _____

THE FACTOR THAT WAS MOST IMPORTANT IN YOUR SELECTION:

☐ THE SYBEX NAME

☐ QUALITY

☐ PRICE

☐ EXTRA FEATURES

☐ COMPREHENSIVENESS

☐ CLEAR WRITING

☐ OTHER _____

OTHER COMPUTER TITLES YOU WOULD LIKE TO SEE IN PRINT:

_____

_____

OCCUPATION

☐ PROGRAMMER   ☐ TEACHER

☐ SENIOR EXECUTIVE   ☐ HOMEMAKER

☐ COMPUTER CONSULTANT   ☐ RETIRED

☐ SUPERVISOR   ☐ STUDENT

☐ MIDDLE MANAGEMENT   ☐ OTHER:

☐ ENGINEER/TECHNICAL   _____

☐ CLERICAL/SERVICE

☐ BUSINESS OWNER/SELF EMPLOYED

CHECK YOUR LEVEL OF COMPUTER USE

☐ NEW TO COMPUTERS

☐ INFREQUENT COMPUTER USER

☐ FREQUENT USER OF ONE SOFTWARE

PACKAGE:

NAME _____

☐ FREQUENT USER OF MANY SOFTWARE

PACKAGES

☐ PROFESSIONAL PROGRAMMER

OTHER COMMENTS:

_____

_____

_____

_____

_____

_____

_____

PLEASE FOLD, SEAL, AND MAIL TO SYBEX

SYBEX, INC.
2021 CHALLENGER DR. #100
ALAMEDA, CALIFORNIA USA
94501

SEAL